AUSTRALIAN VERSE

An Oxford Anthology

AUSTRALIAN VERSE

An Oxford Anthology

Edited by JOHN LEONARD

Melbourne

OXFORD UNIVERSITY PRESS

Oxford   Auckland   New York

OXFORD UNIVERSITY PRESS AUSTRALIA
Oxford New York
Athens Auckland Bangkok Bogotá
Buenos Aires Calcutta Cape Town Chennai
Dar es Salaam Delhi Florence Hong Kong
Istanbul Karachi Kuala Lumpur Madrid
Melbourne Mexico City Mumbai Nairobi
Paris Port Moresby São Paulo Singapore
Taipei Tokyo Toronto Warsaw
and associated companies in
Berlin Ibadan
OXFORD is a trade mark of Oxford University Press

National Library of Australia
Cataloguing-in-Publication data:

Australian verse: an Oxford anthology

Includes index.
ISBN 0 19 550699 5.

Australian poetry. I. Leonard, John, 1940–.

821.08

Cover design by Steve Randles
Typeset by Desktop Concepts P/L, Melbourne
Printed by Kin Keong, Singapore
Published by Oxford University Press,
253 Normanby Road, South Melbourne, Australia

CONTENTS

xii *Contents*

INTRODUCTION

This anthology is a survey of poetry by Australians in English, beginning with a selection of contemporary work by younger poets and going backward in time to the early colonial period. The selection is broad, including recent performance poetry and the words of convict songs and old bush songs as well as the literary — poems equally meant for utterance, but written for printed publication. The 'literary' in this sense is most of the field: a varied continuum from surreal prose poems to early anonymous newspaper verse.

The writing and publication of Australian poetry has a well-debated critical history concerned with themes and influences. Rather than repeat a version of it here I will let the selection make its own critical statement. I hope that the poems will touch against each other in unexpected ways. Poetry is written from an extreme diversity of experience and background, and from conflicting ideas about its proper subject and language. That diversity in turn enlivens reading. In choosing poems for this book, contrast has been a watchword.

For the purpose of study, and for the pleasure of their presence, an extensive selection has been provided from the work of five major twentieth-century poets: Les Murray, Gwen Harwood, Judith Wright, A. D. Hope and Kenneth Slessor. Murray is the obvious choice from among contemporary poets. In view of the historical sweep of this anthology, it has seemed best to select the other four poets from among those whose life's work is complete or mostly so. Generally speaking, contemporary poetry is represented more widely and evenly than that of earlier times, where the bolder claims of priority have already been turned over by more than one generation.

The reverse chronological arrangement opens outward to the past from the vantage of the present. The freshness of that perspective is the reason for its adoption. Of course we read the present through our understanding of the past and the past through our understanding of the present — and most readers, I expect, will read back and forth at will. The order of poets is by date of birth. This means that at times some of the late work of a long-lived poet mixes with another poet's work written at an earlier age. I have let these effects stand, except for slight adjustments in the placing of Mary Fullerton, Mary Gilmore and Jack Mathieu. The date at the foot of each poem is that of first publication in a book by the author; a date in brackets is that of first publication in a newspaper, journal or anthology in cases where no book was published. In a few instances, both dates are provided (and sometimes a date of writing) where this information may be useful.

The anthology begins with the shock of the present in the hands of young artists. The poets represented here in the first thirty pages or so have tended not to divide into literary groupings. Many of them are eclectic in allegiance, free from the intermittent debates of earlier generations about a right and proper style for a modern Australian poetry. At the same time, in many cases they share a poetic rhetoric that is open and hard-edged. (Peter Boyle and Aileen Kelly, who have recently begun to publish in mid-life, belong with their younger peers in this respect.) Some of this newer poetry also shows a strong awareness of violence. This has been a theme in Australian poetry since early days, though it has been sometimes screened out in literary memory. The opening of the anthology with a poetry of youth provides a cue for the full selection: I have watched out for good poems written when their authors were in their twenties and thirties, work that can be overlooked among the poetry of the finesse of age.

No poem has been chosen simply for its historical value. This is a survey of poetry rather than a meditation on Australia, and the aim of the book is the aim of poetry: to delight the mind. But Australian poetry, like that of other countries, is to an extent a local art — it speaks often from Australian perspectives. In much of the poetry of the nineteenth century, up to Federation in 1901, the very question of the newness and nature of Australian perspectives was rarely far from the surface. Twentieth-century poetry has by and large been more outward in its reach, but it frequently engages with Australian experience at hand. This is richly explicit in the keynote meditation of J. S. Harry's 'Picking the Nits' and Murray's 'The Buladelah-Taree Holiday Song Cycle' for example; and in the remembered details of childhood in Brisbane in Harwood's 'Return of the Native' and David Malouf's 'Early Discoveries'. The public note is struck in satirical poems by Ania Walwicz and Hope titled 'Australia', and in elegies such as Oodgeroo's 'We Are Going', Slessor's 'Beach Burial' and Leon Gellert's poem for Gallipoli, 'The Last to Leave'.

Australia is associated mythically with its outback landscapes, for which poetry has supplied some of the images. Landscape in Australian poetry, however, frequently means locality: particular places — urban, suburban, rural, outback or coastal — sketched out spatially and culturally, often within wider distances. In the mid-nineteenth century the poetry of Charles Harpur is already physically attentive to place — an attentiveness followed in modern criticism that Harpur was still too early to find language in English for the distinctiveness of Australian vegetation. But he was excellent on the details of light and sounds, and he transformed what he had inherited of the English Romantic sublime. In the world of 'The Creek of the Four Graves' — published in 1853 but set in the 'olden times' of pioneer settlement-invasion — the hinterland was inhabited, but barely knowable by the newcomer, hence perilous. It was particular and solid, yet seemingly unbounded. This speaks a different awe from the pure epiphany of 'Tintern Abbey', set within cooee of an ancient pastoral of 'plots of cottage ground'. The myths of wilderness have since become ecological, but that touch of unbounded space has proved durable in literature, painting and film. For many people it remains current in the vast distances between places in Australia. This can affect the inflections of place itself, even in the cities, where most Australians live.

One domain omitted with regret from this anthology is traditional indigenous poetry in translation. By every account this is a rich Australian poetry in its original languages, and it is understandable why some anthologists have included it. But I agree with those who feel that English translation is too merely approximate without the addition of lengthy commentary. I also believe that, even in the fragment of this poetry so far translated, the variety in form and regional difference would require a large section of any anthology to represent it justly. This is an oral tradition of ceremonial narrative and song in which every region of the land was culturally and spiritually named long before the first colonists arrived in 1788 — a diverse heritage in at least two hundred and fifty separate languages. As with oral traditions elsewhere, an important portion of this poetry had remained little changed over many generations, but it was also still being made in both its sacred and its more daily aspects. Though much of it is now lost, it remains a living tradition in some places.

As early as the 1830s, Eliza Hamilton Dunlop published verse translations of Aboriginal songs in Sydney newspapers. (Her poem 'The Aboriginal Mother', however, is her own. Like 'The Gin' by 'Hugo', it is a colonial attempt to banish the gulf in imaginative understanding that maintained dispossession. It was also a political intervention, being published in the *Australian* on 13 December 1838 amid the controversy surrounding the unexpected sentence of death, executed five days later, on white stockmen responsible for the Myall Creek massacre.) Among more recent translations of traditional Aboriginal poetry, the most valuable include detailed commentary: the mythology and symbolism are often complex, and meaning can depend partly on performance elements of delivery and music, and sometimes mime and dance. Perhaps the best way to represent this poetry would be in an anthology of its own, a needed companion to one such as this, taken from the best annotated translations, and drawing on an understanding of custodianship and necessary secrecy.

Aboriginal poetry written in English is another matter. It is fair to say that the meeting from both directions between Aboriginal culture and the writing of poetry in English has been quieter than in the field of painting. After generations of privation it seems that the language of pigment and visual line has kept extraordinary resources for the encounter. Aboriginal poetry in English, however, is a distinctive, developing tradition in the current resurgence of Aboriginal culture. Kevin Gilbert's 'The Soldier's Lament' and Jack Davis's 'Camping in the Bush' use the democratic form of a bush ballad pared down to a focus of protest. Beginning with the publication in 1964 of *We Are Going* by Kath Walker (later known by her tribal name, Oodgeroo) a number of Aboriginal poets have written in Aboriginal accents and dialects of English. Some recent poems by Lionel G. Fogarty extend this process, disturbing the expectations of Australian English by using dialect and standard versions together. A modest number of white Australian poets — among them Lee Cataldi, Mark O'Connor, Murray, Wright and Roland Robinson — have in their turn written poetry that listens to what Aboriginal values can offer to a thinking of their own culture.

Even when local in its accents and detail, Australian poetry in English is more likely than the novel to be refractory or wayward in relation to its society. One reason for this is that being a less publicly considered art it sometimes takes the privilege of idiosyncrasy; but it is also a matter of artistic focus. At some level, both the writing and reading of poetry involve a hearing of other, distant poetries, other realms of knowledge. Poets are generally conscious of practising an ancient art that visits across translatable boundaries. From Harpur onward, there has been a strong tendency among Australian poets to draw for some of their inspiration on a reading in chosen areas of world literature. This is not surprising as a recovery from colonial and geographical margins; but such outwardness is crucial to the liveliness of any tradition that is no longer part of the religious weave of a community — that is, most poetries today. In recent times it has been positively promoted by the global revolution in information technology and increasing ease of travel. The publication of poetry books, which for some time has been a settled, regional process, seems on the verge of becoming both more international and more fragmented. Regular publishing in Australia is increasingly in the hands of a few international companies who favour a small number of well-known poets who will sell many copies. This is nudging most of poetry towards something like its position in the nineteenth century, when publication was routinely paid for by the poets, up front or by subscription; the new avenues are desktop publication and the Web, and whatever evolves from these. Small public readings also are now an important form of publication, and one that is increasingly diversified by travel. It becomes possible to imagine a large number of poetries proliferating on a local level, and highly accessible across international borders.

This could be of benefit to the art (though apparently no solution to the penury of poets). Orthodoxies should become less easy to sustain. Poetry depends on poets feeling free to take risks of imagination, and on there being readers (including other poets) who are interested in poems where craft is equal to the vision. That critical process is unlikely to change, even with an increase in the amount of poetry made available. Access to diversity remains the key. In the field of Australian poetry this anthology offers a broad overview to be enjoyed and argued with.

I have had generous assistance in the preparation of this book. My thanks go to Ian Morrison and his fellow staff who made the resources of the La Trobe Collection at the State Library of Victoria so readily available; with special gratitude to Shona Dewar for the energy and expertise of her help with research. At the Cairns end of preparation I have a special debt of thanks to Michelle Borzi for practical help with the manuscript and for research and thoughtful suggestions on the text. Work such as this also has earlier dependences. I think particularly of the spirit of intellectual exchange among members of the Department of English at Monash University during my time there in the 1980s: my thanks are due, among many, to Elaine Barry and the late Dennis Davison. That spirit persisted in a leaner time and place with my colleagues Stephen Torre and Lyn Wilson and some very committed students at JCU Cairns Campus. I am grateful for a seedtime as a postgraduate student at Queen's University, especially for conversations on poetry with Charles Pullen and the late George Whalley, and with Robert Moore and other fellow students; and for the Canada Council doctoral fellowships which enabled it. I remain indebted to my earliest teacher in these matters, the late Sam Tully.

REBECCA EDWARDS   *(b 1969)*

Draw a Lion

they said. With a yellow noose I caught one
tassel-tailed, roaring like the sun.

In science we split the caramel eye of an ox
flattened it into charts
which our retinae screened upside down   5
and our forebrains righted.

Where did yellow begin? On the lips of my father,
in the cave of my ear, or at the point
where speech was pinned by my pencil?
The lion yawned and slipped away.   10

What is yellow? Is the word I utter
the colour buzzing in your shuttered eye?
Is yellow in the lidded pot
still yellow?

And what do we know of green   15
if butterflies see more shades in a leaf
than the human mind has language?

And can they see the lion
staring out from their wings?

(1998)

Moonboat

full tide reels you
from my ribbed and bellied boat

one cell
a moon too small to see

flowing out with plankton   5
                    turtle young
                            the ink of a squid
drawn on a shell-lipped wind

my red pearl
sheathed in an oyster of flesh   10

in the moon a gash of teeth
the carapace of a crab
the ghost of a human face

along my spine a shadow
                    cresting   15
(1998)

Eating the Experience: a Reminder

When you nail yourself
to a cross of flesh
don't forget: there are bones
there are veins.
When you strap yourself   5
to a glittering wheel
are you in for a fortune?
A knife?
When you're guillotined
by the thrill   10
don't forget your face.
You'll have to fumble for it later
with big blind hands.

(1998)

JACINTA LE PLASTRIER   *(b 1965)*

as a child I invented a book

as a child I invented a book
under a roof of bracken,
among the dark sweet of damp earth;
the weight of spiders
large as plates suspended between trees;   5
granite outcrops conjured into houses
on which I played for hours with brothers
strung into a wild sprint downhill
at the shudder of a snake;
a small spring with a solitary willow,   10
the far drop of mountains
in our small valley, where fog lived
except for the scalding, blue mouth of summers;
the lake nearby, its unplummetable depths,
both feared and trusted,   15
the sharp cool of its bathings:
surely I was blessed to grow
among such mountains — and already
with the invention of my book
the languid self-chant of symbols   20
the jugular quick of song's sting
stirring, my sole possession

(1998)

Construction Site

I am not talking of the wall's scream, how it screamed
    so whitely.
How the chair turned away.
How every thread that anchored each stone in me snapped.

I had lost my way earlier.   5

And the beauty hurt, of the city belly unearthed, history
    rupturing outwards,
Then paring back into pillars, huge teeth lodged.

I wanted to climb the rubble, find a single stone.
Let its weight convince me my eye was a hand.   10

(1998)

CORAL HULL   *(b 1965)*

Liverpool

liverpool, where is the city? — the grey platforms
glitter/ cigarette butts, sydney headaches & cultural
nooks/ & loudspeakers all moving backwards/ as we
pull out from town hall/ & slowly make our way home/
to the grand destination of being —   5
                               'all stations to
liverpool via granville — first stop central, then
redfern — then all stations to liverpool via
granville'/ all homesick westies board the red
rattlers with elbows & parramatta beanies & scarves   10
hanging out the windows/
                               at night after the hoyts
& hungry jacks/ adolescent girls stare nervously
through glass doors into rocking train corridors/
into the shaky sway of empty green carriages —   15

reebok thieves, masturbators & killers/ & vomit
washing beneath the cabin doors of tired train
drivers, trying not to kill the next suicide on
the tracks/
                               precious carriages guarded by railway   20
detectives/ smashing handcuffs against rails/ FEET
OFF THE FUCKING SEATS!/ smashing fists against fare
evaders, seat slashers & train wreckers/ at the end
of the line is liverpool:
                               where joyce maine is queen/   25
where the man pops up on the tv screen 'up the
road from baulkham hills', & yells 'let me do it

right for you!'/ liverpool, you dump, you hell hole/
you pollen & pollution collector/ you test tube of
heroin, you bucket of liver/   30
                    liverpool, you supermarket
culture, you checkout chick/ you are responsible for
hair gel & hairdressers like 'antons' & 'classiques'/
& donuts & cake shops & fat legs & summer frocks —
rapraprap gear & tracksuits/   35
                    liverpool, you sydney
basin basement/ i find the bargains/ i shop at
k-mart & target every day/ liverpool, where 'the
customer is always right', until ripped off/ where
door knockers for the spastic centre get a kick in   40
the teeth/
                    liverpool, city of little sympathy &
violent video/ city of passing western suburbs
heroes in video ezy aisles/ inbetween new releases,
pornography, action & horror/   45
                    i make eye contact with
an overweight man/ hugging toffee apples, diet coke,
hawaiian crunch & popcorn/ in each other we both see,
we will never come together & we will never leave
this city/ arnold schwarzenegger will make it better/   50

& a house alarm & a gun licence & crook lock &
derryn hinch to shuv it up all the small time crims
& give us all some largeness/ & some good old
fashioned morals & justice/ at least in our own
homes/   55
                    'hinchy' nightly at 7.00 & 'maccas' with two
allbeefpattiespecialsaucelettucecheesepicklesonions
onasesameseedbun & choosycheesechoosersalwayssay
cheesepleasewhentheychoosethecheeseonthecheese
burgersatmcdonalds —   60
                    i learnt that mythology ten
years ago, liverpool, i have never forgotten/ & i
have not forgiven you casula high — you concrete
gaol with your grey face to piss on/
                    you detention   65
centre for growth — with the teachers who fuck the
students & the students who go to prison/ casula in
the cow paddocks behind inghams — an appropriate
backdrop for frozen & suffocated chickens/
                    yep — &   70
the flannelette shirts & indian skirts/ panel vans,
old holdens & V8s/ & cigarette packets pushed up
beneath the sleeves/ peter jacksons, winfield 25s

& a marijuana earring & what are you smilin' at?/
& why doesn't anybody write poetry about us?/   75
                                          super
aggressive — traffic mongers — tow trucks — insurance
— pink slips, green slips/ slip over in the factory —
fracture your neck — claim compo, pension — sore back
— pay rego/ pay your own way into revesby workers,   80
into parents without partners/
                      & if they overtake
you in the peak hour rush on the hume hwy/ on the
canterbury road thru milperra/ then get out — walk
over — punch 'em thru the window — kick in the   85
mudguard — it's aluminium/
                            more carparks than parks,
more sizzlers than books/ & old school friends work
at the pavlova pantry, n.r.m.a./ join the army, the
police force/ or get married in tears in big park   90
or in the divorce & damnation fires of st lukes/

liverpool, it's good to be home/ dazzled by your
cultural desert/ your childhood, your domestic
violence/ your family victims & survivors/ & the
off yellow glow in suburban backyards/ the starlings,   95
the sparrows, the hills hoists, the clark rubber
swimming pools/
                  the guard dogs on chains/ the
thousands of aviary birds/ bull terriers, dobermans
& german shepherds/ overhead wires & telegraph   100
poles/ & where is the city?
                          — the place where
newspaper & tv people come from?/ what is the
aquarius bookshop?/ & how do those people get to sail
on the harbour?/ & should i send my poetry to a   105
publisher?/
              liverpool, you are the shifty hands of
john 'the shoddy mechanic'/ of caryards tuneups &
wreckers/ dyna tune, ultra tune & autoservice/ city
of vacuum cleaner encyclopedia & lawnmower/ & more   110
liquorlands & TABs than you can lay your damn
pay packet on/
                liverpool, city of the damned/ of
lost dreams, tv screens: the unhealthy unwealthy
& unwise of burke's backyard dreaming & the david   115
jones show/
              abusers & losers i'm telling you straight,
'cos i'm a westie': you gotta be rich to live in
sydney — you gotta be smart to go to uni — & you
gotta be famous to be in the movies/   120
                          why it takes

half a day for us just to get to the beach/ & sunday
afternoon on the way home/ one single stream of
summer car metal/ & heavy metal blaring from
metallic blue & purple/   125
                         on the road past lucas
heights & deadman's creek & thru the meccano lights —
& along the hume hwy & canterbury road via the
heathcote turn off/ into no-man's & no-woman's land

                                                                    1996

JOHN KINSELLA   *(b 1963)*

From Syzygy

16 *Chemical*

Boom-arm pod-fed nuzzles teaming foam
out over red earth: new machines
churning chemical seas in-lateral drift-a-round
phenomenally hand-in-hand with tractors
and deranged furrows rippling   5
heavy clods of soil
                         run-off creek river sea
deranged furrowing residual
        when myth hits purchase
who wants clean food?   10
bulimic south anorexic mid-point
        dr i p-fed north
deep-inhaling flyspray
and mosquito coils
fr - ie - ze dried coffee   15
cleaning a particularly
stubborn stove or bad guests
from a party

                                                                    1993

Heartbreak Drive

Heartbreak Drive, Cocos's Boulevard
of Broken Dreams, where all New York 'gals'
would *love to* be, attracts love-struck tourists
as if it were pure paradise. From Cocos
Hospital (where they recover from reef cuts   5
& alcohol), to Unjung Tanjong (where the ferry
takes them over the coral-encrusted lagoon
for brief outings on Home Island where an eyeless
coconut sees their every move & each grain

of sand has a name & is part of a family, where   10
a story is born with every sunset & Allah
stretches over the Indian Ocean towards Mecca),
all muse over the irony of a name. Like 'Lover's
Leap', which in any place, they'll maintain,
must be a place of magnetic beauty. I tell them   15
this coconut-palmed road that leads to snow-white
tropical sands is the place where infidelities
are named, where twelve-month contracts
are reduced to six & whole families book
their flights home. Where a long-term   20
Westerner might say to another 'There's
no room for suicides here' or 'No room
for *singles* on these islands.' There should be signs
along the boulevard — neon flirting with moonless
nights, like New York or somewhere else   25
that's thick with people & seen as a place
as far away from paradise as you can get.

                                                        1996

ALISON CROGGON   *(b 1962)*

Loneliness

loneliness.
it binds me to itself like a lake
eating my face with ripples.
shadows crawl in its thick depths.
I guess their shapes although I lack   5
a saint's disinterested equanimity
which tweezes parasites from stinking sores
forgiving them their nature.
I can guess what they are:
they are armoured and vicious things   10
their mouths are ugly with all the habits of greed.
if I hook them out with steely fingers
they will be small and limp and pallid
disgusting as excuses.
I recognise them all. I do not want to.   15
tonight I can't be passionless and distant.
I want a room of faces blurred with chat
drinking comfortably from shallow glasses.
I find an acid mirror which dissolves me
to the bitter arch of bone.   20

                                                        1991

the angle of your face

the angle of your face
      between my thighs —
           the thousand notes
                of your lucid tongue —
                      the taut fruits   5
            shivering to wakefulness
      against my lips —
o trees may embrace
      as slowly and completely
           the solemn earth   10
              and the unquenchable light
                  and know the joy of sap
            sweetly engorging them —
      but music once
tore their roots with listening   15
      and eyes rustled open
           hungering for Orpheus —
              that instrument of bone
                scoring the blank sky
              with worlds of loss —   20
         its blood foaming
      in the breath
         of angels
                                1997

Ode to Walt Whitman

Did you see me Walt Whitman beside my meagre river where I walk at
      sunset with my children
who whinge and buffet my arms and will not be led in any direction
marching with my sight closed to the rain and skittering seagulls while my
      children shouted look!
as the incandescent leaves shouted look! individual and numberless under
      the sodium light
although I hurried on nagging and impatient: 5
did you see me step off the sad trains in the hastening twilight
turning my face like a mint coin hope stamped on my mouth
to a night ambiguous with satellites
hearing in my secret heart the radio noise of murders half a suburb away
which all the loud news fails to report —   10
Walt Whitman there are evenings when love withers inside me
the beat you thrummed with your syllabled fingers those joyous rebellious
      prosodies:
did you see the muscles of your teeming world
smashing the earth unstringing the massive harp of the sky
when you sang of your body returning alert as grass   15
or thrust out the spokes of your sight into the great unchanging wheels the
      miraculous sun and the tumultuous impersonal sea —

Walt Whitman the gods are tarnished now the cities mourn their dead no
      longer
children roast in the fires of this terrible century
and no love is enough no elegy sufficient:
and yet I imagine you gentle imperfect generous man I would like to
      talk to you   20
perhaps you sit already at my shoulder whispering that nothing changes
that sunset is enough for its brilliance decay enought for its iridescence
old faker with your wise beard your lustful piety:
and truly what is my faith
except a stubborn voice   25
casting out its shining length to where I walk alone
sick and afraid and unable to accept defeat
singing as I was born to

                                                        1997

who was going to save you

who was going to save you
pretty bird o love of mine
the moon fell into pieces
the rain was not a sign:
the air was full of noises   5
the clouds were sudden bruises
and when you tried to make them sing
they broke and all the stars came in
and none of them had faces:
and then your blood was strange to you   10
bristling inside your skin
and strange the lidless eye which burned
your insides out to empty sky
and nothing spoke from that abyss
and no one held your hand: 15
o how you longed for sleep then
little bird o love of mine
the blue horizon split and bled
across the desert of your bed
o how you longed for sleep   20
                                                        1997

EMMA LEW   *(b 1962)*

They Flew Me in on the Concorde from Paris

They flew me in on the Concorde from Paris.
We were fortunate not to burn.
Over Shanghai I observed to my flautist husband,
'Such a metropolis needs a decent opera house.'

He rejected me in late May.   5
I resolved in future to express my feelings through my garden,
With an archway of zucchinis and cucumbers,
A bed of apothecary roses and high-yield grass seeds.

In the carpark at the Institute of Space Research
Women workers were performing their role of holding up half the sky,   10
While shipping companies complained about reserves of grain
Silting up the anchorage and all the sputnik could do was bleep.

I lodged with a senior government official in four elegant pavilions
Named after four seasons and bedecked with imitation sheep carcasses.
It was almost unthinkable not to give,   15
But I had no hard currency and could not afford contraceptives.
Thus I took a tonic in winter to be able to hunt tiger in spring.

I delivered my acceptance speech in the Great Hall of the People.
Citing the Scripture of Mountains and Seas,
I began by calling on steel makers to take up the way of Lamaism.   20
'Let's start calming down!' I cried.
'Let's get off painting and onto banking.
Differences are secondary to common interests,
They should not affect bilateral ties in a larger sense.'

I was applauded by reformists and conservatives alike.   25
Tell that to the lady in the morgue.
And tell her,
'When you get to heaven,
Maybe you'll get some answers.'

                                                                                                1997

Trench Music

There's an old heaven at work in me,
innocent as a cemetery.

It starts with the sound and speed of barricades,
more pillage and more homage.

Dancing with the bones of the lamb   5
near that delicate Stalingrad.

Entombed, bungled, fogged with breath;
naked never naked enough.

I cannot evade these forms in the bone,
the slow tunes from oblivion.   10

I fill up with shooting stars:
let my human half sing out.

                                                                                                1997

JORDIE ALBISTON *(b 1961)*

From Botany Bay Document

Headcount (1788)

so far: 1 Governor (Phillip) and his staff
of 9 - 1 surveyor-general - 1 surgeon
(White) and 4 assistants - 1 chaplain
(Johnson) and Mary his spouse - 2
servants - 211 marines their 27 wives   5
and 19 offspring - 548 male convicts -
187 female convicts - 17 convict kids (4
born on board) - sundry sheep hogs
cats dogs goats poultry (all types) from
England - 1 bull 1 bull-calf 7 cows 1   10
stallion 3 mares 3 colts 44 sheep 4 goats
28 boars and sows from the Cape of
Good Hope - private stock of officers -
varying numbers of natives (*naked and
saucy with spears and tommyhawks*) -   15
strange animals - coloured birds - Space
so much I feel *launched into eternity* -
•and me.

                                                        1996

Letter Home (Margaret Catchpole)

*Margaret Catchpole arrived in Sydney in 1801, transported for stealing a horse on
behalf of her lover. She chose to stay on in Sydney after her sentence expired, and
died in 1819.*

My dear Uncle and Aunt
I am not married almost
fifty years old nor do I

intend. I rent a small farm
of timber and corn I hire   5
men to work for me now.

I have thirty sheep forty
goats thirty pigs and two
dogs they take care of me

for I live all alone not one   10
human friend in the house.
I miss Home and you both

Botany Bay Document a book of poems that explores women's experience in early New South
Wales. Albiston notes that 'Headcount (1788)' is an 'almost entirely found poem'; and that 'Margaret Catchpole's "Letter Home" ... draws on letters she wrote in 1803, 1806 and 1811'.

and dear cousin Charles to
weigh me a pound of tea I
miss fine young Samuel   15

to make me my shoes and
poor Lucy to thread me
my needle. (And my lover

for whom I was caught
and condemned well he   20
rarely crosses my heart.)

My dearest Aunt I kiss
and cry over the hair you
sent I will always keep it

beside. And dear Uncle   25
you must think I walk well
for I went fifty miles in

only two days to pick up
the box that came in. I am
strong but do not grow   30

younger myself and have
lost all my front teeth. I
wish I could include more

news than this but the ship
sails directly and so I   35
conclude with a prayer to

God for you and yours and
not forgetting myself (adieu)
I am: *Margreat Catchpole*.

P.S. I do have a man that   40
keeps me in company but
I am not a one to embrace

the rôle of wife. No wedding
for me but that to this land
no vow but that to survive.   45

1996

DIPTI SARAVANAMUTTU   *(b 1960)*

Like Yeast in Bread

In the old women's ward
at Neringah hospital
an Ukrainian grandmother is requested
to sing a song. She replies:

'In Ukrainian, songs are dreams.'   5
Awake to death, my grandmother
has asked for someone to stay back, each night.
It is the year of Halley's comet.
My grandmother, who may be in her nineties
does not know her age.   10

My aunts have come from England.
A responsible twenty-five-year-old, I stay
my turn overnight, every fourth night,
in the milky blue light
of the night ward, where noise   15
feels like a hard object
dropped into stillness like glass.

Of her, I have a lifetime
of too few memories.
Unlike anyone we ever love   20
she'd never hurt me, giving
serenity rather than contradiction.
'We don't love people because
they are clear water,' she chided gently
once, after she'd observed   25
a familiar clash of temperament.

My mother's mother kicks the hospital sheets
and asks if the sound
of the air-conditioner is a river.
'Mehe gungak lungethe?'   30
The spirit of place
sits waiting for me all day
in the garden, while she sleeps
clutching the reflection of her hand.

Hers will be the first death   35
in the new land.
Before any birth or marriage,
this grief empties me like shock.
Back in Maroubra I stroll around
feelingless, like a mask that   40
has to absorb whatever image comes next —
her raucous laughter,
her mobile face and hands.

I walk through the shopping mall
beside the sea, trying to write   45
an elegy in all or any appropriate form:
like strokes painted by a fool or madwoman
because she needed art, and suddenly
a nine-year-old Vietnamese boy
in the Christmas show is singing   50

'I love Aeroplane Jelly ...'
in an incredibly high octave
before a beaming, bemused audience.

1993

Poem

When a loneliness we'll all believe
gets mistaken for an invitation
                to style
then I will relax my smile
into commonplace wrinkles   5
you'll use to seem older —
So engaging when you look into
my face I can't read you
                and my poems
of identity will continue   10
inviting us both to a picnic
and not much more
while our agents in another sphere
sleep restlessly
drink wine, argue and carouse   15
till 4am.

1993

LIONEL G. FOGARTY   *(b 1959)*

Sue and Du

The spirit of one tribe is all

The Wakka Wakka are there
walking, talking singing
in the land.
The Gabi Gabi are there, walking
talking, singing in the land.   5
The Gurang Gurang are there walking,
talking, singing in the land.
The Dungidau are there walking,
talking, singing in the land.
The Booyooburra are there walking,   10
talking, singing in the land.
They are all full blooded past and
futures. They are looking at us
doing what's wrong — yes they are
listening to us, saying silly things   15
Do you remember dat story
No it was never told. Yes
but can you sit in the bush and

Sue   magic word to effect change   **Du**   spirit of change (author's notes)

think of the chants peace they had.
Can you sit and easy your spirit   20
to feel their presence
can your mind picture what
they looked painted up like.
Yea Murri it's hard when few
are here, but some have   25
spoken long time ago, some are
here today willing to tell us.
Have you ever heard of Fred Embrey?
Well his stories are recorded in
book, may be taped. And have you   30
heard Willie Mackenzie — he gave
knowledge to migglou of lot of
tribes many old are still here
walking, talking, singing. Where
are they dat come from the land?   35
You Murri of today have it here
speaking, telling and reliving.
Wakka, Kabi are still there
they are all there in the wind,
rain, sun, bush morning and night;   40
you will feel proud to be Aboriginal
if you give all your tribes
the POWER TO LIVE.

                                                                    1995

Frisky Poem and Risky

Regarding respects I'm fully
purchased within my own
exchanges
Please give my regards to our
God down and above   5
I would also like more spirits
so the list can be send
Before receiving your hearing
I had to write to a conference
Sincerely I'm yours against   10
all evil co-ordinators
I decided from myself stems
a meaning and a creation
The prices I payed in every
eye ear and tongue will   15
wish they gave the correct addresses
My project have been pulsed
by blacks, and repriced

---

32 migglou   white people (author's note)

rejected too personally politically
This document I place, will be   20
the birth shown
A division by me is true
of knowledge in poetry
I've got history information
My date rave into sane real   25
I am amended then lended
Are you prepared for the
Nee Nee who died
I anticipated my pissed mind
I wish to withdraw all   30
my poems from the
building and put in the
open spaces.
As for gardens of me growing
out to another country   35
I may do honestly
My heart ain't pure love
My brain ain't poison daze
Ngunda Bimiai spoke the message.
All I did was draw this.   40
All I did was pass on
But one thing they gave me
is my own selfing self.

                                                                1995

PHILIP HODGINS   *(1959–95)*

Trip Cancelled

It's happened as they said it would.
While I was shoring up my hopes
and making plans to go abroad
remission has discreetly stopped.

Last night I tentatively pinned   5
a map of Europe on my wall
and dreamt its cities of the mind —
those languages, that sense of scale.

Today the doctor spoke of death
but what I thought of was a day   10
back on the dappled farm beneath
the peppertree a life ago.

The words for death are all too clear.
I write the poem dumb with fear.

                                                                1986

---

39 **Ngunda**   messenger of God (author's gloss)

Ich Bin Allein

Cancer is a rare and still scandalous subject for poetry; and it seems unimaginable to aestheticize the disease.
                    Susan Sontag, Illness as Metaphor

It is in every part. Nothing can be cut off or out.
A steady suddenness.
It isn't Keats
or randomness.
It is this body   5
nurturing its own determined death.
I will find out how much pain is in this body
and I will not behave myself.
It isn't fit for poetry
but since   10
poets create their own mythology
there is no choice.
My friends have all gone home.
I'm in the dank half-light. I am alone.

                                                        1986

After a Dry Stretch

The rain appears, as always, from the west.
Behind the mountain ranges it seems at first
to be a bigger, purpler, more distant range:
a counterpoint for some corellas, their wings
turning whitenesses on and off, unsynchronised.   5
Soon, almost quietly going about its business,
a marriage of elements descends the foothill slopes
and settles in for the day on the flat country.
In minutes your field of view is brought up close:
through rain there is only more rain further back   10
and cow shapes with their colours all washed out.
Reconstituting paddocks, eliminating dust
the rain is what was promised by machines.
Remembering its way by feel down gullies
it gathers colour, plaited milky brown, and reaches   15
the creek all stirred up, back together at last.
Getting through barricades of its own making,
hastily putting up new ones out of any loose wood,
water-rat-matted coats of dead rushes, bright plastics,
it repeats itself, stuttering in the tight situations   20
and growing in confidence over the broad deep lengths,
determined not to be drawn out in the next transition.
Now in the paddocks there are frogs, unpuffed,
still sluggish and flecked with dirt. Their credo
is sequential, 'Add water, reproduce, avoid snakes'.   25
Even the big ones are learning all over again:

they react by mating with the toe of your boot
when you give them a nudge. Their talkback
is regular as the rain, though lower and sharper.
Not far away, in a galvanised machinery shed   30
diesel is cascading into the tractor already hitched
to a ton and a half of crop seed on wheels.
From inside the amplifying shed it sounds like
hard seed is raining down on the corrugated roof.
A nail hole lets in star-small light, and rain drops.   35
More bags of seed are ready on a loading platform:
they might be sandbags stacked before a flood.
The farmer looks out at his unwritten paddocks,
relieved that all the weather-chat is finished
and that soon he'll be out there for days on end   40
filling the fallow space with standard lines.
The yard dog chases the old tab across bags
of seed. They both know it's only a game.
Over at the house too, the rain is happiness
for water is chortling into the big tank,   45
smoke is unravelling from the year's first fire
and mushrooms are forming in the minds of children.

                                                        1993

The Land Itself

Beyond all arguments there is the land itself,
drying out and cracking at the end of summer
like a vast badly-made ceramic, uneven and powdery,
losing its topsoil and its insect-bodied grass seeds
to the wind's dusty perfumes, that sense of the land,   5
then soaking up soil-darkening rains and filling out
with the force of renewal at the savoured winter break.
Sheep and cattle are there with their hard split feet.
They loosen topsoils that will wash away or blow away,
punishing the land for being so old and delicate,   10
and they make walking tracks that run like scars
across the bitten-down paddocks stitched with fences
while the farmers in their cracked and dried-out boots
wait for one good season to make their money green again.
In places where the land has begun to heal itself   15
there are the younger old cuisines, softer footed,
the emu farms and kangaroo farms, both high-fenced
and nurtured by smart restaurants and tax write-offs.
Further out where the colours are all sun-damaged
and the land is sparse and barely held together   20
you find the future waiting for its many names.
Company personnel in mobile labs are already there,
taking readings and bouncing lumps of jargon off satellites.
A field geologist sits in an air-conditioned caravan.

She sees in front of her a computer screen of numbers   25
then through a dust-filtered window the land itself.
She looks back and forth. Something here is unrealised.
It might be an asset. It might be an idea.

1995

SARAH DAY   *(b 1958)*

Chaos

Ovid was wrong. Chaos is no
unordered mass except for those
in its welter. It is hard to see the pattern
when you are the lines that construct
or the lemniscate you are riding.   5
The abyss, for example, could not be louder
than in this room. Strapped to this chair,
I'm at the epicentre of chaos,
now, before the currents bolt.
But if you are on the outside   10
counting away my clanging seconds,
champagne corked, it's all clear;
killer of wives, children, mothers —
Presto! Order has commenced, is restored.
Chaos Ovid, is frigid, calculated   15
as this inert combination of hot wires.
As my hand with a knife raised.
As my mind on most days.
It's only mad, confusing at the centre.

You are the yellow soup   20
in the chrysalis, awaiting a miracle;
blind faith and caterpillar memory
and no foresight. No distance to view
the alchemy from which the moth swims,
substance from will. Etched wing forms   25
folded inchoate in ether, are unseen;
you have no eyes. Process has no eyes.
The confusion is the caterpillar's
as it must have been the earth's.

Deep in primordial swamp
in the blackening peat-bog,
ideas lie enfolded, reversed fossils
of forests, cities, people.
Turn on your TV news,

1–3 See the opening of Ovid's *Metamorphoses*

suspend history a moment on the screen;   35
the present's an impasse of doubt, a koan,
but today's riddles unwound yesterday.
Model of absurdness, the centre,
the subatomic paradox, thoughts turn
at a distance into this chair, this floor,   40
me. A dead hyacinth, a dry gourd —
viewed too close, autumn's over the hill,
a mockery of summer. Those who saw
the first autumn must have seen
the end of everything.   45
On yesterday's news there's a semblance
of shape, coherence,
design is impossible to argue
on the greens of killing fields.
People are the evidence that of time,   50
distance, order is born
though in stepping back to view
the choreography, a foot may whirl
into the gyre of a madder dance.

                                                                        1991

MARCELLA POLAIN   *(b 1958)*

---

astronomy

shell & membrane part
behind thumbnails wide   insistent as my breath
yellows   tense & hemispheric
(dropped into a wide   cracked   deep   blue bowl)
shake as if the earth itself shakes   5
as i whip the whites with sugar
(peaks that form beneath my hand are himalayan)

above
a yolk rich moon slips over
night's upended pannikin   10
(& paradise shines through brilliant
          where its metal has worn thin)

there are women in my marrow
whose bones were cracked
for alchemy   15
like this

                                                                        1996

gastronomy

this day she eats:
a cornflakes-icecream-peanutbutter-pizza sandwich
& then
this day
she starts to eat herself   5
slowly sucks the fat
beneath her skin
(till her tongue could
lick along her bones)
& smiles   10
buys bathers for herself
gift wraps them
plucks her body hairs
one by one
stares naked into mirrors   15
& is very young again
no more tugged blood

but she can not close the holes in her
fill up & polish scars & pores
knit hymen   20
stop up arse & throat
her fingers find their own way in
& penises
& spoons

this day she eats: 25
an allbran-jam-cheese-sourcream-olive fruitcake
                                        fruitcake
& squats & squats before the toilet hole
thighs wrapped around the pedestal
wanting love   30
offers contents of her belly
to her thin thin lover woman
offers fat & blood & hair & tongue
for love

                                                    1996

ANTHONY LAWRENCE   *(b 1957)*

The *Capricorn*

Got my sealegs the second night out on the *Capricorn*,
staggering drunk from rail to rail
with a knife strapped to my hand under the booms.
A floating meatworks, the nets came up with fish

thrashing silver among scallops,   5
floodlit shapes dumped like a glitter of shit
to the sorting tables, someone copping a raysting
on the hand, and a mulloway grunting its life out
on the boards.
                    Now, parked by the Gascoyne River   10
with a bad dose of shucker's wrist and a frozen
bartail flathead steaming on the bonnet,
my wrist thumping, I see the skipper holed up
behind glass, his face pale-green with radar light,
the wipers smearing yelled abuse from his mouth.   15
We were all half cut, the hip-flasks of Bundy rum
going overboard like undersize cod, Guns n' Roses
blaring through the spray and a bong going back
and forth across the tables, its stem smoking
like the funnel of a miniature steamer.   20

Working fifteen hours then collapsing
into bunks that reek of fish guts, sweat and semen,
tattooed arms draped over the sides, and Canadian
Wayne dreamtalking shark attack and blood.
Then too soon the alarm of the engines, up again   25
to be stabbed by the spines of small bright fish,
the pain wicked — a red-hot wire running
from your hand to your underarm, moaning, still
sorting, and no one giving a fuck.
The money's good but you piss it away,   30
riding your stool the first night back at the bar
of the Carnarvon, one hand on the rail, one
around the glass. The crew a hard lot, young
and scarred — a season on the boats then south
to Donnybrook for the apples.   35
                    A couple of hours
to record three weeks at sea, the flathead
thawing out like some gothic hood ornament,
the veins in my wrist ballooning — poems and scallops
ripped out wet and fleshy from their shells.   40
                                                         1993

Mark and Lars

Wind and rain, and sometimes pigeonshit in your eyes
when Sydney's trains had doors you could wrench open,
with guards taking your false name and telling you
to pull your head in.
                    Going over the harbour,   5
you had to watch the pylons — they made a whip
of air as they came at you, but Mark slapped one,
tagging grey steel, and left his finger
like a white finch perched on a rivet. At least

that's how I imagined it, walking back with him   10
over the bridge next morning, a red blur of absence
seeping through the end of his bandage,
but no finger, not even a smear on the pylon
to tell what had happened.
           And years later,   15
older but still reckless, imagination packed it in
when my sad mate Lars lost his head
on the Western Suburbs line, misjudging the space
between two speeding trains — a sound like
a deflated football being booted, and Lars   20
falling back through the door, the original punk
graffitist, spraying the inside of the carriage.
And drunk, we assisted him, throwing up our guts
and hearts, crying for help and Jesus, spinning
the brake-wheel like we'd always promised,   25
the sparks and guards leaping out into the dark.
On Toongabbie station I looked through a crowd
of emergency people — Lars was laid out weirdly
in his black duffel-coat, the collar turned up hugely;
mad Lars, who'd have said *Whoever finds my noggin*   30
they'd better take care of the bastard.
                             1993

The Drive

My father could not look at me
as we sat in the back of a white sedan
on our way to the police station.
But I looked at him. He was staring
straight ahead through all the years   5
his son had disappointed him.

News had come through of the boy
who'd fire-bombed the car outside
the Methodist Church. When the detectives
arrived, I was having a family   10
portrait taken. I saw the suits and ties
in the window, then the doorbell rang.

I smiled into the flash, ran to the bathroom
and vomited my head off. I wanted to make
the Australian team as a fast bowler.   15
I wanted Frances Clarke to love me.
But instead I'd struck a match and immolated
the minister's new Valiant, my breath

punched out of my lungs by the boom.
I ran behind the Sunday-school buildings   20
and confessed to the lawn-raking currawongs.

I watched black smoke like useless prayer
gutter into the Sydney sky.
The sirens were a long time coming.

As we pulled into the station carpark,   25
dead leaves and the two-way static
sounded like years of thrashings: blue
welts across the backs of my legs like
indelible neon, and my mother's weeping
for the times I nailed her with insults   30

to the wall. But now, after breakdowns,
divorce and a distance of eighteen years,
we can talk about the sound a belt makes
as it flies in the bathroom; about
the violent spirit of a teenage son.   35
My mother kisses my eyes to stop

the sadness we've known from breaking
through. My father tells me about his life
instead of brief reports from the office.
I love them, these parents and strangers,   40
these friends who appear from time to time,
sharing their names, their blood.

                                                                1993

JUDITH BEVERIDGE   *(b 1956)*

How to Love Bats

Begin in a cave.
Listen to the floor boil with rodents, insects.
Weep for the pups that have fallen. Later,
you'll fly the narrow passages of those bones.
                              but for now —   5

open your mouth, out will fly names
like *Pipistrelle, Desmodus, Tadarida*. Then,
listen for a frequency
lower than the seep of water, higher
than an ice planet hibernating   10
beyond a glacier of Time.

Visit op shops. Hide in their closets.
Breathe in the scales and dust
of clothes left hanging. To the underwear
and to the crumpled black silks — well,   15
give them your imagination
and plenty of line, also a night of gentle wind.

By now your fingers should have
touched petals open. You should have been dreaming
each night of anthers and of giving   20
to their furred beauty
your nectar-loving tongue. But also,
your tongue should have been practising the cold
of a slippery, frog-filled pond.

Go down on your elbows and knees.   25
You'll need a speleologist's desire for rebirth
and a miner's paranoia of gases —
but try to find within yourself
the scent of a bat-loving flower.

Read books on pogroms. Never trust an owl.   30
Its face is the biography of propaganda.
Never trust a hawk. See its solutions
In the fur and bones of regurgitated pellets.

And have you considered the smoke
yet from a moving train? You can start   35
half an hour before sunset,
but make sure the journey is long, uninterrupted
and that you never discover
the faces of those Trans-Siberian exiles.

Spend time in the folds of curtains.   40
Seek out boarding-school cloakrooms.
Practise the gymnastics of wet umbrellas.

                    Are you
floating yet, thought-light,
without a keel on your breastbone?   45
Then, meditate on your bones as piccolos,
on mastering the thermals
beyond the tremolo; reverberations
beyond the lexical.

                    Become adept   50
at describing the spectacles of the echo —
but don't watch dark clouds
passing across the moon. This may lead you
to fetishes and cults that worship false gods
by lapping up bowls of blood from a tomb.   55

Practise echo-locating aerodromes,
stamens. Send out rippling octaves
into the fossils of dank caves —
then edit these soundtracks
with a metronome of dripping rocks, heartbeats   60
and with a continuous, high-scaled wondering
about the evolution of your own mind.

But look, I must tell you — these instructions
are no manual. Months of practice
may still only win you appreciation   65
of the acoustical moth,
hatred of the hawk and owl. You may need

to observe further the floating black host
through the hills.

1996

GIG RYAN   *(b 1956)*

Loose Red

1

She turns the conversation down to bite-size
and leaves through an evolving door,
taking care of her face like a contract
that it won't spoil. Profiles are serious,
they forget all about you and your thin planets.   5

Her painting is hieroglyphic
and when you've caught on, you can't stay
in a house of social dialogue. The shiny people
say things they've never said before.
A dull psychotic room fills with them.   10
. . . .

It comes to this, a stray kitchen
where you freeze to death. The nice warm people
talk to each other in a way that means exit.
A hanging tree shines in rain.   15
Wipe your face on that, run, as he delivers
a quiet premiss that might've killed thousands
and abolished you.

2

Mozart, opera, and science: I feel I'm a kid,
watching my father.   20
But it's Newtown. I left my father in Melbourne
with god. Here, there're only crazy people
who know what's good for you, men
who never make it, women who want to be loved.
I only like him as a person, she says coyly,   25
with that candid '72 sense of discovery.
You can date each attitude on your tour
of the past tense. It's what happens when you lose
the 'house of your dreams' in Surfers Paradise,

its view of processed water and the recent past   30
lift back into the envelope.
He stands in the door, fit for someone's crumby sentence,
wishing to be a tenor, or an athlete, even you.
Scrape the healthy muck from the fridge.
Everybody thrives on it. She wants space   35
and walks the beach all night.
I look at the stars tensing into position,
the muffled moon, a cloud's chemical slick
that won't be gone tomorrow.

                                                                              1984

Six Goodbyes

1

His cursory So long
To me, shame, dishonour
frazzle down the drain
as truth is eloquent, passive and detached
I plug his mouth with venom   5
the phone's rash
Desire and remorse confess together
past caring
I wade through the grey trees
cradling death   10

2

New streets tinder to the harbour
They clean up simultaneously in the maverick flats
Two streets away, cars droll towards the Cross
Saturday's a trial
Emptiness follows all the yachts   15
The capitalists are friendly when you buy
'Shakespeare saw that it ... was the perfection of a woman
to be characterless' (Coleridge reflects)
My ears are stuffed with men and the noise they make
A girl walks down the used lane with her pay   20

3

The foamy ingenuous girls kiss and flirt
True love grapples with its forceps and ekes out
what sense you had
They clamour for attention
and in the gin dark I think only of you   25
as Consolation heckles
Downstairs, the taps chore, and he bashes off to work
His kisses don't work

4

She laughs with the cherub women
She loses faith and goes   30
after melting the drugs and administering
I stick the union that we had once in my head
but carry home the sorrow root, the sac

5

Surf music seeps from the separated father's flat
A madman in the lane shouts nothing   35
The walls shudder with the traffic
The Government doesn't know you from a bar
I plug my ears with wax to hear the sirens
Every second weekend his kids invent a yard
between stumps of furniture, a tin shed and a gate   40
The bridge is tanked with frost

6

This junk does nothing
The rotating lounge room and the American music
fan out
The flat's coffin works your heart's tin bureau   45
What I eat I throw out like a philanthropist
blasé with the routine
The dangling acquiescent dawn crops up

                                                           1990

The Cross/The Bay

She turns blue in the bathroom
Meanwhile the endless parades of Youth and Beauty
recreationally pop in.
She recalls him, fagging out on a higher plane
when their blank eyes met   5

The visited day lurches forward,
still negative on the blood test, bereft of hope.
The rich embrace a cause
like if you sink, you're guiltless.
He pitches for a fight. The illusion drops.   10
You leave the car. You leave them all.
The cockroach fidgets on the stove's coil.
In another flat a Spanish lament tilts its stealthy ardour
like crumbs. You wriggle on the grave sea wall.
Weddings drop like flies.   15
The city looks at itself.

                                                           1990

PETER ROSE *(b 1955)*

Vantage

Hanging out the stained tablecloth
and several monogrammed handkerchiefs
once belonging to my father, I look up.
It is a high wild imperious handsome day.
I had it to myself for an hour,   5
like an ambivalent character in Conrad,
nautical man alone with his dyspathy.
Now, looking round me, I confront
a universe like an empirical zoo,
everyone watching: a stunned young man   10
washing up in his hungover way,
a calico cat wedged in its tree,
patient for doves, that elderly
Russian woman leaning from her window,
drying her grey magisterial hair.   15
Staring, just staring, everybody staring.
Or is this egoism, morning's fine way
of mocking an unshaved transcendentalist?
Today I feel like greeting each of them singly,
Charlestoning across this concrete courtyard,   20
essaying some ludicrous summery gesture —
though when I venture 'Good morning'
the Russian woman goes on staring,
her mannish mouth ambiguously grave.
Conceivably deaf, incontestably beautiful,   25
this was someone's Beatrice,
leaning now from a window in a suburb
thousands of miles from the known
and the ardent. What is it you would
have me say? she insinuates,   30
unravelling her grey magisterial hair
while I stroke the belled calico cat,
admire the republic of verdure canopying
our shared courtyard. Last night
it was a refuge for insolent possums,   35
maddening my neighbour's Airedale,
forcing an early waking — not unwelcome.
Again I greet my ironic Russian,
sternest of sharers. Again, no answer.
Yes, it is a high wild imperious handsome day.   40
Upstairs my espresso pot has long boiled dry,
the companionable stock flavours the house
with rosemary and celery and thyme.

In a blind room at the end of the hall
a tender guest, laziest of celebrants,   45
wakens in my bed, traces the knots
and fjords of my absence. Calling.

                                                                      1993

The Only Farewell

Now it flowered on you like coral
of a coruscating kind,
and I moved towards you
in a trace of pulleys,
knowing this would be the only farewell,   5
twining expiation on expiation,
as memory, flawed and tuneful memory,
shivered across me like
the voluptuary's most painterly cloud.

                                                                      1993

KEVIN HART   *(b 1954)*

Sunlight in a Room

The silence attending words,
The body firm as a plum
And the spirit now weightless
And willing as a needle,

And gathering around me   5
This summer morning, sunlight
Basking on the wooden floor
With an animal pleasure:

This first, thoughtless joy, the taste
Of chill water, as the sun   10
Places bread upon a sill,
A hand upon my lover.

                                                                      1984

The Black Telephone

An old black telephone rings in the dark.
How far away it is, when heard asleep,
Somewhere across a border, in the hall;

How far away, and if I answer it
My life will shape itself around a voice.   5
Such darkness as before God spoke a word,

And no one should be calling at this hour.
The names of things creep out into the night
But all creation tenses round that phone.

It is the Duke of Cumberland, breathing hard,   10
'Where are you? Leave for Culloden Moor at once!'
I do not want to answer. I know him well,

Let all the drumming stay in 'forty-six,
With all the sleet, with all the filthy snow.
Let famous generals rot in their gilt frames.   15

It is my mother, awake in Brisbane's heat,
Announcing the anniversary of her death.
I do not want to answer. Go to sleep,

I know those stories better than myself:
Old relatives who smell of photo albums,   20
The knotted streets of Brighton where I got lost.

The night is black and full of secret truths;
It wants to tell us something urgently
And has been trying hard for many years:

An emptiness that longs to talk to you,   25
And say, 'Well, first you must do this, then this ...'
But still that telephone rings in the dark.

                                                          1991

The Calm

There is a cancer fiddling with its cell of blood,
A butcher's knife that's frisking lamb for fat,
And then there is the Calm.

All over the world numbers fall off the clocks
But still there is the Calm. There is a sound   5
Of a clock's hands

And then there is the Calm.

Now there are children playing on a beach
Out on the Marshall Islands
With fallout in their hair, a freak snowfall.   10
There is no Calm

But then there is the Calm.

All night I feel my old loves rotting in my heart
But morning brings the Calm

Or else the afternoon.   15

Some days I will say yes, and then odd days
It seems that things say yes to me.
And stranger still, there are those times   18
When I become a yes

(And they are moments of the Calm).   20

                                                          1995

The Room

It is my house, and yet one room is locked.
The dark has taken root on all four walls.
It is a room where knots stare out from wood,
A room that turns its back on the whole house.

At night I hear the crickets list their griefs   5
And let an ancient peace come into me.
Sleep intercepts my prayer, and in the dark
The house turns slowly round its one closed room.

                                                              1995

DOROTHY PORTER   *(b 1954)*

Bull-leaping

Is poetry a strange leftover
of Minoan bull-leaping?

the archaic skill
of flying over the back
of the beast   5

and gracefully surviving,
making it look easy

the bare sweaty breasts
the gilded loin cloth

the crowd enjoying   10
your big sexy risk.

Or is this kind of poetry
a forgotten fresco crumbling
under a mound of prose

the pieces glimmering   15
like snakes skuttling to ground?

                                                              1996

Why I Love Your Body

I put your body
    between me
        and the history of horrors

your sweet tongue
snaking through my lips   5

your heavy breasts
thudding ripe on my ribs

your thin legs climbing mine
like twin grape vines

your creamy wetness   10
creeping through my fingers

when your body bursts over me
my mind goes almost quiet
faintly squeaking to itself
like a fruit bat dozing   15
        upside down.

I put your body
    between me
        and the terrifying future
            of my body   20

tonight I'm a noisy swamp
squelching under your bare toes.

                                                                 1996

The Water

It's the water I remember,
the warm salt-lick silk of it
around my half-grown hand

and the air
crackling with hot holiday smells.   5
sausages, eucalyptus and Aerogard

was it one moment
on that rocking pontoon
or a thousand?

was it one time   10
I chanted to myself
remember, remember, remember?

the water. my hand. summer.
my life cooking up a storm.

and my loneliness   15
electric.
                                                                 1996

JOHN FOULCHER   *(b 1952)*

Innes Foulcher (1897–1984)

The lace curtains in their living room
were like barbed wire, keeping the carpets from fading;
the furniture was sullied with a mineshaft light.

Everywhere, there were pictures of stiff-collared men
and crushed white women in bonnets,   5
cowled about the piano.

Nellie, her sister, lived by the piano
and died by it, never knowing the unstarched hearts of men,
fearing them, perhaps:

she would cycle in wool-heavy heat   10
with her skirt clinging to her calves, the clipped spinnakers of cloth
billowing, like a storm.

I can't recall colours there, in that Christian house.
But Innes took Christ and all the ranting prophets
out of this, led them   15

through the Pacific's wilderness
to Fiji, where she lived thirty years,
scalded with sun and work.

Some photos I've seen: Innes among the natives,
like a pillar of salt   20
or a sharp vein of quartz through their onyx bodies,

splendidly missed
when she returned for Eric, the mongoloid brother
Nellie couldn't cope with, alone.

I remember the early Christmases,   25
our visits after church, and Eric
with his grub-bellied tongue and lizard eyes.

We saw them always together: Nellie and Innes,
grey puffs of hair, and hands chattering with teacups,
words that hovered in the room   30

like blowflies.
How like coming out from underground it was,
running to the gate and the car beyond.

Innes out-lived them both,
moved to Bowden Brae, the retirement village,   35
with its coal-mine corridors and ceilings,

its assumption that age will diminish us.
It was 'modern', but she filled it with her old house,
chipped floral crockery

on the vinyl tabletop.   40
From the window, the road stuttered between trees,
and the wind chanted

among the iron verandah rails;
ingots of sunlight were stacked by the bed
when, finally, she died, the last of the Foulcher girls.   45

How little we knew of her.
At the funeral, a vague succession of Foulchers
lined the front pews,

each having a name
from somewhere in the Christmas conversations   50
of that dark house;

but, after the last prayers, five Fijians stood
and sang for her, all the island's flowers
opening, in their voices.

                                                                    1987

MYRON LYSENKO   *(b 1952)*

Living in Coburg

I'm a silly boy. A lazy city boy,
sitting in my house drinking beer
& reading newspapers,
surrounded by Italian neighbours
who don't understand   5
my weeds & run-down house.
They believe in food & neatness
& photography & families.
They stand in front of their homes
posing for cameras & relatives,   10
making sure they don't block out
the manicured lawns
& the colours of the stylish flowers
or the new car, washed & gleaming
in the pebbled concrete drive-way.   15
They mail their homes to Italy.

They're nice to me; they wave — smile
when I walk past their lives.
They talk to each other about my house —
want to buy it for their daughters.   20
They don't complain about my stereo
don't ask about the strange looking friends
popping in & out of my doors
or too much about my life-style.
They wonder why I'm too weak   25
to push the lawn mower around.
They meander past my house
when they go visiting in the street,
wondering what I'm doing *in here*
with my loud music & closed blinds.   30
They would like to see more of me
in the front yard.

They tempt me with their food smells
& the way they laugh & talk
when they get excited.   35
They knock on my door & ask
if they can cut down the trees
which are tearing up their drive-ways
& pulling down their fences;
& while they're at it   40
could they possibly mow my lawns
or at least the front one, please?
& maybe next week they could plant flowers
because flowers make a house look good;
& if I'd like, they could turn my back yard   45
into a huge vegetable garden,
altho, of course, they'd leave enough room
for me to sunbake.

They carry a bottle of beer up my drive
& they bring their own glasses   50
& they talk about football & unemployment
& their children, studying at uni.
They ask how long I intend to live here
on my own, surrounded by families.
They tell me not to sell the house   55
without talking to them first
& they say goodbye & smile
as they carry the empty bottle down my drive
sweeping the dirt off my path
with their coloured rubber gumboots;   60
& over the kitchen table they tell their families
that I'm thinking of moving to another suburb
to be with people my own age
& they look out their windows
at me, in the back yard, lying in the sun,   65
dreaming about going to Italy.

                                                              1988

Stephen Edgar   *(b 1951)*

Destiny

It was a simple melody on two flutes,
Brief, meagre, somewhat plodding,
Unembellished,
A slight piece, as I thought, concluding
A side of *La Flûte Indienne*. What the notes   5

Said of it I forget, except its title,
Destino — Destiny. Destiny?
How did that name get itself attached
To a tune with so thin a
Resonance, that offered so little? 10

Yet, later, those narrow notes, that solemn fluting,
Playing on, played on the mind,
Thin and cold
As Andean air and its barren ground
That offers so little. And an image was competing, 15
Now recalled and Indian too, a hall
Of mummies, ancestors,
Trussed and rigid, upright underground, marshalled
There, bearing a bleak justice
That could prove perpetual, 20

Their dead mouths singing, singing, round and stretched,
Two opposite dry lines of O's,
Two hollow ranks
Of flutelike ceaseless crying that rose
Above hearing, and brought to mind the things you've wished 25
Never to know, what you hear
In lulls, behind all sounds,
Or when the first bird sings and its little chinks
Gather from the morning air
The whole weight of silence. 30

1988

Yet

Yet weapon-slender wasps
Torment themselves with glass
As though the look of sky
Will let them pass.

Yet mothers go on driving 5
Children in buckled seats,
Seeming to know a way
Through the hard streets.

Yet far across the river
The afternoon applies 10
Slow fire to the water.
It hurts my eyes.

1995

PETER BOYLE   *(b 1951)*

First Shift

The clothes of the absent woman
who is cold and heavy with sleep
rest easy by night in the darkened kitchen.
Numb with tiredness she will stumble and fix their floral delicacy
to her neck and breasts   5
and the loveless day will drag against her eyes.
Over and over she will find
the sink where her teeth are waiting,
find the chill of the open window
where the steam of the kettle escapes.   10
And the single cup of coffee
will be bitter and strong
under the small light she turns on cautiously
so as not to disturb the children
who must wake later on   15
and dress themselves
and eat the breakfast she leaves out
in the bowls she arranges.

The clothes hang from the back of the fridge
to warm themselves.   20
All night they stay awake,
the consciousness of a house without a voice.
Later she will watch the steam rise
against her fingers as she drinks,
will quickly carefully check the latch when leaving.   25
Walking rapidly through the darkness
towards the first train
she won't even think of endings or purposes.

The earth's cold has many names.
To walk and to breathe   30
will have to count as living.

                                                                    1997

Flying by night

Flying over Saudi at night
to my right the burning fires of wealth
fragile palaces of pink whipped cream
then further, beyond the desert's curve,
wide seas more mountains   5
and soon to the left
the fertile islands of the very poor.
Appearing as tiny pinpricks

the spires and domes of the great faiths
can barely be seen from here,   10
vanity shrunk by distance to the shape of a cup
upturned on an empty chair.
The only man-made structure visible from space
is a long wall built to stop vagabonds
and collect taxes.   15
It did neither for very long.

In the walk down to the Prado past the Cafe Aleman
the slow hill dodges the outlet of a parking station
and there beyond the tree-lined boulevard
of nineteenth century Europe   20
is the terrifying luminous vision of Hieronymus Bosch
hung in the white corner of an ordinary room.
It is upstairs and to the right.
I can give directions on how to find it
but not what to make of it.   25
It says something about the landscapes of wealth
the sterile subways of Tokyo
sensuous nights in a Balinese garden
the death of Saigon
the ghost men descending into torture chambers   30
under a garage in Rosario or Baghdad
and the vast cold lands
where cities form tiny pockets of light
in the darkness that cries for them
like an aborted mother.   35
In the picture mechanical devices for prolonging death
stand innocently beside overripe cherries
plucked from the mouths of gigantic birds.
Naked riders sweat under slicked hair
lashed by the fountain's spray.   40
If this picture gives us a map of the world
we cannot read it from the air
travelling at the same speed as the earth decays.

The plane flies from somewhere over Saudi
into the top centre of the painting   45
where it hovers like a demented moth
in the pink eternal twilight.
I pick my way in darkness
along a breakwater of rough concrete,
feeling my way with my one free hand   50
towards the other shore.

1997

ANIA WALWICZ   *(b 1951)*

Australia

You big ugly. You too empty. You desert with your nothing nothing
nothing. You scorched suntanned. Old too quickly. Acres of suburbs
watching the telly. You bore me. Freckle silly children. You nothing much.
With your big sea. Beach beach beach. I've seen enough already. You dumb
dirty city with bar stools. You're ugly. You silly shoppingtown. You copy.   5
You too far everywhere. You laugh at me. When I came this woman gave
me a box of biscuits. You try to be friendly but you're not very friendly.
You never ask me to your house. You insult me. You don't know how to
be with me. Road road tree tree. I came from crowded and many. I came
from rich. You have nothing to offer. You're poor and spread thin. You   10
big. So what. I'm small. It's what's in. You silent on Sunday. Nobody on
your streets. You dead at night. You go to sleep too early. You don't excite
me. You scare me with your hopeless. Asleep when you walk. Too hot to
think. You big awful. You don't match me. You burnt out. You too big
sky. You make me a dot in the nowhere. You laugh with your big healthy.   15
You want everyone to be the same. You're dumb. You do like anybody
else. You engaged Doreen. You big cow. You average average. Cold day
at school playing around at lunchtime. Running around for nothing. You
never accept me. For your own. You always ask me where I'm from. You
always ask me. You tell me I look strange. Different. You don't adopt me.   20
You laugh at the way I speak. You think you're better than me. You don't
like me. You don't have any interest in another country. Idiot centre of
your own self. You think the rest of the world walks around without shoes
or electric light. You don't go anywhere. You stay at home. You like one
another. You go crazy on Saturday night. You get drunk. You don't like   25
me and you don't like women. You put your arm around men in bars.
You're rough. I can't speak to you. You burly burly. You're just silly to
me. You big man. Poor with all your money. You ugly furniture. You ugly
house. Relaxed in your summer stupor. All year. Never fully awake. Dull
at school. Wait for other people to tell you what to do. Follow the leader.   30
Can't imagine. Work horse. Thick legs. You go to work in the morning.
You shiver on a tram.

(1981)

Little Red Riding Hood

I always had such a good time, good time, good time girl. Each and
every day from morning to night. Each and every twenty-four hours I
wanted to wake up, wake up. I was so lively, so livewire tense, such a highly
pitched little. I was red, so red so red. I was a tomato. I was on the lookout for
the wolf. Want some sweeties, mister? I bought a red dress myself. I bought   5
the wolf. Want some sweeties, mister? I bought a red dress for myself. I
bought a hood for myself. Get me a hood. I bought a knife.

1982

The Abattoir

I owe my living to the abattoir. My father, the manager, sat in the office. Red
brick, smelling of death. These dumb and frightened sheep that travelled at
night. So I could eat them. Each stamp, clip in the office, smelled of
slaughter. The purple, indelible pencil left a dot on the pink tongue tip. So
very extra mauve like mark. Number or tattoo. Counted the stamp marks   5
on the flesh pink, alive yesterday. And killed. These white paper sheets
all written neatly and typed. These tiny pencil marks spelled the ending.
The glazed, dumb eyes of the cows waiting. That I ate. That lived inside me.
That I became. My vet dad, giving me needles. Like a pig. Earned money for
my typewriter in the abattoir. Killing thousands of sheep and eating them   10
all and every one. The blood seeping through the oil paper, these presents he
got me. This meat. Red steaks I'd put in my hand. Lovely ladies, each one.
Put my hand in the mince. Flesh squelching inside my fist. That's me. In
here. Pink and gushing. One little scratch. And I'm one pig. Pigs at the cattle
market. Pinks in the abattoir. My father, the artificial inseminator of cows,   15
sits at his desk and kills. With his purple pencil. These healthy butchers.
Very happy. Slicing away. Their stomachs taut. Looked at them, excited
with their knives. The butcher at home, bending wire in his singlet. I had a
cook. Had cooks. Never had the butcher. This butcher cut a piece. Put red
meat in his raw mouth. My father stood next to the cow. The pig squealed.   20
The healthy, young, beautiful butchers sang in their silver room. Hosed the
floor. Sunshine in their mirrors. Lights in their glass. Glistening pink flesh
on their plate. Sausages in my hand. Warm butcher's hands on my breasts.

1982

JENNY BOULT   *(b 1951)*

i'd like to know about the fruit bowl

because you lived here
but didn't live here
because you kept your own place
(we had agreed on that)
it's difficult to know whether or not   5
you still don't live here

the cup i gave you for your birthday
is in the kitchen
so is the fruitbowl you won
in the easter raffle   10
& the thermos i gave you for christmas

but the drill isn't in the laundry
your books aren't in the study
& your trophy's not on the t.v.

your hairbrush is on the sink
there's shaving cream razor toothbrush
your green towel. the bathroom's full of you.
don't you get dandruff at your place?
is the shampoo in the shower a hint?
you've taken the nail clippers   20

i was feeling guilty
about not feeling guilty
i didn't miss you
maybe it was the small change by the bed

if you'd left the keys & taken the rest   25
I'd have known exactly what you meant
i would like to know about the fruit bowl
& whether or not
you still don't live here

                                                    1986

ΠO   *(b 1951)*

vol/fol

i'm working in a job, that pays 10,000
for checking Subdivisions: 'Mr' and 'Mrs' (joint
proprietors) of Vol/Fol, are encroaching on
'Mr' and 'Mrs' (joint proprietors) of Vol/Fol by
.03 metres, — signed by me & dated,   5
i fell in love at close range, stayed up late
got up the same time sang in the stairwells
in one door & in another
shifting one Vol/Fol to check it, against another
'G'day' . 'Morn 'n' . i say   10
in the same boat, surviving on 10,000 or so
'Friend or Lover, choose' she said
but i choose neither, and interrupt to move
Vol/Fols & G-numbers, between 8
& 4:45, or be accountable to the boss   15
the bosses' boss, and so on
cos there's enough Vol/Fols (9,000,000 to be exact)
to keep me busy. & it's easy enough, easy
if you just keep regular hours (& everyone does)
3 people last month, all had children   20
'Hoot' Gibson's wife is, 6 days overdue, so we
joke about it, tell 'im: it'll B
triplets, & he'll call them: 'Beep, 'Beep' & 'Honk'
(that'll make a *nice* family: 'Beep', 'Beep,
'Honk' & 'Hoot')   25

but i throw in 'Rec'/forms . 'Sick' /forms
& since 'Flexi' . 'Flexi' /forms
cos, sitting at my desk, shifting one Vol/Fol for
another Vol/Fol, i keep thinking about her
over & over, thru one cigarette, into another   30
& watch the window, which is either: raining or sunny
but in here, the air conditioner is accurate:
3° above normal, and comfortable.

                                                            1978

PETER GOLDSWORTHY   *(b 1951)*

Alcohol

You are the eighth
and shallowest
of the seven seas,

a shrivelled fragmented ocean
dispersed into bottles, kegs, casks,   5
warm puddles in lanes behind pubs:
a chain of ponds.

Also a kind of spa,
a very hot spring:
medicinal waters to be taken   10
before meals, with meals, after meals,
without meals;

chief cure
for gout, dropsy, phlegm,
bad humours, apoplexy, rheumatism   15
and chief cause of all the same.

At best you make lovely mischief:
wetter of cunts,
drooper of cocks.

At worst you never know when to stop: 20
wife-beater, mugger of innocents,
chief mitigating circumstance
for half the evil in the world.

All of which I know too well
but choose to ignore,   25
remembering each night only this advice:
never eat on an empty stomach;

for always you make me a child again —
sentimental, boring

and for one happy hour very happy —   30
sniffing out my true character like a dog:
my Sea of Tranquillity,
always exactly shallow enough to drown in.

                                                1988

A Statistician to His Love

Men kill women in bedrooms, usually
by hand, or gun. Women kill men,
less often, in kitchens, with knives.
Don't be alarmed, there is understanding
to be sucked from all such hard   5
and bony facts, or at least a sense
of symmetry. Drowned men — an
instance — float face down, women up.
But women, ignited, burn more fiercely.
The death camp pyres were therefore,   10
sensibly, women and children first,
an oily kind of kindling. The men
were stacked in rows on top. Yes,
there is always logic in this world.
And neatness. And the comfort   15
of fact. Did I mention that suicides
outnumber homicides? Recent figures
are reliable. So stay awhile yet
with me: the person to avoid, alone,
is mostly you yourself.   20
                                                1991

ROBERT HARRIS   *(1951–93)*

From Seven Songs for *Sydney*

6 *They Assume the Survivors are Australian*

You, Carnarvon, at Empire's end
     with your one baker
          baking all night,
you wordless
          under too large a moon,   5
making sandwiches by the pound.

Sydney   The cruiser *HMAS Sydney* and the German raider *Kormoran* were both sunk in an engage-
ment off the Western Australian coast on 19 Novemeber 1941. There were no survivors from *Sydney*; 103 of the survivors from *Kormoran*, who landed in lifeboats, were captured and brought
temporarily to Carnarvon.

Some of those women have since died,
        the youngest married long ago,
            some moved interstate
        for the franchises, the chicken farms   10
coin-laundromats
                & sportsgoods stores
    but who hasn't, man or woman, set up
        some urn and trestle and waited
            in aspects, as a line?   15

All hearts have nourished
                    sworn enemies

And the hatred still wanders
        through scholarship, flares
or ebbs in assiduous pendulation.   20
    At the pub they are saying,
            'Lynch them.'
                'Lynch their captain.'
And you, Carnarvon, you have to find,
    unlock and expend the last resource;   25
you only, the smallest town on earth
            must fight into civilization.

You, stone faced, who pushed out a cup.
You, turning,
to hide your tears from their faces.   30
                                            · 1992

Cane-Field Sunday 1959

The children wear shoes today and wait. By the cattle-grid
in the leaf blue shade. Their houses are stilts in this paddock,
they wait to be picked up for church at the paddock gate.
And this is the extent of it. White, pink, powder blue in a line.
Boys in grey. The man in the ute that roars up wears a hat,   5

he is lost to a commonplace adult restraint.
They climb in the back, like Christmas decorations that escape.
I am thinking of white, pink, blue in a line, and grey
climbing over the metal side, one after the other
and one climbing over the back.   10

There are children already inside, they wear khaki.
And the two sides never say anything. One side white and pink,
one black. And the fields are green and the mission house is unpainted.
Congregational, I think. And this is the extent of it,
a ute-load of children who keep their eyes blank.   15
                                            1992

PHILIP SALOM   *(b 1950)*

Bicentennial — Living Other Lives

At a time when the ruler was troubled by the problems of his subjects, a wise man came to court. He ordered a large bowl filled with water and told the ruler to plunge his head into it. The ruler dreamt of many lives in many places, where justice and riches were plentiful. When he lifted his head from the water, only seconds had elapsed. (Persian tale)

1

Which lives shall emerge from the waters? Kelly, the armour
turned back into a ploughshare and all his youth unfallowed,
his gift for language and republic
put down deeply, a furrow across the squatters' country.

Burke and Wills, with their shuffling dreams of continent,   5
survive and tell, their famous buried food rising in gourmet pods
from the desert, so travellers may keep this side of folly
yet know the route of discovery and have the strength to live it.

A murdered woman (the weighed-down backbone of a nation),
who was left behind the humpy or was it the old white Holden —   10
minute by minute she counts the bullets in her body
as if they were intimate, then flings them down, having done.

Albert Facey and all his kind, children with their backs
worked bare by opportunists, but now the scars from beatings
gone that were a second language, the universal one.   15
They are its counter-text, rough, naive, unworldly,
this keeps them new and perhaps even more profound.

Soldiers return from the mud, the Last Post just missed,
as always. These men and women, shock-tourists, loved and drunk,
riotous and a bloody insult to the Empire, thank God.   20
And now awake to that naive willingness to founder for the British.

And all those young lovers, but mostly fathers and mothers —
who died that invisible death on the wrong end of telegrams
burn now those bitter postcards from another country — the strange
handwriting: 'Wish you were here'. (The picture's blank.)   25

Children rise and breathe again, their skins perfect
and all the sad ways fall from those around them;
the mothers that encircled birth but did not survive it
are themselves born back unto their children.

Aborigines pick out the shot that has sizzled there   30
like ancestral gravel (a kind they could never guess at).
The boots float back from heads and ribs, bones
find their shape again and the body's country is lived again.

Trugannini and King Billy and their others, come back into the one flesh
from the bare and callous measurers, from the museums'   35
glass coffins — go back into the place of totem
their white headhunters gone, or utterly uncurious now.

The women are unraped (the man is peeled off like a transfer
or finds every point of contact as he lies over her
burns like a devilish stigmata. She is his electric chair).   40
Now she can put the pain aside, the horror finally gone.

2

What will they dream of, under the magic waters
where once they were dead and alert, never letting the self die;
or dead in some spiritual sense of justice, this other self
suffering has laid down like the rings of cambium?   45

There is no new world. They are refugees, heart-people
from the subtle lands of history. They cannot shock-start
suddenly in a tea-room, the cup nearly at their lips; or in the Ford;
or the next brick laid; a desk of inventions for watering lawns.

Wipe off the water. The impulse of justice is almost   50
a new colonisation, the latter century under a pith helmet,
or the great body of a leech that must be turned inside-out
to expel its victims. It is the wish for a whole identity.

In each of us there is the exercise of justice.
Without righting anything, there is the gritting tilth of republic   55
in all these lives. It is the other-body, each life-form intense
and crucial. And all beneath the surface of our words.

All that can be offered is to put them back gently
into death. Where they have felt past rage, indignity,
dishonour. They have all gone, as finally as Holt beneath the waves.   60
A public peace. Only this second death can give it.

                                                            1987

The Chamber and Chamberlain

The courtroom is underwater opera, aquarium for the deaf.
Counsel and judge flit and pause, mouthing like goldfish,
nuzzling down onto flakes of law, minutiae on the pages
grown like coral. Lines of bubbles stream from the jury —
justice utterly bewilders them, as it should. To compensate,   5
truth leans twelve different ways, attempts the muscle
of concentration, but who is sure if the jury are swimmers
or singers or part of the set. Justice is the biggest
bubble of the lot. The mumbled points of conceptuality
never prick it: here are the sharks grazing against   10
the glass. Only the judge remains exotic, his scales
strobing porphyrian above proceedings, or flashing

from the mirth that no-one else is quite permitted,
putting personality where it isn't. The accused stares
with desperate equanimity. She's an example they won't take.   15

                                                              1989

JOHN FORBES   *(1950–98)*

the best of all possible poems

like a dozing shark
or a very quiet limb
waiting for the lecture
to make it a star the
best of all possible   5
poems relaxes asleep
in the tropical surf
beginning near the
right hand corner of
the room. meanwhile   10
just outside my window
inter-island trade
begins: their supply
of coconuts is endless

                                                              1980

Drugs

for Jenny Baker and in memory of Simon Bronski

Marijuana lets you know
what you really feel about
this, that, these & those

but cigarettes are just
something to breathe against   5

while speed wraps itself around you
the way a speeding car
wraps itself around a telegraph pole

and all cough medicine can do
is make it a pure delight   10
to read the *Times Literary Supplement*

But a wallet full of money
is a different thing entirely

— you know about amyl nitrite,
the Heart Attack Machine?   15

it's far cheaper than cocaine
& the cat's whisker you can afford

won't give you much of a flash
as opposed to the massive rush
of amyl nitrite's darker hit   20

So why bother with coke? Rock stars
I don't mean you! But the best

of all is heroin. One day.
One day you'll own a big house.

Then by way of light relief   25
there's my own favourite, alcohol

which is not really a drug
at all, just as the motto
'lips that touch liquor will never

touch mine' doesn't mean   30
the girl of your dreams won't be

a problem drinker. Even hippies
will, reluctantly, get pissed

& talk about tripping I won't
because real acid is a thing   35
of the past & besides I could

be busy, like you are, drinking
which means we both have
a Reason to be Cheerful. Another

is when you're on mandies   40
you don't need drugs

the body is so calm it could be
a bag of soft expensive stuff

& the brain is as pure
as foam on central ocean tossed   45
or the driven snow

a girl from Sydney
is hoping she'll find in America

along with the drugs I've left out here
because I can't remember   50

a thing about them except
they felt like I was swallowing a pill

washed down with a lot of vodka
so that the pill & I both forgot

that we've been mingled   55
happily ever after. & I've forgotten too

about drugs & music —
how they meet inside you

in pubs & rooms & dances —
blind chemicals to make you freak   60

or sparkle / rock'n'roll music
to bounce you around.

1980

Speed, a pastoral

it's fun to take speed
& stay up all night
not writing those reams of poetry
just thinking about is bad for you
                        — instead your feelings   5
follow your career down the drain
& find they like it there
among an anthology of fine ideas, bound together
by a chemical in your blood
that lets you stare the TV in its vacant face   10
& cheer, consuming yourself like a mortgage
& when Keats comes to dine, or Flaubert,
you can answer their purities
with your own less negative ones — for example
you know Dransfield's line, that once you become a junkie   15
you'll never want to be anything else?
            well, I think he died too soon,
as if he thought drugs were an old-fashioned teacher
& he was the teacher's pet, who just put up his hand
                        & said quietly, 'Sir, sir'   20
            & heroin let him leave the room.

1988

Love Poem

Spent tracer flecks Baghdad's
bright video game sky

as I curl up with the war
in lieu of you, whose letter

lets me know my poems show   5
how unhappy I can be. Perhaps.

But what they don't show, until
now, is how at ease I can be

with military technology: e.g.
matching their *feu d'esprit* I classify   10

---

15 **Dransfield's line**   See p. 64.

the sounds of the Iraqi AA — the
thump of the 85 mil, the throaty

chatter of the quad ZSU 23.
Our precision guided weapons

make the horizon flash & glow   15
but nothing I can do makes you

want me. Instead I watch the west
do what the west does best

& know, obscurely, as I go to bed
all this is being staged for me.   20

1992

ALAN GOULD   *(b 1949)*

Tightrope Walker

He climbs the vertical on all four hands,
discards the third dimension, dances off

as though he were a stick-man drawn on paper.
His mystery? It's simple. Dream a floor,

then walk or climb on it, for space is strung   5
with rafters of theory. Ah, what might he prove

for physics, this hare-brained fellow with his pole,
this baggy-trousered monocycling spirit.

Perhaps one night he'll amble to the moon
along his wire, umbrella on his shoulder,   10

or stretch a line between the now and then
to cycle there and back, his silver girl

astride his narrow shoulders. His family
includes all sparrows perched on telegraph wires,

all pirouettists, and the earth that walks   15
on its invisible rail around the sun.

But now, perhaps because the plains of mind
have bored him, he lies on his one-strand bed

and goes to sleep with one foot dangling in space,
space-shuttler, hung above the slow continents,   20

the sapphire oceans rolling under his rest,
while from below come cheers like call-signs, which

he's not disposed at present to acknowledge.

1986

Demolisher

By six he's started. I wake to a wince and arrh,
the animal protests of my neighbour's iron roof.
Behind a cypress-dark, the February sky

is blue as gin. The house is nineteen twenties;
he moves along its apex removing it,   5
and at this hour he's higher than the sun,

flexing a torso of cinnamon brown, his singlet
dangling whitely from his belt. Slav
or Italian, perhaps, he applies that rigid serpent,

the pinch-bar, to open unconsidered caches   10
of darkness. His work is wholly restoration —
he is recovering horizons, and

with the long arm of Archimedes, bringing
sunlight to gulf the spiders' vertical suburbs,
dense as hairballs in their sudden light.   15

So ridge-cap, gutter, sheet iron are grimaced free
from battens; sheets of fibro drop-shatter,
nails, clenched in the pinch-bar's single knuckle,

come out with a sigh. By lunchtime the house
is a birdcage of timbers; by evening it's gone,   20
and the man sits, gleaming like resin,

rolling cigarettes, drinking water,
looking through a gap at new hills,
peering down the shaft he's made in sixty years.

                                                                  1988

That Move from Shelter

Laughing, we had made a dash for shelter
into some vast workshop, stood in its gloom
among the chainblocks, lathes, heavy vices,
all recently abandoned. I say our mood
was oddly light, expectant, as we breathed   5
the pungencies of oil and metal filings
while for half an hour the downpour's roar
cocooned us deep within its ambient hiss,
urgent, constant like the TV white noise,
so null we felt uncovered when the storm   10
dwindled, and we started, toiled upward
through woods, the heavens huge in aftermath,
cloudwrack glimpsed and sunlight liquid, foliage
bright like brass on a lathe, diaphanous
in places, whippy branches beside the track   15
flicking rain in our faces, at each slight breeze

the canopy pattering, droplets scintillant,
momentary in the air like a storm
of asteroids against the green tumult of leaves.
Our berets, tunics, were rain-darkened, clung   20
to the skin as though they were some loose
reptilian skin, our boots rain-sheeny, slippy,
and the cold of our hands, our faces, which neither
the sun nor our movement seemed to warm,
spread throughout our bodies, like the cold   25
in the tree's heartwood, in the flakes of shale
tumbling from our boots downhill, cold
of the gleaming earth itself, and its creatures
easing cramped limbs as they ghosted themselves
deeper into their small hollows.   30
                            It is,
it is such details near the sense, mundane,
yet filigreed with such cold beauty that
now I cannot distance from the mind
as I state plainly how we then descended   35
into the small untidy village, saw
the evidence report had spoken of,
called up the choppers, zippered the plastic bags,
remarked how the recent rain had slimed the varied
surfaces of all that had been torched   40
within this place into the one black paste
that fouled our uniforms, greased our palms,
making it impossible to tell
what blackness brushed us, clung to us, knew us,
whether it was the charcoal from some roofbeam   45
or some blackened, suppliant human hand.

                                                      1996

JENNIFER MAIDEN   *(b 1949)*

Space Invaders

Shaun knows you mustn't wait
too long behind the barrier.
You are a target anywhere.
You skip, you strike, you kill
bigger bastards and you score.   5
He steers his tick-shaped ship across
the black dog universe until
it hits a jet fleet like
a phalanx of fleas and implodes with
the wan beep of a dying   10
electrocardiograph. He leans
crosslegged in taut boredom,

and hits with sensuous disgust
the infinity of shit he's known
others he's known to need: the stuff   15
you smoke, the stuff you spend,
the stuff you eat, the stuff
you have to suck at school.
He knows it's not as fucked
as the pokies his parents pull   20
next door. No handfuls
of shit fall out. His
second ship survives.
He still needs to use his aim,
his hand, his sight.   25
In spring again he thinks he'll shoot
more wildcats and rabbits with his mate.
He'd like to join the Army soon.
He has a hunter's eye for parasites.

                                                            1988

The Winter Baby

for my daughter Katharine Margot Toohey

So, babies are primal: Moore-sculpted rock
— rock from a flood as sleek as stone —
that has no more, no less than body warmth,
the warmth of the dusk sun.
                            Her strength   5
is absent-minded and wordlessly good,
a sleepsong sung in the key
of a satisfied short groan.
                            Her laugh
is as wide and wise as winter.   10
There is nothing filmy
nor flimsy about her.
She feeds as firmly
as the heart mills blood,
her needs as fair as Milton's God   15
and her eyes like night on water.
                                                            1990

A Summer Emotion

jealousy is a summer emotion
when the skin is hard to handle
and friendship is intimate
as the stain in the armpits
of the dress worn to impress   5
a judging rival. It is a long
slow urge like a silkworm

spinning. Now softly it emerges.
Its wings have been folded
badly like sheets crowded back   10
on a shelf. It uncreases them
slowly with grublike patience.
Once again I have left things
too late to roast it for silk.

1990

EDITH SPEERS   *(b 1949)*

Why I Like Men

mainly i like men because they're different
they're the opposite sex
no matter how much you pretend they're ordinary
human beings you don't really believe it

they have a whole different language and geography   5
so they're almost as good
as a trip overseas when life gets dull
and you start looking for a thrill

next i like men because they're all so different
one from the other   10
and unpredictable so you can never really know
what will happen from
looks alone

like anyone else i have my own taste with regard
to size and shape and color   15
but the kind of style that has nothing to do
with money can make you bet
on an outsider

lastly i guess i like men because they are the other
half of the human race   20
and you've got to start somewhere
learning to live and let live
with strangers

maybe it's because if you can leave your options open
ready to consider love   25
with such an out and out foreigner
it makes other people seem
so much easier

(1986)

Tony Lintermans   *(b 1948)*

A Bone from the Misty Days

For there is much to be learned from dogs.

For the dog is focused upon the immediate, as in the startled rabbit chased,
    or the scent reciprocated.

For the dog goes crabwise through the day, sidewise he goes with prancing joy.

For the dog is aimlessness creatively tuned, exact opposite to a briefcase.

For my first dog was Whisky, a blue heeler who worked with cattle and was
    well trained.   5

For he was a way-back dog, a down-boy, sit-fella skitch-it dog who always did.

For he was my friend in the days of mist, those early school days.

For he was there the day that raincoated Freddy Hayes rode up to the front
    door demanding to know where his cows were.

For Freddy's fences meant well.

For my mother this was the last straw.   10

For the hearts of snapdragons had been bitten out, and the stocks trampled
    by these same cows on earlier visits.

For she answered, 'If I see 'em, I'll shoot 'em!'

For my father was a flower farmer with finicky customers.

For Freddy Hayes turned his horse and rode away, drawling over his shoulder
    'Well shoot 'em!'

For he was nonchalant like his fences, slack tempered.   15

For three days nothing happened.

For the bees in their box on the old wooden dray it was buzzing as usual.

For the kookaburra flying across the dam with a black snake dangling from
    its mouth it was one more long lunch.

For Whisky and me lying in long grass it was Saturday, and cloud-watching
    time.

For we were friends in the misty days, those early school days.   20

For the cows would come back, and they did.

For they were skinny and ridiculous in their wooden head-frames to stop
    them jumping fences.

For they jumped anyway.

For they landed in our newly planted lawn, and went four-stepping all
    through the pouring night.

For the rain called their tune as they waltzed and slithered and squelched in
    the new-raked soil in their ruinous moo-less ignorance.   25

For morning came, and with it my father's wrath.

For he was shouting, 'The pound! This time it's the bloody pound for Hayes'
    cows!'

For it was five miles to the Ferntree Gully pound, with six cows accused.

For I was to help with the droving, and Whisky too on this suddenly blazing
    no-school morning.

For now it was holler time, pick up stick and hurl it time, hoo those cows
    along!   30

For the cows it was incomprehensible hoo-ha, humans going ga-ga time.

For what are we but cows? their sad eyes asked, for what are we but cows?

For their flanks were heaving and soaked with sweat.

For they would stop to eat, or enter someone's driveway before they were hit
    again, or nipped, or barked at.

For it was 'Get along there!' or 'Move you mongrels!' or 'Gorn!' all the way
    along.   35

For righteous anger ruled, like a stirred-up snake it whipped those cows along.

For I was nine years old and innocent, but helping anyway.

For they were Freddy Hayes' cows, the errant ones, the high jumping ones
    with moons in their eyes who'd moseyed neighborwards once
    too often.

For the day was sunny and the gravel road glinted in the morning's dappled
    shuffle.

For mushrooms were pushing up by the bucketful in Thompson's paddocks
    there as we crashed past, but I could not stop.   40

For the creeks were running, three of them in that five mile walk, snug in
    their ti-treed banks winding like dull green ribbons through the
    passing farms.

For the Gully pound was near now, and half the morning gone.

For the bridge where the swaggie slept was passed.

For the acre of pumpkins gone wild was passed.

For Alberni's and Sharp's and the mad lady with the black horses were all
    watching, and were all passed.   45

For the pound was reached at last.

For one father, one son, one old dog and four cows it was 'Phew' time, and
    one exhausted 'Moo'.

For two of the beasts had bolted, got clear away to the paddocks.

For the pound keeper penned the cows while telling my father the rules of
    redemption, the money that was needed to get them back.

For my father nodded.   50

For he nodded again and said he would tell the owner *immediately* where
    his cows were, but did he?

For not on your Nellie, sport.

For let him sweat, thought he, let him sweat like the flanks of his cows.

For I was late for school, too late for 'Show and Tell' but I told them anyway.

For the subject was 'How We Drove The Cows To The Pound' and it was good. 55

For Whisky died soon after, just lay down in the long grass near the dray
    and became disinterested.

For he was buried in the re-raked, re-sown lawn, and a plum tree planted
    to mark the spot.

For the days of mist were finally over.

For I consider there is much to be learned from dogs.

For they nuzzle and nip only what is wholly present.   60

For they zig-zag everywhere, never going direct on their tail-wagging business.

For the world is always teasingly new, and they know it.

For memories of the misty days are buried like bones, and sometimes when
    I dig them up, I know it too.

           1989

The Escape from Youth

My father's discipline closed me like a box.
A hardness hammered shut the lid.
For fifteen years, no matter what he did,
I was unreachable. Venom sealed the locks.

Neutral beauty kept me company. Walking   5
through neighbours' cattle, from moving skies and trees
I learnt the slower, vaster intimacies.
Avoiding the world of men, I stopped talking,

except intensely to myself. Rumours
of happiness sometimes seeped outside the box.   10
'Untrue!' I howled, and double-checked the locks.
In the dark, poetry grew like a tumour.

When the poems were big enough to break
their way out, dragging me behind, I saw
my father's face, more bitten than before,   15
a soft fist eaten by love, impossible to hate.

There is no forgiveness now, nor the need.
Silence bred rich fruits — a known self, those skies —
for which I thank my father. Amnesia lies
behind our peace. Neither of us dares to bleed.   20

                                                                    1989

ALEX SKOVRON   *(b 1948)*

The Hair

Strolling fondling the *Guide* and glad he bought it
he flattens ants below his knowledge / the mouth soon sings
as he cooks / he swallows a warm slice of slaughtered
mammal and a bum of bird for dinner / brings
an axe killing and the latest balaclava rapes to screen   5
with coffee / takes the news depicting the impressive scene

of a military massacre plus the latest promise
fifty thousand in the Persian quakes / yawns / to quell it
he retires to dream of nipples / next morning nearly vomits
when a razor hair gets caught on his palate.   10

                                                                    1998

Glissando

From a train, each act is slowed, made trivial
    in a sadness outside duration. That's the real
wisdom of trains ... You hurtle past a suburb: men limp
    into doorways, schoolgirls stroll the sun, the street
vendors are statuettes with heavy mechanical limbs.   5
    Who was it said time is an engine of cogs and gears?

Look again. This crowded *shtetl* is no vanished world
   from the mists of time, sealed in monochrome sorrow,
but life, poised at the lit leading edge of time. A child
   waves, smiles up at us: as if there's no tomorrow.   10

1998

Almost

There is a quiet substance to things —
The way the world fits together in spite of itself;
You feel it when driving encapsuled in the rain,
Slipping into a silent hospital at night,
Or scanning half-familiar faces on the screen   5
That almost return your strange satellite gaze.

There is a substance also to emptiness,
But it can never truly be exchanged with another;
Like an absence, or the impulse to despair
At the hole in the universe your substance almost fills.   10

1998

Legend

But this was 1969: her father seemed so old that
I expected him to crumple at any moment. Instead he folded

his fat Saturday paper, smiled Nixonically
and, thoughtful, brushed at his shadow like an alcoholic. 'We

eat at six on Saturdays, you're welcome to join us.   5
In the meantime, drive nicely.' At last: we were alone as

a couple of cosy parkers in Lovers' Lane, or almost — this was a
daytime date so we'd have to make do. And because her

Psych project was due Monday, and tonight being the night of
her babysitting debut, most of the weekend was a write-off.   10

So we drove down to this windy deserted beach
halfway along the coast, to a place where they'd converted each

little picnickers' bay into a sheltered virtually one-car
niche, turned off the wipers, the motor, managed to plunk our

starving bodies into the back, where, peeking over at   15
me like a magnet she loosened herself somewhat and 'Gopherit!'

she said. And before we knew it, as the cross-hatched rain
sealed us into our great dream forever, latched in our hot pain

against the wet world, half-naked where it mattered;
and as I watched her effigy unveil, and our teeth chattered   20

---

7 shtetl   little town (Yiddish): a Jewish town or village of the kind that once flourished in eastern
Europe

in the steam of the afternoon downpour, and she unravelled a
hand into my skin, and I sensed her perfect shadowy parabola

remould itself and disappear somewhere and grow ample,
and understood the thrall of Samson as he grasped the temple

pillars with all his love and all of his power; and as I knew all   25
this, I suddenly recalled, absurdly, that the fuel

gauge had been sitting on absolute zero and in a while I'd
have to restart the car; I thought of her dry old dad and I smiled,

and I looked into her spinning, half-open eyes and her arms clung
irreleasably and that was the moment I drowned, there among   30

the pounding waves of rain and her infinite lips ... That and
the radio humming, and 1969; and who cares today if any of this

is anywhere near the way it never quite happened.

(1996)

ALAN WEARNE   *(b 1948)*

From The Nightmarkets

From *Elise McTaggart*

Often we went to the pictures, Jack persevering.   'Soppy!'
he'd laugh. 'How wet!'   True, being Mister and Missus
would beat any Rialto heart-throb. And our kisses!
Dry electric ones, swoony perfumey ones and sloppy
ones that annoyed him and made me giggle.   5
   Yet we knew what could happen, we knew
how far was far enough, anything else a brew
that made you never never never want to stop. He wouldn't niggle
me or whinge; as much as he tried, John laughed and tried.   'One day,
old girl,' he sighed. 'I know, one day. We understand — '   10
   A full moon covered the sea and suburbs. Under its light,
singing G and S, we drove home. Sunday
after church and dinner I tried to nap and
   Oh thank God, I thought, thank God I didn't give in last night!

1986

From Roger

23

   For no one reads an article or book
to think yes, that's the way to run it.
At least I don't. Those reasons some Cosmo-hack
gives in *How Affairs Succeed*? We'd all begun it,

whatever *it* was, generations before.   5
The early-to-mid twenties of this family man
slotted into an inevitable mosaic, sure;
but Barb liked me. She never, per se, planned
to share another's words breath body farewell-kisses:
which seemed the silliest events on earth,   10
at the time. For me simple *going at it*
wasn't simple. I'd other ways to please the missus
if not excite her. Don't try them? Then you're not worth
that pinch of proverbial. No, something better mattered.

24

    Yet, she's seeing someone. Doesn't need a barrage   15
of love-bites to be hit, for one more crater
to pock the moon of your marriage.
Oh you always hear from clever men, years later,
what *they* would do: stay very single, forget
if any kids were ever hatched.   20
    But Barb, I and Sam lived what we had, for *that*?
Pragmatics are too passionate. Try it detached,
you still need to conceive (italics/
capital H) *Him*. Enough contenders bound
from the blocks, most you'll never meet (the price   25
of a good imagination). This issue, the smart alecs
know, requires a more soluble state. They pound
the problem (yes, you have one) with advice.

25

    So when friends mind your business it's an art
to wear their blunt moralising: 30
man-to-man, Rog, you married a tart.
A skill, sure, like Barb disguising
not *Him* but her despair: the hocus-pocus
affairs need to continue. (Or love, who knows?)
    I'd get myself asleep hardly rousing notice   35
at the hour she might return, stoned I suppose.
By Spring Barb seemed caged to the haywire pulley
of infatuation. Near Christmas she came clanging
back: their trysts, assignations, dates
had closed. And I'd the future: enough to sense *bully-*   40
the-lot-of-it: sharing her round, hanging-
out for what's thought martyrdom, by mates.

26

    Since most times we'd adjust. Those nights I'd end
on some past-the-heal edge of the city:
or her quotation marks round 'catching up', 'friend'   45
(fugues that curled out and back to routine).
                        Self pity?

Less happier men can't tell themselves
She's fucking this guy it doesn't matter much
because I say this someone else   50
is only lucky now ... (He was as clutched
to what us kids, for we were kids, believed;
and that was passing.) ... *with all their perks*
of love a highly probable grand finale approaches.
    So much for those ghosted entries heaved   55
into *Open Marriage: How It Works.*
I never over-dupe myself on books, Charley.

                                                          (1989)

JOHN A. SCOTT   *(b 1948)*

The Celebration

(September 11, 1973)
(for John Hughes)

    And so some hundred beasts
of burden were to be chained inside the city bells,
each body's dull sack replacing the tongue. *For*
it should be understood that victory, never gained
without sacrifice, must echo its cost in celebration.   5
And so the night of herding and enclosure. At dawn
the first ropes were pulled, and the low bellowing
of those beasts whose sheer strength enabled them to
survive the hours, gave way to a splintering
of bone. Only an infrequent clash of nose-iron rang   10
out for the Years, unmuted by flesh. And those who
were gathered in the stadium awoke to this frightful
music, and together they threw back their heads,
        as if for slaughter, and for song.

                                                          1981

Pride of Erin

The public telephone is a cage for the exhibition
    of Chrissie.
She comes from Science to the shop.
Saunters with her friends through a suburb of dogs,
    keeping ahead of evening, just beating it inside.   5
Smoke from the slow-combustion heaters.
A sun, low in the sky, giving lamplight and no warmth.

September 11, 1973   date of a violent coup by the armed forces in Chile against the government of
President Salvador Allende

A dying star and the domino theory of barking, when
    light starts to fail.
She has trouble with the door; with instructions.   10
Is afraid of losing her coin; doesn't have another one
    on her right now.
Is afraid of *not at home. Might be round at Greg's.*
And outside, Sharon and Cheryl and Debbie are wearing
    duffle coats, in range.   15
She is a carrier of nomadic truth.
Wishes commitment.
Knows of energies deep within her, under pressure, that
    she squanders on choir or keeping things clean.
No-one guesses them.   20
They are efforts of will.
Soldiers win medals with them.
She watches the duffle coats picking at dusk.
Watches the way teenage girls jostle and shift; are
    non-committal, like baboons.   25
Can't stop herself being like this most times.
Finds herself doing it.
Wonders if noticing things is the essence of growing
    old; and that as we pass some mid-point they fall
    away again, eventually back to nothing.   30
With difficulty, she comes from the booth into what
    is left of today.
Makes her turn.
Watches her friends move on.
In the darkness they seem to float, like objects   35
    displacing their own weight in water.

1984

Polka

    But the park was in trouble long before the man and his dog
arrived. Summer had brought its permanent cushion of
drunkards to the benches, and under the knife-wounded tree
trunks picnics flourished like bird-baths. The dog was excited. It
bounced. It leapt through the hysterical hoops of command.   5
People aren't fond of leaping dogs and advertise them in the
paper as being 'good with children'. I first learned to translate
classified advertisements when looking for a house to rent. That
'sunny' means a Sahara treelessness, and 'students ok' means
contaminated. Once I nearly inspected a house described as   10
'unusual'. Beneath far-away trees loosely bandaged with
newspaper, the man seemed very small — almost the ideal first
home. And his dog, still testing some distant trampoline.
'Olympian'. 'Suit conversationalist'. 'Loves height'.

1984

Reverie

for Helen Williams

For her a kite's appropriate enough
    to go unwinding in the breeze:
an offered rose upon a single stem,
    a postage stamp upon the sky.
For she has learnt from older men across   5
    the common of her pilgrimage
a clue; a tugging at the figure-eights
    of art and their infinities.
A terror of the commonplace that knows
    the vast importance of the line.   10
                                                               1989

MICHAEL DRANSFIELD   *(1948–73)*

Fix

It is waking in the night,
after the theatres and before the milkman,
alerted by some signal from the golden drug tapeworm
that eats your flesh and drinks your peace;
you reach for the needle and busy yourself   5
preparing the utopia substance in a blackened
spoon held in candle flame
by now your thumb and finger are leathery
being so often burned this way
it hurts much less than withdrawal and the hand   10
is needed for little else now anyway.
Then cordon off the arm with a belt,
probe for a vein, send the dream-transfusion out
on a voyage among your body machinery. Hits you like sleep —
sweet, illusory, fast, with a semblance of forever.   15
For a while the fires die down in you,
until you die down in the fires.
Once you have become a drug addict
you will never want to be anything else.
                                                               1970

Bums' rush

Yea, is not even Apollo, with hair and harpstring of gold
A bitter God to follow, a beautiful God to behold.
                                                    Swinburne

Becoming an eskimo isnt hard once you must.
You start by going far away, perhaps another landmass,
into the jungle of cold air and make a room a cave a hole

in the surface with your axe. Furnish it simply like devils island
carve a ledge for effigies and another to sleep on.   5
Land of the midnight sun it keeps you awake turns ice walls blue
    there are blue
ice walls the effigies a bled white silhouette /
wrapt in a fur you try not to remember but its easier just to let go
and be re-tried re-convicted re-crucified after a few years you even
forget to bleed. Blue all year like a duke's veins   10
like her eyes might have been once
when she had eyes. Freezing to death is the cleanest place on earth.
And identity you need not concern yourself with names you are the
    last of your species.
The worst pain is the morphine blue crevasse and real eskimos
never mind that. Their hallucinations are red-etched norse demons   15
they etch those on stone make fifty copies and sell them at cape dorset.
In the early winter mornings
sometimes you will hear the snow winds blowing in on you
soon then you will become impatient as lost souls do
you will think you hear someone calling   20
when it comes to that all you need do is
take a last look at the effigy collection
say farewell to friends you may have made among the graven images
then walk as a human lemming would
out across the bay to where the ice is thinnest and let yourself vanish.   25
                                                               1970

Parnassus mad ward

for Libby

First day she hid in bed
under the covers. Then tried to climb up the wall.
On the third day she was telling a parable:
'There was a dead dog on a road. Rotting. Everyone thought it ugly.
But Christ said, "Its teeth, they are beautiful."'   5
Overcast Thursday, in the garden
she was picking flowers. 'I like pansies,' she said,
'my friends. They have faces.' Pressed one between the pages
of her sculpture book. It rained, we sat on a bench
beneath a maple whose starfish leaves swam in watery   10
afternoon. Wet grassblades green day everything green
this absolutest colour. Speaking later of Heine:
wondering within myself how if poets become mad
there continues to be such colour and how
if gods shall have been discredited forgotten   15
there still can be innocents there still can be love.
                                                               1970

Flying

i was flying over sydney
in a giant dog

things looked bad

1972

Endsight

for Union Carbide, A. D. Hope & Sir P. Hasluck, Askin, Clutha etc.

midnights of consciousness. still, and even
silent, for now the jets are grounded, due to
lack of visibility, & only random thought & squads of
landladies' plaster ducks attempt flight. occasionally
an owl thuds into a building. it is always   5
dark now, the air a factory black
like X-rays of the children's lungs. the coated
earth is brittle, dead horses rot slowly
where they fall. using modified
radar & homing devices, vehicles crowd roads,   10
sightless, to carry workers from their
shelters to factories. a distant, hardly
safer government issues voluminous
decrees which litter the towns like printed snow.
also the works of the Official Poets, whose genteel   15
iambics chide industrialists
for making life extinct.

1972

MARTIN JOHNSTON   *(1947–90)*

The typewriter, considered as a bee-trap

is no doubt less than perfectly adapted
to its function, just as a bee-trap,
if there are such things, would hardly be the ideal contrivance
for the writing of semi-aleatory poems about
bee-traps and typewriters. Why, in any case,   5
you are entitled to ask, should I
want to trap bees at all? What do with them
if caught? But there are times, like today,
when bees hover about the typewriter
more frequently than poems, surely knowing best   10
what best attracts them. And certainly at such times,
considered in terms of function and structure,
the contraption could be argued to be
anything but a typewriter,
the term 'anything' being considered   15
as including, among all else, bee-traps,
softly multiplying in an ideal world.

1984

Esprit de l'escalier

(Cyclops Song 1)

Good manners, sir, are an infernal machine,
and unjuicing your companions a problem in tact
'at the meeting of two value-systems'. If
you complain, so may I. Sir, I am an ogre
not a structural linguist. Even so I understood,   5
of course, your ridiculous alias, and I knew
perfectly well what 'Noman is hurting me' meant,
but I played by the rules. So now my face feels like pork-crackling,
looks like it too, I imagine. You've ruled yourself out,
made yourself Noman indeed. But how would you have done   10
on *my* IQ tests? Did you get my jokes?
Next time around we'll understand each other,
next time I'll ask you round the back.
I, for one, am going to make sure I get it right

                                                                          1984

The Recidivist

(Cyclops Song 6)

But just consider his subsequent career.
Eight years of gluey fucking, interspersed
with the occasional peeved Please miss I wanna go home.
Then the bullyboy muscleman act — gunning down
every younger better-looking bloke for miles around — 'O man   5
of many devices!' — Killa Godzilla, more like it.
And a kink about bondage.
                          The thrushes flutter in the greased noose.
And then after all that the stickybeak gods
had to be flown in from Athens or wherever   10
like a mob of arbitration commissioners. You:
I'm talking about you. But at least,
you bastard, blind as I am, and a hostage
to your stiff-twined cordon of darkness, *I*
am still the one who writes the poems.   15
                                                                          1984

RHYLL MCMASTER   *(b 1947)*

Case Number 5

Mary admired Peter
and Saul wanted
Bob and Janice who
loved the inside of her head
sat apart watching   5

Mary and Sam and their two children
watching Peter and Helen
observing each other
while Brian who loved trees and solitude
watched a silent movie   10
playing behind his eyeballs.

Janice
who also liked observing
the slope of her nose through her eyelashes
by chance saw Saul   15
hugging Bob behind the piano
and gave up any pretence
of becoming familiar
with the interior of *his* mind
took a swift leap inwards   20
and landed in a corner of her brain
directly opposite Brian's secret movie
knocked and entered his bemused smile
and then tucking the corners in
round her chin   25
put out the light.

                                                                          1972

Company Man

Isaac Newton hugged his inventions,
paper lovers, close to his chest.
Dad didn't.
He handed them over at the Company's behest.

The Company gave him a car,   5
a Humber Snipe,
the Company gave him a reason for life.
Mum didn't.

The Company loved him.
So did Mum.   10
But the Company squeezed his heart in a vice,
it was faithless.
It winked and capered.

Dad lugged his soul that the Company bent
to the side of the grave, a short dark bed.   15
'I feel crook,' he said
and lumbered in.

Mum said,
'They've been good to us
considering.'   20

                                                                          1993

KRIS HEMENSLEY *(b 1946)*

From A Mile from Poetry

8

some sounds for you
/

/
            while you were listening
(& i was reading)
John Thorpe wrote a poem & posted it to that
space above (between the lines those   5
mannered slashes).
          It was a poem about some people
fishing, probably in Bolinas, which doesnt even
figure on the Oxford map of California, but is
only one hour's drive from San Francisco, maybe   10
near Salinas, which *is* on the map, Steinbeck
country isnt it? — — longer as the crow flies, as the
fishermen in John's poem travel, longer than it
takes to read or write. As long, perhaps, as it
takes to receive.   15

     anything

     cicadas a
     trapped blow-fly
     a whisper from

     across the Pacific   20
     Ocean! i
     tell a lie!

     a whisper

     do you hear
     me? sa-soon   25
     sa-sigh

1979

DIANE FAHEY   *(b 1945)*

Dressmaker

As a girl I loved fabrics, stitching and moulding them
to fit. I remember a flared dress, pink roses on white.
Wearing it with my first high heels, I tottered past
neighbourhood louts slung on a verandah; from their transistor
Marty Robbins sang, 'A White Sport Coat and a Pink Carnation'.   5
As I blushed, they eyed the smoky summer air.
                                                        At sixteen,
a slippery silk dress with whorls of red and crimson,
pinched in with a cummerbund. With unswerving hips
I passed the greengrocer, an Italian who sighed, whistled,   10
called in one sound, his pregnant wife thrusting beans
and tomatoes into brown paper bags; her look touched mine:
wary, beyond challenge, sisterly.
                                        Ten years of illness next,
when I bundled myself inside coats in summer, wore black   15
as often as not. Hard to stand straight inside a body
so out of kilter.
                        Since then I have put on the garment
of my womanhood. It marks the curves and leanings
of my flesh, holds in, reveals, what I have come to be,   20
beyond promise and blight. I know its weight, its transparency,
its rawness, its flawed smoothness. I wear it now
with something close to ease, with the freedom, almost,
of nakedness.

                                                                    1990

Sacred Conversations

*After seeing Titian's 'St. Mark Enthroned, with SS Cosmas
and Damian, Roch and Sebastian', Venice.*

I am tired of all those Saint Sebastians standing there
at the feet of Madonna or super-saint, among other
saved ones all waiting for the next prayerful utterance
while ruminating on eternity. He is always so undressed
yet so aloof, so helpless yet complacent, so wounded yet whole.   5
I like saints who hide their virtues beneath ample,
jewel-coloured robes, for whom pain is pain, and joy, joy,
not some awful mix-up of the two.
                                        Still, this Sebastian by
Titian stops me. Only one arrow pierces his body;   10
another, fallen from his calf, lies on the floor, abstemiously.
He has a serious, inward gaze, and no blood. But the glory
of the painting is his stance, graceful yet arrogant —
if one could strut while standing still, he's doing it.

My guess is that he was a sixteenth century gondolier,   15
happy to be gaining money for so little effort, but bored
with standing motionless for so long on terra firma.
So he imagines being gazed at by each woman who enters
the church — over four centuries, a tall order,
but time has delivered ...   20
                 Above, Saint Mark is half-shadow:
Moses-like, he holds the book, stares at dark stars;
but this man's face is clear, his body resembles neither
ravaged nor risen saviour's, the knots in that white cloth
can be undone ... For those arrows belong to Eros,   25
and this is not Christ but Dionysus, who has wandered into
a strangely silent conversation.

                                      1990

Despair

Cover the left side of your face, and see it:
an unwilled bitterness in flesh and feature.
Call it an active lack of expectation —
it replaces fear as your ruling passion,
will be lived with equal single-mindedness: 5
the killing logic that's your version of piety.

There's defencelessness in it, too —
as of an unquilled porcupine huddling
in your lap: a once bristly reality
become this shapeless, alive, no-being,   10
utterly at odds with its future.

What to do? Rearrange that face for a start.
Easy: the body is only time-lapse plasticine,
isn't it? Remove all sign of what blocks out
the sorrows of friends, meets the new   15
with boredom, is in a continental drift
away from wherever now is.

And there's no short-circuiting despair
with cheer or compromise; it will not be
got to the bottom of, or written out in poems.   20

This has been sent to you, has arisen from
what you are: a ticking bomb to be defused,
a Trojan horse to outwit. Walk round it slowly.
Deal with it or be diminished, become a self
shivering in your own helpless hands   25
that can make no offering, will damage all gifts.

                                      1995

MARK O'CONNOR   *(b 1945)*

The Beginning

    God himself
having that day planted a garden
walked through it at evening and knew
that Eden was not nearly complex enough.
And he said: 5
'Let species swarm like solutes in a colloid.
Let there be ten thousand species of plankton
and to eat them a thousand zooplankton.
Let there be ten phyla of siphoning animals,
one phylum of finned vertebrates, from   10
white-tipped reef shark to long-beaked coralfish,
and to each his proper niche,
and — no Raphael, I'm not quite finished yet —
you can add seals and sea-turtles & cone-shells & penguins
(if they care) and all the good seabirds your team can devise —   15
oh yes, and I nearly forgot it, I want a special place
for the crabs! And now for parasites to keep
the whole system in balance, let . . .

'. . . In conclusion, I want,' he said
'ten thousand mixed chains of predation —   20
none of your simple rabbit and coyote stuff!
This ocean shall have many mouths, many palates,
many means of ingestion. I want
a hundred ways of death, three thousand regenerations —
all in technicolor naturally. And oh yes, I nearly forgot,   25
we can use Eden again for the small coral cay in the center.

      'So now Raphael, if you please,
just draw out and marshal these species,
and we'll plant them all out in a twelve-hectare patch.'

So for five and a half days God labored   30
and on the seventh he donned mask and snorkel
and a pair of bright yellow flippers.

And, later, the host all peered wistfully down
through the high safety fence around Heaven
and saw God with his favorites finning slowly over the coral   35
in the eternal shape of a grey nurse shark,
and they saw that it was very good indeed.

                                                  1976

Reef

High by the long island's side
the rubble banks swim in the evening light
death-grey and bleached white, speckled together.

The Wind sings over the coelenterate dead
the hollow-gutted stone-sheath-dwellers   5
the lace-masons, the spicule shapers

the island-makers.

                                                                        1976

Mating Day

The alpine grasshopper's low energy-budget
permits two or three leaps to defeat the torpid skink;
mates in full sun, though the female's legs
are too weak to hop the pair from danger.

Walking off through the tussocks, she gets on   5
with her life — that is, food and eggs —
he, immobile jockey, with sex,
squirting his genes into the future

— while *graniticola*, the granite-loving buttercup
explodes its yellow from bare stone   10
richly wearing the Roman word *cola*
that means dweller, husbander and lover.

Today is mating day, high summer for the alpine grasshopper,
all joy and juices bursting at this hour.
From here the year slopes downhill to the ice,   15
to deaths, and a new generation's singing.

                                                                        1996

Stream so quietly, privately

Stream so quietly, privately
collecting your tributaries
along the perched valley
down to the abnegating heights
where you make in your going   5
a great white flourish

so small and swift
the caddis never fears the trout
so clear and shallow one would swear
the rock's not wet but polished   10

till you expand your waters,
ripplets slap-jostling to the edge,

more shaped by the grain of rock behind
than all the drop below:

when was this place last sung,   15
by what clan or owner,
in lyrics of what local speech
its brisk pools and brisker back-eddies caught?

— One of these busy babbling streams
of Bandusia, Bogong, anywhere, that mean   20
so hugely to their local tribes
so nothing to the stock exchange,
draining country so delicate a brumby stampede
can be traced six years later.

                                                                1996

The Grasshopper Man

— Nemargon the thunder-maker
whetting his axe
till his storm will crash,
gusting inside the overhang.

His groin is shaped insectwise   5
like a clutch of axeheads,
stone prisms jangling together.
Antenna'd, breasted,
he grinds the stone axes on his knees
till shivers of lightning leap   10
from clashed genitals.

Barginj his wife, the Lightning Woman,
sprawls beside, in a birth pose;
her groin is a slot, an open mouth
fervently pouring out life;   15
strained inner sinews
binding its purse together.
Her head a skull,
whose round sockets mimic breasts.

In the Wet, cool season for birth,   20
the open cave trembles, walled
by blue electric sheets.
A spidery hand reaches out in white
to touch her electric husband.
Below, a Gagadju woman squats in birth,   25
triangular breasts tilt ripely to each side.

Namandi the evil one squats, legs splayed,
ochre-red, with a dilly bag of harms
for the mother's heart, lungs, kidney.

Never touch the late-Spring grasshopper, 30
messenger and insect-child of Nemargon
— his blue and orange mandibles will sting
like snakes, his bitter whirr explode.

(1994)

ROBERT GRAY   *(b 1945)*

Flames and Dangling Wire

On a highway over the marshland.
Off to one side, the smoke of different fires in a row,
like fingers spread and dragged to smudge:
it is an always-burning dump.

Behind us, the city 5
driven like stakes into the earth.
A waterbird lifts above this swamp
as a turtle moves on the Galapagos shore.

We turn off down a gravel road,
approaching the dump. All the air wobbles 10
in some cheap mirror.
There is a fog over the hot sun.

Now the distant buildings are stencilled in the smoke.
And we come to a landscape of tin cans,
of cars like skulls, 15
that is rolling in its sand dune shapes.

Amongst these vast grey plastic sheets of heat,
shadowy figures
who seem engaged in identifying the dead —
they are the attendants, in overalls and goggles, 20

forking over rubbish on the dampened fires.
A sour smoke
is hauled out everywhere,
thin, like rope. And there are others moving — scavengers.

As in hell the devils 25
might pick about through our souls, for vestiges
of appetite
with which to stimulate themselves,

so these figures
seem to wander, disconsolate, with an eternity 30
in which to turn up
some peculiar sensation.

We get out and move about also.
The smell is huge,

blasting the mouth dry: 35
the tons of rotten newspaper, and great cuds of cloth ...

And standing where I see the mirage of the city
I realize I am in the future.
This is how it shall be after men have gone.
It will be made of things that worked.   40

A labourer hoists an unidentifiable mulch
on his fork, throws it in the flame:
something flaps
like the rag held up in 'The Raft of the *Medusa*'.

We approach another, through the smoke,   45
and for a moment he seems that demon with the long barge pole.
— It is a man, wiping his eyes.
Someone who worked here would have to weep,

and so we speak. The rims beneath his eyes are wet
as an oyster, and red.   50
Knowing all that he does about us,
how can he avoid a hatred of men?

Going on, I notice an old radio, that spills
its dangling wire —
and I realize that somewhere the voices it received   55
are still travelling,

skidding away, riddled, around the arc of the universe;
and with them, the horse-laughs, and the Chopin
which was the sound of the curtains lifting,
one time, to a coast of light.   60
                                                                    1978

Reflection

Evenings, there are people with no intention of buying
who stop to look through the fish shop glass —
men with noses that are soaked full of alcohol,
old women who speak to the hand-led children that pass.

Water runs down this window in clam-shell pattern.   5
Within, there's bounty, stainless fittings, clean light,
heaped prawns, and flounders white as ice cream,
the lairs' highway, the suburb in its mangrove night.
                                                                    1978

Bondi

The waves are a shoal of white fins, in the end of every downhill street,
and along the streets are stacked blunt-faced blocks of flats:
big, plastery, peeling buildings, in cream, with art deco curves and angles.
Behind this, for a thousand acres, the buckled suburbs of dark brick.

Curtains trail outwards on the heat, and a smell of gas leaks, 5
above singed grass in tiny yards, grey palings, chlorine-blue hydrangeas,
gas pipes like creepers over walls.
There are garbage bins left lying about, empty milk bottles on marble steps,
always snail-dribble across the concrete, to the crushed snail shells.
The sun trundles around and around, amongst its flapping fire. 10
In the longest street, out toward the cave-in on the headland, is a children's
　　　park,
where, through empty swings, with their oversized hot chains, the surf swings.
Out here are callow home units of pale brick, fenestrated as that rock face
below the cliff's edge they're built upon.
Beyond a last railing, the sea throws over and spreads its crocheted cloth 15
across the rock table, and (something you can't watch for long — it is like
　　　madness)
draws it off once again.
Around at the beach-front, rattling fun parlours, discos and milk-bars, the
　　　sign-painting
lurid as tattoos, thickly over them.
Cars are tilted along all the gutters, strung together closely as caterpillars, 20
in the colours of children's sweets. The grit settles, coating
windscreens and duco; vinyl seats bake in the sun,
and that smell will sicken the overwrought children in the late afternoon,
　　　going home.
All day these headlands lie spread apart to the pleasurable, treacherous
　　　elements.
The place seems scoured by weather of every other ideal. 25
But then, a white yacht will appear in the ultramarine passage, an icon
of perfect adaptation, and the people along the sand,
as though in a grandstand, or those wading out
through the low waves towards it, seem all of them everywhere over this
like walking moths, that fan its easy passage with their wings. 30
It goes wandering on midway in the spectrum of blue before them, in the
　　　garment of serenity.
This is the only sort of vision we shall have, and it costs money,
and therefore Bondi is lying crammed together, obtuse, with barely a tree,
　　　behind us —
Every cent is firstly for the secure mechanisms of comfort.
It is not pleasure, to be exact, but its appropriation. And not mindlessness,
　　　but the mind. 35
For at the beach, so much that is nature can be seen to have been called
into the one procession of decay. Flesh become crude and brief
as figures shaped out of beach sand. So many of these people
look as though used like Bondi grit, with its scraps and butts and matchsticks.
Still, the young girls are loping on the sea-front, who secretly 40
amaze themselves with an easy skill they've found —
who can swing their breasts and all the shapes that are surging on their bodies
as if the drum majorettes for this parade.
At dusk, the parking spaces above the sea have emptied
and sand blows along the bitumen like smoke. 45

The garbage bins on posts are steep in their slipping litter.
And the gulls, that run and screech and scatter each other amongst it, never make
contented noises — are scrabbling constantly;
only sometimes one of them is carried off by the wind, down the bay, and it goes along
on its outriggers, smoothly; beautiful, particularly in the dusk,   50
when it flows away as smoothly, sideways, as the running shallows —
its whiteness, that is picked up by the whiteness of a wave's single wingbeat
out there on the deep-mauve water, creating a vast space.

                                                                1983

CAROLINE CADDY   *(b 1944)*

Finding My Daughter

For Tas

Sometimes it seems that for years
I was not your mother
that you had had yourself secretly
                          adopted out —
no way I could follow what I didn't know.   5
We lived a geography where two people wade
                          the same river
in different places.
See that machete   imagine a jungle —
          I spent years getting there and back.   10
Now I know each parent has two children —
the one out of me
                and the other
                          spontaneously created
abandoned before birth.   15
This is the pyramid —
half a life explored to get it back together
                                    me
                          and you and you
wrestling the mighty blocks   20
          never believing they would float up
                          by themselves
like a monstrous
hard fought handing over at birth
                    that grew and grew to be   25
                          a prince.
Even now our words are a delicate operation —
a sliding
of two transparent blueprints.
                    that don't have to match   30

                              to be right
and I still don't know what I did or didnt do
                              to get here
but it's as if I'd said to someone
with a fear of flying   35
              that my spirit would go with them
and the person in the seat next to you
              turned out to be my friend.

Solitude

It's something they carry with them
              — explorers   night shifts   seaman —
like a good pair of binoculars
or a camera case
              perfectly and deeply compartmented.   5
It has a quiet patina
that both absorbs and reflects
              like a valuable instrument
                        you have to sign for
— contract with alone —   10
              and at the end of the voyage
                        you get to keep.
Sometimes it's very far away.
Sometimes so close
              at first you think the person next to you   15
is picking up   putting down
              a personal cup
              a book in another language
before you realise what
— when talk has moved off   20
              leaning its arms
                        on someone else's table —
is being
handed to you.

                                              1996

ROBERT ADAMSON   *(b 1944)*

Dead Horse Bay

Quick hands on spinning ropes
at dawn, blood rising
to the jumping cords.

Ice-pack over bad burns
and the catfish venom.   5
Rock salt against gut-slime.

A southerly blowing up
on the full tide, nets
in mud and mesh-gutting snags.

The bread tasting   10
like kero-sponge, crazed gulls
crashing onto the stern.

Mullet at 3 cents a pound
by the time sun hits
the bar of the *Angler's Rest*.   15

Get drunk enough to keep at it,
clean the gear for tonight
and another bash.

Remember that night in '68
how we killed 'em   20
right through the month

couldn't have gone wrong,
so thick you could've
walked over the water.

When the bream are running   25
like that, nothing can touch you
and everything matters

and you don't want 'em to stop
and you can't slow down
you can't imagine.   30

                                                1977

The Home, The Spare Room

I am the poet of the spare room
the man who lives here

with television's
incessant coloured noise

between the ads keeping the children   5
at bay

At night I walk the seagrass
down the hall

my head rolls before me
like some kind of a round dice   10

which room tonight?

I think of my wife-to-be
who has thrown herself down

into a foetal shape onto her bed

I am a hard man, a vicious seer   15
who simply wants

to go on living — love is beyond me

if it exists — my heart,
so called, is as efficient as a bull's

and as desperate   20
for the earth's treasures —

I turn into the spare room
begin to write a poem of infinite tenderness

                                                        1982

Dreaming Up Mother

Understanding is all, my mother would tell me,
and then walk away from the water;

Understanding is nothing I think, as I mumble
embellished phrases of what's left of her story.

Though I keep battering myself against sky,   5
throwing my body into the open day.

Landscapes are to look at, they taught me,
but now the last of the relatives are dead.

Where do these walks by the shore take us
she would say, wanting to clean up,   10

after the picnic, after the nonsense.
I have been a bother all the years from my birth.

Look out — the river pulls through the day
and Understanding like a flaming cloud, goes by.

                                                        1989

JOHN TRANTER   *(b 1943)*

From The Poem in Love

8

You are inside the 'scream'. Yes, it's very like
an empty room with sky-blue holes where the
paintings have been removed for your protection.
No clothing, it's called 'naked' like the 'scream'
in the empty room becoming the house expanding into   5
a sky-blue hole blowing up to the exact size
of your imagination. Think of television with its
cathode snow above the treeline going blue.

You will search for emaciated verbs to stuff up
the cracks of your imagination for imagination read   10
horror of the empty room where love is all you beg for
and the Poem has gone to Acapulco for the Fire Season
of the Acapulco Gold and other aphrodisiacs
of its liking, of its best desire,

9

Yet this loneliness only means that the Poem
has gone off to ponder its resources, so let it alone
in the café where it can meander through the lists
of great men and their works. For isn't it you
who feature so brightly in its wildest dreams?   5
You don't believe it? Yet it's true, for it finds
nothing else to render comfort in that realm
where words tumble into space and get lost

in a cold bigger than a plastic bomb exploding
a silent violet blast in outer space or so   10
you imagine, yet something remains of 'kindness'
for your fortitude in giving nerve kicks to this poem
who rushes out with other 'friendly writers'
and gets totally lost on the fringe of the blast.

1974

From Crying in Early Infancy

89

I'd like to throw an epileptic fit
at the Sydney Opera House and call it Rodent.
That's what separates me from the herd.
The hand forgives the cutting edge
for what the hand guides it to do.   5
The knife has no pleasure in it.
I'm eating my way through my life —
they said it couldn't be done

but here I am in the Palace of Gastronomes
crazy about the flavour!   10
Moonlight along the blade of a kitchen knife
belongs to the ritzy forties, it's nostalgic
like playing the comb and one-hundred-dollar bill
and calling it the blues.

90

As you get purchase the hate vehicle
you take another quick look at your sister
and the whole cataract falls into place
under the idea of economy at sea
along the edges of the truck   5

your sister is playing around smoking
with a nudist drinking pot just
having a real bad time in Jamaica

you know you'll make naked friends
in the twilight you're not sniffing glue   10
between the Principle of Uncertainty
and the invention of Germ Warfare
there you will find your dazed sister
purchase motor conformity.

                                                                          1977

Voodoo

From his rushing-away, from his
ever-receding throne, under a rainy
canopy of trees and scraps of cloud
that topple back, shrink and disappear,
embalmed behind his rear window in a nest of   5
crushed velvet plush, the flash wog's nodding dog
blinks out his witless approval to the vehicles
that shadow him forever.

His twin the dipping bird sips and sips,
tilts back, cools off, dries out,   10
dries out utterly, totters weakly
on the lip of philosophy
then dips again.

These two critics teach us how to live,
rehearsing the gap between the no-no   15
and the drink-again. Their motto? Every day
I will get better at embroidering the lingo
of the tongue-tied doctors of letters; every night,
in the lack of light, I will get better
and better at the negative virtues, telling   20
girls to piss off, who needs them,
swimming off the edge of the rock
ledge into the plunging broth of deeper waters,
soaring up to the stratosphere, bothering the angels
and yarning with God. My left hand does it,   25
my right hand tells me that it's right.

In the pre-dawn rack and bash of winter peak hour
traffic on the Sydney Harbour Bridge you notice them
hefted up over the city like ju-ju dolls
in the trance of a terrible gift. You note   30
the man with gauntlets and the goggled girl
on motorbikes, the nurses' giggles
in the fogged-up Mini Moke, an ambulance weaving
and howling in the rear-view mirror, the tablets

rattling in the Emergency Bucket, the icy rain   35
furious and seething on the road, and Noddy
and his loopy brother brooding on it all
for our sake, so that we can see it whole.

                                                        1988

Debbie & Co.

The Council Pool's chockablock
with Greek kids shouting in Italian.
Isn't it Sunday afternoon?
Half the school's there, screaming,
skylarking, and bombing the deep end.   5
Nicky picks up her Nikon
and takes it all in, the racket
and the glare. Debbie strikes a pose.

In a patch of shade a grubby brat
dabbles ice-cream into the cement.   10
Tracey and Chris are missing,
mucking about behind the dressing sheds,
Nicky guesses. Who cares?
Debbie takes a dive. Emerging like a
porpoise at the edge of the pool   15
she finds a ledge, a covered gutter,
awash with bubbles and chlorine's
chemical gossip. Debbie yells there,
and the rude words echo.
The piss-tinted water slaps the tiles.   20

Debbie dries off, lights a smoke,
and gazes at her friends fading out
around the corner of a dull relationship
and disappearing.
                    Under the democratic sun   25
her future drifts in and out of focus —
Tracey, Nicky, Chris, the whole arena
sinking into silence. Yet this is almost
Paradise: the Coke, the takeaway pizza,
a packet of Camels, Nicky's dark glasses   30
reflecting the way the light glitters on
anything wet. Debbie's tan needs
touching up. She lies back and dozes
on a terry-towelling print of Donald Duck.

She remembers how Brett was such a   35
dreamboat, until he turned into
somebody's boring husband. Tracey
reappears, looking radiant. Nicky

browses through an Adult Magazine.
Debbie goes to sleep. 40

1988

LEE CATALDI *(b 1942)*

if you stay too long in the third world

you learn
to hawk and spit like an old woman
you become
unfit for dinner parties
in the lands of the well fed 5

having dropped out of your original country
into this space from which
the coast with its oceans and gardens
the party on the terrace.
the splash of green water over the bow of the yacht 10
are images projected on a screen
whose unreality you resent
the other side of the coin whose gain
is the loss you see all around

if you stay too long in the third world 15
death becomes a fact of life   the old
die quickly   the young
can't count on being old   this termite death
hollows out the roots of endeavour

as children leave toys you abandon 20
your previous explanations

if you stay too long in the third world
it will fill the space in your psyche
with a different discourse
you will begin to recognise 25
the unfamiliar in the unfamiliar
the outline of a landscape
in a pattern of dots

the faces of relations in the tragic and violent
repetitions of a song   the patterns of daily living 30
in the holy steps of a dance

if you stay too long in the third world
you will become
accustomed to silence and observation
leading to understanding 35
to abundance and malnutrition
immutably hand in hand

when that eager and rational voice
whose creature you are
whose instrument you had volunteered to become   40
grates like the radio on a bad day
you switch if off

if you stay too long in the third world
you will be unable to leave

1990

ROGER MCDONALD   *(b 1941)*

Two summers in Moravia

That soldier with a machinegun bolted
to his motorcycle, I was going to say
ambled down to the pond to take
what geese he wanted; but he didn't.

This was whole days before the horizon trembled.   5

In the farmyard all the soldier did
was ask for eggs and milk.
He and the daughter (mother sweeping)
stood silent, the sky rounded
like a blue dish.   10

This was a day
when little happened,
though inch by inch everything changed.
A load of hay narrowly crossed the bridge,
the boy caught a fish underneath in shade,   15
and ducks quarrelled in the reeds.
Surrounded by wheat, everyone heard the wind
whisper, at evening, as though grain already threshed
was poured from hand to hand.

This was a day possible to locate, years later,   20
on a similar occasion; geese alive,
the sky uncracked like a new dish,
even the wheat hissing with rumour.
I was going to say unchanged
completely, but somewhere behind   25
the soldier had tugged his cap,
kicked the motor to harsh life
and swayed off,
the nose of the machinegun tilted up.

1975

1915

Up they go, yawning,
the crack of knuckles dropped
to smooth the heaving
in their legs, while some,
ashamed, split bile   5
between their teeth,
and hum to drown their stomachs.

Others touch their lips
on splintered wood
to reach for home —   10
'a bloke's a mug'
thinks one (who sees
a ringbarked hill)
another hisses drily
(leaping burrs).   15

All dreaming,
when the whistle
splits the pea, as up
they scramble, pockets fat
with Champion Flake   20
in battered tins,
and letters wadded thick
from Mum (who says
'always keep
some warm clothes on . . .')   25

Up from slits in dirt
they rise, and here they stop.
A cold long light swings over.

Hard like ice
it cracks their shins —   30
they feel a drill and mallet
climb their bones, then cold
then warmth as blood spills out from pockets,
chests, and mouths.
No mother comes to help, although   35
a metal voice is whining
'boys, relax', as one
by one they totter to their knees.

                                                          1975

The hollow thesaurus

Names for everything I touch
were hatched in bibles, in poems cupped by madmen
on rocky hills, by marks on sheets of stone,
by humped and sticky lines in printed books.

Lexicographers burned their stringy eyeballs black   5
for the sake of my knowing. Instinctive generations
hammered their victories, threaded a chain,
and lowered their strung-up wisdom in a twist
of molecules. But with me in mind
their time was wasted.   10

When the bloodred, pewter, sickle, sick or meloned moon
swells from nowhere,
the chatter of vast informative print
spills varied as milk. Nothing prepares me
even for common arrivals like this.   15

Look. The moon comes up. Behind certain trees are bats
that wrench skyward like black sticks.
Light falls thinly on grass, from moon and open door.
This has not happened before.

                                                                           1975

In the event of autumn

The big summer weeds, like adolescent eucalypts,
obligingly sway as the old dog noses up the gully.
The air sweats like a slice of clay.

These are the months of dry-retching moonlight, beams full stretch
on the dry tubs of creekbeds. Dust fuses together   5
and stubs the toe. Water steams in waterbags.

Lightning rattles a box of sticks on the white-hot horizon,
but exhausts itself there. The dog finds maggots
with its lazy paw, or stirs ticks from their slumber.

We planned cool tubs of mangoes, and freezing beer.   10
But a scorching wind arrived on the first day of spring
and shrivelled the mango flowers. The beer evaporated in froth.

Where do we go from here? The sun is maliciously intent
on baking the undersides of stones. We'd climb
gratefully to our coffins if the cemetery weren't smouldering.   15

In any case, a man down the road shot himself for relief, but lived
to tell the tale. The bullet melted, striking the roof of his mouth
like a splash of hot pudding, so he said.

Before my brain cracks and my fingers shrivel to ash
I'll leave these lines wedged in a slice of asbestos   20
for you to find, with luck, in the event of autumn.

                                                                           1975

GEOFFREY LEHMANN   *(b 1940)*

The Two Travellers

A girl was picking parsley near a church,
An old man fished the summer stream for perch,

There was a pear tree; but we had to ride
Through heath and furze and up a mountainside ...

We crossed the snowline, lit a fire and sang   5
That night and the deserted valley rang.

We slew a dragon, travelled up the pass,
Went through a town of broken boards and glass.

Dead spirits swarmed across a sandy plain.
Dry lightning, and a blind man gasped for rain.   10

Years later in a stream we washed our hair
And swam one night, then slept beneath a pear.

A parsley field and church shone in the sun,
The girl was there. We diced and my friend won.

1972

The Old Rifle

In the long school holidays in summer
I'd be out in the orchard
with an old rifle Mr Long fixed up,
shooting at rosellas
that were raiding fruit.   5
As each bird fell I'd watch
where the blue and red flickered down,
then I'd drop the rifle and run.
That way I stocked my aviary
with broken-winged rosellas,   10
And somewhere in my childhood
I dropped and forgot that rifle.

A year of grass grew over it.
Men were working in the orchard one day,
and my brother, the dentist, four years old,   15
was playing in the grass and found the rifle,
rusted all over — a wreck —
as though it had lain there for years.
My brother knew how to hold a gun
and pointing it at Jim Long, said,   20
'I'll shoot you Mr Long.'

The Old Rifle   from *Spring Forest*, a sequence of poems in the voice of Ross, a farmer

He said, 'Oh don't shoot me, Barry —
shoot Bill over there.'
Barry pointed the gun at Bill.
'I'll shoot you Uncle Bill.'   25
'Don't shoot me, Barry,' Bill said,
'Shoot Ted here.' And Ted said,
'Why not shoot Jip?'

Jip was a good sort of dog,
my black and white fox terrier cross,   30
who was racing around the orchard,
looking for rabbits.
Barry dropped to one knee and squinting took aim.
Jip dropped dead on the spot.
They buried him, telling no one,   35
but in their haste
made the hole too shallow,
and a few days later the story came out
when the fowls scratched him up.

'You know, Barry's quite a fair shot,'   40
Mr Long said,
out in the bush with Barry and me.
'My word I am,' said Barry.
'I can hit anything.'
'Can you, Barry, well — see what you can do.'   45
Barry took the rifle,
went down on one knee
and aimed at Mr Long's billy hanging
from a distant branch.
He fired,   50
and a stream of brown tea came spurting out.

                                                        1976

GEOFF PAGE   *(b 1940)*

Inscription at Villers-Bretonneux

The dead at Villers-Bretonneux
rise gently on a slope towards
the sky. The land is trim — skylines

of ploughed earth and steeples; unfallen
rain still hanging in the air;   5
confusion smoothed away

Villers-Bretonneux   a town in northern France where Australian troops suffered heavy casualties in
1918

and everything put back — the village
too   (red brick/white sills)   in nineteen
twenty, unchanged since. Headstones

speak a dry consensus. Just one   10
breaks free: 'Lives Lost, Hearts Broken —
And for What?' I think of the woman

and those she saddened by insisting —
the Melbourne clerk
who must have let it through.   15

                                                         1978

Clarence Lyric

For Alec and Penelope Hope

Surrounded by his
Pills and bottles
The old man's heaped
In bed at last
Washed in sidelong   5
From the world
Which circles seaward
With his past

Carpet snakes
With rats and swallows   10
Weave their close
Dependent lives
Silverfish
Invade the paintings
Whiteants hollow   15
Out the piles

A grandson and his
Wife move in
Rational with
Paint and saw   20
Three children spread
Into the rooms
Banging through the
Cedar doors

One soon lost   25
To outer paddocks
Another buoyant
On her smile
A third obscurely
Stalled by fiction   30
In a chair not
Quite in style

Snakes slide from
The long verandah
Rats go back   35
To tractor sheds
All morning through
The polished glass
A man stares outwards
From the dead   40

Sees the river
Skimmed with wind
Hears the children
Start to fight
The afternoon   45
Goes on forever
The westward pools
Are filled with light

                                                    1988

Kokoda Corrective

*It was here young Australian men fought for the first time
against the prospect of the invasion of their country ...*
                    Paul Keating, Kokoda, Anzac Day 1992

... Or first that could be counted any rate
all lined up here underground
and numbered from the right.

The others were a good bit sooner
hundred years or so   5
their skulls much further out of sight

or overseas in glass.
Old Pemulwuy of the Eora,
now he gave trouble for a time,

dozen years to be exact,   10
and Yagan on the Upper Swan —
his head was souvenired as well, if I recall.

And Windradyne out Bathurst way
required a whiff of martial law
before he saw the light   15

and Pigeon in the Kimberley
now there's a bloke who liked a fight.
Good that you could make it, Paul.

Nice to see that someone came.
Not actually the first, not quite,   20
but damn fine all the same.

                                                    1996

JAN OWEN *(b 1940)*

Schoolgirls Rowing

Five twelve-year-olds in short white skirts,
skinny, long-legged, filling out
but chattering with treble voices still,
are teetering over the edge of adolescence
and the slender yellow boat.   5
'Sir!' says blonde bunches, 'What are we 'sposed to do?
There's water up to the clogs. It's practically full!'
'It's disgusting, Sir,' adds brown plaits.
'How are we 'sposed to row?'
'Shut up, girls,' the coach says, 'and get out.'   10
The *Dickie Richards*, with due fuss, is turned and drained.
Smiling now, back in, they push off well.
'Square your blade, Four,' says the cox,
'I keep telling you, Danielle!'
Coincidence or foul play from Prince's passing by   15
sends duck-weed and a snigger or two their way.
'Don't buck your oar, Jane,' calls the coach.
'Kim, you're taking too much reach
and watch that feathering height!'
As Saint's, ship-shape in white and gold,   20
draw level in the *Piping Shrike*,
their number three looks sideways, washing out;
they steer right through the weed.
The girls stay straight faced, lift their chins
and pull more smoothly with each stroke;   25
sleekly the *Dickie Richards* cuts the murky green.
Past the boys and under the bridge
skim Alison, Danielle, Rebecca, Kim and Jane;
the ripples in their wake
touch *Popeye* at the river's edge   30
with alpha waves of light.
You're on the bank, just sitting in the sun,
but suddenly happiness has you by the throat.

                                                              1986

The Kiss

I love the way
a Pole will take your hand
in both of his
and straighten with the merest hint
of a military click   5
and bow his head
and tighten his grip
and press his moist and fervent lips

to your skin,
also the gentle after-caress   10
of his moustache.
Most, I love the dark
and frankly soulful look
(still holding your hand)
he'll fix you with   15
for exactly three seconds after:
the look that says
   this, we understand, means nothing
and everything —
   you are a stranger I salute   20
across the eternal silence of this space,
   you are Baila, my first love,
in her blue cotton dress,
   you are my mother
holding back her tears,   25
   you are garrulous Mrs Zukowski
who gave us eggs,
   you are all our grandmothers
waving after the train,
   you are woman,   30
we may never meet again.

                                                        1994

Gone

Straw-coloured sun
floods over the year's
first blackberries,
the children's fruit.
Cat-slither of fur,   5
thorns at my skin —
the silk and sharp of this world
using me,
its bitter leafy edge
breathed in.   10
Now, the thrush's startling
rupture of air,
bright red, spilt gold.
I was swelling with you already
when the membrane split,   15
small death
I do not forget.
Gone, this slope of apple-trees,
a valleyful of sky,
the sea.   20
The blood thuds on
its timpani of perfume and stain,
a drunken drummer in Ulysses' hold.

                                                        1994

KATE LLEWELLYN   *(b 1940)*

Stupid

I'd say it is surprising
a girl like me
can clean a chook
unbog a truck
fight a fire   5

lay out the dead
make the bread

deliver babies
write a poem
move a man to tears   10
rear the kids
and keep on
acting stupid

1982

Finished

There'll be no more
lying on your shoulder love
or listening for your car

there'll be no more
drinking on the verandah love   5
or eating roasted veal

there'll be no more
my legs around your neck love
and howling at the moon

there'll be no more   10
hits across my mouth love
and crawling on the floor

there'll be no more
smoking listening to you curse love
or smiling drinking more   15

there'll be no more
crying because you rage love
or dancing up your drive

there's no more
love love   20

1982

AILEEN KELLY   *(b 1939)*

Substance

Sometimes china she belongs on the secure span of mantelpiece over solid
        brick and tile against the wall
or craves the shut glass of a cabinet, tucked back in triangular dark unseen
        unless someone bends and reaches.
Instead she is perched absurdly on the coffee table while children and dog
        tumble and yell, hurting
themselves and each other in their rage to find out muscle and light and
        strength and control and brain and interaction and domination.
Hurts that no china figurine can prevent or mend, while at a hundred
        near-misses she compacts her stillness to its lowest centred balance   5
waiting for the next thoughtless nearness to miss missing and become a
        casual hit;
for herself to become a crunch of fragments underfoot in the own lives to
        which they are of course entitled.

Lattertimes stone she stands integral on the side of the birdbath, an
        outstretched hand offering refreshment to the thirsty and the dusty.
Equally unaffected by weather, wattlebirds dive and shower and take nectar from
        the feeder above, striated feathers clear striped by a linger of damp.
Higher yet a blackbird sings in an endless spring, cockblack on the rooftip.   10
She knows his lyric and his busy wife; brown and black sip here together at
        evening.
She knows where their nest is hidden each year among the camellias.
She knows the neighbour's cat seeking and the soft shaping of fur and claw
        through foliage.
She has learnt to make no judgement between them, holding herself in
        her own familiarity, warmed by sun, collecting and freed from debris
        according to the wind.

Sometimes she is required instantly to be human,   15
a bright loving woman among her independent offspring
to fill a lull in their preoccupations.

                                                1994

Looking for Andy

The police knocked early at my daughter's door
looking for Andy, just wanting to check.
Politely. Once inside suddenly more
like a drugbust. She and her husband took
deep breaths, sat still. There's nothing in that house,   5
no secrets and no drugs, not even coffee.
My deaf grandson watched a stranger browse
through his clean socks, and made the sign for crazy.
Later my daughter came to ask me where
Andy might be, what sort of trouble, how   10

they could help. I wish I had an answer.
There's only been a phone-voice: 'Listen, cow,
your Andy really ripped us off, the bastard.
Tell him we're gonna break his fucking legs
soon as we find him.'   15
                   Andy, please call home.
Andy? This is an urgent message whispered
into old dark space. With love from Mum.

                                  1994

Cross country

At dawn over the ridge I circled with the wedge-tail and her mate
sunpowered at spin-brain height. I woke in my skull
headed for the hills where the monk mind can buzz in its cell
or lie quiet, looking down and back over smog and burglar alarms
or soar in bone-space, hanging on the cold attentive air. I woke   5

in my body, heart-city of graffiti:
MUTATE NOW AND AVOID THE RUSH;
REAL PUNKS CANT SPELL QUEECHE;
THE MEEK DONT WANT IT.
Pun-scutted, chrome-eyed, the city's rodent peeps   10
from its burrow reamed in the heart's right chamber
and tucks its back legs ready for a practised skitter
under the pounding traffics of wheel and dealer.

Warm as a sunned puppy I flop
over from fuzzy and wake in the creak of my skin-naked self.   15
With coffee I take in my window's terraced garden,
the fishpond to the right, shaped as one hemisphere
of the brain, a pool troubled by the casual ascent of angels
or a couple of wandering ducks washing their feet.

                               (1998)

PETER STEELE   *(b 1939)*

April Fool

Done with Herod and the glittering robe,
     the zinfandel in Pilate's bowl,
the scarlet thorned together at his breast,
     he went, what was left of him, after
the lashed bone and lead toggles were finished   5
     making completely clear who
was who and what was what, out of the city,
     a day's work still to do.

A retrospective piety would have him
      gaze down the novel vistas   10
of Flodden Field, Antietam, Gallipoli,
      the flaming butter of napalm, the gulf
made in the air when atoms boil, the hiss
      of gas to deal with other Jews:
but he may have found it saving grace enough   15
      not to be hating bloody fools.

                                                (1997)

Brother

No day goes by without your haunting me,
You, whose tongue was always heavy with silence.

Watching myself taped, a mouth pouring
Word on crested word, I am ashamed

To have outlived you, whom first I saw huddled   5
Behind glass some wars and loves ago.

There is, as your brooding gaze always implied,
Nothing to say. But as I back towards

Your veiled country, let me say only
That you were never slight, nor I the rock.   10

                                              (1998)

Playwright

Wrong about almost the whole damn thing except horror,
He got this right, that in memory everything seems
To happen to music. Off-stage or on, the performers
Move as though swayed by another planet's trajection,
The modes taking them out on the plains of Mars,   5
Or to where pitiless Venus winds her tourbillion.

Each of them — hind, aristo, the manic, the feckless —
Is attended and glozed by a species of cosmic murmur.
Shadowless all, none of them lacks a vestige,
An air in the air, the leavings of undulant sound   10
That used to sway like so much wheat in the breeze
Begun in the void by all that crystalline spinning.

And still we are matched with some of Orpheus' children,
Menaced by those who detest his ways. The middle
Movement of the Moonlight Sonata, said Liszt,   15
Is 'a flower between two abysses': and Ovid,
'Songs have immunity from death': and Elizabeth,
Coldly, 'Hang the harpers wherever found.'

If the blithe gods in their blue country have music
Instead of memory, and if the tireless demons   20
Truffle for chaos, all of them walled in a now,

We have nothing to say to each other. A blessed fireball
Mounts from its chasm, making a gift of shadows,
Each of them singing to the lost years it carries.

(1998)

J. S. HARRY   *(b 1939)*

Selling Ethiopia

After he had carved up Ethiopia as if it were
a private cloth and not a commonalty
all may walk to — he sold it by pretending faded remnants
were the relics of some great and holy traveller —

he sold it — piece by piece — wailing in the market —   5
          — in shoddy raw-edged segments —
as if there were a glittering whole of which
the pieces were only a reminder,

it occurred to him that what he'd sold
was all there was   or would be   of glitter or unity   10
                    that he'd
ever get close to. There was only one
shoddy voyaged end-piece.

After he had noticed   from a distance
                    himself and others   15
in small luminous segments — wondrous as earthworms
                    or marble —

he began again to paddle, bearing the storms
of which no extrinsic proof existed,
as if he might meet some other traveller —   20

as if the storms might make a final gift

1979

Mousepoem

Her lover departed
to the warm purry
bed of his wife,
with pale blue hands
in the cold dawnlight   5
she has written a poem so slight
she thinks if a mouse breathed on it,
it would collapse (the
poem, not
          the mouse which is made   10
of tough, mouse material, whiskers, ears,

small, quick, risk-assessing eyes; the poem
is so light it seems to float, not stand;
the mouse ... stands on firm mouse-muscles
& potato-crispy, cat-delighting   15
bones). Who would ever   think of fucking
a mouse, but its lover? Who would ever
want to be fucked by a mouse but another?
Who would wish for blind, hairless
mouse-children, but a mousy mother?   20
Does a mouse wish
or are children merely what happens to it
wishless but wanting?
Time: is a moment
a mouse at rest? Pick it up? You cannot.   25
Relativity (by neither Newton's nor Einstein's
mechanics): when a human moves
a live mouse refuses arrest.
Even a blind mouse
will feel the great weight   30
of a malnutritioned
skinny human
& dart for the soot-stinky hole
behind a dead fire's
cold grate.   35

What has her slight poem
to do with a dead fire?
                              Ah ...

                                                                   1995

Picking the Nits

Tied to a streetlamp post as in the past
        people hitched horses, and now
park dogs, two royal blue, three white
        and two liverwurst-coloured balloons
salute the Vietnam veterans,   5
        who walk, in 1987, some in patched bodies,
on semi-functional legs,
        to remember ... the unreturning, and to prove
as if adjusting Descartes —
        je marche, donc je suis, giving themselves to the day   10
as weather gives itself to the ground, without stint.
Beside the solid, lumpen Opera House, and the light,
        wind-lunged yachts on the harbour
that sail, from Bennelong Point as the wind breathes
        in, out, under the bridge, wherever sails are pushed,   15
today the vets walk by choice. They have been solicited.

---

10 'I march, therefore I am.'

Crowds cheer, and people weep, as if
they are forgiving.
    Sun, which gives itself utterly to the day,
without meaning anything by it, dries the veterans' skins   20
    without defoliating them. Time has blotted some
    of every body's atrocities
into dried ink, on written pages, in books of
    je t'accuse, je m'accuse.

    Behind eyes ride the paling colours   25
of flaming children, of murderous children.
    Behind eyes rides war, with all its defoliants
of the human heart, war with all its drugs
    of the rituals of action —
    the drugging, mechanical actions   30
of people on firing ranges, and at sideshows —
    toy rises, you shoot, hit toy falls, another rises,
you shoot — or bomb, or flame-throw. In wars
    all the live toys
shoot back: sometimes the target-shooter falls,   35
    sometimes the target. In wars you are ordered
    to put your blocking-piece,
between the forces you are with,
    that are hopefully, behind you, and the forces
you are opposing. Lose your life-toy, no one will pat you   40
    on the back, say bad luck soldier, you've lost
your toy, here's another. Exactly the same
    one-birth-one-death deal as you get in peace, except
in peace, it is not the same — you are not
    ordered to kill. Few die, in peace or in war,   45
on ground they have chosen. The selector
    of a battleground is seldom called upon
to kill on it, or to fertilize it
    with the blood and bones of his body.

Cochineal-pink   50
    and white azaleas, mounted against a
sandstone rockface, do not lose the petals of their skins
    like people peeled by chemicals. War lives
behind people's eyes like some surrealist film, and with
    the eyes of the blind, we salute   55
    where we think you stand, on ground that
hurts because it is so unforgiving. In the sixties
    I knew a countryboy from the Vic. wheatlands
who carried his army gun, as a boy his
    rabbit-shooting rifle, marked by a knife   60

---

24 'I accuse you, I accuse myself.' 'J'accuse' was the heading of an open letter in which Emile Zola
in 1898 challenged the conviction of Alfred Dreyfus for treason. The 'Dreyfus affair' became the focus of bitter division in France.

with a notch for each
    known Vietnamese he'd scored. He was proud
of his tally. Whether the target came
    from the North or South, of the paddock,
age, or sex, of the rabbit, was not something   65
    he'd bothered overly much about at home;
at home or in 'Nam he'd done
  what he was told,
whether by dad or the sergeant.
    Had not shot, by mistake, Australians. If he is   70
alive now, he will be marching, belly-paunched, older,
    amazed   at his life as one of his rabbits would be
if it were left alive, if   it could think.

The rest of their day goes by
    in the physical fashion of Sydney. As in the rest   75
of some brewer's dream of Australia,
    tin cans slant, tilted
up to mouths, and drunks slant angled
    ogling out at traffic.

Elsewhere,   80
out in the scrub, beetles sail like small brown
    furniture-polished *objets d'art*
from one side of the hiking track to the other.
    Some click, as the rifle bolt does, into its breech,
and some go zzzz.   85
    Heavy black power shift and gear-change, overhead
in the hard black wing shuffle of a bird's dark
    swerve, sideways from the scrub, to check what is:
people moving over ground so hard it sends
    its pain upward, each further   90
step you limp sends bruised feet's message
    through your body. The centre of pain,
where the message
    comes from, is the brain. However feeble.

Dog with brown saliva-and-dirt-sodden ball   95
    that it is carrying in its mouth so the two
humans with it won't forget
    its most precious
joy-tool. A toy, which is not
    its life, but which   100
puts a polish of joy on shared living. Honeysuckle's
    little penises — cream and corn-yellow
on the same tendril — drench the air
    with their sweet potent song. This
honeysuckle's leaves are the playgrounds   105
    of small insects; the leaves' elongated ovals
are the green of a watered lawn on sandy soil.

Picked, these leaves
    curl and turn inwards, as they die. They die twisting
and twisted.   110
    Some people pick honeysuckle and put it
between the pages of a book, to remind
themselves of something. Lost between the pages
    of a book, when they find it, they've forgotten
what such honeysuckle meant. In your mind   115
    as on a picked and dying tendril, the scent
of honeysuckle lingers.

It has been fashionable   for America to see itself
    as the literate Ape
conscientiously picking the nits   120
    of its acts in Vietnam
from the fur of its belly, to examine them
    and crack them, censuring itself with its teeth.
Now, it is into acceptance. Perhaps Australia too
    is past its nit-picking ... into acceptance.   125

The Vietnam War too has been picked.
    It is the past.
It smells of horror terror flesh on fire.
Water on ash, flame gone out, steam rising.
The scent of faded flesh on fire   130
sticks, peeling and clinging, to the flesh of memory.
                                                      1995

MUDROOROO   *(b 1939)*

Lightning Travels

Dunno who he was, that brother with the hammer,
With the mallet in his fist, just a brother,
One of us mob, who liked travelling on and light
And heavy, smashing his legs, moving his toes, stumping out
A sign for us to follow along behind his ancestral ways.   5
Always moving, travelling light, pushing out,
Ahead into foreign lands, and hands and arms,
And experiences, lush and barren, flickering with lightning,
Lightning from his hammer, our brother's hammer,
Our father's hammer, our grandfather's hammer,   10
Our children's children's hammer hammering out.
Namaragan, sweep us together in your lightning flashes,
Namaragan, as my clapsticks mark out the rhythm
Your hammer crashes and in the wind spirit children whisper
Out the consternation of their line, of our line, of your line.   15
                                                   1991

Aussie Dreams a Wakey-wake Time 2

Suburban house wiles the time in fitful dozes of Nyoongah
Dodging how it is as the flowers grow scattering sleep-seeds
Over my faint snores mowing the lawns and stretching out lines
Jailing the quietness, sunny Aussie dream fought over,
Punching out sneerers, king-hitting the cynical bastards.   5
Holding on to my dream in my sleek arms, in my limp fists,
In my growing belly spawning the Aussie dream,
Life-time mortgage dream, earthquaking titles to my dream
In which insecurity lurks, in which adventures huddle,
Though the sounds of midnight blows sweeten my desire for   10
A city street rancid with a beer-smell of wilderness.
I'll seek a bridge to shelter my shivering body,
My vomit will stream away the debris of the gutters,
My saliva will rain down over this city blurring
The dancing lights hazy in my bleary eyes,   15
Playing over the loneliness of an old man's room
In which my toothless gums mutter dribbling past dentures.
Some folk don't make it to the suburbs,
Some folk one day button their jackets over past sorrows,
Holding out against excessive dreams and penthouse posturings.   20

1991

LES MURRAY   *(b 1938)*

Once in a Lifetime, Snow

For Chris and Mary Sharah

Winters at home brought wind,
black frost and raw
grey rain in barbed-wire fields,
but never more

until the day my uncle   5
rose at dawn
and stepped outside — to find
his paddocks gone,

his cattle to their hocks
in ghostly ground   10
and unaccustomed light
for miles around.

And he stopped short, and gazed
lit from below,
and half his wrinkles vanished   15
murmuring *Snow.*

A man of farm and fact
he stared to see
the facts of weather raised
to a mystery   20

white on the world he knew
and all he owned.
Snow? Here? he mused. I see.
High time I learned.

Here, guessing what he meant   25
had much to do
with that black earth dread old men
are given to,

he stooped to break the sheer
crust with delight   30
at finding the cold unknown
so deeply bright,

at feeling it take his prints
so softly deep,
as if it thought he knew   35
enough to sleep,

or else so little he
might seek to shift
its weight of wintry light
by a single drift,   40

perceiving this much, he scuffed
his slippered feet
and scooped a handful up
to taste, and eat

in memory of the fact   45
that even he
might not have seen the end
of reality ...

Then, turning, he tiptoed in
to a bedroom, smiled,   50
and wakened a murmuring child
and another child.

                                    1969

The Broad Bean Sermon

Beanstalks, in any breeze, are a slack church parade
without belief; saying *trespass against us* in unison,
recruits in mint Air Force dacron, with unbuttoned leaves.

Upright with water like men, square in stem-section
they grow to great lengths, drink rain, keel over all ways,
kink down and grow up afresh, with proffered new greenstuff.

Above the cat-and-mouse floor of a thin bean forest
snails hang rapt in their food, ants hurry through several dimensions:
spiders tense and sag like little black flags in their cordage.

Going out to pick beans with the sun high as fence-tops, you find   10
plenty, and fetch them. An hour or a cloud later
you find shirtfulls more. At every hour of daylight

appear more than you missed: ripe, knobbly ones, fleshy-sided,
thin-straight, thin-crescent, frown-shaped, bird-shouldered, boat-keeled ones,
beans knuckled and single-bulged, minute green dolphins at suck,   15

beans upright like lecturing, outstretched like blessing fingers
in the incident light, and more still, oblique to your notice
that the noon glare or cloud-light or afternoon slants will uncover

till you ask yourself Could I have overlooked so many, or
do they form in an hour? unfolding into reality   20
like templates for subtly broad grins, like unique caught expressions,

like edible meanings, each sealed around with a string
and affixed to its moment, an unceasing colloquial assembly,
the portly, the stiff, and those lolling in pointed green slippers ...

Wondering who'll take the spare bagfulls, you grin with happiness   25
— it is your health — you vow to pick them all
even the last few, weeks off yet, misshapen as toes.

                                                                    1977

The Buladelah-Taree Holiday Song Cycle

1

The people are eating dinner in that country north of Legge's Lake;
behind flywire and venetians, in the dimmed cool, town people eat Lunch.
Plying knives and forks with a peek-in sound, with a tuck-in sound,
they are thinking about relatives and inventory, they are talking about
          customers and visitors.
In the country of memorial iron, on the creek-facing hills there,   5
they are thinking about bean plants, and rings of tank water, of growing a
          pumpkin by Christmas;
rolling a cigarette, they say thoughtfully Yes, and their companion nods,
          considering.

Fresh sheets have been spread and tucked tight, childhood rooms have been
      seen to,
for this is the season when children return with their children
to the place of Bingham's Ghost, of the Old Timber Wharf, of the Big Flood
      That Time,   10
the country of the rationalized farms, of the day-and-night farms, and of the
      Pitt Street farms,
of the Shire Engineer and many other rumours, of the tractor crankcase
      furred with chaff,
the places of sitting down near ferns, the snake-fear places, the
      cattle-crossing-long-ago places.

2

It is the season of the Long Narrow City; it has crossed the Myall, it has
      entered the North Coast,
that big stunning snake; it is looped through the hills, burning all night
      there.   15
Hitching and flying on the downgrades, processionally balancing on the climbs,
it echoes in O'Sullivan's Gap, in the tight coats of the flooded-gum trees;
the tops of palms exclaim at it unmoved, there near Wootton.
Glowing all night behind the hills, with a north-shifting glare, burning
      behind the hills;
through Coolongolook, through Wang Wauk, across the Wallamba,   20
the booming tarred pipe of the holiday slows and spurts again; Nabiac
      chokes in glassy wind,
the forests on Kiwarrak dwindle in cheap light; Tuncurry and Forster swell
      like cooking oil.
The waiting is buffed, in timber villages off the highway, the waiting is buffeted:
the fumes of fun hanging above ferns; crime flashes in strange windscreens,
      in the time of the Holiday.
Parasites weave quickly through the long gut that paddocks shine into;   25
powerful makes surging and pouncing: the police, collecting Revenue.
The heavy gut winds over the Manning, filling northward, digesting the
      towns, feeding the towns;
they all become the narrow city, they join it;
girls walking close to murder discard, with excitement, their names.
Crossing Australia of the sports, the narrow city, bringing home the children.   30

3

It is good to come out after driving and walk on bare grass;
walking out, looking all around, relearning that country.
Looking out for snakes, and looking out for rabbits as well;
going into the shade of myrtles to try their cupped climate, swinging by one
      hand around them,
in that country of the Holiday ...   35
stepping behind trees to the dam, as if you had a gun,
to that place of the Wood Duck,
to that place of the Wood Duck's Nest,

proving you can still do it; looking at the duck who hasn't seen you,
the mother duck who'd run Catch Me (broken wing) I'm Fatter (broken
     wing), having hissed to her children.   40

4

The birds saw us wandering along.
Rosellas swept up crying out *we think we think*; they settled farther along;
knapping seeds off the grass, under dead trees where their eggs were,
     walking around on their fingers,
flying on into the grass.
The heron lifted up his head and elbows; the magpie stepped aside a bit,   45
angling his chopsticks into pasture, turning things over in his head.
At the place of the Plough Handles, of the Apple Trees Bending Over, and of
     the Cattlecamp,
there the vealers are feeding; they are loosely at work, facing everywhere.
They are always out there, and the forest is always on the hills;
around the sun are turning the wedgetail eagle and her mate, that dour
     brushhook-faced family: 50
they settled on Deer's Hill away back when the sky was opened,
in the bull-oak trees way up there, the place of fur tufted in the grass, the
     place of bone-turds.

5

The Fathers and the Great-grandfathers, they are out in the paddocks all the
     time, they live out there,
at the place of the Rail Fence, of the Furrows Under Grass, at the place of the
     Slab Chimney.
We tell them that clearing is complete, an outdated attitude, all over;   55
we preach without a sacrifice, and are ignored; flowering bushes grow dull
     to our eyes.
We begin to go up on the ridge, talking together, looking at the kino-coloured
     ants,
at the yard-wide sore of their nest, that kibbled peak, and the workers
     heaving vast stalks up there,
the brisk compact workers; jointed soldiers pour out then, tense with acid;
     several probe the mouth of a lost gin bottle;
Innuendo, we exclaim, *literal minds!* and go on up the ridge, announced by
     finches;   60
passing the place of the Dingo Trap, and that farm hand it caught, and the
     place of the Cowbails,
we come to the road and watch heifers,
little unjoined Devons, their teats hidden in fur, and the cousin with his
     loose-slung stockwhip driving them.
We talk with him about rivers and the lakes; his polished horse is stepping
     nervously,
printing neat omegas in the gravel, flexing its skin to shake off flies;   65
his big sidestepping horse that has kept its stones; it recedes gradually,
     bearing him;
we murmur *stone-horse* and *devilry* to the grinners under grass.

6

Barbecue smoke is rising at Legge's Camp; it is steaming into the midday air,
all around the lake shore, at the Broadwater, it is going up among the
      paperbark trees,
a heat-shimmer of sauces, rising from tripods and flat steel, at that place of
      the cone shells,   70
at that place of the Seagrass, and the tiny segmented things swarming in it,
      and of the Pelican.
Dogs are running around disjointedly; water escapes from their mouths,
confused emotions from their eyes; humans snarl at them
Gwanout and Hereboy, not varying their tone much;
the impoverished dog people, suddenly sitting down to nuzzle themselves;
      toddlers side with them: 75
toddlers, running away purposefully at random, among cars, into big
      drownie water (come back, Cheryl-Ann!).
They rise up as charioteers, leaning back on the tow-bar; all their attributes
      bulge at once:
swapping swash shoulder-wings for the white-sheeted shoes that bear them,
they are skidding over the flat glitter, stiff with grace, for once not travelling
      to arrive.
From the high dunes over there, the rough blue distance, at length they come
      back behind the boats,   80
and behind the boats' noise, cartwheeling, or sitting down, into the lake's
      warm chair;
they wade ashore and eat with the families, putting off that uprightness, that
      assertion,
eating with the families who love equipment, and the freedom from equipment,
with the fathers who love driving, and lighting a fire between stones.

7

Shapes of children were moving in the standing corn, in the child-labour
      districts;   85
coloured flashes of children, between the green and parching stalks,
      appearing and disappearing.
Some places, they are working, racking off each cob like a lever, tossing it on
      the heaps;
other places, they are children of child-age, there playing jungle:
in the tiger-striped shade, they are firing hoehandle machine-guns, taking
      cover behind fat pumpkins;
in other cases, it is Sunday and they are lovers.   90
They rise and walk together in the sibilance, finding single rows irksome,
      hating speech now,
or, full of speech, they swap files and follow defiles, disappearing
      and appearing;
near the rain-grey barns, and the children building cattleyards beside them;
the standing corn, gnawed by pouched and rodent mice; generations are
      moving among it,

the parrot-hacked, medicine-tasselled corn, ascending all the creek flats, the
 wire-fenced alluvials,   95
going up in patches through the hills, towards the Steep Country.

8

Forests and State Forests, all down off the steeper country; mosquitoes are
 always living in there:
they float about like dust motes and sink down, at the places of the Stinging
 Tree,
and of the Staghorn Fern; the males feed on plant-stem fluid, absorbing that
 watery ichor;
the females meter the air, feeling for the warm-blooded smell, needing blood
 for their eggs.   100
They find the dingo in his sleeping-place, they find his underbelly and
 his anus;
they find the possum's face, they drift up the ponderous pleats of the fig
 tree, way up into its rigging,
the high camp of the fruit bats; they feed on the membranes and ears of
 bats; tired wings cuff air at them;
their eggs burning inside them, they alight on the muzzles of cattle,
the half-wild bush cattle, there at the place of the Sleeper Dump, at the
 place of the Tallowwoods.   105
The males move about among growth tips; ingesting solutions, they crouch
 intently;
the females sing, needing blood to breed their young; their singing is in the
 scrub country;
their tune comes to the name-bearing humans, who dance to it and irritably
 grin at it.

9

The warriors are cutting timber with brash chainsaws; they are trimming
 hardwood pit-props and loading them;
Is that an order? they hoot at the peremptory lorry driver, who laughs; he is
 also a warrior.   110
They are driving long-nosed tractors, slashing pasture in the dinnertime sun;
they are fitting tappets and valves, the warriors, or giving finish to
 a surfboard.
Addressed on the beach by a pale man, they watch waves break and are
 reserved, refusing pleasantry;
they joke only with fellow warriors, chaffing about try-ons and the police,
 not slighting women.
Making Timber a word of power, Con-rod a word of power, Sense a word
 of power, the Regs. a word of power,   115
they know belt-fed from spring-fed; they speak of being *stiff*, and being
 history;
the warriors who have killed, and the warriors who eschewed killing,
the solemn, the drily spoken, the life peerage of endurance; drinking water
 from a tap,
they watch boys who think hard work a test, and boys who think it is not a
 test.

10

Now the ibis are flying in, hovering down on the wetlands,   120
on those swampy paddocks around Darawank, curving down in ragged
        dozens,
on the riverside flats along the Wang Wauk, on the Boolambayte pasture
        flats,
and away towards the sea, on the sand moors, at the place of the Jabiru
        Crane;
leaning out of their wings, they step down; they take out their implement at
        once,
out of its straw wrapping, and start work; they dab grasshopper and
        ground-cricket   125
with nonexistence ... spiking the ground and puncturing it ... they swallow
        down the outcry of a frog;
they discover titbits kept for them under cowmanure lids, small slow things.
Pronging the earth, they make little socket noises, their thoughtfulness
        jolting down and up suddenly;
there at Bunyah, along Firefly Creek, and up through Germany,
the ibis are all at work again, thin-necked ageing men towards evening; they
        are solemnly all back   130
at Minimbah, and on the Manning, in the rye-and-clover irrigation fields;
city storemen and accounts clerks point them out to their wives,
remembering things about themselves, and about the ibis.

11

Abandoned fruit trees, moss-tufted, spotted with dim lichen paints; the fruit
        trees of the Grandmothers,
they stand along the creekbanks, in the old home paddocks, where the
        houses were,   135
they are reached through bramble-grown front gates, they creak at dawn
        behind burnt skillions,
at Belbora, at Bucca Wauka, away in at Burrell Creek,
at Telararee of the gold-sluices.
The trees are split and rotten-elbowed; they bear the old-fashioned summer
        fruits,
the annual bygones: china pear, quince, persimmon;   140
the fruit has the taste of former lives, of sawdust and parlour song, the tang
        of Manners;
children bite it, recklessly,
at what will become for them the place of the Slab Wall, and of the Coal Oil
        Lamp,
the place of moss-grit and swallows' nests, the place of the Crockery.

12

Now the sun is an applegreen blindness through the swells, a white blast
        on the sea face, flaking and shoaling;   145
now it is burning off the mist; it is emptying the density of trees, it is
        spreading upriver,
hovering about the casuarina needles, there at Old Bar and Manning Point;

flooding the island farms, it abolishes the milkers' munching breath
as they walk towards the cowyards; it stings a bucket here, a teatcup there.
Morning steps into the world by ever more southerly gates; shadows
      weaken their north skew   150
on Middle Brother, on Cape Hawke, on the dune scrub toward Seal Rocks;
steadily the heat is coming on, the butter-water time, the clothes-sticking
      time;
grass covers itself with straw; abandoned things are thronged with spirits;
everywhere wood is still with strain; birds hiding down the creek galleries,
      and in the cockspur canes;
the cicada is hanging up her sheets; she takes wing off her music-sheets.   155
Cars pass with a rational zoom, panning quickly towards Wingham,
through the thronged and glittering, the shale-topped ridges, and the
      cattlecamps,
towards Wingham for the cricket, the ball knocked hard in front of
      smoked-glass ranges, and for the drinking.
In the time of heat, the time of flies around the mouth, the time of the west
      verandah;
looking at that umbrage along the ranges, on the New England side;   160
clouds begin assembling vaguely, a hot soiled heaviness on the sky, away
      there towards Gloucester;
a swelling up of clouds, growing there above Mount George, and above
      Tipperary;
far away and hot with light; sometimes a storm takes root there, and fills the
      heavens rapidly;
darkening, boiling up and swaying on its stalks, pulling this way and that,
      blowing round by Krambach;
coming white on Bulby, it drenches down on the paddocks, and on the wire
      fences;   165
the paddocks are full of ghosts, and people in cornbag hoods approaching;
lights are lit in the house; the storm veers mightily on its stem, above the
      roof; the hills uphold it;
the stony hills guide its dissolution; gullies opening and crumbling down,
      wrenching tussocks and rolling them;
the storm carries a greenish-grey bag; perhaps it will find hail and send it down,
      starring cars, flattening tomatoes,
in the time of the Washaways, of the dead trunks braiding water, and of the
      Hailstone Yarns.   170

13

The stars of the holiday step out all over the sky.
People look up at them, out of their caravan doors and their campsites;
people look up from the farms, before going back; they gaze at their year's
      worth of stars.
The Cross hangs head-downward, out there over Markwell;
it turns upon the Still Place, the pivot of the Seasons, with one shoulder
      rising: 175
'Now I'm beginning to rise, with my Pointers and my Load ...'
hanging eastwards, it shines on the sawmills and the lakes, on the glasses of
      the Old People.

Looking at the Cross, the galaxy is over our left shoulder, slung up highest in
    the east;
there the Dog is following the Hunter; the Dog Star pulsing there above
    Forster; it shines down on the Bikies,
and on the boat-hire sheds, there at the place of the Oyster; the place of the
    Shark's Eggs and her Hide;   180
the Pleiades are pinned up high on the darkness, away back above the
    Manning;
they are shining on the Two Blackbutt Trees, on the rotted river
    wharves, and on the towns;
standing there, above the water and the lucerne flats, at the place of the
    Families;
their light sprinkles down on Taree of the Lebanese shops, it mingles with the
    streetlights and their glare.
People recover the starlight, hitching north,   185
travelling north beyond the seasons, into that country of the Communes,
    and of the Banana:
the Flying Horse, the Rescued Girl, and the Bull, burning steadily above that
    country.
Now the New Moon is low down in the west, that remote direction of
    Cattlemen,
and of the Saleyards, the place of steep clouds, and of the Rodeo;
the New Moon who has poured out her rain, the moon of the Planting-times. 190
People go outside and look at the stars, and at the melon-rind moon,
the Scorpion going down into the mountains, over there towards Waukivory,
    sinking into the tree-line,
in the time of the Rockmelons, and of the Holiday ...
the Cross is rising on his elbow, above the glow of the horizon;
carrying a small star in his pocket, he reclines there brilliantly,   195
above the Alum Mountain, and the lakes threaded on the Myall River,
    and above the Holiday.

                                             1977

Bent Water in the Tasmanian Highlands

Flashy wrists out of buttoned grass cuffs, feral whisky burning gravels,
jazzy knuckles ajitter on soakages, peaty cupfuls, soft pots overflowing,
setting out along the great curve, migrating mouse-quivering water,
mountain-driven winter water, in the high tweed, stripping off its mountains
to run faster in its skin, it swallows the above, it feeds where it is fed on,   5
it forms at many points and creases outwards, pleated water
shaking out its bedding soil, increasing its scale, beginning the headlong
   — Bent Water, you could call this level
between droplet and planetary, not as steered by twisting beds laterally
but as upped and swayed on its swelling and outstanding own curvatures,   10
its floating top that sweeps impacts sidelong, its event-horizon,
a harelip round a pebble, mouthless cheeks globed over a boulder, a
finger's far-stretched holograph, skinned flow athwart a snag
   — these flexures are all reflections, motion-glyphs, pitches of impediment,
say a log commemorated in a log-long hump of wave,   15

a buried rock continually noted, a squeeze-play
through a cracked basalt bar, maintaining a foam-roofed two-sided
overhang of breakneck riesling; uplifted hoseless hosings, fully circular water,
flattened water off rock sills, sandwiched between an upper
and a lower whizzing surface, trapped in there with airy scatter   20
and mingled high-speed mirrorings; water groined, produced and spiralled
— Crowded scrollwork from events, at steepening white velocities
as if the whole outline of the high country were being pulled out
along these joining channels, and proving infinite, anchored deeply as it
is in the groundwater scale, in the silence around racy breccia   25
yet it is spooling out; the great curve, drawing and driving,
of which these are the animal-sized swells and embodiments
won't always describe this upland; and after the jut falls, the inverse
towering on gorges, these peaks will be hidden beneath
rivers and tree-bark, in electricity, in cattle, on the ocean   30
— Meditation is a standing wave, though, on the black-green inclines
of pouring and cascading, slate-dark rush and timber-worker's tea
bullying the pebble-fans; if we were sketched first at this speed,
sheaths, buttocks, wings, it is mother and history and swank here
till our wave is drained of water. And as such it includes the writhing   35
down in a trench, knees, bellies, the struggling, the slack bleeding
remote enough perhaps, within its close clean film,
to make the observer a god; do we come here to be gods?
or to watch an alien pouring down the slants of our anomaly
and be hypnotized to rest by it? So much detail's unlikely, for hypnosis;   40
it looks like brotherhood sought at a dreamer's remove
and, in either view, laws of falling and persistence:
the continuous ocean round a planetary stone, braiding uptilts
after swoops, echo-forms, arches built from above and standing
on flourish, clear storeys, translucent honey-glazed clerestories —   45

                                                                                1983

The Quality of Sprawl

Sprawl is the quality
of the man who cut down his Rolls-Royce
into a farm utility truck, and sprawl
is what the company lacked when it made repeated efforts
to buy the vehicle back and repair its image.   5

Sprawl is doing your farming by aeroplane, roughly,
or driving a hitchhiker that extra hundred miles home.
It is the rococo of being your own still centre.
It is never lighting cigars with ten-dollar notes:
that's idiot ostentation and murder of starving people.   10
Nor can it be bought with the ash of million-dollar deeds.

Sprawl lengthens the legs; it trains greyhounds on liver and beer.
Sprawl almost never says Why not? with palms comically raised
nor can it be dressed for, not even in running shoes worn

with mink and a nose ring. That is Society. That's Style.   15
Sprawl is more like the thirteenth banana in a dozen
or anyway the fourteenth.

Sprawl is Hank Stamper in *Never Give an Inch*
bisecting an obstructive official's desk with a chainsaw.
Not harming the official. Sprawl is never brutal   20
though it's often intransigent. Sprawl is never Simon de Montfort
at a town-storming: Kill them all! God will know his own.
Knowing the man's name this was said to might be sprawl.

Sprawl occurs in art. The fifteenth to twenty-first
lines in a sonnet, for example. And in certain paintings;   25
I have sprawl enough to have forgotten which paintings.
Turner's glorious *Burning of the Houses of Parliament*
comes to mind, a doubling bannered triumph of sprawl —
except, he didn't fire them.

Sprawl gets up the nose of many kinds of people   30
(every kind that comes in kinds) whose futures don't include it.
Some decry it as criminal presumption, silken-robed Pope Alexander
dividing the new world between Spain and Portugal.
If he smiled *in petto* afterwards, perhaps the thing did have sprawl.

Sprawl is really classless, though. It's John Christopher Frederick Murray   35
asleep in his neighbours' best bed in spurs and oilskins
but not having thrown up:
sprawl is never Calum who, drunk, along the hallways of our house,
reinvented the Festoon. Rather
it's Beatrice Miles going twelve hundred ditto in a taxi,   40
No Lewd Advances, No Hitting Animals, No Speeding,
on the proceeds of her two-bob-a-sonnet Shakespeare readings.
An image of my country. And would that it were more so.

No, sprawl is full-gloss murals on a council-house wall.
Sprawl leans on things. It is loose-limbed in its mind.   45
Reprimanded and dismissed
it listens with a grin and one boot up on the rail
of possibility. It may have to leave the Earth.
Being roughly Christian, it scratches the other cheek
and thinks it unlikely. Though people have been shot for sprawl.   50

                                                                       1983

The Tin Wash Dish

Lank poverty, dank poverty,
its pants wear through at fork and knee.
It warms its hands over burning shames,
refers to its fate as Them and He
and delights in things by their hard names   5

---

33 in petto   term indicating a secret clause in a papal document

rag and toejam, feed and paw —
don't guts that down, there ain't no more!
Dank poverty, rank poverty,
it hums with a grim fidelity
like wood-rot with a hint of orifice,   10
wet newspaper jammed in the gaps of artifice,
and disgusts us into fierce loyalty.
It's never the fault of those you love:
poverty comes down from above.
Let it dance chairs and smash the door,   15
it arises from all that went before
and every outsider's the enemy —
Jesus Christ turned this over with his stick
and knights and philosophers turned it back.
Rank poverty, lank poverty,   20
chafe in its crotch and sores in its hair,
still a window's clean if it's made of air,
not webby silver like a sleeve.
Watch out if this does well at school
and has to leave and longs to leave: 25
someone, sometime, will have to pay.
Shave with toilet soap, run to flesh,
astound the nation, rule the army,
still you wait for the day you'll be sent back
where books or toys on the floor are rubbish   30
and no one's allowed to come and play
because home calls itself a shack
and hot water crinkles in the tin wash dish.

                                                               1990

The Last Hellos

Don't die, Dad —
but they die.

This last year he was wandery:
took off a new chainsaw blade
and cobbled a spare from bits.   5
Perhaps if I lay down
my head'll come better again.
His left shoulder kept rising
higher in his cardigan.

He could see death in a face.   10
Family used to call him in
to look at sick ones and say.
At his own time, he was told.

The knob found in his head
was duck-egg size. Never hurt.   15
Two to six months, Cecil.

I'll be right, he boomed
to his poor sister on the phone
I'll do that when I finish dyin.

*

Don't die, Cecil.   20
But they do.

Going for last drives
in the bush, odd massive
board-slotted stumps bony white
in whipstick second growth.   25
I could chop all day.

*I could always cash
a cheque, in Sydney or anywhere.
Any of the shops.*

Eating, still at the head   30
of the table, he now missed
food on his knife side.

*Sorry, Dad, but like
have you forgiven your enemies?
Your father and all them?*   35
All his lifetime of hurt.

I must have, (grin). *I don't
think about that now.*

*

People can't say goodbye
any more. They say last hellos.   40

Going fast, over Christmas,
he'd still stumble out
of his room, where his photos
hang over the other furniture,
and play host to his mourners.   45

The courage of his bluster,
firm big voice of his confusion.

Two last days in the hospital:
his long forearms were still
red mahogany. His hands   50
gripped steel frame. *I'm dyin.*

On the second day:
*You're bustin to talk
but I'm too busy dyin.*

*

Grief ended when he died,   55
the widower like soldiers who
won't live life their mates missed.

Good boy Cecil! No more Bluey dog.
No more cowtime. No more stories.
We're still using your imagination,   60
it was stronger than all ours.

Your grave's got littler
somehow, in the three months.
More pointy as the clay's shrivelled,
like a stuck zip in a coat.   65

Your cricket boots are in
the State museum! Odd letters
still come. Two more's died since you:
Annie, and Stewart. Old Stewart.

On your day there was a good crowd,   70
family, and people from away.
But of course a lot had gone
to their own funerals first.

Snobs mind us off religion
nowadays, if they can.   75
Fuck thém. I wish you God.

                                                              1996

Cotton Flannelette

Shake the bed, the blackened child whimpers,
O shake the bed! through beak lips that never
will come unwry. And wearily the iron-
framed mattress, with nodding crockery bulbs,
jinks on its way.   5
                Her brothers and sister take
shifts with the terrible glued-together baby
when their unsleeping absolute mother
reels out to snatch an hour, back to stop
the rocking and wring pale blue soap-water   10
over nude bladders and blood-webbed chars.

Even their cranky evasive father
is awed to stand watches rocking the bed.
Lids frogged shut, *O please shake the bed*,
her contour whorls and braille tattoos   15
from where, in her nightdress, she flared
out of hearth-drowse to a marrow shriek

pedalling full tilt firesleeves in mid air,
                   are grainier with repair
than when the doctor, crying *Dear God, woman!*   20
No one can save that child. Let her go!
spared her the treatments of the day.

Shake the bed. Like: count phone poles, rhyme,
classify realities, bang the head, any
iteration that will bring, in the brain's forks,   25
the melting molecules of relief,
and bring them again.
                   O rock the bed!

Nibble water with bared teeth, make lymph
like arrowroot gruel, as your mother grips you   30
for weeks in the untrained perfect language,
till the doctor relents. Salves and wraps you
in dressings that will be the fire again,
ripping anguish off agony,
                   and will confirm   35
the ploughland ridges in your woman's skin
for the sixty more years your family weaves you
on devotion's loom, rick-racking the bed
as you yourself, six years old, instruct them.

                                   1996

The Instrument

Who reads poetry? Not our intellectuals:
they want to control it. Not lovers, not the combative,
not examinees. They too skim it for bouquets
and magic trump cards. Not poor schoolkids
furtively farting as they get immunized against it.   5

Poetry is read by the lovers of poetry
and heard by some more they coax to the cafe
or district library for a bifocal reading.
Lovers of poetry may total a million people
on the whole planet. Fewer than the players of *skat*.   10

What gives them delight is a never-murderous skim
distilled, to verse mainly, and suspended in fulfilment
on the surface of paper. The rest of poetry
to which this was once integral still rules
continents, as it always did. But on condition now   15

that its true name is never spoken. This feral poetry,
the opposite but also the secret of the rational,
who reads that? Ah, the lovers, the schoolkids,
debaters, generals, crime-lords, everybody reads it:
Porsche, lift-off, Gaia, proletariat, Celebes.   20

That's the kind which may demand your flesh
to embody itself. Only the serried verses,
being fully made, can dance you, blushing, still seated,
pirouetting through the larger poems you are in.
Being outside all poetry is an unreachable void.   25

Why write poetry? For the unemployment.
For the painless headaches, that must be tapped to strike
down along your writing arm at the cumulative moment.
For the adjustments after, aligning facets inside a verb
before the trance leaves you. For working always beyond   30

your own intelligence. For not needing to rise
and betray the poor to do it. For a non-devouring fame.
Little in politics resembles it: perhaps
the Australian colonists' devising of that snide
secret ballot in which deflation could hide   35

and, as a welfare bringer, shame the mass-grave Revolutions,
so axe-edged, so lictor-y.
Was that moral cowardice's one shining world victory?
Breathing in dream-rhythm awake and far from bed
evinces the gift. Being tragic with a book on your head.   40

                                                        (1997)

JUDITH RODRIGUEZ   *(b 1936)*

Towards fog

The quality of fog is that it has style but no detail.
Though detected in a state of nuance, it cannot be caught at it.
I try with a 2B — softly — with a 6 or 8B — I am gradual as growing —
still there are lines, parts, separations. Fog has none.
When was a photograph of fog, a film of fog moving,   5
ever so diffuse, directionless, and all-round-clammy?
And the incuriosity of fog is beyond everything.

There are times I want to go back to somewhere like beginning.
The concept of a cell is too advanced for what I want to be, sometimes.
Words are cellular, and baulk at it: fog is not-saying.   10
Fog engulfs. Devours, with no process. Fog is instead of.
Fog extends. Fog bulks. It is nothing you ever see in profile, yet there ...

What is *there*? I put out my hand. Is that a handful of fog?

---

35 secret ballot. The use of a secret ballot was pioneered by Australian colonies in the 1850s.

Does it flow through? And can I expel it with a willed clenching?
Or invite it with nebulous fingers, tendons in concert — the hand
    half-opening?   15

Mind revving up to understand, body boggling
at the falling to inorganic, the going nerveless;
both fall short, bailed up on recognised borders.
The true photograph of fog would disappear,
its corners sucked into monochrome lack of point.   20
And the drawing of fog would be made with
horizonless sky and land for a pencil.
And the poem of fog would fold
round the wire-thin word *today-as-usual*
all the sounds, ideas of all kinds of being   25
in a more than pastoral silence.

The man as fog does not bear thinking of.
Green though the slopes are, after.

I displace fog, yet it is inward with me.
I can't do fog. Never, perhaps, to be done with it —   30
exhalations from a deep place, earth-rumours
fragile and huge, a beauty of a threat
there's no dealing with.

                                  1976

Eskimo occasion

I am in my Eskimo-hunting-song mood,
Aha!
The lawn is tundra   the car will not start
the sunlight is an avalanche   we are avalanche-struck at our breakfast
struck with sunlight through glass   me and my spoonfed daughters   5
out of this world in our kitchen.

I will sing the song of my daughter-hunting,
Oho!
The waves lay down   the ice grew strong
I sang the song   of dark water under ice   10
the song of winter fishing   the magic for seal rising
among the ancestor-masks.

I waited by water to dream new spirits,
Hoo!
The water spoke   the ice shouted   15
the sea opened   the sun made young shadows
they breathed my breathing   I took them from deep water
I brought them fur-warmed home.

I am dancing the years of the two great hunts,
Ya-hay!   20
It was I who waited   cold in the wind-break

I stamp like the bear   I call like the wind of the thaw
I leap like the sea spring-running.   My sunstruck daughters splutter
and chuckle and bang their spoons:

Mummy is singing at breakfast and dancing!   25
So big!

1976

The mudcrab-eaters

Nothing lovers in their forties do together
      that they don't, you'd say, repeat.
      But then, this day, what others here
      so feast, rising on the lean threat
      of the night apart? Or so taste   5
      and toast their exquisite lot?

      Who else at Gambaro's is happy?
      With dolphin glances serving
      each other, the lovers sit, sea-delight
      lightening air. And though   10
they night and morning years-long sat down to mudcrab,
      they have never eaten mudcrab before.

1980

In-flight note

Kitten, writes the mousy boy in his neat
fawn casuals sitting beside me on the flight,
neatly, *I can't give up everything just like that.*
Everything, how much was it? and just like what?
Did she cool it or walk out? loosen her hand from his tight   5
white-knuckled hand, or not meet him, just as he thought
You mean far too much to me. I can't forget
the four months we've known each other. No, he won't eat,
finally he pays — pale, careful, distraught —
for a beer, turns over the pad on the page he wrote   10
and sleeps a bit. Or dreams of his Sydney cat.
The pad cost one dollar twenty. He wakes to write
It's naive to think we could be just good friends.
Pages and pages. And so the whole world ends.

1988

MAL MORGAN   *(b 1936)*

Some Dream It

      Some dream it   some think it
up   some ask God or Beethoven   hold it
tight   in their minds   in their tight blue
jeans   in their DNA   some hold onto their

letting go of it   beat their wives   5
for it   fall in a heap over it   some find it
in the corner shop   in the butterfly house
wave goodbye to it   from a 767   from the deck
of a great ocean liner   some go overboard
draw a line on it   lateralize it   doctorate it   10
cut it fine   smoke it   some see it   once
in a lifetime   in a blue moon   a Leunig
cartoon   some say it with flowers   with scud
missiles   some soap it   cheat on it
beat their meat on it   read it in Matthew   15
Sartre   Pound   drink it   down down down
bring it back up   some take it off the back of a
truck   fake it   dangle it   nail their hands
for it   some soldier it   spit and polish it
hide it in the back shed   some snails have it   20
some trees have more of it than some snails
and some of us   some smell it in a black rose
a hairy armpit   some feel it in their bones
their Shakespeare   King Kong   Teddy Bear
some think they'll find it   at the end of the   25
ocean   at the top of the stairs   in the attic
in Piccadilly Circus   in East Timor
some do

                                                            1992

Opening Myself

Seven days I sat
after her death
   bewildered by life.
Seven days I listened
   to Hebraic music   5
and questioned
   all my questions.
Moments fell about me,
   a bible's torn white pages.
The week closed around me.   10
   It was a prayer shawl
its fringes on fire.
   Fifteen years later
I come to this work,
   open myself to it   15
to trees and wine,
   to children.

                                                            1992

THOMAS SHAPCOTT   *(b 1935)*

Near the School For Handicapped Children

His hat is rammed on
his shirt jerks at his body
his feet cannot hold in
    the sway   he cannot keep
                still.   5
When I see his face it is freckled
to remind me of nephews
his limbs remind me of how straight
is my own spine and that I take my fingers
for granted.   10
He is waiting for the green light.
        My fingers clench
    I am hurt by my wholeness
    I cannot take my eyes from him
    I fear my daughter may be watching   15
He has been dressed carefully
    I'm here I'm here I'm here
his whole struggle rasps me like a whisper

and when the lights do change
  he skips across the road he   20
    skips he skips he dances and skips
      leaving us all behind like a skimming tamborine
      brittle with music.

                            1975

Those who have seen visions

Those who have seen visions do not smile.
They speak. They take a ripe peach and bite
straight through the furzy skin to the juice. They shit
as the body directs. They have seen visions while
at just such functional tasks. You cannot tell   5
and yet you tell at once. Is it an absence of light
or a presence? It is a burden. Even the night
cannot ease knowledge. There is no escape at all.

On an obscure wall with quick strokes on wet plaster
Piero della Francesca painted Christ   10
lifting his heavy torso, released at last
into vision. The painter was concentrating his cluster
of geometric tokens to clamp like a bite
against the neck of absence. We flinch alright.

                            1983

RANDOLPH STOW   *(b 1935)*

Portrait of Luke

For Catherine Broom-Lynne

The infant Buddha — his hair like dying palms,
his eyes (look) portholes, framing the Timor Sea —
opal-blue, dolphin-carved, tenders his wakeless mind.

Dhows, frigates, lákatois pass and repass unhailed.
In his waters we fly no flags. Strange mariners come   5
dressed in the simple skin of the one sun.

Though the season will change and give place to another year
of customs houses, passports, dues, officials,
for today, for a while, his eyes are open harbours

and the dolphins of his thoughts cannot obscure   10
(look down) the coral bones of all our ancestors.

                                        1962

Ruins of the City of Hay

The wind has scattered my city to the sheep.
Capeweed and lovely lupins choke the street
where the wind wanders in great gaunt chimneys of hay
and straws cry out like keyholes.

Our yellow Petra of the fields: alas!   5
I walk the ruins of forum and capitol,
through quiet squares, by the temples of tranquillity.
Wisps of the metropolis brush my hair.
I become invisible in tears.

This was no ratbags' Eden: these were true haystacks.   10
Golden, but functional, our mansions sprang from dreams
of architects in love (*O my meadow queen!*).
No need for fires to be lit on the yellow hearthstones;
our walls were warmer than flesh, more sure than igloos.
On winter nights we squatted naked as Esquimaux,   15
chanting our sagas of innocent chauvinism.

In the street no vehicle passed. No telephone,
doorbell or till was heard in the canyons of hay.
No stir, no sound, but the sickle and the loom,
and the comments of emus begging by kitchen doors   20
in the moonlike silence of morning.

Though the neighbour states (said Lao Tse) lie in sight of the city
and their cocks wake and their watchdogs warn the inhabitants
the men of the city of hay will never go there
all the days of their lives.   25

But the wind of the world descended on lovely Petra
and the spires of the towers and the statues and belfries fell.
The bones of my brothers broke in the breaking columns.
The bones of my sisters, clasping their broken children,
cracked on the hearthstones, under the rooftrees of hay.   30
I alone mourn in the temples, by broken altars
bowered in black nightshade and mauve salvation-jane.

And the cocks of the neighbour nations scratch in the straw.
And their dogs rejoice in the bones of all my brethren.

                                                        1962

The Utopia of Lord Mayor Howard

*Lord Mayor Howard ... said that the trees on the corner had grown so tall that they
had lost their attraction. Neat rose gardens would be much more attractive.*
                                        The West Australian

His delicate fingers, moving among the roses,
became a symbol. His words, a battle-cry.
'Nothing shall be taller than Lord Mayor Howard
but insurance buildings.'

A fanatical army, wild with Cromwellian zeal,   5
laid waste Kings Park, denuded Darlington.
Guerillas of Pemberton fried alive in their forests,
as mile on mile, that the giant unattractive karri
had once encumbered, fell thrall to triumphant Peace.

And not Peace alone, but also Dame Edith Helen,   10
Comtesse Vandal, and even a brand new strain:
Mrs Lord Mayor Howard.

Only you and I, my subversive and admirable brethren,
did not join in the celebrations. A malicious rumour
that some of us had been seen to spit on roses   15
obliged us to fly the land.

On Kerguelen, New Amsterdam and such friendly islands
pitching our tents, and on each one planting one karri,
under the name of Yggdrasil we worshipped them.
— Tenderly, humbly, as became the last plants on earth   20
that were taller than Lord Mayor Howard.

And although the news of our ruthless persecution
of every breed of rose caused shudders in Guildford,
and although our faith, known as anti-Rosaceanism,
was condemned in the United Nations and *The Times*,   25

the remembrance of our trees so sighs in their sleep
that the immigrants have been more than we can handle.
And in truth, we half expect to see Lord Mayor Howard.

                                                        1962

DAVID MALOUF *(b 1934)*

Difficult Letter

And what should I write to you across
five oceans, who to me were nearer
once than my own breath? If you were set
at distance of mere enmity, I
might with casual phrases, cold polite-   5
ness bridge the gap; but what dark words can
scrawl these oceans now that flow like time
between us? What can I say to you,
my neither enemy nor friend, when
once, between our lips, were printed word-   10
less psalms of praise, when once I signed
my scribbles in the ocean of your blood?

                                                                      1962

Early Discoveries

I find him in the garden. Staked tomato-plants are what
he walks among, the apples of paradise. He is eighty
and stoops, white-haired in baggy serge and braces. His moustache,

once warrior-fierce for quarrels in the small town of Zahle,
where honour divides houses, empties squares, droops and is thin   5
from stroking. He has come too far from his century to care

for more than these, the simplest ones: Webb's Wonders, salad-harmless,
stripped by the birds. He pantomimes a dervish-dance
among them and the birds creak off, his place at evening filled

by a stick that flares and swipes at air, a pin-striped waistcoat stuffed 10
with straw. It cuffs and swivels, I'm scared of it. Such temper-tantrums
are unpredictable; blind buffeting of storms that rattle

venetians, hiss off pavements in the sun. Grandpa is milder,
but when he hefts us high his white hairs prickle and the smell
is foreign. Is it garlic or old age? They are continents   15

I have not happened on, their time will come. Meanwhile he mutters
blessings. I watch him practice his odd rites, hatchet in hand
as he martyrs chickens in the woodblock's dark, an old man struggling

with wings, or shakes a sieve while bright grain showers in a heap
and blown chaff flies and glitters, falling to the other mouths.   20
He comes and goes with daylight. He is the lord of vegetables,

the scourge of birds and nuns, those shoo-black crows his sullen daughters
taunt him with. His black-sheep son feeds rabbits live to greyhounds
in a cage behind choko-vines. The girls too go to the bad

in a foreign land, consorting with Carmelites, on hot nights tossing   25
on their high beds in a riot of lace doilies, painted virgins,
unwed. They dwell in another land. As I do, his eldest

grandson, aged four, where I nose through dusty beanstalks searching
for brothers under nine-week cabbages. He finds me there
and I dig behind his shadow down the rows. This is his garden,   30

a valley in Lebanon; you can smell the cedars on his breath
and the blood of massacres, the crescent flashing from ravines
to slice through half a family. He rolls furred sage between

thumb and stained forefinger, sniffs the snowy hills: bees shifting
gold as they forage sunlight among stones, churchbells wading   35
in through pools of silence. He has never quite migrated,

the weather in his head still upside-down as out of season
snow falls from his eyes on Queensland's green, and January's
midwinter still. These swelling suns are miracles. Tomatoes

in invisible glass-houses sweat in the heat of his attention,   40
like islands Colombus happens on. And me, whom he also finds
squatting, egg-plant tall and puzzled by his dark hands parting

the stems. Where am I? This is Brisbane, our back yard. We let him
garden here behind a lattice wall. This house is ours
and home. He comes like a stranger, warrior-mustachioed,   45

un-English. These days I find him at all turns. One morning early
in Chios, I raise the shutter, and his garden, re-discovered,
shines: cucumbers, spinach, trellised vines. The old man finds me

watching; smiles and nods. Later, fresh on the marble step
in yesterday's newspaper (words of a tongue I cannot read)   50
his offering: two heads of new spring cabbage. I look under

the leaves (an ancient joke), there's nothing there. Just a sprinkling
of black soil on the headlines of another war, shaken
from the roots. That night I eat them, boiled, with oil and vinegar.
                                                                                    1974

MARGARET SCOTT   *(b 1934)*

Grandchild

Early this morning, when workmen were switching on lights
in chilly kitchens, packing their lunch boxes
into their Gladstone bags, starting their utes in the cold
and driving down quiet streets under misty lamps,
my daughter bore a son. Nurses sponged him clean   5
as the glittering shingle of suburbs beside the river
waned to a scattered glimmer of pale cubes.
We met at half-past twelve in a ward crowded
with people busy with parcels and extra chairs.
A bunch of flowers fell on the floor. We passed   10
the baby round. His dark head lay in my hand
like a fruit. He seemed to be dwelling on something
half-remembered, puckering his brow, occasionally
flexing fingers thin and soft as snippets of mauve string.
Far below in the street lunch-time crowds flowed out   15
among the traffic. Girls went arm in arm on high
heels. An ambulance nosed into a ground-floor bay.
A clerk strode in the wind with a streaming tie.
Beyond the office blocks and the estuary, in Santa Fe,
Northampton or the other side of town, a young man   20
may be gripping a girl's hand as they climb upstairs.
She is wearing a cotton dress. Her sandals slip
on metal treads. She laughs, embarrassed, excited
at being desired so urgently in the
minutes before this grandchild's wife is conceived.   25
And his best friend, whose parents quarrel all day
about leaving Greece, is lying perhaps in his cot
on a balcony, watching his fat pink hands and woolly sleeves
swatting at puffs of cloud in the airy blue.
News he may break to our boy in some passage-way   30
in a house we've never seen is breeding now
in the minds of pensive children queuing by Red Cross
trucks, or curled like foetuses deep under warm quilts
as the long ship-wrecking roar of the distant sea
slides to the coming of night and fades away.   35

                                                    1988

Surfers

Far out, down heaving green glass hills
The surfers ride the summer seas.
Their taut brown bodies, arms upraised,
Slide through an Egyptian frieze.

High and dry upon the beach,   5
Pinned to my rug by a glaring sun
I sit among the picnic things,
Alone and fat and forty-one.

And idly through the memory's hand
Stream visions of a Cornish day   10
When effervescent waves and air
Sparkled into glinting play.

The breakers crash, a board flies up.
A boy runs laughing on the land,
Then, turning, wades to ride again.   15
I close the fingers of my hand.

                                                          1988

CHRIS WALLACE-CRABBE   *(b 1934)*

Losses and Recoveries

I

There he goes, went, catch him,
small boy in a beret, nervously smiling, taken
for tourist walks on the wrong end of a leash
in that snow-white stretch of life I can't remember:
half-timbered Munich, strudelplatz Berlin,   5
droppings of history mounded high above me,
over those pigeons the Leica had me feed.
Where's it all gone, that Deutschland culture-fodder
that I soaked up in travel, a willing sponge?

Crusty surfaces in half-tone,   10
brick, stone, snow, inked crosses marking
a bit of myself on this or that hotel
and here's the window where I heard the Rhineland
cobbles re-echo to military geese,
but I can't know whatever I could tell,   15
what strands were plaited by which war, which peace.

II

A drive flashes from the thick meat of my bat,
leaving extra cover for dead. All around us,
touched by a pastoral brush,
midges hover and glint: 20
chiaroscuro daubs the river-gums.
The serene hour brims with oceanic feeling,
drowning these four green ovals deep as dream
in which I move at ease, for Morrison's off-spinners
aren't going to turn an inch this afternoon.   25

Goings and dwindlings: my stupid adolescence,
bone-dry years of hollowness and blank,
thirsting, fills out again with fields and games
till my lifelong model
of happiness or poise becomes   30
a well-timed leg glance taken off my toes.

III *For Bruce Dawe*

Film has no tenses, the latest pundit says,
poems have tenses and nostalgias though
like anything, and when I get to think
of the mid-fifties, flashing through my slides,   35
I see you slope past Chemistry, blue-chinned
in military shirt and a maroon
figured art-silk tie with look-I'm-right
Ciardi's *Inferno* splitting away to cantos
and well-thumbed pages in your jacket pocket,   40
verse on your tongue of mice in evening dress.

In memory's yellow eye it's always summer,
nobody ever worked, the grass grew thick,
coffee cups, unlike women, had no bottoms
and there you grin, old-fashioned Carlton shepherd   45
dry-wittedly enjoying
the Arcadian lull between Joey Cassidy stories.

IV

Looms up the liner's rivetty white side,
streamers droop overhead,
our good friends go. There are many folk we love   50
this way and that, struggling to find a balance
where the high side fills with a charge of shadows
and wharfside waters lap quietly below.
Dulled along splintery boards we walk away.

Melbourne holds us: hands, lips, bodies, all   55
that we are it feeds — and feeds upon;
many would go, but drag the city with them
world-wide, wherever they push and flee.
Here, look now, all this is ourselves and
up over the dull blue skyline dangles   60
a bright eastering T-jet the colour of hope.

1971

---

39 Ciardi's *Inferno*   John Ciardi's translation of Dante
47 Joey Cassidy stories   short fiction by Bruce Dawe

There

At the bottom of consciousness there is a clear lake
The waters of which throb ever so lightly
(Like the bodies of lovers after their spasm ends)
Throwing dimpled distortion across the rocky bed,
Greenish round rocks, the size of a grapefruit, say,   5
And through these cold waters fish are swimming
Seeming quite continuous with their medium
As sexual love flows directly through God.
Here water moves the slubbing barabble of language,
Gust and pith, cacophony, glossolalia,   10
Gift of the gab and purple rhetoric,
Moaning in rut, scream, snicker, and the rip
That is sheer pain.
                  Yes, these are of language
But not yet *it*. They are the pool,   15
Its diamonds and yabbies, ripple and scale,
Insatiable glittering ...
         I'm afraid I don't know what paths
Lead up from the pool to where I think and talk;
By what stony track with landslip and synapse   20
Distracted everywhere, choked with scrubby thorns
We got to where we are. Conscious.
                  Aren't we?
Oh hell, we seem to think we understand:
When I ask at the ticket-box they sell me a ticket   25
But I do not know what the recently dead will ask us
When they walk through the scrub again like sunbeams.

                                             1985

Genius Loci

When I can't sleep and prove
a pain in the neck to myself
I will sneak downstairs, dress up warmly
and squeeze into whelming darkness
or piccaninny daylight, where   5
I may just glimpse at a corner
one of the Jika Jika slipping away
lapped in a possumskin rug.

I will hurry like steam to the corner,
ever so much wanting to say,   10
'Hey, wait. I have so much that I ...'
But there will only be
broad street, creamy houses, dew
and a silence of black shrubs.

Maybe if I got up   15
a little more smartly next time,
got out on the road quick,
I could sneak up closer
on that dark tribesman in his furry cloak
and ask him ...   20
                    oh, something really deep:

something off the planet.

                                                                   1985

JENNIFER STRAUSS   *(b 1933)*

Loving Parents

Sometimes, night-waking, they made love
As if two strangers frantic to be known,
As if unfeaturing darkness stripped away
Affectionate disguises, long-term habits
Which daylight coupling decently assumed,   5
And laid the fierce nerves of loving bare.

Such times, they moved about their morning chores
Abstracted, in a sensual shadowed glow
Where suckling babies might bask mindlessly
But awkward older children, growing wise,   10
Looked askance, and bruised their egos' fists
Against that dark complicity which gave them being.

                                                                   1975

Life 201: Essay after the Seminar

I'm trying to appreciate
My Life as Structure,
Seeing an earlier topic
(Life as Story)
Dead-ended by naivety   5
Of interest in the teller:
Fearing to fall among intentionalists
Nipped speculation as to what he meant,
Then came this notion of the absolutely
Not-to-be-trusted narrator.   10

Trust me, my first love said,
We can get nowhere without trust.
How right he was. Untrusted —
Provident, malicious, or inane —
My fool/god is dead.   15

Trust then the tale? Frankly,
I'd like mine taller; as I read it now,
Love's a potent source of irony,
And death the structure's donnée.

1981

Wife to Horatio

You didn't know Horatio had a wife?
Of course he did. To marry is the fate
Of ordinary men. And his wife says:
'No interviews! They are forbidden.
My husband is a private citizen,   5
And ill. You think I'd let vultures like you
Rip open that old wound? Why would you want
To dig up all that buried agony?
Hamlet's skull whitens like Yorick's now
And on those walls where once the dead king stalked   10
The sturdy sons of Fortinbras play ball.
His rule is well enough. Was it surprising
That he grew restive hearing Hamlet praised
Perpetually? Not that I'd criticize
My husband's friend; I'm told that friendship's noble,   15
Ophelia was my friend — we laughed a lot.
I know that Hamlet had great difficulties,
And when the great have problems, we all know,
It is the ordinary lives that pay.
Ophelia was my friend — but she was dead,   20
And the live child in my belly jumped
When the king frowned. I found that I had wits
(My family too was not uninfluential):
We sought permission to withdraw from court.
It came readily, and as a bonus   25
Horatio was appointed (a neat move)
To write the official life of the late Prince —
Oh yes, the work's in progress. There came too
The settlement of this estate. The king
Is not ungenerous. He sent birth gifts,   30
The boy a handsome set of fencing foils,
My daughter pearls. Yes, that's Ophelia
Playing by the river. Aren't we afraid?
Not more than ordinary parents are.
Horatio, it's true, was rather anxious,   35
And no, we didn't talk it out. Come, come,
You've lived in Denmark, surely you must know
What miseries breed from talk. We needed
Action. There'll be no drowning here.
I've seen to it that she knows how to swim.'   40

1988

FAY ZWICKY *(b 1933)*

Summer Pogrom

Spade-bearded Grandfather, squat Lenin
In the snows of Donna Buang.
Your bicycle a wiry crutch, nomadic homburg
Alien, black, correct. Beneath, the curt defiant
Filamented eye. Does it count the dead   5
Between the Cossack horses' legs in Kovno?

Those dead who sleep in me, me dry
In a garden veiled with myrtle and oleander,
Desert snows that powder memory's track
Scoured by burning winds from eastern rocks,   10
Flushing the lobes of mind,
Fat white dormant flowrets.

Aggressive under dappled shade, girl in a glove;
Collins street in autumn,
Mirage of clattering crowds: Why don't you speak English?   15
I don't understand, *I don't understand!*
Sei nicht so ein Dummerchen, nobody cares.
Not for you the upreared hooves of Nikolai,
Eat your icecream, Kleine, *may his soul rot,*
These are good days.   20

Flared candles; the gift of children; love,
Need fulfilled, a name it has to have — how else to feel?
A radiance in the garden, the Electrolux man chats,
Cosy spectre of the afternoon's decay.
My eye his eye, the snows of Kovno cover us.   25
Is that my son bloodied against Isaac the Baker's door?

The tepid river's edge, reeds creak, rats' nests fold and quiver;
My feet sink in sand: the children splash and call, sleek
Little satyrs diamond-eyed reined to summer's roundabout,
Hiding from me. Must I excavate you,   30
Agents of my death? Hushed snows are deep, the
Dead lie deep in me.

                                                                                    1975

Tiananmen Square June 4, 1989

Karl Marx, take your time,
looming over Highgate on your plinth.
Snow's falling on your beard,
exiled, huge, hairy, genderless.

---

2 **Highgate** Highgate cemetery in London has Marx's grave and monument.

Terminally angry, piss-poor,   5
stuffed on utopias and cold,
cold as iron.

I'm thinking of your loving wife,
your desperate children and your grandchild
dead behind the barred enclosure of your brain.   10
Men's ideas the product, not the cause
of history, you said?

The snow has killed the lilacs.
Whose idea?
The air is frozen with theory.   15

What can the man be doing all day
in that cold place?
What can he be writing?
What can he be reading?
What big eyes you have, mama!   20
Next year, child, we will eat.

I'm thinking of my middle-class German grandmother
soft as a pigeon, who wept
when Chamberlain declared a war.
Why are you crying, grandma?   25
It's only the big bad wolf, my dear.
It's only a story.

There's no end to it.
The wolves have come again.
What shall I tell my grandchildren?   30

No end to the requiems, the burning trains,
the guns, the shouting in the streets,
the outraged stars, the anguished face
of terror under ragged headbands
soaked in death's calligraphy.   35

Don't turn your back, I'll say.
Look hard.
Move into that frozen swarming screen.
How far can you run with a bullet in your brain?

And forgive, if you can, the safety of a poem   40
sharpened on a grieving night.

A story has to start somewhere.

                                                                    1990

Letting Go

Tell the truth of experience
they say they also
say you must let
go learn to let go
let your children   5
go

and they go
and you stay
letting them go
because you are obedient and   10
respect everyone's freedom
to go and you stay

and you want to tell the truth
because you are yours truly
its obedient servant   15
but you can't because
you're feeling what you're not
supposed to feel you have
let them go and go and

you can't say what you feel   20
because they might read
this poem and feel guilty
and some post-modern hack
will back them up
and make you feel guilty   25
and stop feeling which is
post-modern and what
you're meant to feel

so you don't write a poem
you line up words in prose   30
inside a journal trapped
like a scorpion in a locked
drawer to be opened by
your children let go
after lived life and all the time   35
a great wave bursting
howls and rears and

you have to let go
or you're gone you're
gone gasping you   40
let go
till the next wave
towers crumbles
shreds you to lace —

When you wake   45
your spine is twisted
like a sea-bird
inspecting the sky,
stripped by lightning.

                                                       1992

KEVIN GILBERT   *(1933–93)*

'Consultation'

Me, mate?
You'll get no views from me!
Where did I ever go?
Who did I ever meet?
What did I ever see?   5
Nothin' just the old river, the gumtree
The mission. Me seven kids, four grandkids
Blacks gamblin' drunk, fightin', laughin', cryin'
Mostly gamblin'. Playin' 'pups' wild deuces game
Doin' it, risking their twenty cents to try to win thirty   10
Price of bread, you know. You know, life ain't too bad here
No runnin' water, no fireplaces, huh, no houses even
Jus' the kerosene tin and hessian bag humpies.
They say there's 'welfare' for Blacks these days
But the mission looks the same to me. Seven I got   15
An' another one in the barrel — put there by the 'manager'
'Cause his wife cut him short or somethin'
Nothin' changes. I don't ever see nothin' much
An' no-one asked me my view before.

                                                       1978

The Soldier's Reward

I'm Gerry Ivan James Chickenmar Grantling
I'm five foot four or is it three?
Joined the forces as a Private
Weren't no blue-arsed flies on me!
Worked as stockman on a station   5
Always earnt me meat 'n bread
I'm as good as any whiteman
Yet I'm here stone cold and dead
In the stinkin' cell at Condo
I was drunk and I was brash   10
Bought meself some plonk an' devon
Staggered up the street . . . then crash!

Local sergeant and constable
Read the riot act out loud
Law said Abos can't have liquor   15
I was doin' what's not allowed.
They forget that I'm a Private
Fought for freedom — two great wars
They threw me on the cold stone cell floor
Broke me neck — the rotten whores!   20

                                          1978

Jim B.

Sure, they all come here to listen
And tape with a cassette
I'm the one who knows the 'language'
I'm the last one you can bet
Speak eight languages — all tribal   5
And they listen to me, mate
Anthropologists, students, teachers
None ever see the hate
Pearls to Gideon swine I cast them
Pearls — beneath the feet of pigs   10
For their avaricious seeking
I just couldn't give two figs
But our words are all that's left now son
Man's memory soon grows dim
The whiteman's sons may become *men* some day —   15
And we'll leave those pearls for him!!

                                          1978

PHILIP MARTIN   *(b 1931)*

A Sacred Way

The God his father preached was a harsh God.
Then as he grew to manhood he must face
Desire as horror: the female legs gaped wide,
The whirlpool sucked him to its hell-black centre.
But there was no escape from womankind,   5
And past the middle of life the dark wood thinned,
Sunlight among the limbs, and overhead
Leaves swaying in wind the hair of dancers.
He found the woman in himself, and found
In every woman he embraced the earth: 10
It was from her he came and he would soon
Re-enter her. His father's God was dead
Long since. It was a goddess whom he served.
She spread dark honey on his lips. They sang.

                                          1982

Nursing Home

Incontinence, and the mind going. Where?
The place is all it should be. Not enough.
She's had such spirit. *No more advice, thank you!*
And she'd slam down the receiver. Hated drudging:
The house is crawling away with dirt, but I'm   5
Going out to garden. Thwarted, self-thwarted:
Gave up the piano when her marriage failed,
Should have had a career. Instead she moved:
Twenty houses in forty years. And always
Well, dear son, at last we've found the right one.   10
Never. And now, this one room, to be shared
With a woman still as a stonefish.

                              Sunday morning:
Outside, the trees wrestle with spring wind.
She sits here in her chair beating her tray: 15
Sister sister sister sister sister!
Clenches her lips, hums against them. And again
Sister sister sister sister sister!
High, scratched voice: *Behind me behind me behind me!*
What is, Mother? A pause. *I don't know.*   20
And again the drumming: *Sister sister sister!*

              *   *   *

The mind going, and coming back, and going.
Each ebb, a little further. She says one evening
A bit flat today. Long pause, and then
I don't like this place. (What is *this place?*)   25
And slowly: *All that way along that wall!*
Too far to go.

                  I stand smoothing her forehead,
Her child's become her parent, saying with her
The night prayers. She's growing peaceful now.   30
I'm drawn to the edge of a mystery. The mind
I cannot know, what does it know? She seems
Listening. As a remote landscape listens
To its river in a circle of hills. As a boat
Far out may heed the current beneath,   35
Bearing it further. What sounds? To us, silence.

                                     1982

A Certain Love

There's no gainsaying this:
We're blessed. We know it.
And if God came to me today and said
'You must give her up', I'd answer
'Ridiculous. Why contradict yourself?'   5

                                     ·   1988

EVAN JONES   *(b 1931)*

Generations

I go to see my parents,
we chew the rag a bit;
I turn the telly on
and sit and look at it.

Not much gets said: 5
there doesn't seem much point.
But still they like to have
me hanging round the joint.

I go to see my son,
I'm like a Santa Claus: 10
he couldn't like me more;
mad about him, of course.

Still years before he learns
to judge, condemn, dismiss.
I stand against the light   15
and bleed for both of us.

                                                            1967

Eurydice Remembered

The shadows of your cheek
deepened and were defined
under your cloud of hair:
I called you into being out of air
because you filled my mind;   5
I almost made you speak.

I sang, and there you stood;
I stopped, and you were still:
in that echoing cave
I played and sang with all the craft I have   10
to bring you to my will,
to wake your frozen blood.

We trod a winding path,
my music led your feet.
And then I failed: I turned   15
to speak, not sing: and all at once you burned
to air. Now I must meet
all women in their wrath.

                                                            1967

Him

Why does he never sleep, when sleep is healing?
All night while I lie still, not feeling feeling,
He walks the networks of my little city,
Swinging his lantern, crying out the time.

Later and later. When I swing awake   5
I try to trace his movements, but he goes
Always by back ways and the hidden places,
Fugitive, cautious, undiscernible.

Persistently I strive to meet him, whether,
When he at last obtrudes on my short sight,   10
He prove dog-faced or radiant, standing in
Insanity, or on the shores of light.

                                                                  1967

BRUCE DAWE   *(b 1930)*

Drifters

One day soon he'll tell her it's time to start packing.
and the kids will yell 'Truly?' and act wildly excited for no reason,
and the brown kelpie pup will start dashing about, tripping
                                        everyone up,
and she'll go out to the vegetable-patch and pick all the green   5
                                        tomatoes from the vines,
and notice how the oldest girl is close to tears because she was
                                        happy here,
and how the youngest girl is beaming because she wasn't.
And the first thing she'll put on the trailer will be the bottling-set   10
                        she never unpacked from Grovedale,
and when the loaded ute bumps down the drive past the blackberry-
                        canes with their last shrivelled fruit,
she won't even ask why they're leaving this time, or where
                                        they're heading for   15
— she'll only remember how, when they came here,
she held out her hands bright with berries,
the first of the season, and said:
'Make a wish, Tom, make a wish.'

                                                                  1968

The Raped Girl's Father

The buzz-saw whine of righteous anger rose
murderously in his throat throughout the night,
long after she had watched her mother close
the door to, and the honeyed wedge of light
was eaten by the dark, his voice whirred on,   5
and in that darker dark in which she lay

she felt his jaws rasp on the naked bone
of time and place and what she'd need to say
and how, if he were judge, by Christ, he'd cut …
She knew that glare of blindness that came down   10
upon him like a weather-wall and shut
him off from pity — hunched inside her gown
she shrank from what the morning held, the fresh assault
of reason that his manic shame would make,
the steady rape wished on her for her fault   15
in being the unlucky one to take
the fancy of another man who'd said:
'OK, this one will do …' and swung the wheel.
Somebody sobbed. Grief mimed out in her head
the ritual she did not dare to feel.   20
Bones, she was dice-bones, shaken, rolled on black,
wishing her frenzied suitors might re-pass,
and at this stage be merciful, take her back,
and leave her, shuddering, blank-faced, on the grass.

                                                      1969

Homecoming

All day, day after day, they're bringing them home,
they're picking them up, those they can find, and bringing them home.
they're bringing them in, piled on the hulls of Grants, in trucks, in convoys.
they're zipping them up in green plastic bags,
they're tagging them now in Saigon, in the mortuary coolness   5
they're giving them names, they're rolling them out of
the deep-freeze lockers — on the tarmac at Tan Son Nhut
the noble jets are whining like hounds,
they are bringing them home
— curly-heads, kinky-hairs, crew-cuts, balding non-coms   10
— they're high, now, high and higher, over the land, the steaming *chow
      mein*
their shadows are tracing the blue curve of the Pacific
with sorrowful quick fingers, heading south, heading east,
home, home, home — and the coasts swing upward, the old ridiculous
      curvatures
of earth, the knuckled hills, the mangrove-swamps, the desert emptiness …   15
in their sterile housing they tilt towards these like skiers
— taxiing in, on the long runways, the howl of their homecoming rises
surrounding them like their last moments (the mash, the splendour)
then fading at length as they move
on to small towns where dogs in the frozen sunset   20
raise muzzles in mute salute,
and on to cities in whose wide web of suburbs
telegrams tremble like leaves from a wintering tree
and the spider grief swings in his bitter geometry
— they're bringing them home, now, too late, too early.   25

                                                      1969

Morning Becomes Electric

Another day
roars up at you out of the east
in an expressway of birds gargling their first
antiseptic song, where clouds are
bumper-to-bumper all the way back to the horizon.   5

Once seen, you know
something formidable, news-worthy,
is about to happen, a gull hovers
like a traffic-report helicopter over the bank-up,
one-armed strangers wave cigarette hellos from their cars,   10
an anxious sedan's bellow floats above the herd
— the odour of stalled vehicles
wickedly pleasant like an old burned friend,
still whispering to you from the incinerator.

Broad day is again   15
over you with its hooves and re-treads,
its armies, its smoke, its door-to-door salesmen,
irrational, obsessed, opening sample cases in the kitchen,
giving you an argument of sorts
before you have even assembled your priorities,   20
properly unrolled your magic toast
or stepped into the wide eyes of your egg.

                                                                   1974

Going

for my mother-in-law, Gladys

Mum, you would have loved the way you went!
One moment, at a barbecue in the garden
— the next, falling out of your chair,
hamburger in one hand,
and a grandson yelling.   5

Zipp! The heart's roller blind
rattling up, and you, in an old dress,
quite still, flown already from your dearly-loved
Lyndon, leaving only a bruise like a blue kiss
on the side of your face, the seed-beds incredibly tidy,   10
grass daunted by drought.

You'd have loved it, Mum, you big spender! The relatives,
eyes narrowed with grief, swelling the rooms
with their clumsiness, the reverberations of tears, the endless
cuppas and groups revolving blinded as moths.   15

The joy of your going! The laughing reminiscences
snagged on the pruned roses
in the bright blowing day!

                                                                   1974

Doctor to Patient

Please sit down. I'm afraid I have some
rather bad news for you: you are now seventeen
and you have contracted an occupational disease called
unemployment. Like others similarly afflicted
you will experience feelings of   5
shock, disbelief, injustice, guilt, apathy, and aggression
(although not necessarily in that order)
and you'll no doubt be urged to try the various
recommended anodynes: editorials in newspapers,
voluntary unpaid work for local charities, booze,   10
other compulsive mind-destroyers, prayer, comforting
talks with increasingly less-interested friends.
It is small comfort to know that the disease
is universal and can accommodate
the middle-aged and thirtyish and strikes down   15
those in camps in Kompong Sam and Warsaw.
However you will discover, as time passes,
that your presence in itself will make others
obviously uncomfortable. Try not to let
your shadow, at this stage,   20
fall across your neighbour's plate; eat
with the right hand only; do not touch
others in public (this can be easily
misconstrued); keep always
down-wind, if possible. Please remember   25
you have now become our common vulnerability
personified. Oh yes, and, by the way,
you will be relieved to know the disease
is only in a minority of cases terminal.

Most, that is, survive. Next, please.   30

                                                                    1986

BRUCE BEAVER   *(b 1929)*

From Lauds and Plaints

III

To the memory of him who wrote the word ETERNITY
so carefully on Sydney's pavements.

eternity on street corners
   so obviously belonging in such
   a setting

in a clerk's copperplated script
   with surveyor's yellow crayon   the one   5
   big word

nobody ever saw you at it
   until near the end you were lumbered and warned
   indulgently

to keep out of the way of young cops   10
   who may not understand why an
   elderly gent

in a grey dust coat would practise calligraphy
   at just such a time in this suspicious
   manner   15

none of our business whether you were that
   paradox in a higher tax bracket
   a single man

or if you had a home in some concrete
   and grass suburb away from the black-board   20
   bitumen

that took your message to heart   that vanished
   with the tread of vanishing feet beneath
   the juggernaut

time   thirty years ago   25
   when too many young men and women
   too soon

were finding out about your word
   I first saw it on corner after
   corner   30

of the grey by day blacked-out city
   when I pushed a messenger's trolley
   or lugged

an overload of parcels from warehouse
   to shop   fourteen years old   finished   35
   with schooling

in words   what has become known as
   a drop-out   but a poet already
   in intent

a home-made magician's kit of other men's   40
   spells sizzling and bubbling in
   my serpentine

mind   my tongue dumb for three more
   years until two place-names fierily
   atomised   45

in far-off Nippon fructified
   my early loving/hating liaison
   with words

yellow days of years   the one
   real word in an unreal world   50
   eternity

I knew it was here already surrounding
   us   adding to subtracting from
   our moments

crossing and dotting our *Is* and lives   55
   with its big beautiful script looping
   volute

that was before I learned of the commonest
   agony of all   time's rape of
   the timeless   60

as I watched the generations of dogs
   excreting religiously over it
   the myriad

leather soles taking a little of it
   with them into homes shops   65
   offices

and the closest thing to sanctuaries
   of grass stone leaf sand
   wave-lapped

rock   out of the streets and into   70
   their lives blindly underfoot
   always

say that you had retired from packing-bench
   shop-counter   something modest
   enough   75

inflating skimped dreams with such
   grandeur of forever   so conscious
   a glimpse

of that *other* we hover about as a gnat-
   cloud of scintillant lives in a shaft   80
   of sun

if you meant an inkling of hell that's not
   your fault   familiarity
   breeds fear

as often as contempt   pain's ever-   85
   present to help us stay awake
   the big sleep

of the partly living isn't quite death
   for wherever life is is
   forgetfulness   90

and memory   remember yourselves
  you said over and over for over
  thirty

livelong years   not long in eternity
  yet what statistics of shoe-leather   95
  knee-bending

miles of yellow crayon stretching
  from Sydney to Parramatta to
  eternity

towards the close of your circuit you came   100
  into the salty streets of Manly
  the lettering

fainter   less forceful   a little shaky
  but still as clear as ever the word
  forever   105

did you pay the ferry man with those four
  syllables and did he splash
  the while

impatiently with an oar   a dream
  on a boat trip back to the darker side   110
  of the harbour

on this much lauded isthmus between
  the tides that rose and lapsed before
  your word

was ever enunciated the seasons   115
  stir and flex   go rigid or lurch
  swashbuckling

through the perennial montage   now
  is forever three years after you
  wrote finis   120

to infinity   but there's always a message
  in all our frenetic or soporific
  actions

even in this my noising of
  these all-too-soluble somethings of utterance   125
  into

the silence you now inhabit   just
  to say haltingly somehow or other
  the message

inescapably got there   got over   130
  to a number for what it was pricelessly worth
  your chapter

of obsessional effort   our paragraphs of
   approaching and passing   the one real word
   remaining   135
                                                    1974

Machine

The bicycle on the balcony,
resplendently blue in the wan weather,
reclines in the cornice, the handlebars
horning over a thirty foot drop,
perched on by unbelievably gaudy   5
lorikeets whose slate pencil scratching
shrieks undo their beauty. The balcony
suffers the bicycle like a metal haemorrhoid
despite its angular attractiveness, its wiry
wheeled being of speed and jaunty games.   10
It does not beg to be straddled, to have
somebody bunching or cupping its bony
seat, it is in the best tradition of bachelor-
or spinster-dom. It stays alone and likes it.
So far this morning it has suffered the edges   15
of a storm and does not look wet or seem
ready to fantasise about rusting. Soon enough
someone will come and commandeer
its unforlorn integrity; will bounce and push it
down the felted concrete stairs and back into   20
the tacky tarsealed street of holes and bumps
where it will override indignity
and be itself admirably, elegantly.
                                                    1988

PETER PORTER   *(b 1929)*

Print Out: Apocalypse

When the army of ecologists
has scraped the last shellfish
from the lagoon,

When all the cars on
the urban overpasses are towed   5
to adventure playgrounds,

When the phrase 'fossil fuel'
is considered too holy to be used
in crossword puzzles,

When 'Thirties hats and hairdos   10
have come back into fashion
for the tenth time,

When archivists have stored
reserve prints of every manifestation
of popular culture,   15

When software and hardware
have swapped places in our
advanced computers,

When these words are fed in
for me to consider, I will come again,   20
says the Lord ...

                                                        1975

An Exequy

In wet May, in the months of change,
In a country you wouldn't visit, strange
Dreams pursue me in my sleep,
Black creatures of the upper deep —
Though you are five months dead, I see   5
You in guilt's iconography,
Dear Wife, lost beast, beleaguered child,
The stranded monster with the mild
Appearance, whom small waves tease,
(Andromeda upon her knees   10
In orthodox deliverance)
And you alone of pure substance,
The unformed form of life, the earth
Which Piero's brushes brought to birth
For all to greet as myth, a thing   15
Out of the box of imagining.

This introduction serves to sing
Your mortal death as Bishop King
Once hymned in tetrametric rhyme
His young wife, lost before her time;   20
Though he lived on for many years
His poem each day fed new tears
To that unreaching spot, her grave,
His lines a baroque architrave
The Sunday poor with bottled flowers   25
Would by-pass in their mourning hours,
Esteeming ragged natural life
('Most dearly loved, most gentle wife'),
Yet, looking back when at the gate
And seeing grief in formal state   30

17–20 Porter's poem is close in form and subject to 'The Exequy' by Henry King (1657).

Upon a sculpted angel group,
Were glad that men of god could stoop
To give the dead a public stance
And freeze them in their mortal dance.

The words and faces proper to   35
My misery are private — you
Would never share your heart with those
Whose only talent's to suppose,
Nor from your final childish bed
Raise a remote confessing head —   40
The channels of our lives are blocked,
The hand is stopped upon the clock,
No one can say why hearts will break
And marriages are all opaque:
A map of loss, some posted cards,   45
The living house reduced to shards,
The abstract hell of memory,
The pointlessness of poetry —
These are the instances which tell
Of something which I know full well,   50
I owe a death to you — one day
The time will come for me to pay
When your slim shape from photographs
Stands at my door and gently asks
If I have any work to do   55
Or will I come to bed with you.
O scala enigmatica,
I'll climb up to that attic where
The curtain of your life was drawn
Some time between despair and dawn —   60
I'll never know with what halt steps
You mounted to this plain eclipse
But each stair now will station me
A black responsibility
And point me to that shut-down room,   65
'This be your due appointed tomb.'

I think of us in Italy:
Gin-and-chianti-fuelled, we
Move in a trance through Paradise
Feeding at last our starving eyes,   70
Two people of the English blindness
Doing each masterpiece the kindness
Of discovering it — from Baldovinetti
To Venice's most obscure jetty.
A true unfortunate traveller, I   75
Depend upon your nurse's eye
To pick the altars where no Grinner
Puts us off our tourists' dinner

And in hotels to bandy words
With Genevan girls and talking birds,   80
To wear your feet out following me
To night's end and true amity,
And call my rational fear of flying
A paradigm of Holy Dying —
And, oh my love, I wish you were   85
Once more with me, at night somewhere
In narrow streets applauding wines,
The moon above the Apennines
As large as logic and the stars,
Most middle-aged of avatars,   90
As bright as when they shone for truth
Upon untried and avid youth.

The rooms and days we wandered through
Shrink in my mind to one — there you
Lie quite absorbed by peace — the calm   95
Which life could not provide is balm
In death. Unseen by me, you look
Past bed and stairs and half-read book
Eternally upon your home,
The end of pain, the left alone.   100
I have no friend, or intercessor,
No psychopomp or true confessor
But only you who know my heart
In every cramped and devious part —
Then take my hand and lead me out,   105
The sky is overcast by doubt,
The time has come, I listen for
Your words of comfort at the door,
O guide me through the shoals of fear —
'Fürchte dich nicht, ich bin bei dir.'   110

                                                                    1978

Non Piangere, Liù

A card comes to tell you
you should report
to have your eyes tested.

But your eyes melted in the fire
and the only tears, which soon dried,   5
fell in the chapel.

---

110 'Fear not, I am with you': from J. S. Bach, Motet No. 4
Non Piangere, Liù   'Don't cry, Liù': from Puccini, *Turandot*

Other things still come —
invoices, subscription renewals,
shiny plastic cards promising credit —
not much for a life spent   10
in the service of reality.

You need answer none of them.
Nor my asking you for one drop
of succour in my own hell.

Do not cry, I tell myself,   15
the whole thing is a comedy
and comedies end happily.

The fire will come out of the sun
and I shall look in the heart of it.

                                                      1978

How Important is Sex?

Not very. Even if it plays a not
Inconsiderable part in misery,
You can be unhappy without reference
To its intervention or its absence.

Our researchers have discovered even   5
Species whose reproductive processes
Are quite unsexual — and usually these
Are the more efficient and uncomplicated.

But, says the man waiting for a letter
And trying to read an article in a liberated   10
Magazine, I haven't been able to keep
My mind off sex since I was seven.

Others' minds go further back. Perhaps
Our evolution took the one track
(As the mind has it) into love and found   15
That those innovatory machines

The genitals, once in place, wouldn't
Be denied their significance. The sight
Of mummy's hair puts us on the spot,
A cave more mysterious than the mouth.   20

Now flow from it plays and operas
And the horrible spoutings of rancid
Kitchens: a world of novels awaits
The boy taught things by his jokey schoolmates.

But you are talking about love, you'll say.   25
Yes, and I know the difference,
Taking down a wank magazine,
Then a note more fingered than any photo.

Nevertheless, I am a respecter
Of power, having seen a skinny girl   30
Screaming in the playground, oblivious
Of boys, wake to her hormonal clock

As Juliana or as Mélisande —
Even the great gods and captains
Might relax with a plaything   35
As bold and changeable as this.

                                                       1981

At Schubert's Grave

They took their calipers and measured
        Dead Schubert's skull,
So Science was by Music pleasured,
        The void made null.

What could that space of fleshly tatters   5
        Say of its time,
Of keyboard lords and kindred matters
        Of the sublime?

The integers took up the story
        In fields of snow   10
And dreams through every category
        Were leased to go.

His was the head which notes had chosen
        To move within —
What gods and scientists had frozen   15
        Melted in him.

                                                       1992

JILL HELLYER   *(b 1925)*

Living With Aunts

1

Passed to two maiden aunts, the quiet child
absorbed the trinity of their beliefs;
only in adolescence she learned to cry
and later, much later, to analyse her griefs.

Her thoughts were tracts they never visited: 5
the child became myself, always unknown
but present, obedient, silent. I watched them eat
slowly, talk slowly, and the seeds were sown

of the divinity of the *Sydney Morning Herald*,
the British Empire, and the ABC: 10
I was always told how fortunate I was
as though my needs were met by literacy.

My aunt once saw reviewed in her Saturday *Herald*
The Rise and Fall of the British Empire. She
read it to us in helpless disbelief.   15
(It wasn't mentioned on the ABC)

2

I'd always thought Soames Forsyte was a cousin,
I'd heard so much about him. One aunt read
all of the Saga, the other had poor eyesight
so she and I both painstakingly were fed   20

news of the Forsytes slowly at the table.
I knew Soames better than I knew my father
whose death I learned about in secret from
a *Herald* clipping. I was the child left over.

3

I was always a bother to them, and they'd say   25
You're not a proper Hellyer, not with brown eyes
(as though it were a crime). I was the wrong
dreamer of wrong dreams, was the wrong size,

never came first in the class for them nor brandished
my energy for causes they considered noble.   30
But the British Empire after all had fallen
too while they ate so slowly at the table.

                                                          1981

Englynion for Two Friends, and another

1

Urgent for sharp stars, believing one kiss
        could be storm and haven
        for the flinting of verses,
        that night she found it proven.

2

Still your eyes, deep and mutable,   5
        subtly calm and knowing,
        steady the tides that lash my shores
        in their ebb and flowing.

---

17 **Soames Forsyte**   a principal character in *The Forsyte Saga* (1906–21), a series of novels by John
Galsworthy set in late Victorian England

3

It is customary to smile at neighbours
    and postmen, but to weave   10
    disquieter threads in the fabric
    of the grave gaze of love.

                                                        1981

VINCENT BUCKLEY   *(1925–88)*

From Stroke

V

Indoors and out, weather and winds keep up
Time's passion: paddocks white for burning.
As usual, by his bed, I spend my time
Not in talk, but restless noticing:
If pain dulls, grief coarsens.   5
Each night we come and, voyeurs of decay,
Stare for minutes over the bed's foot,
Imagining, if we think at all,
The body fuming ash, the near insane
Knowledge when, in the small hours,   10
Alone under the cold ceiling, above
The floor where the heating system keeps its pulse,
He grows accustomed to his own sweat
And sweats with helplessness, remembering
How, every day, at eight o'clock   15
The Polish nurse kisses him goodnight.
His arms are bent like twigs; his eyes
Are blown to the door after her; his tears
Are squeezed out not even for himself.
Where is the green that swells against the blade   20
Or sways in sap to the high boughs? To the root
He is dry wood, and in his sideways
Falling brings down lights. Our breath
Mingles,
Stirs the green air of the laurel tree.   25

VI

The roofs are lit with rain.
Winter. In that dark glow,
Now, as three months ago,
I pray that he'll die sane.

On tiles or concrete path   5
The old wheeling the old,
For whom, in this last world,
Hope is an aftermath,

And the damp trees extend
Branch and thorn. We live   10
As much as we believe.
All things covet an end.

Once, on the Kerrie road,
I drove with him through fire.
Now, in the burnt cold year,   15
He drains off piss and blood,

His wounded face tube-fed,
His arm strapped to a bed.

VII

At the merest handshake I feel his blood
Move with the ebb-tide chill. Who can revive
A body settled in its final mood?
To whom, on what tide, can we move, and live?

Later I wheel him out to see the trees:
Willows and oaks, the small plants he mistakes   6
For rose bushes; and there
In the front, looming, light green, cypresses.
His pulse no stronger than the pulse of air.

Dying, he grows more tender, learns to teach
Himself the mysteries I am left to trace.   11
As I bend to say 'Till next time', I search
For signs of resurrection in his face.

                                                       1966

Small Brown Poem for Grania Buckley

Paleface, small fume of fire,
flame that burns nobody,
each time you come into the room
you compose a new colour.

You have mastered the trick   5
of hovering in doorways
with the fury of the eavesdropper,
peacemaker, magpie at nesting,

Your cardigan worn like an argument,
your runner's legs in straight trousers,   10
as you stand there, being praised,
as if your whole figure had just been brushed.

Even in the rashness of the close
night, you ask questions about space,
as we watch the black spread like lava   15
and the stars keep their grip on it
in the pale, pale cold of Kildare.

                                                       1991

The Too-Lateness

for George Russell

What I hate most
is the too-lateness: when you come
to touch or accept even the smallest
good your life relishes,
you find it slipped   5
out of its proper time
into some other pace of being,
lost, gone; and you are left dreading
each familiar season, caught
in the mind's alternative society.   10

And the best, the best, you can
have then, is that freedom
which comes closest, most dear,
when all the best are dead
or dying, or love grown so late   15
it fastens to you, like a cry
heard decades after,
drilling the sleepless ear,
a child's wail lasting for ever.

Mute freedom of the hospital   20
or of the sidelines,
the unused time, vacuous with omens
mistaken for sanctity.

Heaven (the name so lovely,
the idea so distant)   25
lies about us, yes,
but where? From the first light
into which the town
clicks open, and the tussocks
purple like wildflowers, to the last   30
red tincture in the sunsetting wave,
it moves steady as a clock's
alarming throb, keeping
around us like our own heartbeat;
night jasmine, soft bluebeard mint,   35
the cool roots of the heat; as you stand
among them, appalled by their completeness
you'd think heaven the longing for a present
that slips keenly away:
a moment's glow   40
a figment of the weather.

So Christ, when he outfaced them,
or when he harried his own
with quick asperities: *You know not*
the day nor the hour, 45
meant: you have not come up to it,
have barely approached it,
or have dreamed past it. Here
I am, I am here,
he taught them: My time a learned time. 50

There's plenty of time, we said.
There was no time.
The sunny afternoons
were short as blows.

Tomorrows rushed, with less 55
time to count them
than to drink to their passing.
And that glow in the grass
was where it all started,
cold, with the unearthly 60
blood-chill of the salt life-forms,
sucked into walls porous as limestone,
to stay there, like a leaf-fossil
mimicking eternity:
the Oldest Animals. 65
And you and I go on, mazed
in the Byzantine closed mesh of nature
when all we wanted
was some place in a story.

1991

Seeing Romsey

I see Romsey through a hole in the wind
as I used to in late autumn, in the southern gales,
just there, not vibrating with changes
but like a model that has grown to its full height.
The timber houses have roofs of painted iron, 5
the brick ones are lowering with warm tiles.
The tree near me is the one I climbed
fifty-three years ago. I smell *roses* on the fence
where once the whole air was brushed with cypress.
Proust's madeleine, nothing. Even the smell 10
of trains that haven't run here
for forty years. Smelling strong as they slow down.
Smell of the comics they brought each Saturday.
Proust's madeleine was nothing to this,
or Eliot's hyacinths and lilacs 15

or that great heap of blossom in Yeats's window.
Nothing to this. To the firesmell of the forge,
squeezing into the smell of burning hoof. Incense
through the voices singing O *Salutaris hostia*
that never sing Latin any more.   20
I smell the printer's ink, and books,
and dust that flashes when the raindrops hit it
as it takes the rain into itself.

                                                                    1991

FRANCIS WEBB   *(1925–73)*

The Gunner

When the gunner spoke in his sleep the hut was still,
Uneasily strapped to the reckless wheel of his will;
Silence, humble, directionless as fog,
Lifted, and minutes were rhythmical on the log;

While slipstream plucked at a wafer of glass and steel,   5
Engines sliced and scooped at the air's thin wall,
And those dim spars dislodged from the moon became
Red thongs of tracer whipping boards aflame.

Listening, you crouched in the turret, watchful and taut
— *Bogey two thousand, skipper, corkscrew to port* —   10
Marvellous, the voice: driving electric fires
Through the panel of sleep, the black plugs, trailing wires.

The world spoke through its dream, being deaf and blind,
Its words were those of the dream, yet you might find
Forgotten genius, control, alive in this deep   15
Instinctive resistance to the perils of sleep.

                                                                    1952

Morgan's Country

This is Morgan's country: now steady, Bill.
(Stunted and grey, hunted and murderous.)
Squeeze for the first pressure. Shoot to kill.

Five: a star dozing in its cold cavern.
Six: first shuffle of boards in the cold house.   5
And the sun lagging on seven.

The grey wolf at his breakfast. He cannot think
Why he must make haste, unless because their eyes
Are poison at every well where he might drink.

---

19 **O Salutaris hostia**   hymn for the Eucharist in the Catholic Latin rite: 'Health-giving host'
Morgan   Daniel Morgan (?1830–65), a bushranger who roamed areas of south-central NSW and
northern Victoria

Unless because their gabbling voices force   10
The doors of his grandeur — first terror, then only hate.
Now terror again. Dust swarms under the doors.

Ashes drift on the dead-sea shadow of his plate.
Why should he heed them? What to do but kill
When his angel howls, when the sounds reverberate   15

In the last grey pipe of his brain? At the window sill
A blowfly strums on two strings of air:
Ambush and slaughter tingle against the lull.

But the Cave, his mother, is close beside his chair,
Her sunless face scribbled with cobwebs, bones   20
Rattling in her throat when she speaks. And there

The stone Look-out, his towering father, leans
Like a splinter from the seamed palm of the plain.
Their counsel of thunder arms him. A threat of rain.

Seven: and a blaze fiercer than the sun.   25
The wind struggles in the arms of the starved tree,
The temple breaks on a threadbare mat of glass.

Eight: even under the sun's trajectory
This country looks grey, hunted and murderous.

                                                                                        1952

End of the Picnic

When that humble-headed elder, the sea, gave his wide
Strenuous arm to a blasphemy, hauling the girth
And the sail and the black yard
Of unknown *Endeavour* towards this holy beach,
Heaven would be watching. And the two men. And the earth,   5
Immaculate, illuminant, out of reach.

It must break — on sacred water this swindle of a wave.
Thick canvas flogged the sticks. Hell lay hove-to.
Heaven did not move.
Two men stood safe: even when the prying, peering   10
Longboat, the devil's totem, cast off and grew,
No god shifted an inch to take a bearing.

It was Heaven-and-earth's jolting out of them shook the men.
It was uninitiate scurf and bone that fled.
Cook's column holds here.   15
Our ferry is homesick, whistling again and again;
But still I see how the myth of a daylight bled
Standing in ribbons, over our heads, for an hour.

                                                                                        1953

End of the Picnic 'It is likely that at the time of Cook's landing, Kurnell was holy ground to the local aboriginals' (author's note)

Five Days Old

(For Christopher John)

Christmas is in the air.
You are given into my hands
Out of quietest, loneliest lands.
My trembling is all my prayer.
To blown straw was given   5
All the fullness of Heaven.

The tiny, not the immense,
Will teach our groping eyes.
So the absorbed skies
Bleed stars of innocence.   10
So cloud-voice in war and trouble
Is at last Christ in the stable.

Now wonderingly engrossed
In your fearless delicacies,
I am launched upon sacred seas,   15
Humbly and utterly lost
In the mystery of creation,
Bells, bells of ocean.

Too pure for my tongue to praise,
That sober, exquisite yawn   20
Or the gradual, generous dawn
At an eyelid, maker of days:
To shrive my thought for perfection
I must breathe old tempests of action

For the snowflake and face of love,   25
Windfall and word of truth,
Honour close to death.
O eternal truthfulness, Dove,
Tell me what I hold —
Myrrh? Frankincense? Gold?   30

If this is man, then the danger
And fear are as lights of the inn,
Faint and remote as sin
Out here by the manger.
In the sleeping, weeping weather   35
We shall all kneel down together.

1961

Bells of St Peter Mancroft

Gay golden volleys of banter
Bombard the clockwork grief;
A frisson of gold at the centre
Of prayer, bright core of life.

Who knew the old lofty tower,   5
The ancient holy eye,
To come open like a flower,
To roll and wink with joy?

Townspeople, who wear
Shrewd colours and know the move,   10
Now blunder and wander, I swear,
In a transport of love.

And the belfry, hale and blest:
Picture the jolly hand
Milking each swinging breast   15
Of its laughing golden sound.

                                             1961

The Horses

The vegetative soul is the dedicated rhetorician:
Yellow knuckles of gorse are eloquent; motion
Is the psyche entire whose fullness is a naked growing
Ungirt with passion or reflection.
Grass meanders intoxicate in green simple action,   5
Little hills troll the pastoral catches, allowing
Hosannas of Saints in sober gesture alive
As flowering cherry along a drive.   .

With the Wensum comes consecrated ordered Wish.
From weedy tenements the spying suburban fish.   10
Dace, roach, carp, dart or loiter with tingling gills
In subaqueous blackout, neon,
Discuss certain shadows, suns as wool or rayon,
Choose certain baits as tranquillizers, pills.
Plucked from his element, each convulsed dreamer beats   15
Agony for his city streets.

A phylum apart these two old horses stand.
(Flies conspire to transfix the sweating land.)
The pair of them will stand an hour together
Licking each other's sides with great slow tongues.   20
Minds, as bodies, are ancient galls and wrongs.
Flies would erode this hackneyed summer weather.

The Horses   one of ten poems with the overall title 'Around Costessey' set in Norfolk, England
9 Wensum   a river in Norfolk

Memory, rumour, and an hour spin in the guise
Of the buzzing swarming flies.

He will give his body to the gesticulating   25
Green grass without forethought. He will lie beating, awaiting
The perfect town of water, going, gone.
He is the listing hulk or bale of straw
In silt of the inorganic; pang of law
Tides him into the rivers and the sun.   30
Light plays throughout his muddied floating things,
His action, desire, his gift of tongues.

                                                                    1964

Harry

It's the day for writing that letter, if one is able,
And so the striped institutional shirt is wedged
Between this holy holy chair and table.
He has purloined paper, he has begged and cadged
The bent institutional pen,   5
The ink. And our droll old men
Are darting constantly where he weaves his sacrament.

Sacrifice? Propitiation? All are blent
In the moron's painstaking fingers — so painstaking.
His vestments our giddy yarns of the firmament,   10
Women, gods, electric trains, and our remaking
Of all known worlds — but not yet
Has our giddy alphabet
Perplexed his priestcraft and spilled the cruet of innocence.

We have been plucked from the world of commonsense,   15
Fondling between our hands some shining loot,
Wife, mother, beach, fisticuffs, eloquence,
As the lank tree cherishes every distorted shoot.
What queer shards we could steal
Shaped him, realer than the Real: 20
But it is no goddess of ours guiding the fingers and the thumb.

She cries: *Ab aeterno ordinata sum.*
He writes to the woman, this lad who will never marry.
One vowel and the thousand laborious serifs will come
To this pudgy Christ, and the old shape of Mary.   25
Before seasonal pelts and the thin
Soft tactile underskin
Of air were stretched across earth, they have sported and are one.

Harry   one of eight poems with the overall title 'Ward Two', which arose from Webb's stay in Parramatta Psychiatric Hospital in 1960–61

Ab aeterno ordinata sum   'I was set up from everlasting': words spoken by Wisdom in Proverbs
8:23. Christian liturgy applies these words to Mary.

Was it then at this altar-stone the mind was begun?
The image besieges our Troy. Consider the sick   30
Convulsions of movement, and the featureless baldy sun
Insensible — sparing that compulsive nervous tic.
Before life, the fantastic succession,
An imbecile makes his confession,
Is filled with the Word unwritten, has almost genuflected.   35

Because the wise world has for ever and ever rejected
Him and because your children would scream at the sight
Of his mongol mouth stained with food, he has resurrected
The spontaneous thought retarded and infantile Light.
Transfigured with him we stand   40
Among walls of the no-man's-land
While he licks the soiled envelope with lover's caress

Directing it to the House of no known address.

1964

DOROTHY HEWETT   *(b 1923)*

Grave Fairytale

I sat in my tower, the seasons whirled,
the sky changed, the river grew
and dwindled to a pool.
The black Witch, light as an eel,
laddered up my hair   5
to straddle the window-sill.

She was there when I woke, blocking the light,
or in the night, humming, trying on my clothes.
I grew accustomed to her; she was as much a part of me
as my own self; sometimes I thought, 'She is myself!'   10
a posturing blackness, savage as a cuckoo.

There was no mirror in the tower.

Each time the voice screamed from the thorny garden
I'd rise and pensively undo the coil,
I felt it switch the ground, the earth tugged at it,   15
once it returned to me knotted with dead warm birds,
once wrapped itself three times around the tower —
                              the tower quaked.
Framed in the window, whirling the countryside
with my great net of hair I'd catch a hawk,   20
                    a bird, and once a bear.
One night I woke, the horse pawed at the walls,
the cell was full of light, all my stone house

suffused, the voice called from the calm white garden,
                             'Rapunzel'.   25
I leant across the sill, my plait hissed out
                        and spun like hail;
he climbed, slow as a heartbeat, up the stony side,
we dropped together as he loosed my hair,
his foraging hands tore me from neck to heels: 30
the witch jumped up my back and beat me to the wall.

Crouched in a corner I perceived it all,
the thighs jack-knifed apart, the dangling sword
                        thrust home,
pinned like a specimen — to scream with joy.   35

I watched all night the beasts unsatisfied
roll in their sweat, their guttural cries
made the night thick with sound.
Their shadows gambolled, hunchbacked, hairy-arsed,
and as she ran four-pawed across the light,   40
the female dropped coined blood spots on the floor.

When morning came he put his armour on,
kissing farewell like angels swung on hair.
I heard the metal shoes trample the round earth
                        about my tower.   45
Three times I lent my hair to the glowing prince,
hand over hand he climbed, my roots ached,
the blood dribbled on the stone sill.
Each time I saw the framed-faced bully boy
                        sick with his triumph.   50

The third time I hid the shears,
a stab of black ice dripping in my dress.
He rose, his armour glistened in my tears,
the convex scissors snapped,
the glittering coil hissed, and slipped   55
                        through air to undergrowth.
His mouth, like a round O, gaped at his end,
his finger-nails ripped out, he clawed through space.
His horse ran off flank-deep in blown thistles.
Three seasons he stank at the tower's base.   60
A hawk plucked out his eyes, the ants busied his brain,
the mud-weed filled his mouth, his great sword rotted,
his tattered flesh-flags hung on bushes for the birds.

Bald as a collaborator I sit walled
                        in the thumb-nosed tower,   65
wound round three times with ropes of autumn leaves.
And the witch ... sometimes I idly kick
a little heap of rags across the floor.
I notice it grows smaller every year.

                                                                        1975

I've Made My Bed, I'll Lie on It

With legs apart I lie on mother's bed,
disturbing dust that shrouds the mighty dead.
You stake me out; as I begin to moan
her hairbrush beats us like a metronome.
She snicks her death's head over us with pins,   5
we fall apart, the bed's small hell begins.
An epitaph to end the fearful ride,
my heart, recalcitrant, leaps from my side:
seizing a chance I plagiarise a line,
'With thee contending I forget all time;'   10
staking a bid for permanence I weep,
you give me up, roll over, fall asleep.

My tongue's a broken clapper in a bell,
with book and candle I roll down to Hell,
and circling back upon my mother's bed,   15
gift-wrapped receive the Kingdom of the Dead.

1975

Anniversary

Death is in the air —

today is the anniversary of his death in October
(he would have been thirty-one)
I went home to High Street
& couldn't feed the new baby   5
my milk had dried up
so I sat holding him numbly
looking for the soft spot on the top of his head
while they fed me three more librium
you're only crying for yourself he said   10
but I kept on saying *It's the waste I can't bear.*

All that winter we lived
in the longest street in the world
he used to walk to work in the dark
on the opposite side of the street   15
somebody always walked with him but they never met
he could only hear the boots
& when he stopped they stopped.

The new baby swayed in a canvas cot lacing his fingers
I worried in case he got curvature of the spine   20
Truby King said a baby needed firm support
he was a very big bright baby
the cleaner at the Queen Vic said every morning
you mark my words that kid's been here before.

The house was bare & cold with a false gable   25
we had no furniture only a double mattress
on the floor a big table & two deal chairs
each morning I dressed the baby in a shrunken jacket
& caught the bus home to my mother's to nurse the child
who was dying   the house had bay windows   30
hidden under fir trees smothered in yellow roses
the child sat dwarfed at the end of the polished table
pale as death in the light of his four candles
singing 'Little Boy Blue'.

I pushed the pram to the telephone box   35
I'm losing my milk I told her   *I want to bring him*
home to die   Home she said   *you left*
home a long time ago to go with that man.

I pushed them both through the park
over the dropped leaves (his legs were crippled)   40
a magpie swooped down black out of the sky
& pecked his forehead   a drop of blood splashed on
his wrist   he started to cry

It took five months & everybody was angry
because the new baby was alive & cried for attention   45
pollen sprinkled his cheeks under the yellow roses.

When he died it was like everybody else
in the public ward with the screens around him
the big bruises spreading on his skin
his hand came up out of the sheets *don't cry*   50
he said   *don't be sad*
I sat there overweight in my Woolworth's dress
not telling anybody in case they kept him alive
with another transfusion —

          Afterwards I sat by the gas fire
in my old dressing-gown turning over the photographs
wondering why I'd drunk all that stout
& massaged my breasts every morning to be
          a good mother.

                                                                                1979

From Alice in Wormland

10

In the Dream Girl's Garden
there were dolls & rocking horses
gilt hornets built clay houses on the verandah
tom-tits swung dry grass nests in almond trees.

This was Eden   perfect   circular   5
the candid temples of her innocence
the homestead in the clearing
ringed with hills
the paddocks pollened deep in dandelions
the magic forest dark & beckoning   10

Giants & marvels would she ever go there?
Alice ringed   her hair & wrists with chains
He loves me   loves me not
what did it mean?

There was some point   15
where picture books dissolved
& prophecy was rampant
the shearing shed giddy as blown glass
teetered on the edge of the known world
blue heelered swaggies shell-shocked   20
mocked and blind
fell down the tunnel of this nothingness
horned toads & dugites hid in hollyhocks
the spotted snake spoke as she leaned to listen
his hooded world-sick eyes instructed her   25
Alice was driven howling from the garden.

21

Alice rose up
& went looking for love
but didn't find it
she tried
the Lecturer in Zoology   5
who'd once played the lead
in   *Waiting for Lefty*

the Associate Professor of History
who'd led the party split
in Melbourne   10
the thermometer
under her tongue
recorded her first hot flush

the marbles fell for Vietnam
& spared her son   15
the Buddhists burned
in pillars of wildfire
Alice fought
the dictatorship of the proletariat
abandoned socialist realism   20
(her lectures on Blake were famous)

tried to put democracy
back into centralism
the Russsian tanks
rumbled through Czechoslovakia   25
she stood on the platform
in tears   resigning
the Jewish Party Secretary
with a wattled neck
stared out the window   30
a veteran called her
the lady with the sob story.

                                                                  1987

NANCY KEESING   *(1923–93)*

Old Hardware Store, Melbourne

Being un-organic, non-macrobiotic, lazy
I do not wish to return to the honest names
Or the slow, outmoded, heavy, intractable objects
As: mincers, mangles, mowers, mattocks, hames;
Collars and saddles of horsehair-padded leather;   5
Pots of cast and enamelled iron; hones
For sharpening blades of shares, shears, scythes and sickles;
Hafted axes; burrs and grinding stones.
      But I value verbs: to mill, till, harrow, harvest, burnish,
Hew, strip, beat, toss, tether, render, comb,   10
Roast, brew, knead, prove dough — one returns to bread,
To meat, to bellies and bowels, to prick and womb —
To bear, be born, to suck, piss, shit, to cry,
To work, sweat, live, sing, love, pray, die.

                                                                  1977

Darlo and the Cross

1

As we walked home from school today
Past Darlinghurst Fire Station,
One lady took off her high-heeled shoe
And ripped another's cheek right through.
Gee, ladies fight like children do.   5

Ladies don't fight. You soon must learn
That every head of bottle blonde
Is not by any means true gold.
Please walk straight home as you've been told
Or you'll be sorry when you're old. 10

2

Near Lister Hospital this morning
A lady from an upstairs flat
Threw some prawn shells out the window
Onto the brim of Mary Lou's hat.
'What did she do?' 15
Oh, Mary Lou
Just tossed her head and they went on the path
And she trod them into a nice pink squash.
'How very dirty
Feckless and naughty 20
To make such a litter
She should have known better.'
The lady who threw?
'Yes, *and* Mary Lou.'

3

Right-thinking parents fear Mary Lou 25
They cannot imagine how she slipped through
The interviews for an exclusive school,
Her mother had broken every rule,
So I overheard, and the man's a fool.

I went to Mary Lou's flat one day 30
If I didn't tell where I went to play
What harm? She has a key of her own,
She can spin what she likes on the gramophone,
She eats pink bought cakes and has fun alone.

Mary Lou's mother wears swami scanties, 35
Mary Lou has lace on her weekend panties,
She can colour her lips and paint her nails
And wear patent shoes; she has kissed grown males
Who are not related. And if she fails

To pass the Inter they won't mind 40
By then she'll be old enough to find
A flat for herself and have cocktails and fun.
But she topped the school. Every prize she won
Including religion. She's now a nun.

1995

GEOFFREY DUTTON   *(b 1922)*

From A Body of Words

8 *Happy*

Happiness is a persecuted word,
Not safe for a moment from the advertising man
Glueing it with 'is' to something sticky,
Nor from the politician with his teargas
Spraying the greatest number and calling it good.   5

But just right for lovers, who never bought each other,
Whose secret votes are counted on their fingers,
And who never need to ask
'Has it been said before?'
Any more than the earth questions the spring rain.   10

Lovers crush happiness till it bleeds
Like a strawberry eaten mouth to mouth.
There are also easier implications of gaiety,
As when he eats a strawberry from her navel
Or somewhere else, joy beyond skin,   15
Ecstasy deeper than love, and pleasure,
Simply, the pleasure of your company.
This is the time, without lifting a cork,
When 'happy' means '*colloq. (joq.)*. Slightly drunk 1770.'

Lovers and children are happy because they praise,   20
They say so, with their lips and eyes,
Knowing and unknowing, for children are on parole
And lovers are all escaped prisoners,
'Wanted', 'Reward', by those who claim to need them.

She opens no dictionary to know   25
That for six or seven hundred years
'Happy' is 'having good hap',
And that 'hap' is 'chance or fortune (good or bad);
Luck, lot; often, an unfortunate event, mishap.'

That is why they give thanks (to that kind goddess   30
Who pitches her shrine in any old bed)
To the luck that out of millions
Brought them together.

And when he draws the sunlight of her face
From the tent of her hair   35
The shadows are still there, mishap, bad luck,
But at this moment having no power at all,
The persecuted, in each others' arms
Having become '2. b. Blessed, beatified.'

9 Body

She threw the dictionary out the window
Cursing him for a semantic, pedantic
Man of words, words, and it was spring,
A chalice of scent the red rose of her navel
Honeysuckle hiding behind her earlobes   5
The gold iris waking to the tan of summer
Pink nipples lifting from the caps of gumblossom
Her feet lost in the simplicities of daisies
Her hands twining columns with wistaria
The brown earth succouring red radishes   10
Everything fermenting, every bubble of the champagne air
Bursting against the frothing clouds
And the land throwing scarlet and green fountains
Of whirring parrots into the infinite blue.

Defying words, she reinterpreted   15
The illiterate spring by the pure vowels
Of birdsong and the consonants of bees.

When they were together as an arum lily
No one wanted a history of the spring.
They were silent as the sun through the rise and fall of day.   20

Yet words shake out of the past
From roots, on stems, with leaves and flowers.

Their bodies are the bearers of all those messages
And finally, when they wake from the trance
They open each other like letters, being lovers   25
Words are their sap and their electricity.

Definitions are a game of absence,
Like old ladies behind lace curtains
Playing patience, the dictionary is solitaire.

As soon as she moves, she has redefined all words.   30

BODY. The word has died out of German, its place being taken by *leib*,
orig. 'life', and *körper* from Latin: but, in English, *body* remains a great
and important word.

                                                     O.E.D.

                                                            1977

DIMITRIS TSALOUMAS   *(b 1921)*

The Return

The war's been over now for forty years
and you've still to take the enemy off the wire.
Who opened up his back so that his lungs hung out
from behind? Haven't you tired of his shallow moans
in a whole lifetime? I sent you word to empty out   5
the bucket with the arm and other bits,
to stop up all the cracks. The house
stinks like a shambles. You haven't even sealed
the holes in the cellar and who knows what
might suddenly creep out on us? I don't like   10
this weather at all. Already my sleep is taking
water, and there are tentacles stretching out,
feeling in the dark. I'm sorry to tell you,
brother, but I'm not spending summer here.
At our age some caution is called for.   15

                                        1983

Falcon Drinking

Awakened to this other bleakness
I sit to read my daily portion

of the wall. Sometimes it's voices:
women disputing a place at the head

of public fountains in years of drought,   5
Orpheus pleading in the basement,

the anguished bidding at the 'Change.
Sometimes it's touch:

shuddering flesh and silken skin,
the clammy passage of darkness   10

in night corridors, forgotten scars
and varnishes on old violins.

Today is seeing time. Knife-sharp,
a cruel blade of light cuts through

the brain's greyness, sweeps over mists   15
and hints at ridges, distantly.

Close in, at the stone-trough
hard by the spring of language where

the cypress stands, a falcon drinks.
The cypress ripples in shattered water   20

nights of many moons and nightingales.
The bird stoops shivering to sip

then tilts its head back skywards.
stammers its beak and trills

the narrow tongue. Spilt drops
hang bright in midair, hard as tears.   26
                                          1988

Elegy

You had always been young
and impatient. The angel
who came that day to part the crowd
looked edgy too
as you walked the cleared path   5
in a haze of cypress blossom
and were gone,
a sprig of mint in your hand.

These lines bend like light
through taut infinity   10
but fetch no image fit for worship
in my shrine of vespertine
abstractions. What's far
is near enough,   14
sharper than knives.

That night I spat at the sea
and stamped the ground in blasphemy,
and from my roof I stoned
the screaming mare of the wind.   19
But it's the other element
that has you. Secret
beneath the cinders of many years,
it flares up suddenly
and from my chest   24
it drives frightened birds
and words
into the madness of each spring.
                                          1993

ROSEMARY DOBSON   *(b 1920)*

In A Café

She clasps the cup with both her hands,
Over the rim her glance compels;
(A man forgets his hat, returns,
The waitress leans against the shelves).

And Botticelli, painting in the corner,   5
Glances absorbed across a half-turned shoulder
Thinking of lilies springing where she walks
As now she rises, moves across the room,
(The yawning waitress gathers up the stalks,
The ash, the butt-ends and the dregs of tea).   10
Pausing between the gesture and the motion,
Lifting her hand to brush away her hair,
He limns her in an instant, always there
Between the doorway and the emphatic till
With waves and angels, balanced on a shell.   15

                                                             1944

The Bystander

I am the one who looks the other way,
In any painting you may see me stand
Rapt at the sky, a bird, an angel's wing,
While others kneel, present the myrrh, receive
The benediction from the radiant hand.   5

I hold the horses while the knights dismount
And draw their swords to fight the battle out;
Or else in dim perspective you may see
My distant figure on the mountain road
When in the plains the hosts are put to rout.   10

I am the silly soul who looks too late,
The dullard dreaming, second from the right.
I hang upon the crowd, but do not mark
(Cap over eyes) the slaughtered Innocents,
Or Icarus, his downward-plunging flight.   15

Once in a Garden — back view only there —
How well the painter placed me, stroke on stroke,
Yet scarcely seen among the flowers and grass —
I heard a voice say, 'Eat,' and would have turned —
I often wonder who it was that spoke.   20

                                                             1955

The Birth

A wreath of flowers as cold as snow
Breaks out in bloom upon the night:
That tree is rooted in the dark,
It draws from dew its breath of life,
It feeds on frost, it hangs in air   5
And like a glittering branch of stars
Receives, gives forth, its breathing light.

Eight times it flowered in the dark,
Eight times my hand reached out to break
That icy wreath to bear away   10
Its pointed flowers beneath my heart.
Sharp are the pains and long the way
Down, down into the depths of night
Where one goes for another's sake.

Once more it flowers, once more I go   15
In dream at midnight to that tree,
I stretch my hand and break the branch
And hold it to my human heart.
Now, as the petals of a rose
Those flowers unfold and grow to me —   20
I speak as of a mystery.

1955

Cock Crow

Wanting to be myself, alone,
Between the lit house and the town
I took the road, and at the bridge
Turned back and walked the way I'd come.

Three times I took that lonely stretch,   5
Three times the dark trees closed me round,
The night absolved me of my bonds;
Only my footsteps held the ground.

My mother and my daughter slept,
One life behind and one before,   10
And I that stood between denied
Their needs in shutting-to the door.

And walking up and down the road
Knew myself, separate and alone,
Cut off from human cries, from pain,   15
And love that grows about the bone.

Too brief illusion! Thrice for me
I heard the cock crow on the hill
And turned the handle of the door
Thinking I knew his meaning well.   20

1965

The Rape of Europa

Beautiful Europa, while the billy boils
Underneath the she-oaks, underneath the willows,
Underneath the sky like a bent bow of silver,
Like the arms of a god embracing a mortal —
Beautiful Europa has set out a picnic.   5

All her father's paddocks that slope to the water
Are singing with runnels and freshets of crystal
And the voice of the river is loud as it plunges
By boulders of granite and shouldering basalt —
On a spit of white sand she is boiling the billy.   10

The cattle come down to the sand by the river,
Europa is plaiting green willows and buttercups,
Daisies and water-weeds: mocking, she crowns them
With wreaths and festoons, with dripping green garlands,
And climbs to the back of the dark one, the leader.   15

Europa, Europa, the billy is boiling,
Down from the woolsheds your brothers come riding.
There's a splash in the shallows, a swirl, a commotion,
He has leapt, he is swept in the rush of the current,
And the riders draw rein on the hillside, astounded.   20

Oh wave to Europa for far she is faring
Past farmyard and homestead, past township and jetty,
And many will say that they saw them go riding,
The girl and the bull on the back of the river
Down to the harbour and over the ocean.   25

And distant indeed are the coasts of that country
Where the god was revealed in splendour and ardour.
Europa, Europa, as you lay quiet
In sunshine and shadow, under a plane-tree,
Did you remember the river, the she-oaks?   30

                                                            1965

The Sailor: May 1960

The sailor settled the oar at his back,
Over the hills he took the track
And the blue sea dipped behind him.
Whenever he saw beneath his palm
The shimmering roofs of a country town   5
He rubbed his hands and hoisted his oar —
But those who came to gape at the door
Cried out, 'Well, look at the sailor!'

May 1960 'a time of threats of war' (from the author's note in *Collected Poems* 1991)

Over the crests of the Great Divide,
Down the slopes on the other side   10
Across the plains out westward —
And still as he walked through one-horse towns
Or droving-camps or mining-claims
The folk came out to watch him pass
And chewing a stalk of summer grass   15
Said, 'What do you know — a sailor!'

Way out west where the red sand spins
And the plains lie down under gibber-stones
He followed the stock-routes inland.
The stockmen shouted, 'Sailor, hey!'   20
But he came at last to the end of his way
For he heard a voice from a humpy croak
'What's that, mate, tied up on your back?'
And, 'Here I stay' cried the sailor.

I've half a mind to hoist a gun   25
And follow the way that sailor's gone . . .

                                                                    1965

GWEN HARWOOD   *(1920–95)*

Home of Mercy

By two and two the ruined girls are walking
at the neat margin of the convent grass
into the chapel, counted as they pass
by an old nun who silences their talking.

They smooth with roughened hands the clumsy dress   5
that hides their ripening bodies. Memories burn
like incense as towards plaster saints they turn
faces of mischievous children in distress.

They kneel: time for the spirit to begin
with prayer its sad recourse to dream and flight   10
from their intolerable weekday vigour.
Each morning they will launder, for their sin,
sheets soiled by other bodies, and at night
angels will wrestle them with brutish vigour.

                                                                    1963

In the Park

She sits in the park. Her clothes are out of date.
Two children whine and bicker, tug her skirt.
A third draws aimless patterns in the dirt.
Someone she loved once passes by — too late

to feign indifference to that casual nod.   5
'How nice,' et cetera. 'Time holds great surprises.'
From his neat head unquestionably rises
a small balloon ... 'but for the grace of God ...'

They stand a while in flickering light, rehearsing
the children's names and birthdays. 'It's so sweet   10
to hear their chatter, watch them grow and thrive,'
she says to his departing smile. Then, nursing
the youngest child, sits staring at her feet.
To the wind she says, 'They have eaten me alive.'

                                                          1963

Boundary Conditions

'At the sun's incredible centre
    the atomic nuclei
with electrons and light quanta
    in a burning concord lie.
All the particles that form   5
    light and matter, in that furnace
keep their equilibrium.
    Once we pass beyond the surface
of the star, sharp changes come.
    These remarks apply as well   10
to the exploding atom bomb,'
    said Professor Eisenbart
while his mistress, with a shell
    scored an arrow and a heart
in the sand on which they lay   15
    watching heat and light depart
from the boundaries of day.

'Sprung from love's mysterious core
    soul and flesh,' the young girl said,
'restless on the narrow shore   20
    between the unborn and the dead,
split from concord, and inherit
    mankind's old dichotomy:
mind and matter; flesh and spirit;
    what has been and what will be;   25
desire that flares beyond our fate:
    still in the heart more violence lies
than in the bomb. Who'll calculate
    that tough muscle's bursting size?'

Tongues of darkness licked the crust   30
    of pigment from the bowl of blue.
Thought's campaniles fell to dust
    blown by the seawind through and through.

                                                          1963

An Impromptu for Ann Jennings

Sing, memory, sing those seasons in the freezing
    suburb of Fern Tree, a rock-shaded place
with tree ferns, gullies, snowfalls and eye-pleasing
    prospects from paths along the mountain-face.

Nursing our babies by huge fires of wattle,   5
    or pushing them in prams when it was fine.
exchanging views on diet, or Aristotle,
    discussing Dr Spock or Wittgenstein,

cleaning up infants and the floors they muddied,
    bandaging, making ends and tempers meet —   10
sometimes I'd mind your children while you studied,
    or you'd take mine when I felt near defeat;

keeping our balance somehow through the squalling
    disorder, or with anguish running wild
when sickness, a sick joke from some appalling   15
    orifice of the nightwatch, touched a child;

think of it, woman: each of us gave birth to
    four children, our new lords whose beautiful
tyrannic kingdom might restore the earth to
    that fullness we thought lost beyond recall   20

when, in the midst of life, we could not name it,
    when spirit cried in darkness, 'I will have ...'
but what? have what? There was no word to frame it,
    though spirit beat at flesh as in a grave

from which it could not rise. But we have risen.   25
    Caesar's we were, and wild, though we seemed tame.
Now we move where we will. Age is no prison
    to hinder those whose joy has found its name.

We are our own. All Caesar's debts are rendered
    in full to Caesar. Time has given again   30
a hundredfold those lives that we surrendered,
    the love, the fruitfulness; but not the pain.

Before the last great fires we two went climbing
    like gods or blessed spirits in summer light
with the quiet pulse of mountain water chiming   35
    as if twenty years were one long dreaming night,

above the leafy dazzle of the streams
    to fractured rock, where water had its birth,
and stood in silence, at the roots of dreams,
    content to know: our children walk the earth.   40

                                      1975

---

8 Dr Spock Benjamin Spock (b 1903), author of influential books on child-rearing who became a prominent activist in the USA against the Vietnam War

Barn Owl

Daybreak: the household slept.
I rose blessed by the sun.
A horny fiend, I crept
out with my father's gun.
Let him dream of a child   5
obedient, angel-mild —

old No-Sayer, robbed of power
by sleep. I knew my prize
who swooped home at this hour
with daylight-riddled eyes   10
to his place on a high beam
in our old stables, to dream

light's useless time away.
I stood, holding my breath,
in urine-scented hay,   15
master of life and death,
a wisp-haired judge whose law
would punish beak and claw.

My first shot struck. He swayed,
ruined, beating his only   20
wing, as I watched, afraid
by the fallen gun, a lonely
child who believed death clean
and final, not this obscene

bundle of stuff that dropped,   25
and dribbled through loose straw
tangling in bowels, and hopped
blindly closer. I saw
those eyes that did not see
mirror my cruelty   30

while the wrecked thing that could
not bear the light nor hide
hobbled in its own blood.
My father reached my side,
gave me the fallen gun.   35
'End what you have begun.'

I fired. The blank eyes shone
once into mine, and slept.
I leaned my head upon
my father's arm, and wept,   40
owl-blind in early sun
for what I had begun.

                                          1975

Oyster Cove

Dreams drip to stone. Barracks and salt marsh blaze
opal beneath a crackling glaze of frost.
Boot-black, in graceless Christian rags, a lost
race breathes out cold. Parting the milky haze
on mudflats, seabirds, clean and separate, wade.   5
Mother, Husband and Child: stars which forecast
fine weather, all are set. The long night's past
and the long day begins. God's creatures, made
woodcutters' whores, sick drunks, watch the sun prise
their life apart: flesh, memory, language all   10
split open, featureless, to feed the wild
hunger of history. A woman lies
coughing her life out. There's still blood to fall,
but all blood's spilt that could have made a child.

1975

The Sharpness of Death

Leave me alone. — You will?
That's your way with us women.
You've left my mother so,
desolate in my father's house.
But that's not what I mean.   5
Suppose we come to terms:
you take one day for each
day that I've wished to die.
Give me more time for time
that was never long enough.   10
Look, here's a list of names.
Take these, the world will bless you.
Death, you've become obscene.
Nobody calls you *sweet* or *easeful* now.
You're in the hands of philosophers   15
who cut themselves, and bleed,
and know that knives are sharp,
but prove with complex logic
there's no such thing as sharpness.

Heidegger

Like Wittgenstein, he found much cause to wonder   20
　　'that there are things in being'.
Searching for roots, he thought all words were names.
　　Given the German language
and his training as a Jesuit seminarian

he could talk about God's *Dasein*,   25
and in untranslatable reasonings maintain
   that the human concept *Being*
and the question 'What is Being?' are essential:
   since man's a language user
he must say things *are*, or cannot speak at all.   30
   He called philosophy,
in his late works, 'the enemy of thinking'.
   Rilke said song was Dasein.
Heidegger left ontology for Hölderlin
   and his blessed Grecian world,   35
'the language in which Being speaks to us'.
   Untranslatable as ever!
Was it significant nonsense or deep insight
   flowed from his pen? He thought
much about dying. No one could die for him.   40
   Poetry led him
close to the Logos. Nothing could be proved,
   but much was hinted.
Death, he said, was 'the ultimate situation'.
   I hope he found some light   45
beyond that field of black everlasting flowers.

Nasturtiums

Purest of colours, how they shone
while we talked in your studio.
Light like a noble visitor
stayed with us briefly and moved on.   50
A schoolgirl bringing flowers, an artist
accepting colour and crazy love,
we stand among the plaster mouldings
of figures from an earlier time.
How would you ever know me now   55
if I came to your grave and called you,
unless I brought those flowers, those colours,
that ray of light descending through
the room's eccentric fenestration?

---

25 Dasein   in German, 'existence': literally, 'being there'. In the tradition of Western philosophy God's 'Dasein' is his (infinite) 'existence'. Martin Heidegger (1889–1976) questioned the concept, arguing that Dasein is properly thought of as finite: he referred the term to the 'being' proper to the human, for whom 'to be' is to be in and to understand a particular world. The opening of such being occurs in language — likewise finite and temporal. Harwood's poem, concerning a thinker who takes the 'human concept' of the being of 'things' seriously, was written at a time when academic analytic philosophy tended to confine 'being' to the connections of grammar.

31–36 For Heidegger, poetic language is language at its most originating; hence his study of Rilke, Hölderlin and the Greek pre-Socratic thinkers.

42 Logos   in Christian theology, the divine creating Word (John 1:1); in classical Greek philosophy, language, discourse, the ordering of things

Seed of the seed of countless seasons
blossoms to hold the light that's gone. 60

Death, I will tell you now:
my love and I stood still
in the roofless chapel. My
body was full of him, my 65
tongue sang with his juices, I
grew ripe in his blond light.
If I fall from that time,
then set your teeth in me.

1981

The Sea Anemones

Grey mountains, sea and sky. Even the misty
seawind is grey. I walk on lichened rock
in a kind of late assessment, call it peace.
Then the anemones, scarlet, gouts of blood.
There is a word I need, and earth was speaking. 5
I cannot hear. These seaflowers are too bright.
Kneeling on rock, I touch them through cold water.
My fingers meet some hungering gentleness.
A newborn child's lips moved so at my breast.
I woke, once, with my palm across your mouth. 10
    The word is: *ever*. Why add salt to salt?
    Blood drop by drop among the rocks they shine.
    Anemos, wind. The spirit, where it will.
Not flowers, no, animals that must eat or die.

1981

Religious Instruction

My friend and I, put out
from the Old Testament
lesson for giggling, went
and made ourselves from clay
a fine hermaphrodite 5
idol: huge breasts, the lot.

We sought protection from
teachers and clergymen,
but most, two goatish boys
who took the same road home 10
calling, 'You've got a womb!
Girls have got wombs!' and worse.

---

13 **Anemos** wind (Greek: 'anemone' means 'daughter of the wind'). **The spirit** See John 3:8 (Revised Standard Version): 'The wind blows where it wills, and you hear the sound of it, but you do not know whence it comes or whither it goes; so it is with every one who is born of the Spirit.' In Latin, 'spiritus' can denote spirit, wind, or breath.

Immediate success!
That self-same day the first
caught smoking was well thrashed,   15
and the second savaged by
a dog he used to tease.
Versions of this got round.

So we reigned in a blessed
communion of young sinners,   20
queens of the underworld.
But in secret crumbled God
back to his elements
among riddles never guessed.

                                                                1981

A Music Lesson

Kröte's not well. His mood is bloody.
A pupil he can hardly stand
attacks a transcendental study.
— Lord, send me one real pianist.
Soul of a horse! He shapes her hand   5
and breathes apologies to Liszt.

'Reflect: in order to create
we must know how to. Think about
the balance between height and weight,
shoulder to fingertip; a hanging   10
bridge, resilient, reaching out
with firm supports. Let's have no banging!

'Playing begins inside your brain.
Music's much more than flesh and bone.
Relax, and listen. If you strain   15
your muscles *here* and *here* contract.
You get a stiff, unlovely tone.'
His pupil says, 'Is that a fact?'

She plays the passage louder, faster;
indeed deliberately tries   20
to infuriate her music master.
'The year that Liszt was born, a comet
blazed over European skies.'
'Am I to draw conclusions from it?

'And, if so, what?' the tyro sneers.   25
— Cold heart, stiff hands. How to explain?
'When a new genius appears
it's like that fiery head of light
drawing us in its golden train.
Now, shall we try to get it right?   30

'Does it give you no pride to say
"My teacher's teacher learned from Liszt?"
Feel in your hands, before you play,
the body's marvellous architecture:
the muscles between hand and wrist   35
kept flexible; now try to picture

the finger forming, from the point
where it rests on the key, an arc
curving through every finger-joint,
supporting the whole arm's free weight.   40
Now the least effort makes its mark.
The instrument can sing.'
                             'I'm late,'

the pupil whines. The lesson's over.
The teacher pours himself a gin,   45
pats the piano like a lover
(— Dear mistress, we're alone once more).
Liszt, with his upper lip gone in,
beams from the cover of a score.

Abbé, forsooth! A toast to you,   50
old friend, old fiend in monkish dress.
I know you had your off days too.
At Schumann's, Clara said, you played
his work so badly once (confess!)
that only her good manners made   55

her sit in silence in that room.
— Have mercy on all pianists,
Architect of the world, of whom
I ask that I may live to see
Halley's Comet.   60
              If God exists
then music is his love for me.

                                              1981

Thoughts before Sunrise

The season for philosophy draws on.
Pentameters flow smoothly from the pen.
The crops are in, the autumn work is done.
Earth settles down to die and rise again.

The last of the year's sweetness: time to write   5
long letters home, says Rilke. (This is home.)
The Chinese claim to know the pitch of night,
the mixture of all sound, earth's general hum,

F above middle C. I can't respond.
The house creaks, possums chatter, plover scream,   10
the geese scream back. Such croaking in the pond!
Hector crows for the sun to colour him

'Ab-so-LUTE-ly! Ab-so-LUTE-ly!' — that bird
never sings Cock-a-doodle. Once he caught
a whipsnake in his beak. Well, there's a word   15
he offers, very suitable for thought.

The Absolute, the unlimited perfect Being.
In Hector's case, the sun, which gilds his ruff
and sets his green and russet feathers glowing,
absolutely. His life is long enough.   20

I think of those for whom there'll be no letter
now or in any season, whom no sound
will reach, however pitched. I think of water
frozen to grassblades. Wheatgrains underground.

                                                              1981

Death Has No Features of His Own

Death has no features of his own.
He'll take a young eye bathed in brightness
and the raging cheekbones of a raddled queen.
Misery's cured by his appalling taste.
His house is without issue. He appears   5
garlanded with lovebirds, hearts and flowers.
Anything, everything.
                        He'll wear my face and yours.
Not as we were, thank God. As we shall be
when we let go of the world, late ripe fruit falling.   10
What we are is beyond him utterly.

                                                              1981

Return of the Native

The big house is turned into flats, the last camphor laurel
cut down, alas; the street paved, the cool weatherboard suburb
gone trendy with fancy brick; but new roses spill
their old abundance of scent, and across the kerb

as if this were a film, a Mintie wrapper blows.   5
So cut to two freckled children unwrapping Minties
in their camphor laurel house, and from wide windows
let the sounds of teacups and voices and laughter rise.

It is late afternoon, and the towering cumulus gather
over city, suburb and treehouse as everyone tells   10
silly stories. A pause. A rich baritone voice is clear:
'Well, a gentleman knows where he is if the police own the brothels.'

The grown-ups shriek, and repeat the curious line.
Heaven cracks open. The children run, drenched, inside,
and the girl, who learns like a parrot, repeats it again
and is slapped into tears without knowing how she has offended.

And Freddy, who said it while managing his tea
with his hand and his hook says, 'She didn't understand,'
and talks about Little Pitchers and says he's sorry.
(He told me once: 'When the Germans shot off my hand

'God gave me this hook, it's much better for carrying parcels.'
I believed the curving steel grew out of his arm.)
But it's time for some good old songs, and music quells
the world's injustice, and clears away the storm.

My taxi is waiting. The driver puts down his book.
It's Volume Two of the brick-red paperback Popper.
I say, 'Full Marx?' He grins, 'Half. Have you had a good look?
Was that your old home? Do you like what they've done to her?

'Do you like what they've done to this old State of yours?
I'm a useless M.A. It's no use whingeing, but.
You can't sing hymns in the park, and the police own the parlours.
But I've a sick wife and a kid, so I keep my mouth shut.

'Ban Uranium, one bald tyre, they'll have you off.
If you're sporting a Jesus Saves they'll let you go
without tyres or lights. You'd better go back down south.'
I remember Freddy singing 'My old Shako',

and would like to say, he'd given a hand for freedom
and would use his hook if anyone threatened his rights.
But the truth is, he'd have voted to build the Bomb
and to clean the long-haired larrikins out of the streets.

Turn like a jewel that small clear scene in your head:
cloud-blaze, leaf-glitter, loved faces, a radiant voice
singing 'Fifty years ago ...' Though you summon the dead
you cannot come as a child to your father's house.

15

20

25

30

35

40

1981

A Simple Story

A visiting conductor
        when I was seventeen,
took me back to his hotel room
        to cover the music scene.

I'd written a composition.
        Would wonders never cease —
here was a real musician
        prepared to hold my piece.

5

He spread my score on the counterpane
    with classic casualness,   10
and put one hand on the manuscript
    and the other down my dress.

It was hot as hell in The Windsor.
    I said I'd like a drink.
We talked across gin and grapefruit,   15
    and I heard the ice go clink

as I gazed at the lofty forehead
    of one who led the band,
and guessed at the hoarded sorrows
    no wife could understand.   20

I dreamed of a soaring passion
    as an egg might dream of flight,
while he read my crude sonata.
    If he'd said, 'That bar's not right,'

or, 'Have you thought of a coda?'   25
    or, 'Watch that first repeat,'
or, 'Modulate to the dominant,'
    he'd have had me at his feet.

But he shuffled it all together,
    and said, 'That's *lovely*, dear,'   30
as he put it down on the washstand
    in a way that made it clear

that I was no composer.
    And I being young and vain,
removed my lovely body   35
    from one who'd scorned my brain.

I swept off like Miss Virtue
    down dusty Roma Street,
and heard the goods trains whistle
    WHO? WHOOOOOO? in aching heat.   40
                              1981

Mother Who Gave Me Life

Mother who gave me life
I think of women bearing
women. Forgive me the wisdom
I would not learn from you.

It is not for my children I walk   5
on earth in the light of the living.
It is for you, for the wild
daughters becoming women,

anguish of seasons burning
backward in time to those other 10
bodies, your mother, and hers
and beyond, speech growing stranger

on thresholds of ice, rock, fire,
bones changing, heads inclining
to monkey bosom, lemur breast, 15
guileless milk of the word.

I prayed you would live to see
Halley's Comet a second time.
The Sister said, When she died
she was folding a little towel. 20

You left the world so, having lived
nearly thirty thousand days:
a fabric of marvels folded
down to a little space.

At our last meeting I closed 25
the ward door of heavy glass
between us, and saw your lace
crumple, fine threadbare linen

worn, still good to the last,
then, somehow, smooth to a smile 30
so I should not see your tears.
Anguish: remembered hours:

a lamp on embroidered linen,
my supper set out, your voice
calling me in as darkness 35
falls on my father's house.

1981

The Twins

Three years old when their mother died
in what my grandmother called
accouchement, my father labour,
they heard the neighbours intone
'A mercy the child went with her.' 5

Their father raised them somehow.
No one could tell them apart.
At seven they sat in school
in their rightful place, at the top
of the class, the first to respond 10
with raised arm and finger-flick.

When one gave the answer, her sister
repeated it under her breath.
An inspector accused them of cheating,
but later, in front of the class,   15
declared himself sorry, and taught us
a marvellous word: *telepathic.*

On Fridays, the story went,
they slept in the shed, barred in
from their father's rage as he drank   20
his dead wife back to his house.
For the rest of the week he was sober
and proud. My grandmother gave them
a basket of fruit. He returned it.
'We manage. We don't need help.'   25

They could wash their own hair, skin rabbits,
milk the cow, make porridge, clean boots.

Unlike most of the class I had shoes,
clean handkerchiefs, ribbons, a toothbrush.
We all shared the schoolsores and nits   30
and the language I learned to forget
at the gate of my welcoming home.

One day as I sat on the fence
my pinafore goffered, my hair
still crisp from the curlers, the twins   35
came by. I scuttled away
so I should not have to share
my Saturday sweets. My mother
saw me, and slapped me, and offered
the bag to the twins, who replied   40
one aloud and one sotto voce,
'No thank you. We don't like lollies.'

They lied in their greenish teeth
as they knew, and we knew.
                  Good angel   45
give me that morning again
and let me share, and spare me
the shame of my parents' rebuke.

                                 1988

OODGEROO OF THE TRIBE NOONUCCAL   *(1920–93)*

We are Going

For Grannie Coolwell

They came in to the little town
A semi-naked band subdued and silent,
All that remained of their tribe.
They came here to the place of their old bora ground
Where now the many white men hurry about like ants.   5
Notice of estate agent reads: 'Rubbish May Be Tipped Here'.
Now it half covers the traces of the old bora ring.
They sit and are confused, they cannot say their thoughts:
'We are as strangers here now, but the white tribe are the strangers.
We belong here, we are of the old ways.   10
We are the corroboree and the bora ground,
We are the old sacred ceremonies, the laws of the elders.
We are the wonder tales of Dream Time, the tribal legends told.
We are the past, the hunts and the laughing games, the wandering camp fires.
We are the lightning-bolt over Gaphembah Hill   15
Quick and terrible,
And the Thunder after him, that loud fellow.
We are the quiet daybreak paling the dark lagoon.
We are the shadow-ghosts creeping back as the camp fires burn low.
We are nature and the past, all the old ways   20
Gone now and scattered.
The scrubs are gone, the hunting and the laughter.
The eagle is gone, the emu and the kangaroo are gone from this place.
The bora ring is gone.
The corroboree is gone.   25
And we are going.'

                                                                    1964

No More Boomerang

No more boomerang
No more spear;
Now all civilized —
Colour bar and beer.

No more corroboree,   5
Gay dance and din.
Now we got movies,
And pay to go in.

Oodgeroo of the tribe Noonuccal   formerly known as Kath Walker

No more sharing
What the hunter brings.   10
Now we work for money,
Then pay it back for things.

Now we track bosses
To catch a few bob,
Now we go walkabout   15
On bus to the job.

One time naked,
Who never knew shame;
Now we put clothes on
To hide whatsaname.   20

No more gunya,
Now bungalow,
Paid by higher purchase
In twenty year or so.

Lay down the stone axe,   25
Take up the steel,
And work like a nigger
For a white man meal.

No more firesticks
That made the whites scoff.   30
Now all electric,
And no better off.

Bunyip he finish,
Now got instead
White fella Bunyip,   35
Call him Red.

Abstract picture now —
What they coming at?
Cripes, in our caves we
Did better than that.   40

Black hunted wallaby,
White hunt dollar;
White fella witch-doctor
Wear dog-collar.

No more message-stick;   45
Lubras and lads
Got television now,
Mostly ads.

Lay down the woomera,
Lay down the waddy.   50
Now we got atom-bomb.
End *every*body.

1966

Gifts

'I will bring you love,' said the young lover,
'A glad light to dance in your dark eye.
Pendants I will bring of the white bone,
And gay parrot feathers to deck your hair.'

But she only shook her head.   5

'I will put a child in your arms,' he said,
'Will be a great headman, great rain-maker.
I will make remembered songs about you
That all the tribes in all the wandering camps
Will sing for ever.'   10

But she was not impressed.

'I will bring you the still moonlight on the lagoon,
And steal for you the singing of all the birds;
I will bring down the stars of heaven to you,
And put the bright rainbow into your hand.'   15

'No,' she said, 'bring me tree-grubs.'

1966

ANNE ELDER   *(1918–76)*

At Amalfi

She climbed slowly in her black worn
not for mourning but as a custom, garb
to cover scars, inadequacies, repel
strangers and wipe hands. In the high square
the moorish cupola of a toy cathedral   5
winked gold and verdigris. With diffident
deliberation she approached the table and chair
of the town scribe.

       'I wish a letter written.
       With delicacy ... ' and she faltered   10
       and then, quick and low
       because she was poor:
       'What is the cost?'

       'A letter from the heart, Signora?
       The cost is high and no bargaining.   15
       Take it or leave it. Mille lire.'

       'I will take it,' she said,
       'when it is written and read
       to my satisfaction.'

For a moment their eyes met   20
in a clash of respect. She sat
and watched his hand as he wrote
dashingly the stock effusion
and read it to her with great
propriety. Mille lire   25
passed between them. She left
the letter on the table for him, a thing
as pale and fluttering and lovelorn
as a womanish glance.
By nature courteous he waited   30
until she was out of sight
to have to smile.

Italy. Where the tongue is easy
in plausible flower towards a reluctant caesura;
where the belvederes of the crumbling villas   35
hang over haze over turquoise enamel
of bays over emerald caverns: and where
the old gods of broken stone
recline discourteously in their grottoes
and do not smile. In a certain light   40
their pitted eyeballs roll
deploringly as though they had foreseen
through the wreaths of time
no laughing matter.

                                                           1976

The White Spider

Something white scuttled
into this black hole,
the body soft as a blob of pus,
the legs rapidly working.

This is a creature without camouflage,   5
its only weapon
being that it is impossible to kill
because of the squash,
so deep a revulsion shakes us
when something white scuttles   10
into a black hole.

It is a ghost of horror,
so small but of great power,
and horror terror horror terror
go its legs rapidly working.   15

                                                           1976

'ERN MALLEY'   ('1918–43')

Culture as Exhibit

'Swamps, marshes, borrow-pits and other
Areas of stagnant water serve
As breeding-grounds ...' Now
Have I found you, my Anopheles!
(There is a meaning for the circumspect)   5
Come, we will dance sedate quadrilles,
A pallid polka or a yelping shimmy
Over these sunken sodden breeding-grounds!
We will be wraiths and wreaths of tissue-paper
To clog the Town Council in their plans.   10
Culture forsooth! Albert, get my gun.

I have been noted in the reading-rooms
As a borer of calf-bound volumes
Full of scandals at the Court. (Milord
Had his hand upon that snowy globe   15
Milady Lucy's sinister breast ...) Attendants
Have peered me over while I chewed
Back-numbers of Florentine gazettes
(Knowst not, my Lucia, that he
Who has caparisoned a nun dies   20
With his twankydillo at the ready? ...)
But in all of this I got no culture till
I read a little pamphlet on my thighs
Entitled: 'Friction as a Social Process.'
What?   25
Look, my Anopheles,
See how the floor of Heav'n is thick
Inlaid with patines of etcetera ...
Sting them, sting them, my Anopheles.

                                                        1944

Petit Testament

In the twenty-fifth year of my age
I find myself to be a dromedary
That has run short of water between
One oasis and the next mirage
And having despaired of ever   5
Making my obsessions intelligible
I am content at last to be
The sole clerk of my metamorphoses.
Begin here:

In the year 1943   10
I resigned to the living all collateral images
Reserving to myself a man's
Inalienable right to be sad
At his own funeral.
(Here the peacock blinks the eyes   15
of his multipennate tail.)
In the same year
I said to my love (who is living)
Dear we shall never be that verb
Perched on the sole Arabian Tree   20
Not having learnt in our green age to forget
The sins that flow between the hands and feet
(Here the Tree weeps gum tears
Which are also real: I tell you
These things are real)   25
So I forced a parting
Scrubbing my few dingy words to brightness.

Where I have lived
The bed-bug sleeps in the seam, the cockroach
Inhabits the crack and the careful spider   30
Spins his aphorisms in the corner.
I have heard them shout in the streets
The chiliasms of the Socialist Reich
And in the magazines I have read
The Popular Front-to-Back.   35
But where I have lived
Spain weeps in the gutters of Footscray
Guernica is the ticking of the clock
The nightmare has become real, not as belief
But in the scrub-typhus of Mubo.   40

It is something to be at last speaking
Though in this No-Man's-language appropriate
Only to No-Man's-Land.
Set this down too:
I have pursued rhyme, image, and metre,   45
Known all the clefts in which the foot may stick,
Stumbled often, stammered,
But in time the fading voice grows wise
And seizing the co-ordinates of all existence
Traces the inevitable graph   50
And in conclusion:
There is a moment when the pelvis
Explodes like a grenade. I
Who have lived in the shadow that each act
Casts on the next act now emerge   55

As loyal as the thistle that in session
Puffs its full seed upon the indicative air.
I have split the infinitive. Beyond is anything.

1944

JACK DAVIS   *(b 1917)*

Camped in the Bush

Wind in the hair
Of a sleeping child
And the tree-tops wavering,
The starlight mild.

The moon's first peep   5
On the sand-plain rise,
And the fox in the shadows
With flashing eyes.

Over the campfire
The bat cries shrill   10
And a 'semi' snarls
On the Ten Mile Hill.

And the lonely whistle
Of the train at night,
Where my kingdom melted   15
In the city's light.

1983

Black Life

The howl of a dingo
Holden or Valiant
Talkin in lingo
That's life

Gettin security   5
Social I mean
Just out of puberty
jacket and jeans
My life

Knowing who friends are   10
enemies too
Uniforms uniforms
jackets of blue
Scum life

Gotta listen to music   15
gotta listen to song
sick of listening to people
saying I'm wrong
Crap life

Lethargic at sunrise   20
alive after dark
hauntin the fun dives
for a joint and a lark
Dream life

Blood in my nostrils   25
a nightmare afloat
a mosaic of meaning
caught in my throat
Black life

                                                    1992

JAMES MCAULEY   *(1917–76)*

Envoi

There the blue-green gums are a fringe of remote disorder
And the brown sheep poke at my dreams along the hillsides;
And there in the soil, in the season, in the shifting airs,
Comes the faint sterility that disheartens and derides.

Where once was a sea is now a salty sunken desert,   5
A futile heart within a fair periphery;
The people are hard-eyed, kindly, with nothing inside them,
The men are independent but you could not call them free.

And I am fitted to that land as the soul is to the body,
I know its contractions, waste, and sprawling indolence;   10
They are in me and its triumphs are my own,
Hard-won in the thin and bitter years without pretence.

Beauty is order and good chance in the artesian heart
And does not wholly fail, though we impede;
Though the reluctant and uneasy land resent   15
The gush of waters, the lean plough, the fretful seed.

                                                    1946

In the Twentieth Century

Christ, you walked on the sea,
But cannot walk in a poem,
Not in our century.

There's something deeply wrong
Either with us or with you.   5
Our bright loud world is strong

And better in some ways
Than the old haunting kingdoms:
I don't reject our days.

But in you I taste bread,   10
Freshness, the honey of being,
And rising from the dead:

Like yolk in a warm shell —
Simplicities of power,
And water from a well.   15

We live like diagrams
Moving on a screen.
Somewhere a door slams

Shut, and emptiness spreads.
Our loves are processes   20
Upon foam-rubber beds.

Our speech is chemical waste;
The words have a plastic feel,
An antibiotic taste.

And yet we dream of song   25
Like parables of joy.
There's something deeply wrong.

Like shades we must drink blood
To find the living voice
That flesh once understood.   30

1969

Because

My father and my mother never quarrelled.
They were united in a kind of love
As daily as the *Sydney Morning Herald*,
Rather than like the eagle or the dove.

I never saw them casually touch,   5
Or show a moment's joy in one another.
Why should this matter to me now so much?
I think it bore more hardly on my mother,

Who had more generous feelings to express.
My father had dammed up his Irish blood   10
Against all drinking praying fecklessness,
And stiffened into stone and creaking wood.

His lips would make a switching sound, as though
Spontaneous impulse must be kept at bay.
That it was mainly weakness I see now,   15
But then my feelings curled back in dismay.

Small things can pit the memory like a cyst:
Having seen other fathers greet their sons,
I put my childish face up to be kissed
After an absence. The rebuff still stuns   20

My blood. The poor man's curt embarrassment
At such a delicate proffer of affection
Cut like a saw. But home the lesson went:
My tenderness thenceforth escaped detection.

My mother sang *Because*, and *Annie Laurie*,   25
White Wings, and other songs; her voice was sweet.
I never gave enough, and I am sorry;
But we were all closed in the same defeat.

People do what they can; they were good people,
They cared for us and loved us. Once they stood   30
Tall in my childhood as the school, the steeple.
How can I judge without ingratitude?

Judgment is simply trying to reject
A part of what we are because it hurts.
The living cannot call the dead collect: 35
They won't accept the charge, and it reverts.

It's my own judgment day that I draw near,
Descending in the past, without a clue,
Down to that central deadness: the despair
Older than any hope I ever knew.   40
                                                                    1969

Pietà

A year ago you came
Early into the light.
You lived a day and night,
Then died; no-one to blame.

Once only, with one hand,   5
Your mother in farewell
Touched you. I cannot tell,
I cannot understand

A thing so dark and deep,
So physical a loss: 10
One touch, and that was all

She had of you to keep.
Clean wounds, but terrible,
Are those made with the Cross.

                                                                    1969

Childhood Morning — Homebush

The half-moon is a muted lamp
Motionless behind a veil.
As the eastern sky grows pale,
I hear the slow-train's puffing stamp

Gathering speed. A bulbul sings,   5
Raiding persimmon and fig.
The rooster in full glossy rig
Crows triumph at the state of things.

I make no comment; I don't know;
I hear that every answer's No,   10
But can't believe it can be so.

                                                    1971

In Northern Tasmania

Soft sodden fields. The new lambs cry,
And shorn ewes huddle from the cold.
Wattles are faintly tinged with gold.
A raven flies off silently.

Bare hawthorn thickets pearled with rain   5
Attract the thornbill and the wren.
Timber-trucks pass now and then,
And cows are moving in the lane.

At dusk I look out through old elms
Where mud-pools at the gatepost shine.   10
A way of life is in decline,

And only those who lived it know
What it is time overwhelms,
Which they must gradually let go.

                                                    1973

JUDITH WRIGHT   *(b 1915)*

The Cycads

Their smooth dark flames flicker at time's own root.
Round them the rising forests of the years
alter the climates of forgotten earth
and silt with leaves the strata of first birth.

Only the antique cycads sullenly   5
keep the old bargain life has long since broken;
and, cursed by age, through each chill century
they watch the shrunken moon, but never die,

for time forgets the promise he once made,
and change forgets that they are left alone.   10
Among the complicated birds and flowers
they seem a generation carved in stone.

Leaning together, down those gulfs they stare
over whose darkness dance the brilliant birds
that cry in air one moment, and are gone;   15
and with their countless suns the years spin on.

Take their cold seed and set it in the mind,
and its slow root will lengthen deep and deep
till, following, you cling on the last ledge
over the unthinkable, unfathomed edge   20
beyond which man remembers only sleep.

                                                       1949

The Child

To be alone in a strange place in spring
shakes the heart. The others are somewhere else;
the shouting, the running, the eating, the drinking —
never alone and thinking,
never remembering the Dream or finding the Thing,   5
always striving with your breath hardly above the water.
But to go away, to be quiet and go away,
to be alone in a strange place in spring
shakes the heart.

To hide in a thrust of green leaves   10
with the blood's leap and retreat
warm in you;
burning, going and returning
like a thrust of green leaves
out of your eyes, out of your hands and your feet —   15
like a noise of bees, growing, increasing;
to turn and to look up,
to find above you the enfolding, the exulting
may-tree
shakes the heart.   20

Spring is always the red tower of the may-tree,
alive, shaken with bees, smelling of wild honey,
and the blood a moving tree of may;
like a symbol for a meaning; like time's recurrent morning
that breaks and beckons, changes and eludes,   25
that is gone away;
that is never gone away.

                                                       1949

Camphor Laurel

Here in the slack of night
the tree breathes honey and moonlight.
Here in the blackened yard
smoke and time and use have marred,
leaning from that fantan gloom   5
the bent tree is heavy in bloom.

The dark house creaks and sways;
'Not like the old days.'
Tim and Sam and ragbag Nell,
Wong who keeps the Chinese hell,   10
the half-caste lovers, the humpbacked boy,
sleep for sorrow or wake for joy.

Under the house the roots go deep,
down, down, while the sleepers sleep;
splitting the rock where the house is set,   15
cracking the paved and broken street.
Old Tim turns and old Sam groans,
'God be good to my breaking bones;'
and in the slack of tideless night
the tree breathes honey and moonlight.   20
                                                        1949

Woman to Man

The eyeless labourer in the night,
the selfless, shapeless seed I hold,
builds for its resurrection day —
silent and swift and deep from sight
foresees the unimagined light.   5

This is no child with a child's face;
this has no name to name it by:
yet you and I have known it well.
This is our hunter and our chase,
the third who lay in our embrace.   10

This is the strength that your arm knows,
the arc of flesh that is my breast,
the precise crystals of our eyes.
This is the blood's wild tree that grows
the intricate and folded rose.   15

This is the maker and the made;
this is the question and reply;
the blind head butting at the dark,
the blaze of light along the blade.
Oh hold me, for I am afraid.   20
                                                        1949

Woman to Child

You who were darkness warmed my flesh
where out of darkness rose the seed.
Then all a world I made in me;
all the world you hear and see
hung upon my dreaming blood.   5

There moved the multitudinous stars,
and coloured birds and fishes moved.
There swam the sliding continents.
All time lay rolled in me, and sense,
and love that knew not its beloved.   10

O node and focus of the world;
I hold you deep within that well
you shall escape and not escape —
that mirrors still your sleeping shape
that nurtures still your crescent cell.   15

I wither and you break from me;
yet though you dance in living light
I am the earth, I am the root,
I am the stem that fed the fruit,
the link that joins you to the night.   20
                                              1949

Train Journey

Glassed with cold sleep and dazzled by the moon,
out of the confused hammering dark of the train
I looked and saw under the moon's cold sheet
your delicate dry breasts, country that built my heart;

and the small trees on their uncoloured slope   5
like poetry moved, articulate and sharp
and purposeful under the great dry flight of air,
under the crosswise currents of wind and star.

Clench down your strength, box-tree and ironbark.
Break with your violent root the virgin rock.   10
Draw from the flying dark its breath of dew
till the unliving come to life in you.

Be over the blind rock a skin of sense,
under the barren height a slender dance ...

I woke and saw the dark small trees that burn   15
suddenly into flowers more lovely than the white moon.
                                              1953

At Cooloolah

The blue crane fishing in Cooloolah's twilight
has fished there longer than our centuries.
He is the certain heir of lake and evening,
and he will wear their colour till he dies,

but I'm a stranger, come of a conquering people.   5
I cannot share his calm, who watch his lake,
being unloved by all my eyes delight in,
and made uneasy, for an old murder's sake.

Those dark-skinned people who once named Cooloolah
knew that no land is lost or won by wars,   10
for earth is spirit: the invader's feet will tangle
in nets there and his blood be thinned by fears.

Riding at noon and ninety years ago,
my grandfather was beckoned by a ghost —
a black accoutred warrior armed for fighting,   15
who sank into bare plain, as now into time past.

White shores of sand, plumed reed and paperbark,
clear heavenly levels frequented by crane and swan —
I know that we are justified only by love,
but oppressed by arrogant guilt, have room for none.   20

And walking on clean sand among the prints
of bird and animal, I am challenged by a driftwood spear
thrust from the water; and, like my grandfather,
must quiet a heart accused by its own fear.

                                                    1955

Eve to Her Daughters

It was not I who began it.
Turned out into draughty caves,
hungry so often, having to work for our bread,
hearing the children whining,
I was nevertheless not unhappy.   5
Where Adam went I was fairly contented to go.
I adapted myself to the punishment: it was my life.

But Adam, you know ...!
He kept on brooding over the insult,
over the trick They had played on us, over the scolding.   10
He had discovered a flaw in himself
and he had to make up for it.

Outside Eden the earth was imperfect,
the seasons changed, the game was fleet-footed,
he had to work for our living, and he didn't like it.   15
He even complained of my cooking
(it was hard to compete with Heaven).

So he set to work.
The earth must be made a new Eden
with central heating, domesticated animals,   20
mechanical harvesters, combustion engines,
escalators, refrigerators,
and modern means of communication
and multiplied opportunities for safe investment
and higher education for Abel and Cain   25
and the rest of the family.
You can see how his pride had been hurt.

In the process he had to unravel everything,
because he believed that mechanism
was the whole secret — he was always mechanical-minded.   30
He got to the very inside of the whole machine
exclaiming as he went, So this is how it works!
And now that I know how it works, why, I must have invented it.
As for God and the Other, they cannot be demonstrated,
and what cannot be demonstrated   35
doesn't exist.
You see, he had always been jealous.

Yes, he got to the centre
where nothing at all can be demonstrated.
And clearly he doesn't exist; but he refuses   40
to accept the conclusion.
You see, he was always an egotist.

It was warmer than this in the cave;   43
there was none of this fall-out.
I would suggest, for the sake of the children,   45
that it's time you took over.

But you are my daughters, you inherit my own faults of character;
you are submissive, following Adam   48
even beyond existence.
Faults of character have their own logic   50
and it always works out.
I observed this with Abel and Cain.

Perhaps the whole elaborate fable   53
right from the beginning
is meant to demonstrate this; perhaps it's the whole secret.   55
Perhaps nothing exists but our faults?
At least they can be demonstrated.

But it's useless to make   58
such a suggestion to Adam.
He has turned himself into God,   60
who is faultless, and doesn't exist.

                                                        1966

A Document

'Sign there.' I signed, but still uneasily.
I sold the coachwood forest in my name.
Both had been given me; but all the same
remember that I signed uneasily.

Ceratopetalum, Scented Satinwood: 5
a tree attaining seventy feet in height.
Those pale-red calyces like sunset light
burned in my mind. A flesh-pink pliant wood

used in coachbuilding. Difficult of access
(those slopes were steep). But it was World War Two.   10
Their wood went into bomber-planes. They grew
hundreds of years to meet those hurried axes.

Under our socio-legal dispensation
both name and woodland had been given me.
I was much younger then than any tree   15
matured for timber. But to help the nation

I signed the document. The stand was pure
(eight hundred trees perhaps). Uneasily
(the bark smells sweetly when you wound the tree)
I set upon this land my signature.   20

1966

To Another Housewife

Do you remember how we went,
on duty bound, to feed the crowd
of hungry dogs your father kept
as rabbit-hunters? Lean and loud,
half-starved and furious, how they leapt   5
against their chains, as though they meant
in mindless rage for being fed,
to tear our childish hands instead!

With tomahawk and knife we hacked
the flyblown tatters of old meat,   10
gagged at their carcass-smell, and threw
the scraps and watched the hungry eat.
Then turning faint, we made a pact
(two greensick girls), crossed hearts and swore
to touch no meat forever more.   15

How many cuts of choice and prime
our housewife hands have dressed since then —
these hands with love and blood imbrued —
for daughters, sons, and hungry men!
How many creatures bred for food   20
we've raised and fattened for the time

they met at last the steaming knife
that serves the feast of death-in-life!

And as the evening meal is served
we hear the turned-down radio
begin to tell the evening news
just as the family joint is carved.
O murder, famine, pious wars ...
Our children shrink to see us so,
in sudden meditation, stand
with knife and fork in either hand.

1966

This Time Alone

Here still, the mountain that we climbed
when hand in hand my love and I
first looked through one another's eyes
and found the world that does not die.

Wild fuchsia flowered white and red,   5
the mintbush opened to the bee.
Stars circled round us where we lay
and dawn came naked from the sea.

Its holy ordinary light
welled up and blessed us and was blessed.   10
Nothing more simple, nor more strange,
than earth itself was then our rest.

I face the steep unyielding rock,
I bleed against the cockspur's thorn,
struggling the upward path again,   15
this time alone. This time alone,

I turn and set that world alight.
Unfurling from its hidden bud
it widens round me, past my sight,
filled with my breath, fed with my blood;   20

the sun that rises as I stand
comes up within me gold and young;
my hand is sheltered in your hand,
the bread of silence on my tongue.

1970

Lament for Passenger Pigeons

(*'Don't ask for the meaning, ask for the use.'* — *Wittgenstein*)

The voice of water as it flows and falls
the noise air makes against earth-surfaces
have changed; are changing to the tunes we choose.

What wooed and echoed in the pigeon's voice?
We have not heard the bird. How reinvent   5
that passenger, its million wings and hues,

when we have lost the bird, the thing itself,
the sheen of life on flashing long migrations?
Might human musics hold it, could we hear?

Trapped in the fouling nests of time and space,   10
we turn the music on; but it is man,
and it is man who leans a deafening ear.

And it is man we eat and man we drink
and man who thickens round us like a stain.
Ice at the polar axis smells of me.   15

A word, a class, a formula, a use:
that is the rhythm, the cycle we impose.
The sirens sang us to the ends of sea,

and changed to us; their voices were our own,
jug jug to dirty ears in dirtied brine.   20
Pigeons and angels sang us to the sky

and turned to metal and a dirty need.
The height of sky, the depth of sea we are,
sick with a yellow stain, a fouling dye.

Whatever Being is, that formula,   25
it dies as we pursue it past the word.
We have not asked the meaning, but the use.

What is the use of water when it dims?
The use of air that whines of emptiness?
The use of glass-eyed pigeons caged in glass?   30

We listen to the sea, that old machine,
to air that hoarsens on earth-surfaces
and has no angel, no migrating cry.

What is the being and the end of man?
Blank surfaces reverb a human voice   35
whose echo tells us that we choose to die:

or else, against the blank of everything,
to reinvent that passenger, that bird-
siren-and-angel image we contain
essential in a constellating word.   40
To sing of Being, its escaping wing,
to utter absence in a human chord
and recreate the meaning as we sing.

                                                        1973

Smalltown Dance

Two women find the square-root of a sheet.
That is an ancient dance:
arms wide: together: again: two forward steps: hands meet
your partner's once and twice.
That white expanse   5
reduces to a neat
compression fitting in the smallest space
a sheet can pack in on a cupboard shelf.

High scented walls there were of flapping white
when I was small, myself.   10
I walked between them, playing Out of Sight.
Simpler than arms, they wrapped and comforted —
clean corridors of hiding, roofed with blue —
saying, Your sins too are made Monday-new;
and see, ahead   15
that glimpse of unobstructed waiting green.
Run, run before you're seen.

But women know the scale of possibility,
the limit of opportunity,
the fence,   20
how little chance
there is of getting out. The sheets that tug
sometimes struggle from the peg,
don't travel far. Might symbolise
something. Knowing where danger lies   25
you have to keep things orderly.
The household budget will not stretch to more.

And they can demonstrate it in a dance.
First pull those wallowing white dreamers down,
spread arms: then close them. Fold   30
those beckoning roads to some impossible world,
put them away and close the cupboard door.

                                                                1985

For a Pastoral Family

I *To my brothers*

Over the years, horses have changed to land-rovers.
Grown old, you travel your thousands of acres
deploring change and the wickedness of cities
and the cities' politics; hoping to pass to your sons
a kind of life you inherited in your generation.   5
Some actions of those you vote for stick in your throats.
There are corruptions one cannot quite endorse;
but if they are in our interests, then of course . . .

Well, there are luxuries still,
including pastoral silence, miles of slope and hill,   10
the cautious politeness of bankers. These are owed
to the forerunners, men and women
who took over as if by right a century and a half
in an ancient difficult bush. And after all
the previous owners put up little fight,   15
did not believe in ownership, and so were scarcely human.

Our people who gnawed at the fringe
of the edible leaf of this country
left you a margin of action, a rural security,
and left to me   20
what serves as a base for poetry,
a doubtful song that has a dying fall.

II *To my generation*

A certain consensus of echo, a sanctioning sound,
supported our childhood lives. We stepped
on sure and conceded ground.   25
A whole society
extended a comforting cover of legality.
The really deplorable deeds
had happened out of our sight, allowing us innocence.
We were not born, or there was silence kept.   30

If now there are landslides, if our field of reference
is much eroded, our hands show little blood.
We enter a plea: Not Guilty.
For the good of the Old Country,
the land was taken; the Empire had loyal service.   35
Would any convict us?
Our plea has been endorsed by every appropriate jury.

If my poetic style, your pastoral produce,
are challenged by shifts in the market
or a change of taste, at least we can go down smiling   40
with enough left in our pockets
to be noted in literary or local histories.

III *For today*

We were always part of a process. It has expanded.
What swells over us now is a logical spread
from the small horizons we made —   45
the heave of the great corporations
whose bellies are never full.
What sort of takeover bid
could you knock back now if the miners,
the junk-food firms or their processors want your land?   50

Or worse, leave you alone to hoe
small beans in a dwindling row?

The fears of our great-grandfathers —
apart from a fall in the English market —
were of spearwood, stone axes. Sleeping 55
they sprang awake at the crack
of frost on the roof, the yawn and stretching
of a slab wall. We turn on the radio
for news from the U.S.A. and U.S.S.R.
against which no comfort or hope 60
might come from the cattle prizes at the Show.

IV *Pastoral lives*

Yet a marginal sort of grace
as I remember it, softened our arrogant clan.
We were fairly kind to horses
and to people not too different from ourselves. 65
Kipling and A. A. Milne were our favourite authors
but Shelley, Tennyson, Shakespeare stood on our shelves —
suitable reading for women,
to whom, after all, the amenities had to be left.

An undiscursive lot (discourse is for the city) 70
one of us helped to found a university.
We respected wit in others,
though we kept our own for weddings,
unsure of the bona fides of the witty.

In England, we called on relatives, 75
assuming welcome for the sake of a shared bloodline,
but kept our independence.
We would entertain them equally, if they came
and with equal hospitality —
blood being thicker than thousands of miles of waters — 80
for the sake of Great-aunt Charlotte and old letters.

At church, the truncate, inarticulate
Anglican half-confession
'there is no health in us'
made us gag a little. We knew we had no betters 85
though too many were worse.
We passed on the collection-plate
adding a reasonable donation.

That God approved us was obvious.
Most of our ventures were prosperous. 90
As for the *Dies Irae*
we would deal with that when we came to it.

---

91 Dies Irae Latin hymn on the Last Judgement: 'Day of wrath'

V *Change*

At best, the men of our clan
have been, or might have been,
like Yeats' fisherman. 95
A small stream, narrow but clean,

running apart from the world.
Those hills might keep them so,
granite, gentle and cold.
But hills erode, streams go 100

through settlement and town
darkened by chemical silt.
Dams hold and slow them down,
trade thickens them like guilt.

All men grow evil with trade 105
as all roads lead to the city.
Willie Yeats would have said,
perhaps, the more the pity.

But how can we be sure?
Wasn't his chosen man 110
as ignorant as pure?
Keep out? Stay clean? Who can?

VI *Kinship*

Blue early mist in the valley. Apricots
bowing the orchard trees, flushed red with summer,
loading bronze-plaqued branches; 115
our teeth in those sweet buttock-curves. Remember
the horses swinging to the yards, the smell
of cattle, sweat and saddle-leather?
Blue ranges underlined the sky. In any weather
it was well, being young and simple, 120
letting the horses canter home together.

All those sights, smells and sounds we shared
trailing behind grey sheep, red cattle,
from Two-rail or Ponds Creek
through tawny pastures breathing pennyroyal. 125
In winter, sleety winds bit hands and locked
fingers round reins. In spring, the wattle.

With so much past in common,
on the whole we forgive each other
for the ways in which we differ — 130
two old men, one older woman.

95ff See W. B. Yeats's poem 'The Fisherman'.

When one of us falls ill,
the others may think less
of today's person, the lined and guarding face,

than of a barefoot child running careless through   135
long grass where snakes lie, or forgetting
to watch in the paddocks for the black Jersey bull.
Divisions and gulfs deepen
daily, the world over
more dangerously than now between us three.   140
Which is why, while there is time (though not our form at all)
I put the memories into poetry.

                                                            1985

Summer

This place's quality is not its former nature
but a struggle to heal itself after many wounds.

Upheaved ironstone, mudstone, quartz and clay
drank dark blood once, heard cries and the running of feet.

Now that the miners' huts are a tumble of chimney-stones   5
shafts near the river shelter a city of wombats.

Scabs of growth form slowly over the rocks.
Lichens, algae, wind-bent saplings grow.

I'll never know its inhabitants. Evening torchlight
catches the moonstone eyes of big wolf-spiders.   10

All day the jenny-lizard dug hard ground
watching for shadows of hawk or kookaburra.

At evening, her pearl-eggs hidden, she raked back earth
over the tunnel, wearing a wide grey smile.

In a burned-out summer, I try to see without words   15
as they do. But I live through a web of language.

                                                            1985

DAVID CAMPBELL   *(1915–79)*

We Took the Storms to Bed

We took the storms to bed at night
When first we loved. A spark
Sprang outward from our loins to light
Like genesis the dark.

On other things our minds were bent,   5
We did not hear the Word,

But locked like Sarah in her tent
The listening belly heard.

And though we wept, she laughed aloud
And fattened on her mirth: 10
As strange as creatures from a cloud
Our children walk the earth.

1962

Song for the Cattle

Down the red stock route
Hock-deep in mirage
Rode the three black drovers
Singing to the cattle.

And with them a young woman,   5
Perhaps some squatter's daughter
From homestead or township,
Who turned her horse easily.

To my mind she was as beautiful
As the barmaid in Brewarrina   10
Who works at the Royal. Men
Ride all day to see her.

Fine-boned as a brigalow
Yet ample as a granary,
She has teeth good for laughing   15
Or biting an apple.

I'm thinking of quitting
My mountain selection,
The milking at morning
And the lonely axe-echoes;   20

Of swapping my slab hut
For a rolled-up blanket
And heading north-westward
For a life in the saddle —

For the big mobs trailing   25
Down the empty stock routes,
A horned moon at evening
And songs round the campfire.

Yes, I'll soon be drinking
At the Royal in Brewarrina   30
And ambling through mirage
With the squatter's daughter.

1962

---

7 **Sarah**   See Genesis 18 and 21.

Among the Farms

May He who sent His only Son
To torment on a cross of wood,
Look twice on animal and man
Caught in the narrow ways of blood.
The moonlit fox who hunts by night　　　　　　5
The lambs that dance these frosted hills,
Hunts first from need and appetite,
Then for his own delight he kills.
I knew a man with violet eyes,
A countryman who loved his ewes　　　　　　10
And swore, by God, he'd put him wise,
And when the fox was in his noose,
He stripped the russet pelt for prize
And set the living creature loose.

　　　　　　　　　　　　　　　　1962

Mothers and Daughters

The cruel girls we loved
Are over forty,
Their subtle daughters
Have stolen their beauty;

And with a blue stare　　　　　　5
Of cool surprise,
They mock their anxious mothers
With their mothers' eyes.

　　　　　　　　　　　　　　　　1962

The Australian Dream

The doorbell buzzed. It was past three o'clock.
The steeple-of-Saint-Andrew's weathercock
Cried silently to darkness, and my head
Was bronze with claret as I rolled from bed
To ricochet from furniture. Light! Light　　　　　　5
Blinded the stairs, the hatstand sprang upright,
I fumbled with the lock, and on the porch
Stood the Royal Family with a wavering torch.

'We hope,' the Queen said, 'we do not intrude.
The pubs were full, most of our subjects rude.　　　　　　10
We came before our time. It seems the Queen's
Command brings only, "Tell the dead marines!"
We've come to you.' I must admit I'd half
Expected just this visit. With a laugh

That put them at their ease, I bowed my head.   15
'Your Majesty is most welcome here,' I said.
'My home is yours. There is a little bed
Downstairs, a boiler-room, might suit the Duke.'
He thanked me gravely for it and he took
Himself off with a wave. 'Then the Queen Mother?   20
She'd best bed down with you. There is no other
But my wide bed. I'll curl up in a chair.'
The Queen looked thoughtful. She brushed out her hair
And folded up *The Garter* on a pouf.
'Distress was the first commoner, and as proof   25
That queens bow to the times,' she said, 'we three
Shall share the double bed. Please follow me.'

I waited for the ladies to undress —
A sense of fitness, even in distress,
Is always with me. They had tucked away   30
Their state robes in the lowboy; gold crowns lay
Upon the bedside tables; ropes of pearls
Lassoed the plastic lampshade; their soft curls
Were spread out on the pillows and they smiled.
'Hop in,' said the Queen Mother. In I piled   35
Between them to lie like a stick of wood.
I couldn't find a thing to say. My blood
Beat, but like rollers at the ebb of tide.
'I hope your Majesties sleep well,' I lied.
A hand touched mine and the Queen said, 'I am   40
Most grateful to you, Jock. Please call me Ma'am.'

                                                                            1968

From Ku-ring-gai Rock Carvings

The Lovers

Making love for ten thousand years on a rockledge:
    The boronia springs up purple
   From the stone, and we lay together briefly
   For as long as those two lovers.

Spring

The Chase is mad with sex. Flowered trees sustain
    The act of love a season;
   While from stone loins wild orchids spring
   Whose pleasure is in intercourse with beetles.

Tench, 1791

Flesh carvings: for theft, before the assembled tribes,
     A convict was flogged. Daringa,
   Her nets forgotten, wept: while Barangaroo
   Threatened the lasher. A feckless if tender people.

The Underground

The underground is stirring. Orchid and bird
     Rise from the ashes, seed
   Spread beetle wings; and August's student tribes
   Step out between the blackened trees.

Hands

An artist blew ruddy ochre to outline his hand
     In a cave the water glazed.
   You can shake hands with this dead man.
   It teases the mind like John Keats' hand.

Baiame

Baiame, the All-father, is a big fellow with a big dong
     And the rayed crown of a god.
   He looks at his Sunday children who snigger and drive
   Home to their home-units. The god is not surprised.

                                                          1970

Crab

The crab sidled out
From its hiding place
Beneath my shoulder-blade

Fending with one enlarged claw
It scuttled sideways   5
And settled in an outcropping elbow

It left tiptoe tracks
In the hard sands of the ulna
Pain broke on the white beach

The crab has reached my hand   10
In the dreck at the high-tide line
Look what I have found.

                                                          1979

DOROTHY AUCHTERLONIE *(1915–91)*

Present Tense

'Nothing can ever come of it', he said.
— Outside the window, the white rose waved its head,
A late bird sang, insouciant, in the tree,
The sunset stained the river red.

'There is no future, none at all', he said.   5
— She stretched her arms up from the tumbled bed:
'What future has the river or the rose?' said she,
'The bird's song is, and nothing comes of red.'

He held her as the river holds the red
Stain of sunset; as, when the bird has fled,   10
The tree holds the song. 'Listen,' said she,
'Bird, rose and sunlit water sing from this bed.'

                                                                      1967

Chess by the Sea

The tide is rising with the wind,
Wave answers wind in the black pines,
The dolphin dies upon the beach —
Behind your head, the darkness shines.

Cold, cold upon the widowed sand,   5
Death opens up his ancient game;
His hooded face is white and wise.
He moves a pawn and names my name.

The firelight stains the squares you drew,
Teach me to play, the night is long: 10
The dolphin's eye is wild and sad,
The surf beats loud, the wind is strong.

Move for move you play Death's game;
Outside, I see his shadowed hand.
Love knows no rules, my moves are blind,   15
The dolphin dies upon the sand.

A game I have not played before:
Make all the moves, but tell no lies . . .
The first is last, a castle falls,
The queen is taken by surprise.   20

The queen is taken, now the king
Falls to your strategy of fear:
Death sweeps the pieces from the board.
The dolphin dies, you shed no tear.

                                                                      1967

JOHN MANIFOLD   *(1915–85)*

To Lucasta

On seeing no immediate hope of returning from the wars

The facts may be a bit obscure
   But all the legends show
A poet's blood is good manure
   Where freedom is to grow.

One dies at Zutphen, one in Greece,   5
   Dozens in France and Spain,
And now it looks, by all one reads,
   Like Greece's turn again.

The mode is exigent, my sweet;
   I cannot well refuse   10
To stoop and buckle to my feet
   My pair of dead men's shoes.

                         1948

Camouflage

Because the paint is not the shadow of branches
But dies like a fish on the concrete in the sun's glare,
Leaving the mechanical outline bare
To fool only the plane's mechanical glances;

Because this bonhomie is a skinny false   5
Mask on the iron skeleton of constraint
And freedom in newsprint only a smear of paint
Across the ancient menace, 'Believe, or else ...'

Therefore if I must choose I prefer to sing
The tommy gun, the clean, functional thing,   10
The singlehander, deadly to the rigid line,
Good at a job it doesn't attempt to conceal.

Give me time only to teach this hate of mine
The patience and integrity of the steel.

                         1948

Making Contact

Crazy as hell and typical of us:
The blackout bus-light stippling the passengers' shoulders,
Rumbling through darkness, and a whistling behind me smoulders
Into recognition — 'Comrade' — like that, in the bus.

So that minutes later I am talking across a table   5
At a tall girl laughing with friendliness and relief —
Soldier with pickup? Not likely. Nothing so brief.
I have found my footing, that's all; I am standing stable.

Oh, I was hungry for this! I needed reminding
What countless comrades are mine for the seeking and finding.   10
The numbness of isolation falls off me like sleep,

Something a light wind or a word could abolish;
And the girl comrade smiles, disclaiming the knowledge
That at any moment I could put my head in her lap and weep.

                                                                                          1948

Incognito

Every station in the country keeps a pony that was sent
     Late at night to fetch a doctor or a priest,
And has lived the life of Riley since that faraway event,
     But the stories don't impress me in the least;

For I once owned Incognito — what a jewel of a horse!   5
     He was vastly better bred than many men!
But they handicapped so savagely on every local course
     I was forced to dye him piebald now and then.

For I needed all the money that a sporting life entails,
     Having found the cost of living rather dear,   10
And my wife, the very sweetest little girl in New South Wales,
     Was presenting me with children every year.   12

We were spreading superphosphate one October afternoon
     When the missus said she felt a little sick:
We were not expecting Septimus (or Septima) so soon,   15
     But I thought I'd better fetch the doctor quick,

So I started for the homestead with the minimum delay,
     Where I changed, and put pomade on my moustache;
But before I reached the sliprails Incognito was away,
     And was heading for the township like a flash.   20

First he swam a flooded river, then he climbed a craggy range,
     And they tell me, though I haven't any proof,
That he galloped thro' the township to the telephone exchange,
     Where he dialled the doctor's number with his hoof.

Yes, he notified the doctor, and the midwife, and the vet,   25
     And he led them up the mountain to my door
Where he planted, panting, pondering, in a rivulet of sweat,
     Till he plainly recollected something more.

Then he stretched his muzzle towards me. He had something in his teeth,
 Which he dropped with circumspection in my hand;   30
And I recognised his offering as a contraceptive sheath,
 So I shot him. It was more than I could stand.

But I've bitterly repented that rash act of injured pride —
 It was not the way a sportsman should behave!
So I'm making my arrangements to be buried at his side,   35
 And to share poor Incognito's lonely grave.

               1971

JOHN BLIGHT   *(1913–95)*

The Oyster-eaters

I had heard the bird's name and searched with intent
the oyster banks, and a bird with a red bill
and a hingeing, unoiled note gave a high call
in a flat treble. Whatever the bird-voice meant,
it sounded ajar — a door protestingly forced,   5
a bivalve opening — shell from shell divorced.

I saw the oyster-bird with red cockade-like beak
 — white, blue, red (a tricolour) plump as a chef;
and it could well prepare banquets to last a week:
oysters — hors-d'oeuvres. Somewhere around a cliff,   10
a door's answering squeak, and two birds dined together
at turn of the tide, with wind blowing us salty weather.

               1954

Crab

Shellfish and octopus and all the insane
thinking of the undersea to us is lost;
at most is food, in our higher plane.
But what of this submarine ghost-
life, without its meddling monkey? Can   5
the crab regenerate into prototype merman?
Sea, of nightmare pressure and mask-
green faces in the gloom — what is your task
in creation, or is it over? Has space
such a tragedy of planets trapped? Was   10
Eden thus? Oh, pressures which the lace
sponge of the brain survives! What has
the life of the sea of my ignorance
but such creatures; much of this wild-shaped chance?

               1963

Sea Level

Over this flat-pan sea, this mud haven,
this shelf of the sea-floor, sea-birds paddle
and the red mud raddles the sea.
You are on creation's level. Proven
your lowly origin, where, in one puddle,   5
sea-snails and your toes agree —
the same spasms and rhythms. Stub
on a rock, or a sharp stab of a beak;
they draw in. Pain is the one language
spoken to them. You, in the sky, snub   10
your feet. Impediments! But can you take
your brain's cloud and drift, disengage
those 'body's worms'? Try: disconnect
the thought from their feeling, and soon the soul is wrecked.

1963

DOUGLAS STEWART   *(1913–85)*

Flying Ants

Pouring straight up in their excited millions
Like smoke from the hot earth in narrow rings
The flying termites, blind in their own bright shower,
Whirl in a crystal tower not there at all:
For while the glimmering column holds them safe   5
To dance their delirious dance of summer and love
How frail and small it floats in the evening's brilliance:
And, striking in shafts of light that burn their wings,
Infinite space pierces the crystal wall
Where thought itself floats glinting in that tower.   10

1952

The Fungus

Leave it alone. Don't touch it! Oh, but don't touch it.
That crimson is nature's warning, those specks that blotch it
Reek with their leathery stench of corruption and poison.
And say it is only a fungus, speckled and crimson
With gaping throat and tentacles wavering out   5
Under a log in the sun; but then how it loves
To hide in the dark where the grass is thick and sour —
Leave it alone! For white like the egg of a snake
In its shell beside it another begins to break,
And under those crimson tentacles, down that throat,   10
Secret and black still gurgles the oldest ocean
Where, evil and beautiful, sluggish and blind and dumb,

Life breathes again, stretches its flesh and moves
Now like a deep-sea octopus, now like a flower,
And does not know itself which to become.   15

                                                                1952

B Flat

Sing softly, Muse, the Reverend Henry White
Who floats through time as lightly as a feather
Yet left one solitary gleam of light
Because he was the Selborne naturalist's brother

And told him once how on warm summer eves   5
When moonlight filled all Fyfield to the brim
And yearning owls were hooting to their loves
On church and barn and oak-tree's leafy limb

He took a common half-a-crown pitch-pipe
Such as the masters used for harpsichords   10
And through the village trod with silent step
Measuring the notes of those melodious birds

And found that each one sang, or rather hooted,
Precisely in the measure of B flat.
And that is all that history has noted;   15
We know no more of Henry White than that.

So, softly, Muse, in harmony and conformity
Pipe up for him and all such gentle souls
Thus in the world's enormousness, enormity,
So interested in music and in owls: 20

For though we cannot claim his crumb of knowledge
Was worth much more than virtually nil
Nor hail him for vast enterprise or courage,
Yet in my mind I see him walking still

With eager ear beneath his clerical hat   25
Through Fyfield village sleeping dark and blind,
Oh surely as he piped his soft B flat
The most harmless, the most innocent of mankind.

                                                                1967

---

4 **Selborne naturalist**   Gilbert White (1720–93), English naturalist, who wrote *The Natural History and Antiquities of Selborne*

KENNETH MACKENZIE   *(1913–55)*

The Snake

Withdrawing from the amorous grasses
from the warm and luscious water
the snake is soul untouched by both
nor does the fire of day through which it passes
mark it or cling. Immaculate navigator   5
it carries death within its mouth.

Soul is the snake that moves at will
through all the nets of circumstance
like the wind that nothing stops,
immortal movement in a world held still   10
by rigid anchors of intent or chance
and ropes of fear and stays of hopes.

It is the source of all dispassion
the voiceless life above communion
secret as the spring of wind   15
nor does it know the shames of self-confession
the weakness that enjoys love's coarse dominion
or the betrayals of the mind.

Soul is the snake the cool viator
sprung from a shadow on the grass   20
quick and intractable as breath
gone as it came like the everlasting water
reflecting god in immeasurable space —
and in its mouth it carries death.

                                        (written 1951) 1972

Two Trinities

Are you ready? soul said again
smiling deep in the dark
where mind and I live passionately
grain rasping across grain
in a strangled question-mark   5
— or so we have lived lately.

I looked through the hollow keyhole
at my wife not young any more
with my signature on her forehead
and her spirit hers and whole   10
unsigned by me — as before
we knew each other, and wed.

I looked at my grown daughter
cool and contained as a flower
whose bees I shall not be among —   15
vivid as white spring water
full of womanish power
like the first phrases of a song.

I looked at my son, and wept
in my mouth's cave to see   20
the seed ready for sowing
and the harvest unready to be reaped —
green fruit shocked from the tree,
the bird killed on the wing.

Well? soul said and I said,   25
Mind and I are at one
to go with you now — finally
joined now to be led —
for our place here is gone:
we are not among those three.   30

Soul said, *Now come with me.*

                                                   (written 1952) 1972

BARBARA GILES   *(b 1912)*

In the park, looking

I'm not too old to like the shape of a man,
his walk, the set of his head on his shoulders,
the strong legs, well fleshed and that bright
black-browed glance. There's a nose that I like,
admiring blank-faced. If you should   5
see me looking, if you saw me at all,
you'd think I'm reminded of someone,
husband, son, grandson, not that I look at you
as a woman looks at a man who stirs her.

The heart lifts, it's good to see a fine man,   10
to think, there goes a man I could love.
I'm looking at you, not remembering.
But as I well know, you don't see me,
old women are almost invisible. If I do catch your eye,
likely enough you'll be thinking, 'She has a look of my mother.'   15
                                                                  1984

Moonlighting

After the children are grown and gone,
long nights of love,
the house once more their own.

And now there seems no measure
to love's artfulness,
no limits to their pleasure.   5

The honeyed fruit hangs low,
plucked, infant-innocent,
its taste sophisticate.

They had no inklings of such late-won rapture   10
and no words for it,
only their joyous laughter.

1993

Stuff

The thingness, thusness, whatness
of this and that — continual ravishment,
now cool and smooth, now soft and furry
and these, perfumed and those, how crisp to bite.

And there's a chair, relaxing while it waits   5
with such delicious curve of leg:
This gleaming bowl, the indifferent mirror — needing
nothing — no smudge-fingered exploration.

These knives, aligned, so excellent in sharpness
with handle ready for hand, require no flesh,
unlike the gluttonous users, hungry-eyed,   10
voracious, butcherly, complacent,

which surely I am not, but frangible,
frail as your gift, that vase
of particoloured glass, which of itself   15
sundered last night, doubting its quiddity.

1997

ROLAND ROBINSON   *(1912–92)*

Inscription

I made my verses of places where I made my fires;
of the dark trees standing against the blue-green night
with the first stars coming; of the bare plains where a bird
broke into running song, and of the wind-cold scrub
where the bent trees sing to themselves, and of the night   5
dark about me, the fire dying out, and the ashes left.

1944

And the Blacks are Gone

But this sea will not die, this sea that brims
beyond the grass-tree spears and the low, close scrub,
or lies at evening limitless after rain,
or breaks in languorous lines to the long golden beach
that the blacks called Gera, before the white man came.   5
And the blacks are gone, and I frighten the crimson-wing
and the wallaby in gullies where the rock-pools lie
fringed by acacias and stunted gums, and I come
out onto open ridges flowering before this sea.
And the blacks are gone, and we are not more than they,   10
tonight as I make my camp by the rain-stilled sea.

                                                        1944

The Cradle

A corrugated iron shack. One room.
Tree-posts its uprights, saplings, axe-
trimmed, its beams and rafters. It stands
fast, no matter how the huge hands
of mountain winds grasp it. Rain   5
is tumult, deafening peace on the roof.

Rain-forest rises behind it, a maze
of cicada-sound. Tonight you will hear
the creek like rain as, just on dark,
the cat-bird meows and yowls from the edge   10
of the jungle-forest. Your eyes will daze,
close in lamplight over your book.

The kettle sings on the 'Waratah' stove.
Pots and pans gleam on their ledge
above. You will wish dawn not to come.   15
You will sleep, a child, as the hoarse wind
cradles you in the trees, as the arm
of the mountain holds the light of the farm.

                                                        1967

The Two Sisters

Related by Manoowa from Milingimbi

On the Island of the Spirits of the Dead,
one of two sisters talks.
'We must make a canoe and follow the way
the sun walks.'

The Two Sisters   This and the next three poems are lightly rewritten into verse from the stories as told to Robinson.

They've filled the canoe with sacred   5
rannga things,
and paddled away into the night
singing ritual songs.

'Sister, look back!' the first sister calls.
'Do you see the morning star?'   10
Her sister looks out along their wake.
'Nothing. Nothing's there.'

The little sister has fallen asleep.
Again her sister calls,
'Sister, look back for the morning star.'   15
'Nothing. Nothing at all.'

A spear of light is thrown across
the sea and lies far
ahead upon the sisters' course.
'Sister, the morning star.'   20

The sun comes up and walks the sky.
A fish with whiskers swims
ahead, and leaps out of the sea,
while the sisters sing.

Day and night, and day and night,   25
the sisters are gone
with the morning star and the leaping fish
and the sky-walking sun.

The sisters, hoar with dried salt spray,
the semen of the sea,   30
make landfall where parrots scream
from paperbark trees.

The sisters beach the bark canoe,
unload the *rannga* things.
They thrust one in the earth. From there   35
the first goanna comes.

They've gone inland. Their digging sticks
make sacred springs.
They leave behind them *rannga* forms
for all living things.   40

Out gathering food, the sisters have hung
their dilly-bags in a tree.
While they're away, men come and steal
their sacred ceremonies.

The sisters hear men singing and   45
song-sticks' 'tjong-tjong'.
'Cover your ears. We cannot hear
the sacred song.'

'O, all our sacred ceremonies
belong now to the men.   50
We must gather food, and bear
and rear children.'

                                                                  1970

Mapooram

Related by Fred Biggs, Ngeamba tribe, Lake Carjelligo

Go out and camp somewhere. You're lying down.
A wind comes, and you hear this *Mapooram*.
'What's that?' you say. Why, that's a *Mapooram*.
You go and find that tree rubbing itself.
It makes all sorts of noises in the wind.
It might be like a sheep, or like a cat
or like a baby crying, or someone calling,
a sort of whistling-calling when the wind
comes and swings and rubs two boughs like that.

A *wirreengun*, a clever-feller, sings
that tree. He hums a song, a *Mapooram*:
a song to close things up, or bring things out,
a song to bring a girl, a woman from that tree.
She's got long hair, it falls right down her back.
He's got her for himself. He'll keep her now.

One evening, it was sort of rainy-dark,
they built a mia-mia, stripping bark.
You've been out in the bush sometime and seen
them old dry pines with loose bark coming off.
You get a lot of bark from those old dry pines,
before they rot and go too far, you know.
That woman from the tree, she pulled that bark.
It tore off, up and up the tree. It pulled
her up, into the tree, up, up into the sky.
Well, she was gone. That was the end of it.
No more that *wirreengun* could call her back.

'*Mapooram. Mapooram.*' 'What's that?' you say.
Why, that's two tree boughs rubbing in the wind.

                                                                  1970

Billy Bamboo

Related by Billy Bamboo, Wallaga Lake

This wild cherry tree makes a good shade.
I lie down under it and go to sleep.
By and by I hear a roaring sound.
'Oh, thunder storm coming up. I'll soon
fix him.' I break a branch off this tree   5
and burn it. The smoke goes straight up
into the sky. Those big rolling clouds
divide, one cloud goes one way, one cloud
the other way. You hear thunder rolling
down the sky.   10

This is our sacred tree.
It belongs to all the blackfellers. You're a bit
of a blackfeller, you try it. You'll say,
'That's true what old Billy Bamboo says.'

Well, my tribe got shot up. A white man found   15
a baby near the camp and took it back
to the station on his horse. That baby grew up
to be my father.

A Victorian tribe fought
the Wallaga Lake tribe. An old man and his wife   20
were running away along a path, carrying
a baby with them.
They saw a big log hollowed out
by fire. They put the baby inside the log
and ran on.   25

A white man was riding his horse.
He heard a baby crying in the bush.
He came to the big log and listened.
He saw the pale feet of the baby sticking out.
He took the child and reared it and gave it
his name. And that baby was my mother.

Me? I'm Billy Bamboo. Anyone will tell you.
The buckjump rider, the bare knuckle fighter.
We used to stand toe to toe. We'd go down
to the creek and wash the blood off our faces
and come back and into it again. I was a flash
young feller in jodhpurs, riding boots and hat.

No, I can't see as well as I used to,
and I have to get about with this stick now.
You should have seen the old people. They would
have told you what the emu told the kangaroo.
Those old people are all gone from this mission.
They're all ghosts walking around in this place.

1970

Captain Cook

Related by Percy Mumbulla, Wallaga Lake

Tungeei, that was her native name.
She was a terrible tall woman
who lived at Ulladulla.
She had six husbands,
an' buried the lot.   5

She was over a hundred, easy,
when she died.
She was tellin' my father,
they were sittin' on the point
that was all wild scrub.   10

The big ship came and anchored
out at Snapper Island.
He put down a boat
an' rowed up the river
into Bateman's Bay.   15

He landed on the shore of the river,
the other side from where the
church is now.
When he landed he gave the Kurris clothes,
an' those big sea-biscuits.   20
Terrible hard biscuits they was.

When they were pullin' away to go back
to the ship, these wild Kurris
were runnin' out of the scrub.
They'd stripped right off again.   25
They were throwin' the clothes an' biscuits
back at Captain Cook
as his men were pullin' away in the boat.

                                                    1970

WILLIAM HART-SMITH   *(1911–90)*

Kellerberin 6410

'Where civilisation is a remote
glint of roofshine
in one vast sea of wheat.'

    Civilisation is a house
    sixteen miles as the road runs   5
    out of town as the crow cries
    as the black and white magpies
    yodel in the afternoon.

The main road runs right through
these wheatbelt towns with their   10
sagging wooden houses and their
one storey shops with fly-spotted
plastic strips over open doorways
and the smell of fish and chips.

    A small winking glint   15
    in the hot distance
    is the house.

'One longed for someone to come.'

    Scarify the sandy soil in May
    put in the Super and sow   20
    watch the landscape turn to
    green under the May rains
    on into June and September
    when the rains go
    and the grain ripens   25
    and the heat
    would bake the ripe wheat
    as grain still in head
    before it is bread.

'The stillness.   30
One longed for someone to come.'

    There's a silo down at Tammin
    where the quotas go.

And now the scrub-cover's gone
when the harvest's in   35
the fields of brittle stubble
give nothing back to the sky
but the sweet acrid smell of dusty hay.

'Annual rainfall's down
on what it was.'   40

    It's a resentful landscape
    and a bored town. Neutral.
    I bring you all a message from the sun.

'Open the gate. This was the garden
Those were   45
roses. Even the cactus is dead.'

    There's a gaping hole in the side
    of the implement shed
    and through it I see
    I see   50
    someone looking

'One longed for someone to come.'

an old brass bedstead
a child's tricycle
and a tin kettledrum.   55

'Mother said,
"I won't go back because
I'd rather see the garden as it was."'

1975

Relativity

The main reason why dogs
love to sit in cars
is because
when a dog's inside
a car doesn't move   5

When the doors
of the small intimate room
with master and mistress in it
close

the room bucks   10
and barks and makes
most unusual noises
and odours

then houses get up and run
trees get up and run   15
posts get up and run
and telegraph poles

in fact everything does

With his nose thrust out
bang in the eye of the galloping wind   20
his right ear streaming
like a strip of rag in a gale

he for a change can sit still
chin on the window-sill

and let the world do all the running about   25

1985

ELIZABETH RIDDELL   *(b 1910)*

The Soldier in the Park

All day he slept, his mouth on pennyroyal,
His eyelids couched on clover,
His fingers twined around the stems of grass,

Doves near him, and the sun upon his shoulder.
The earth drowsed under him,   5
And the clouds slid over.
The boats on the bay rocked, the willows sighed.

How long ago was that?

That was in summer, some time before he died.

1948

The Letter

I take my pen in hand
> *there was a meadow*
beside a field of oats, beside a wood,
beside a road, beside a day spread out
green at the edges, yellow at the heart.   5
The dust lifted a riffle, a finger's breadth;
the word of the wood pigeon travelled slow,
a slow half pace behind the tick of time.

To tell you I am well and thinking of you
and of the walk through the meadow, and of another walk   10
along the neat piled ruin of the town
under a pale heaven empty of all but death
and rain beginning. The river ran beside.

It has been a long time since I wrote. I have no news.
I put my head between my hands and hope   15
my heart will choke me. I put out my hand
to touch you and touch air. I turn to sleep
and find a nightmare, hollowness and fear.

And by the way, I have had no letter now
For eight weeks, it must be   20
a long eight weeks
because you have nothing to say, nothing at all,
not even to record your emptiness
or guess what's to become of you, without love.

I know that you have cares   25
ashes to shovel, broken glass to mend
and many a cloth to patch before the sunset.

Write to me soon and tell me how you are
if you still tremble, sweat and glower, still stretch
a hand for me at dusk, play me the tune,   30
show me the leaves and towers, the lamb, the rose.

Because I always wish to hear of you
and feel my heart swell and the blood run out
at the ungraceful syllable of your name
said through the scent of stocks, the little snore of fire,   35
the shoreless waves of symphony, the murmuring night.

I will end this letter now. I am yours with love.
Always with love, with love.

1948

Occasions of Birds

I

I heard on the radio how birds in Assam
lifted like a cloud over the camellia forest
and flew to a village in the last light.
There it was warm and filled with other wings
transparent and flickering.   5
They dashed their bodies against the smoking lamps and fell
into the street
onto the trodden stems of water hyacinth.

Women who had been picking tea
all day on the hillside   10
came down to the village
holding their baskets against their muslin skirts
and their skirts away from the bleeding feathers
in fear and surprise. There was hardly a sound
when the wings ceased to beat.   15

It was south of the Kahsi hills where the Brahmaputra flows
the birds flowed to their death in the soft night.

II

In Dar-es-Salaam the morning lay on us like wet silk.
We bought fruit in thin slices, and yellow bead rings,
waiting for the news of the tornado, the hurricane,   20
the cyclone, the typhoon
crouched in the opaque sky.

We ran before the wind
to Malagasy, to Reunion, to Mauritius
where it caught us, cast us on the beach   25
beside the tourist cabins and the sugar cane,
both with rats.

Port Louis was under water, we saw with dismay.
The corpses of duck dinners
floated in the dark gutter under the blind windows   30
and past closed schools.
Reflected in this aberrant lake, old cool houses
suitable for provincial nobles and for slaves
brooded under wisteria. Their columns were erected
in memory of the Loire.   35

I remembered about the pink pigeons of Mauritius.
They have tiny heads and supplicating voices,

poor flakes of pink driven out when the forest was felled
to make way for the chateaux.
There is not one left to complain. 40

III

Governor Hunter despatched
many a live bird to England
to bleach in the fog, attempt a trill
in Hove or Lockerbie
and marvel through the bars 45
at rain on the pale honeyed flowers
and honeyeaters dancing on the rain.

As Governor Hunter and his men marched west
the sun struck gold from epaulettes
and sparkled on the cages ready for the feather, 50
the bright eye, the tender claw, the beak
of the lyrebird and the cockatoo
(the rosy one, the sulphur-crested screamer, the shining black)
and the paradise parrot of which Leach says
'it is an exquisite creature, 55
in general green below and blue above'
(like forest, like sky)
'with red shoulders'
(at sunset out-sparkling the governor's gold)
'and a red forehead. It nests in sandhills.' 60

One hundred and eighty years later
a man is out there in the dunes
searching for the paradise parrot.
Listen as he walks, crab-scuttle on the sand.
He has not much to offer this bird 65
which saw the gold and heard the sound of fife and drum.

IV

We were in a foreign country
reading about another foreign country —
well, hardly foreign at all
since once we saw it from a deck, 70
a smudge of cloud on cloud,
Mangere Island in the lonely Chathams
twelve thousand miles away in the long fall
of grey seas — reading about its five black robins
last of their race, 75
news because they were about to die.
As with a few Indians along the Amazon,
robins and Indians, it's all news,
small items only because so far away,
and small. 80

Rain sluiced the colonnades
where they sell the *International Herald Tribune*
(how to rent a palazzo, share a car to Munich, learn Chinese)
with baseball scores from home.
Rare robins, the item said,   85
rare black robins, three females and two males,
the usual ratio, we're used to it.

It's cold on Mangere. The waves swing in across the rocks
great shawls of kelp.
Three men were on Mangere   90
with tents and playing cards and paperbacks,
a radio, tins of butter, binoculars
to watch the robins, and suddenly spied
after fifteen years the orange-breasted parakeet
risen again, a flame rekindled from the phoenix fire.   95
What next? The black stilt or the kakapo?
The parrot like an owl that walks, stately, instead of flying?
We doubt if they'll turn up.

The birds will be reprogrammed. Not much to do
with chirping, building nests or catching flies   100
or even flying. It's cold on Mangere
for orange-breasted parakeets and such.

                                                                                                   1987

A. D. HOPE   *(b 1907)*

Australia

A Nation of trees, drab green and desolate grey
In the field uniform of modern wars,
Darkens her hills, those endless, outstretched paws
Of Sphinx demolished or stone lion worn away.

They call her a young country, but they lie: 5
She is the last of lands, the emptiest,
A woman beyond her change of life, a breast
Still tender but within the womb is dry.

Without songs, architecture, history:
The emotions and superstitions of younger lands,   10
Her rivers of water drown among inland sands,
The river of her immense stupidity

Floods her mountainous tribes from Cairns to Perth.
In them at last the ultimate men arrive
Whose boast is not: 'we live' but 'we survive',   15
A type who will inhabit the dying earth.

And her five cities, like five teeming sores,
Each drains her: a vast parasite robber-state
Where second-hand Europeans pullulate
Timidly on the edge of alien shores.   20

Yet there are some like me turn gladly home
From the lush jungle of modern thought, to find
The Arabian desert of the human mind,
Hoping, if still from the deserts the prophets come,

Such savage and scarlet as no green hills dare   25
Springs in that waste, some spirit which escapes
The learned doubt, the chatter of cultured apes
Which is called civilization over there.

(written 1939) 1960

Flower Poem

Not these cut heads posed in a breathless room,
Their crisp flesh screaming while the cultured eye
Feeds grublike on the double martyrdom:
The insane virgins lusting as they die!
Connoisseurs breathe the rose's agony;   5
Between their legs the hairy flowers in bloom

Thrill at the amorous comparison.
As the professor snips the richest bud
For his lapel, his scalpel of reason
Lies on the tray; the class yawns for its food —   10
Only transfusion of a poem's blood
Can save them, bleeding from their civilization —

Not this cut flower but the entire plant
Achieves its miracle from soil and wind,
Rooted in dung, dirt, dead men's bones; the scent   15
And glory not in themselves an end; the end:
Fresh seeding in some other dirty mind,
The ache of its mysterious event

As its frail root fractures the subsoil, licks
At the damp stone in passing, drives its life   20
Deeper to split the ancient bedded rocks
And penetrates the cave beneath, it curls
In horror from that roof. There in its grief
The subterranean river roars, the troll's knife
Winks on his whetstone and the grinning girls   25
Sit spinning the bright fibre of their sex.

(written 1940) 1955

The Gateway

Now the heart sings with all its thousand voices
To hear this city of cells, my body, sing.
The tree through the stiff clay at long last forces
Its thin strong roots and taps the secret spring.

And the sweet waters without intermission   5
Climb to the tips of its green tenement;
The breasts have borne the grace of their possession,
The lips have felt the pressure of content.

Here I come home: in this expected country
They know my name and speak it with delight.   10
I am the dream and you my gates of entry,
The means by which I waken into light.

(written 1942) 1955

Ascent into Hell

Little Henry, too, had a great notion of singing.
        History of the Fairchild family

I, too, at the mid-point, in a well-lit wood
Of second-rate purpose and mediocre success,
Explore in dreams the never-never of childhood,
Groping in daylight for the key of darkness;

Revisit, among the morning archipelagoes,   5
Tasmania, my receding childish island;
Unchanged my prehistoric flora grows
Within me, marsupial territories extend:

There is the land-locked valley and the river,
The Western Tiers make distance an emotion,   10
The gum trees roar in the gale, the poplars shiver
At twilight, the church pines imitate an ocean.

There, in the clear night, still I listen, waking
To a crunch of sulky wheels on the distant road;
The marsh of stars reflects a starry croaking;   15
I hear in the pillow the sobbing of my blood

As the panic of unknown footsteps marching nearer,
Till the door opens, the inner world of panic
Nightmares that woke me to unawakening terror
Birthward resume their still inscrutable traffic.   20

Memory no more the backward, solid continent,
From island to island of despairing dream
I follow the dwindling soul in its ascent;
The bayonets and the pickelhauben gleam

Among the leaves, as, in the poplar tree,   25
They find him hiding. With an axe he stands

Above the German soldiers, hopelessly
Chopping the fingers from the climbing hands.

Or, in the well-known house, a secret door
Opens on empty rooms from which a stair   30
Leads down to a grey, dusty corridor,
Room after room, ominous, still and bare.

He cannot turn back, a lurking horror beckons
Round the next corner, beyond each further door.
Sweating with nameless anguish then he wakens;   35
Finds the familiar walls blank as before.

Chased by wild bulls, his legs stick fast with terror.
He reaches the fence at last — the fence falls flat.
Choking, he runs, the trees he climbs will totter.
Or the cruel horns, like telescopes, shoot out.   40

At his fourth year the waking life turns inward.
Here on his Easter Island the stone faces
Rear meaningless monuments of hate and dread.
Dreamlike within the dream real names and places

Survive. His mother comforts him with her body   45
Against the nightmare of the lions and tigers.
Again he is standing in his father's study
Lying about his lie, is whipped, and hears

His scream of outrage, valid to this day.
In bed, he fingers his stump of sex, invents   50
How he took off his clothes and ran away,
Slit up his belly with various instruments;

To brood on this was a deep abdominal joy
Still recognized as a feeling at the core
Of love — and the last genuine memory   55
Is singing 'Jesus Loves Me' — then, no more!

Beyond is a lost country and in vain
I enter that mysterious territory.
Lit by faint hints of memory lies the plain
Where from its Null took shape this conscious I   60

Which backward scans the dark — But at my side
The unrecognized Other Voice speaks in my ear,
The voice of my fear, the voice of my unseen guide;
'Who are we, stranger? What are we doing here?'

And through the uncertain gloom, sudden I see   65
Beyond remembered time the imagined entry,
The enormous Birth-gate whispering, *'per me,*
per me si va tra la perduta gente.'

                                          (written 1943–44) 1955

---

68 See Dante's *Inferno* 3: 'Through me the way among the lost people'.

The Brides

Down the assembly line they roll and pass
Complete at last, a miracle of design;
Their chromium fenders, the unbreakable glass,
The fashionable curve, the air-flow line.

Grease to the elbows Mum and Dad enthuse,   5
Pocket their spanners and survey the bride;
Murmur: 'A sweet job! All she needs is juice!
Built for a life-time — sleek as a fish. Inside

'He will find every comfort: the full set
Of gadgets; knobs that answer to the touch   10
For light or music; a place for his cigarette;
Room for his knees; a honey of a clutch.'

Now slowly through the show-room's flattering glare
See her wheeled in to love, console, obey,
Shining and silent! Parson with a prayer   15
Blesses the number-plate, she rolls away

To write her numerals in his book of life;
And now, at last, stands on the open road,
Triumphant, perfect, every inch a wife,
While the corks pop, the flash-light bulbs explode.   20

Her heavenly bowser-boy assumes his seat;
She prints the soft dust with her brand-new treads,
Swings towards the future, purring with a sweet
Concatenation of the poppet heads.

(written 1951) 1955

Imperial Adam

Imperial Adam, naked in the dew,
Felt his brown flanks and found the rib was gone.
Puzzled he turned and saw where, two and two,
The mighty spoor of Jahweh marked the lawn.

Then he remembered through mysterious sleep   5
The surgeon fingers probing at the bone,
The voice so far away, so rich and deep:
'It is not good for him to live alone.'

Turning once more he found Man's counterpart
In tender parody breathing at his side.   10
He knew her at first sight, he knew by heart
Her allegory of sense unsatisfied.

The pawpaw drooped its golden breasts above
Less generous than the honey of her flesh;
The innocent sunlight showed the place of love;   15
The dew on its dark hairs winked crisp and fresh.

This plump gourd severed from his virile root,
She promised on the turf of Paradise
Delicious pulp of the forbidden fruit;
Sly as the snake she loosed her sinuous thighs,   20

And waking, smiled up at him from the grass;
Her breasts rose softly and he heard her sigh —
From all the beasts whose pleasant task it was
In Eden to increase and multiply

Adam had learned the jolly deed of kind: 25
He took her in his arms and there and then,
Like the clean beasts, embracing from behind,
Began in joy to found the breed of men.

Then from the spurt of seed within her broke
Her terrible and triumphant female cry,   30
Split upward by the sexual lightning stroke.
It was the beasts now who stood watching by:

The gravid elephant, the calving hind,
The breeding bitch, the she-ape big with young
Were the first gentle midwives of mankind;   35
The teeming lioness rasped her with her tongue;

The proud vicuña nuzzled her as she slept
Lax on the grass; and Adam watching too
Saw how her dumb breasts at their ripening wept,
The great pod of her belly swelled and grew,   40

And saw its water break, and saw, in fear,
Its quaking muscles in the act of birth,
Between her legs a pigmy face appear,
And the first murderer lay upon the earth.

(written 1952) 1955

The Return of Persephone

Gliding through the still air, he made no sound;
Wing-shod and deft, dropped almost at her feet,
And searched the ghostly regiments and found
The living eyes, the tremor of breath, the beat
Of blood in all that bodiless underground.   5

She left her majesty; she loosed the zone
Of darkness and put by the rod of dread.
Standing, she turned her back upon the throne
Where, well she knew, the Ruler of the Dead,
Lord of her body and being, sat like stone;   10

Stared with his ravenous eyes to see her shake
The midnight drifting from her loosened hair,
The girl once more in all her actions wake,

The blush of colour in her cheeks appear
Lost with her flowers that day beside the lake.   15

The summer flowers scattering, the shout,
The black manes plunging down to the black pit —
Memory or dream? She stood awhile in doubt,
Then touched the Traveller God's brown arm and met
His cool, bright glance and heard his words ring out: 20

'Queen of the Dead and Mistress of the Year!'
— His voice was the ripe ripple of the corn;
The touch of dew, the rush of morning air —
'Remember now the world where you were born;
The month of your return at last is here.'   25

And still she did not speak, but turned again
Looking for answer, for anger, for command:
The eyes of Dis were shut upon their pain;
Calm as his marble brow, the marble hand
Slept on his knee. Insuperable disdain   30

Foreknowing all bounds of passion, of power, of art,
Mastered but could not mask his deep despair.
Even as she turned with Hermes to depart,
Looking her last on her grim ravisher
For the first time she loved him from her heart.   35

                                        (written 1953) 1955

Crossing the Frontier

Crossing the frontier they were stopped in time,
Told, quite politely, they would have to wait:
Passports in order, nothing to declare,
And surely holding hands was not a crime;
Until they saw how, ranged across the gate,   5
All their most formidable friends were there.

Wearing his conscience like a crucifix,
Her father, rampant, nursed the Family Shame;
And, armed with their old-fashioned dinner-gong,
His aunt, who even when they both were six,   10
Had just to glance towards a childish game
To make them feel that they were doing wrong.

And both their mothers, simply weeping floods,
Her head-mistress, his boss, the parish priest,
And the bank manager who cashed their cheques;   15
The man who sold him his first rubber-goods;
Dog Fido, from whose love-life, shameless beast,
She first observed the basic facts of sex.

They looked as though they had stood there for hours;
For years; perhaps for ever. In the trees   20

Two furtive birds stopped courting and flew off;
While in the grass beside the road the flowers
Kept up their guilty traffic with the bees.
Nobody stirred. Nobody risked a cough.

Nobody spoke. The minutes ticked away;   25
The dog scratched idly. Then, as parson bent
And whispered to a guard who hurried in,
The customs-house loudspeakers with a bray
Of raucous and triumphant argument
Broke out the wedding march from *Lohengrin*.   30

He switched the engine off: 'We must turn back.'
She heard his voice break, though he had to shout
Against a din that made their senses reel,
And felt his hand, so tense in hers, go slack.
But suddenly she laughed and said: 'Get out!   35
Change seats! Be quick!' and slid behind the wheel.

And drove the car straight at them with a harsh,
Dry crunch that showered both with scraps and chips,
Drove through them; barriers rising let them pass;
Drove through and on and on, with Dad's moustache   40
Beside her twitching still round waxen lips
And Mother's tears still streaming down the glass.

                                              (written 1963) 1966

Advice to Young Ladies

A.U.C. 334: about this date
For a sexual misdemeanour, which she denied,
The vestal virgin Postumia was tried.
Livy records it among affairs of state.

They let her off: it seems she was perfectly pure;   5
The charge arose because some thought her talk
Too witty for a young girl, her eyes, her walk
Too lively, her clothes too smart to be demure.

The Pontifex Maximus, summing up the case,
Warned her in future to abstain from jokes,   10
To wear less modish and more pious frocks.
She left the court reprieved, but in disgrace.

What then? With her the annalist is less
Concerned than what the men achieved that year:
Plots, quarrels, crimes, with oratory to spare!   15
I see Postumia with her dowdy dress,

Stiff mouth and listless step; I see her strive
To give dull answers. She had to knuckle down.
A vestal virgin who scandalized that town
Had fair trial, then they buried her alive.   20

Alive, bricked up in suffocating dark;
A ration of bread, a pitcher if she was dry,
Preserved the body they did not wish to die
Until her mind was quenched to the last spark.

How many the black maw has swallowed in its time!   25
Spirited girls who would not know their place;
Talented girls who found that the disgrace
Of being a woman made genius a crime;

How many others, who would not kiss the rod,
Domestic bullying broke or public shame?   30
Pagan or Christian, it was much the same:
Husbands, St Paul declared, rank next to God.

Livy and Paul, it may be, never knew
That Rome was doomed; each spoke of her with pride.
Tacitus, writing after both had died,   35
Showed that whole fabric rotten through and through.

Historians spend their lives and lavish ink
Explaining how great commonwealths collapse
From great defects of policy — perhaps
The cause is sometimes simpler than they think.   40

It may not seem so grave an act to break
Postumia's spirit as Galileo's, to gag
Hypatia as crush Socrates, or drag
Joan as Giordano Bruno to the stake.

Can we be sure? Have more states perished, then,   45
For having shackled the enquiring mind,
Than those who, in their folly not less blind,
Trusted the servile womb to breed free men?

                                            (written 1965) 1966

On an Engraving by Casserius

For Dr John Z. Bowers

Set on this bubble of dead stone and sand,
Lapped by its frail balloon of lifeless air,
Alone in the inanimate void, they stand,
These clots of thinking molecules who stare
Into the night of nescience and death,   5
And, whirled about with their terrestrial ball,
Ask of all being its motion and its frame:
This of all human images takes my breath;
Of all the joys in being a man at all,
This folds my spirit in its quickening flame.   10

Casserius   Giulio Casserio (?1552–1616), anatomist

Turning the leaves of this majestic book
My thoughts are with those great cosmographers,
Surgeon adventurers who undertook
To probe and chart time's other universe.
This one engraving holds me with its theme: 15
More than all maps made in that century
Which set true bearings for each cape and star,
De Quiros' vision or Newton's cosmic dream,
This reaches towards the central mystery
Of whence our being draws and what we are.   20

It came from that great school in Padua:
Casserio and Spiegel made this page.
Vesalius, who designed the *Fabrica*,
There strove, but burned his book at last in rage;
Fallopius by its discipline laid bare   25
The elements of this humanity,
Without which none knows that which treats the soul;
Fabricius talked with Galileo there:
Did those rare spirits in their colloquy
Divine in their two skills the single goal?   30

'One force that moves the atom and the star,'
Says Galileo; 'one basic law beneath
All change!' 'Would light from Achernar
Reveal how embryon forms within its sheath?'
Fabricius asks, and smiles. Talk such as this,   35
Ranging the bounds of our whole universe,
Could William Harvey once have heard? And once
Hearing, strike out that strange hypothesis,
Which in *De Motu Cordis* twice recurs,
Coupling the heart's impulsion with the sun's?   40

Did Thomas Browne at Padua, too, in youth
Hear of their talk of universal law
And form that notion of particular truth
Framed to correct a science they foresaw,
That darker science of which he used to speak   45
In later years and called the Crooked Way
Of Providence? Did *he* foresee perhaps
An age in which all sense of the unique
And singular dissolves, like ours today,
In diagrams, statistics, tables, maps?   50

21ff **great school in Padua**   Vesalius, Fallopius, Fabricius, Casserius and Spiegel (Spigelius) presided successively over the advances in the science of anatomy at Padua in the late 16th and early 17th centuries. Vesalius' *Fabrica* (1543) was a pioneer work on the subject. Spiegel's *Tabulae Anatomicae* (1627) posthumously incorporated copperplate engravings by Casserius, including the one described in this poem.

37 **William Harvey**   (1578–1657) author of a treatise on the circulation of the blood, *De Motu Cordis*. He studied anatomy at Padua under Casserius.

41 **Thomas Browne**   (1605–82) British physician and writer

Not here! The graver's tool in this design   51
Aims still to give not general truth alone,
Blue-print of science or data's formal line:
Here in its singularity he has shown
The image of an individual soul;   55
Bodied in this one woman, he makes us see
The shadow of his anatomical laws.
An artist's vision animates the whole,
Shines through the scientist's detailed scrutiny
And links the person and the abstract cause.   60

Such were the charts of those who pressed beyond
Vesalius their master, year by year
Tracing each bone, each muscle, every frond
Of nerve until the whole design lay bare.
Thinking of this dissection, I descry   65
The tiers of faces, their teacher in his place,
The talk at the cadaver carried in:
'A woman — with child!'; I hear the master's dry
Voice as he lifts a scalpel from its case:
'With each new step in science, we begin.'   70

Who was she? Though they never knew her name,
Dragged from the river, found in some alley at dawn,
This corpse none cared, or dared perhaps, to claim,
The dead child in her belly still unborn,
Might have passed, momentary as a shooting star,   75
Quenched like the misery of her personal life,
Had not the foremost surgeon of Italy,
Giulio Casserio of Padua,
Bought her for science, questioned her with his knife,
And drawn her for his great *Anatomy*;   80

Where still in the abundance of her grace,
She stands among the monuments of time
And with a feminine delicacy displays
His elegant dissection: the sublime
Shaft of her body opens like a flower   85
Whose petals, folded back expose the womb,
Cord and placenta and the sleeping child,
Like instruments of music in a room
Left when her grieving Orpheus left his tower
Forever, for the desert and the wild.   90

Naked she waits against a tideless shore,
A sibylline stance, a noble human frame
Such as those old anatomists loved to draw.
She turns her head as though in trouble or shame,
Yet with a dancer's gesture holds the fruit   95
Plucked, though not tasted, of the Fatal Tree.
Something of the first Eve is in this pose

And something of the second in the mute
Offering of her child in death to be
Love's victim and her flesh its mystic rose.   100

No figure with wings of fire and back-swept hair
Swoops with his: Blessed among Women!; no sword
Of the spirit cleaves or quickens her; yet there
She too was overshadowed by the Word,
Was chosen, and by her humble gift of death   105
The lowly and the poor in heart give tongue,
Wisdom puts down the mighty from their seat;
The vile rejoice and rising, hear beneath
Scalpel and forceps, tortured into song,
Her body utter their magnificat.   110

Four hundred years since first that cry rang out:
Four hundred years, the patient, probing knife
Cut towards its answer — yet we stand in doubt:
Living, we cannot tell the source of life.
Old science, old certainties that lit our way   115
Shrink to poor guesses, dwindle to a myth.
Today's truths teach us how we were beguiled;
Tomorrow's how blind our vision of today.
The universals we thought to conjure with
Pass: there remain the mother and the child.   120

Loadstone, loadstar, alike to each new age,
There at the crux of time they stand and scan,
Past every scrutiny of prophet or sage,
Still unguessed prospects in this venture of Man.
To generations, which we leave behind,   125
They taught a difficult, selfless skill: to show
The mask beyond the mask beyond the mask;
To ours another vista, where the mind
No longer asks for answers, but to know:
What questions are there which we fail to ask?   130

Who knows, but to the age to come they speak
Words that our own is still unapt to hear:
'These are the limits of all you sought and seek;
More our yet unborn nature cannot bear.
Learn now that all man's intellectual quest   135
Was but the stirrings of a foetal sleep;
The birth you cannot haste and cannot stay
Nears its appointed time; turn now and rest
Till that new nature ripens, till the deep
Dawns with that unimaginable day.'   140

(written 1967) 1969

Moschus Moschiferus

A Song for St Cecilia's Day

In the high jungle where Assam meets Tibet
The small Kastura, most archaic of deer,
Were driven in herds to cram the hunters' net
And slaughtered for the musk-pods which they bear;

But in those thickets of rhododendron and birch   5
The tiny creatures now grow hard to find.
Fewer and fewer survive each year. The search
Employs new means, more exquisite and refined:

The hunters now set out by two or three;
Each carries a bow and one a slender flute.   10
Deep in the forest the archers choose a tree
And climb; the piper squats against the root.

And there they wait until all trace of man
And rumour of his passage dies away.
They melt into the leaves and, while they scan   15
The glade below, their comrade starts to play.

Through those vast listening woods a tremulous skein
Of melody wavers, delicate and shrill:
Now dancing and now pensive, now a rain
Of pure, bright drops of sound and now the still,   20

Sad wailing of lament; from tune to tune
It winds and modulates without a pause;
The hunters hold their breath; the trance of noon
Grows tense; with its full power the music draws

A shadow from a juniper's darker shade;   25
Bright-eyed, with quivering muzzle and pricked ear,
The little musk-deer slips into the glade
Led by an ecstasy that conquers fear.

A wild enchantment lures him, step by step,
Into its net of crystalline sound, until   30
The leaves stir overhead, the bowstrings snap
And poisoned shafts bite sharp into the kill.

Then, as the victim shudders, leaps and falls,
The music soars to a delicious peak,
And on and on its silvery piping calls   35
Fresh spoil for the rewards the hunters seek.

But when the woods are emptied and the dusk
Draws in, the men climb down and count their prey,

St Cecilia   a martyr of the early Church and patron saint of music. Poems for music on her feast
day, 22 November, have been written by a number of poets, including Dryden, Pope and Auden.

Cut out the little glands that hold the musk
And leave the carcasses to rot away.   40

A hundred thousand or so are killed each year;
Cause and effect are very simply linked:
Rich scents demand the musk, and so the deer,
Its source, must soon, they say, become extinct.

Divine Cecilia, there is no more to say!   45
Of all who praised the power of music, few
Knew of these things. In honour of your day
Accept this song I too have made for you.

(written 1967) 1969

Inscription for a War

Stranger, go tell the Spartans
we died here obedient to their commands.
                    Inscription at Thermopylae

Linger not, stranger; shed no tear;
Go back to those who sent us here.

We are the young they drafted out
To wars their folly brought about.

Go tell those old men, safe in bed,   5
We took their orders and are dead.

1981

Trees

For Penelope

Since you left me forever, I find my eyes
See things less clearly than they used to do.
All that I view lacks that hint of surprise
That once I shared with you.

They are merely looked at; they are not completely seen.   5
Only some evenings I sit on our terrace and turn
To watch our trees, rustling, vividly green,
Come fully alive. I discern

That we see them together with joy as once we did,
And wonder if it could possibly be true   10
That there still lives on, that in their foliage hid,
Those trees remember you.

Our fifty years together, I should have thought
Would have left great gaps and so they have for sure.
What I learn now is: moments of this sort   15
Are those that most endure.

1991

The Mayan Books

Diego de Landa, archbishop of Yucatan
— The curse of God upon his pious soul —
Placed all their Devil's picture-books under ban
And, piling them in one sin-heap, burned the whole;

But took the trouble to keep the calendar   5
By which the Devil had taught them to count time.
The impious creatures had tallied back as far
As ninety million years before Eve's crime.

That was enough: they burned the Mayan books,
Saved souls and kept their own in proper trim.   10
Diego de Landa in heaven always looks
Towards God: God never looks at him.

                                        1991

ROBERT D. FITZGERALD   *(1902–87)*

In Personal Vein

Speaking from the heart, rather than with that heed
for accuracy, reason (cowardice, veiled),
which somewhat the years have taught me, somewhat failed
in teaching, I would say there is certain need
even at this hour to remember that men bleed   5
much the same blood, attackers and assailed;
that shattered dams pour death; that those discs nailed
flush to the earth were cities, whether the deed
were guilt or the judgement on it. This heart's-word
I would not match against logic; there's no doubt   10
only the one-eyed man walks straight through his brain,
and some considerations are better deferred
ten years, twenty years hence; but, in personal vein,
it is well that the heart sees and still speaks out.

                                (written 1945) 1953

The Wind at Your Door

(To Mary Gilmore)

My ancestor was called on to go out —
a medical man, and one such must by law
wait in attendance on the pampered knout
and lend his countenance to what he saw,
lest the pet, patting with too bared a claw,   5
be judged a clumsy pussy. Bitter and hard,
see, as I see him, in that jailhouse yard.

Or see my thought of him: though time may keep
elsewhere tradition or a portrait still,
I would not feel under his cloak of sleep   10
if beard there or smooth chin, just to fulfil
some canon of precision. Good or ill
his blood's my own; and scratching in his grave
could find me more than I might wish to have.

Let him then be much of the middle style   15
of height and colouring; let his hair be dark
and his eyes green; and for that slit, the smile
that seemed inhuman, have it cruel and stark,
but grant it could be too the ironic mark
of all caught in the system — who the most,   20
the doctor or the flesh twined round that post?

There was a high wind blowing on that day;
for one who would not watch, but looked aside,
said that when twice he turned it blew his way
splashes of blood and strips of human hide   25
shaken out from the lashes that were plied
by one right-handed, one left-handed tough,
sweating at this paid task, and skilled enough.

That wind blows to your door down all these years.
Have you not known it when some breath you drew   30
tasted of blood? Your comfort is in arrears
of just thanks to a savagery tamed in you
only as subtler fears may serve in lieu
of thong and noose — old savagery which has built
your world and laws out of the lives it spilt.   35

For what was jailyard widens and takes in
my country. Fifty paces of stamped earth
stretch; and grey walls retreat and grow so thin
that towns show through and clearings — new raw birth
which burst from handcuffs — and free hands go forth   40
to win tomorrow's harvest from a vast
ploughland — the fifty paces of that past.

But see it through a window barred across,
from cells this side, facing the outer gate
which shuts on freedom, opens on its loss   45
in a flat wall. Look left now through the grate
at buildings like more walls, roofed with grey slate
or hollowed in the thickness of laid stone
each side the court where the crowd stands this noon.

One there with the officials, thick of build,   50
not stout, say burly (so this obstinate man
ghosts in the eyes) is he whom enemies killed
(as I was taught) because the monopolist clan

found him a grit in their smooth-turning plan,
too loyally active on behalf of Bligh.   55
So he got lost; and history passed him by.

But now he buttons his long coat against
the biting gusts, or as a gesture of mind,
habitual; as if to keep him fenced
from stabs of slander sticking him from behind,   60
sped by the schemers never far to find
in faction, where approval from one source
damns in another clubroom as of course.

This man had Hunter's confidence, King's praise;
and settlers on the starving Hawkesbury banks   65
recalled through twilight drifting across their days
the doctor's fee of little more than thanks
so often; and how sent by their squeezed ranks
he put their case in London. I find I lack
the hateful paint to daub him wholly black.   70

Perhaps my life replies to his too much
through veiling generations dropped between.
My weakness here, resentments there, may touch
old motives and explain them, till I lean
to the forgiveness I must hope may clean   75
my own shortcomings; since no man can live
in his own sight if it will not forgive.

Certainly I must own him whether or not
it be my will. I was made understand
this much when once, marking a freehold lot,   80
my papers suddenly told me it was land
granted to Martin Mason. I felt his hand
heavily on my shoulder, and knew what coil
binds life to life through bodies, and soul to soil.

There, over to one corner, a bony group   85
of prisoners waits; and each shall be in turn
tied by his own arms in a human loop
about the post, with his back bared to learn
the price of seeking freedom. So they earn
three hundred rippling stripes apiece, as set   90
by the law's mathematics against the debt.

These are the Irish batch of Castle Hill,
rebels and mutineers, my countrymen
twice over: first, because of those to till
my birthplace first, hack roads, raise roofs; and then   95
because their older land time and again
enrolls me through my forbears; and I claim
as origin that threshold whence we came.

One sufferer had my surname, and thereto
'Maurice', which added up to history once;   100
an ignorant dolt, no doubt, for all that crew
was tenantry. The breed of clod and dunce
makes patriots and true men: could I announce
that Maurice as my kin I say aloud
I'd take his irons as heraldry, and be proud.   105

Maurice is at the post. Its music lulls,
one hundred lashes done. If backbone shows
then play the tune on buttocks! But feel his pulse;
that's what a doctor's for; and if it goes
lamely, then dose it with these purging blows —   110
which have not made him moan; though, writhing there,
'Let my neck be,' he says, 'and flog me fair.'

One hundred lashes more, then rest the flail.
What says the doctor now? 'This dog won't yelp;
he'll tire you out before you'll see him fail;   115
here's strength to spare; go on!' Ay, pound to pulp;
yet when you've done he'll walk without your help,
and knock down guards who'd carry him being bid,
and sing no song of where the pikes are hid.

It would be well if I could find, removed   120
through generations back — who knows how far? —
more than a surname's thickness as a proved
bridge with that man's foundations. I need some star
of courage from his firmament, a bar
against surrenders: faith. All trials are less   125
than rain-blacked wind tells of that old distress.

Yet I can live with Mason. What is told
and what my heart knows of his heart, can sort
much truth from falsehood, much there that I hold
good clearly or good clouded by report;   130
and for things bad, ill grows where ills resort:
they were bad times. None know what in his place
they might have done. I've my own faults to face.

                                                            1959

From Eleven Compositions: Roadside

III

Having said that all the gums have not been cut
and dry sticks break beneath them; and having said
the grass is good this year, but shows a rut
developing here and there and looking red

along worn sides of hills; that as I walked   5
kicking up dust and powdered dung of sheep,

a hare came loping towards me, saw me, baulked,
crouched — then lost his nerve and fled with a leap;

that magpies gossiped above me on big boughs;
that tanks are three parts full though hard earth bakes;   10
that there are sheep, of course, a few dry cows,
not many rabbits, and I stirred no snakes;

having said this much I know and regret my loss,
whose eye falls short of my love for just this land,
too turned within for the small flower in the moss   15
and birds my father all but brought to his hand.

                                                                    1962

KENNETH SLESSOR   *(1901–71)*

Nuremberg

So quiet it was in that high, sun-steeped room,
So warm and still, that sometimes with the light
Through the great windows, bright with bottle-panes,
There'd float a chime from clock-jacks out of sight,
    Clapping iron mallets on green copper gongs.   5

But only in blown music from the town's
Quaint horologe could Time intrude ... you'd say
Clocks had been bolted out, the flux of years
Defied, and that high chamber sealed away
    From earthly change by some old alchemist.   10

And, oh, those thousand towers of Nuremberg
Flowering like leaden trees outside the panes:
Those gabled roofs with smoking cowls, and those
Encrusted spires of stone, those golden vanes
    On shining housetops paved with scarlet tiles!   15

And all day nine wrought-pewter manticores
Blinked from their spouting faucets, not five steps
Across the cobbled street, or, peering through
The rounds of glass, espied that sun-flushed room
    With Dürer graving at intaglios.   20

O happy nine, spouting your dew all day
In green-scaled rows of metal, whilst the town
Moves peacefully below in quiet joy ...
O happy gargoyles to be gazing down
    On Albrecht Dürer and his plates of iron!   25

                                                                    1924

The Night-Ride

Gas flaring on the yellow platform; voices running up and down;
Milk-tins in cold dented silver; half-awake I stare,
Pull up the blind, blink out — all sounds are drugged;
The slow blowing of passengers asleep;
Engines yawning; water in heavy drips;   5
Black, sinister travellers, lumbering up the station,
One moment in the window, hooked over bags;
Hurrying, unknown faces — boxes with strange labels —
All groping clumsily to mysterious ends,
Out of the gaslight, dragged by private Fates.   10
Their echoes die. The dark train shakes and plunges;
Bells cry out; the night-ride starts again.
Soon I shall look out into nothing but blackness,
Pale, windy fields. The old roar and knock of the rails
Melts in dull fury. Pull down the blind. Sleep. Sleep.   15
Nothing but grey, rushing rivers of bush outside.
Gaslight and milk-cans. Of Rapptown I recall nothing else.

                                                                      1926

From Five Visions of Captain Cook

V

After the candles had gone out, and those
Who listened had gone out, and a last wave
Of chimney-haloes caked their smoky rings
Like fish-scales on the ceiling, a Yellow Sea
Of swimming circles, the old man,   5
Old Captain-in-the-Corner, drank his rum
With friendly gestures to four chairs. They stood
Empty, still warm from haunches, with rubbed nails
And leather glazed, like agéd serving-men
Feeding a king's delight, the sticky, drugged   10
Sweet agony of habitual anecdotes.
But these, his chairs, could bear an old man's tongue,
Sleep when he slept, be flattering when he woke,
And wink to hear the same eternal name
From lips new-dipped in rum.   15

'Then Captain Cook,
I heard him, told them they could go
If so they chose, but he would get them back,
Dead or alive, he'd have them,'
The old man screeched, half-thinking to hear 'Cook!   20
Cook again! Cook! It's other cooks he'll need,
Cooks who can bake a dinner out of pence,
That's what he lives on, talks on, half-a-crown
A day, and sits there full of Cook.
Who'd do your cooking now, I'd like to ask,   25

If someone didn't grind her bones away?
But that's the truth, six children and half-a-crown
A day, and a man gone daft with Cook.'

That was his wife,
Elizabeth, a noble wife but brisk,   30
Who lived in a present full of kitchen-fumes
And had no past. He had not seen her
For seven years, being blind, and that of course
Was why he'd had to strike a deal with chairs,
Not knowing when those who chafed them had gone to sleep   35
Or stolen away. Darkness and empty chairs,
This was the port that Alexander Home
Had come to with his useless cutlass-wounds
And tales of Cook, and half-a-crown a day —
This was the creek he'd run his timbers to,   40
Where grateful countrymen repaid his wounds
At half-a-crown a day. Too good, too good,
This eloquent offering of birdcages
To gulls, and Greenwich Hospital to Cook,
Britannia's mission to the sea-fowl.   45

It was not blindness picked his flesh away,
Nor want of sight made penny-blank the eyes
Of Captain Home, but that he lived like this
In one place, and gazed elsewhere. His body moved
In Scotland, but his eyes were dazzle-full   50
Of skies and water farther round the world —
Air soaked with blue, so thick it dripped like snow
On spice-tree boughs, and water diamond-green,
Beaches wind-glittering with crumbs of gilt,
And birds more scarlet than a duchy's seal   55
That had come whistling long ago, and far
Away. His body had gone back,
Here it sat drinking rum in Berwickshire,
But not his eyes — they were left floating there
Half-round the earth, blinking at beaches milked   60
By suck-mouth tides, foaming with ropes of bubbles
And huge half-moons of surf. Thus it had been
When Cook was carried on a sailor's back,
Vengeance in a cocked hat, to claim his price,
A prince in barter for a longboat.   65
And then the trumpery springs of fate — a stone,
A musket-shot, a round of gunpowder,
And puzzled animals, killing they knew not what
Or why, but killing ... the surge of goatish flanks
Armoured in feathers, like cruel birds: 70
Wild, childish faces, killing; a moment seen,
Marines with crimson coats and puffs of smoke
Toppling face-down; and a knife of English iron,

Forged aboard ship, that had been changed for pigs,
Given back to Cook between the shoulder-blades.   75
There he had dropped, and the old floundering sea,
The old, fumbling, witless lover-enemy,
Had taken his breath, last office of salt water.

Cook died. The body of Alexander Home
Flowed round the world and back again, with eyes   80
Marooned already, and came to English coasts,
The vague ancestral darknesses of home,
Seeing them faintly through a glass of gold,
Dim fog-shapes, ghosted like the ribs of trees
Against his blazing waters and blue air.   85
But soon they faded, and there was nothing left,
Only the sugar-cane and the wild granaries
Of sand, and palm-trees and the flying blood
Of cardinal-birds; and putting out one hand
Tremulously in the direction of the beach,   90
He felt a chair in Scotland. And sat down.

                                                        1932

Country Towns

Country towns, with your willows and squares,
And farmers bouncing on barrel mares
To public-houses of yellow wood
With '1860' over their doors,
And that mysterious race of Hogans   5
Which always keeps General Stores ...

At the School of Arts, a broadsheet lies
Sprayed with the sarcasm of flies:
'The Great Golightly Family
Of Entertainers Here To-night' —   10
Dated a year and a half ago,
But left there, less from carelessness
Than from a wish to seem polite.

Verandas baked with musky sleep,
Mulberry faces dozing deep,   15
And dogs that lick the sunlight up
Like paste of gold — or, roused in vain
By far, mysterious buggy-wheels,
Lower their ears, and drowse again ...

Country towns with your schooner bees,   20
And locusts burnt in the pepper-trees,
Drown me with syrups, arch your boughs,
Find me a bench, and let me snore,
Till, charged with ale and unconcern,
I'll think it's noon at half-past four!   25

                                                        1932

A bird sang in the jaws of night

A bird sang in the jaws of night,
Like a star lost in space —
O, dauntless molecule to smite
With joy that giant face!

I heard you mock the lonely air,   5
The bitter dark, with song,
Waking again the old Despair
That had been dead so long,

That had been covered up with clay
And never talked about,   10
So none with bony claws could say
They'd dig my coffin out.

But you, with music clear and brave,
Have shamed the buried thing;
It rises dripping from the grave   15
And tries in vain to sing.

O, could the bleeding mouth reply,
The broken flesh but moan,
The tongues of skeletons would cry,
And Death push back his stone!   20

1932

Up in Mabel's Room

The stairs are dark, the steps are high —
    Too dark and high for YOU —
Where Mabel's living in the sky
    And feeding on the view;
Five stories down, a fiery hedge,   5
    The lights of Sydney loom,
But the stars burn on the window-ledge
    Up in Mabel's room.

A burning sword, a blazing spear,
    Go floating down the night,   10
And flagons of electric beer
    And alphabets of light —
The moon and stars of Choker's Lane,
    Like planets lost in fume,
They roost upon the window-pane   15
    Up in Mabel's room.

And you with fifty-shilling pride
    Might scorn the top-floor back,
But, flaming on the walls outside,
    Behold a golden track!   20

Oh, bed and board you well may hire
  To save the weary hoof,
But not the men of dancing fire
  Up on Mabel's roof.

There Mr Neon's nebulae   25
  Are constantly on view,
The starlight falls entirely free,
  The moon is always blue,
The clouds are full of shining wings,
  The flowers of carbon bloom —   30
But you — YOU'LL never see these things
  Up in Mabel's room.

                                                      1933

Out of Time

I

I saw Time flowing like the hundred yachts
That fly behind the daylight, foxed with air;
Or piercing, like the quince-bright, bitter slats
Of sun gone thrusting under Harbour's hair.

So Time, the wave, enfolds me in its bed,   5
Or Time, the bony knife, it runs me through.
'Skulker, take heart,' I thought my own heart said,
'The flood, the blade, go by — Time flows, not you!'

Vilely, continuously, stupidly,
Time takes me, drills me, drives through bone and vein,   10
So water bends the seaweeds in the sea,
The tide goes over, but the weeds remain.

Time, you must cry farewell, take up the track,
And leave this lovely moment at your back!

II

Time leaves the lovely moment at his back,   15
Eager to quench and ripen, kiss or kill;
To-morrow begs him, breathless for his lack,
Or beauty dead entreats him to be still.

His fate pursues him; he must open doors,
Or close them, for that pale and faceless host   20
Without a flag, whose agony implores
Birth, to be flesh, or funeral, to be ghost.

Out of all reckoning, out of dark and light,
Over the edges of dead Nows and Heres,
Blindly and softly, as a mistress might,   25
He keeps appointments with a million years.

I and the moment laugh, and let him go,
Leaning against his golden undertow.

III

Leaning against the golden undertow,
Backward, I saw the birds begin to climb   30
With bodies hailstone-clear, and shadows flow,
Fixed in a sweet meniscus, out of Time,

Out of the torrent, like the fainter land
Lensed in a bubble's ghostly camera,
The lighted beach, the sharp and china sand,   35
Glitters and waters and peninsula —

The moment's world, it was; and I was part,
Fleshless and ageless, changeless and made free.
'Fool, would you leave this country?' cried my heart,
But I was taken by the suck of sea.   40

The gulls go down, the body dies and rots,
And Time flows past them like a hundred yachts.

                                                    1939

South Country

After the whey-faced anonymity
Of river-gums and scribbly-gums and bush,
After the rubbing and the hit of brush,
You come to the South Country

As if the argument of trees were done,   5
The doubts and quarrelling, the plots and pains,
All ended by these clear and gliding planes
Like an abrupt solution.

And over the flat earth of empty farms
The monstrous continent of air floats back   10
Coloured with rotting sunlight and the black,
Bruised flesh of thunderstorms:

Air arched, enormous, pounding the bony ridge,
Ditches and hutches, with a drench of light,
So huge, from such infinities of height,   15
You walk on the sky's beach

While even the dwindled hills are small and bare,
As if, rebellious, buried, pitiful,
Something below pushed up a knob of skull,
Feeling its way to air.   20

                                                    1939

Five Bells

Time that is moved by little fidget wheels
Is not my Time, the flood that does not flow.
Between the double and the single bell
Of a ship's hour, between a round of bells
From the dark warship riding there below,   5
I have lived many lives, and this one life
Of Joe, long dead, who lives between five bells.

Deep and dissolving verticals of light
Ferry the falls of moonshine down. Five bells
Coldly rung out in a machine's voice. Night and water   10
Pour to one rip of darkness, the Harbour floats
In air, the Cross hangs upside-down in water.

Why do I think of you, dead man, why thieve
These profitless lodgings from the flukes of thought
Anchored in Time? You have gone from earth,   15
Gone even from the meaning of a name;
Yet something's there, yet something forms its lips
And hits and cries against the ports of space,
Beating their sides to make its fury heard.

Are you shouting at me, dead man, squeezing your face   20
In agonies of speech on speechless panes?
Cry louder, beat the windows, bawl your name!

But I hear nothing, nothing ... only bells,
Five bells, the bumpkin calculus of Time.
Your echoes die, your voice is dowsed by Life,   25
There's not a mouth can fly the pygmy strait —
Nothing except the memory of some bones
Long shoved away, and sucked away, in mud;
And unimportant things you might have done,
Or once I thought you did; but you forgot,   30
And all have now forgotten — looks and words
And slops of beer; your coat with buttons off,
Your gaunt chin and pricked eye, and raging tales
Of Irish kings and English perfidy,
And dirtier perfidy of publicans   35
Groaning to God from Darlinghurst.
                              Five bells.

Then I saw the road, I heard the thunder
Tumble, and felt the talons of the rain
The night we came to Moorebank in slab-dark,   40
So dark you bore no body, had no face,
But a sheer voice that rattled out of air
(As now you'd cry if I could break the glass),

Five Bells   ship's signal for ten-thirty

A voice that spoke beside me in the bush,
Loud for a breath or bitten off by wind,   45
Of Milton, melons, and the Rights of Man,
And blowing flutes, and how Tahitian girls
Are brown and angry-tongued, and Sydney girls
Are white and angry-tongued, or so you'd found.
But all I heard was words that didn't join   50
So Milton became melons, melons girls,
And fifty mouths, it seemed, were out that night,
And in each tree an Ear was bending down,
Or something had just run, gone behind grass,
When, blank and bone-white, like a maniac's thought,   55
The naphtha-flash of lightning slit the sky,
Knifing the dark with deathly photographs.
There's not so many with so poor a purse
Or fierce a need, must fare by night like that,
Five miles in darkness on a country track,   60
But when you do, that's what you think.

                                        Five bells.

In Melbourne, your appetite had gone,
Your angers too; they had been leeched away
By the soft archery of summer rains   65
And the sponge-paws of wetness, the slow damp
That stuck the leaves of living, snailed the mind,
And showed your bones, that had been sharp with rage,
The sodden ecstasies of rectitude.
I thought of what you'd written in faint ink,   70
Your journal with the sawn-off lock, that stayed behind
With other things you left, all without use,
All without meaning now, except a sign
That someone had been living who now was dead:
'At Labassa. Room 6 x 8   75
On top of the tower; because of this, very dark
And cold in winter. Everything has been stowed
Into this room — 500 books all shapes
And colours, dealt across the floor
And over sills and on the laps of chairs;   80
Guns, photoes of many differant things
And differant curioes that I obtained ...'

In Sydney, by the spent aquarium-flare
Of penny gaslight on pink wallpaper,
We argued about blowing up the world,   85
But you were living backward, so each night
You crept a moment closer to the breast,
And they were living, all of them, those frames
And shapes of flesh that had perplexed your youth,
And most your father, the old man gone blind,   90
With fingers always round a fiddle's neck,
That graveyard mason whose fair monuments

And tablets cut with dreams of piety
Rest on the bosoms of a thousand men
Staked bone by bone, in quiet astonishment   95
At cargoes they had never thought to bear,
These funeral-cakes of sweet and sculptured stone.

Where have you gone? The tide is over you,
The turn of midnight water's over you,
As Time is over you, and mystery,   100
And memory, the flood that does not flow.
You have no suburb, like those easier dead
In private berths of dissolution laid —
The tide goes over, the waves ride over you
And let their shadows down like shining hair,   105
But they are Water; and the sea-pinks bend
Like lilies in your teeth, but they are Weed;
And you are only part of an Idea.
I felt the wet push its black thumb-balls in,
The night you died, I felt your eardrums crack,   110
And the short agony, the longer dream,
The Nothing that was neither long nor short;
But I was bound, and could not go that way,
But I was blind, and could not feel your hand.
If I could find an answer, could only find   115
Your meaning, or could say why you were here
Who now are gone, what purpose gave you breath
Or seized it back, might I not hear your voice?

I looked out of my window in the dark
At waves with diamond quills and combs of light   120
That arched their mackerel-backs and smacked the sand
In the moon's drench, that straight enormous glaze,
And ships far off asleep, and Harbour-buoys
Tossing their fireballs wearily each to each,
And tried to hear your voice, but all I heard   125
Was a boat's whistle, and the scraping squeal
Of seabirds' voices far away, and bells,
Five bells. Five bells coldly ringing out.
                                            Five bells.
                                                                    1939

Beach Burial

Softly and humbly to the Gulf of Arabs
The convoys of dead sailors come;
At night they sway and wander in the waters far under,
But morning rolls them in the foam.

Between the sob and clubbing of the gunfire   5
Someone, it seems, has time for this,
To pluck them from the shallows and bury them in burrows
And tread the sand upon their nakedness;

And each cross, the driven stake of tidewood,
Bears the last signature of men,   10
Written with such perplexity, with such bewildered pity,
The words choke as they begin —

'*Unknown seaman*' — the ghostly pencil
Wavers and fades, the purple drips,
The breath of the wet season has washed their inscriptions   15
As blue as drowned men's lips,

Dead seamen, gone in search of the same landfall,
Whether as enemies they fought,
Or fought with us, or neither; the sand joins them together,
Enlisted on the other front.   20

El Alamein

                                                              (1944) 1957

LEON GELLERT   *(1892–1977)*

A Night Attack

Be still. The bleeding night is in suspense
    Of watchful agony and coloured thought,
And every beating vein and trembling sense
    Long-tired with time, is pitched and overwrought.
And for the eye, the darkness holds strange forms,   5
    Soft movements in the leaves, and wicked glows
That wait and peer. The whole black landscape swarms
    With shapes of white and grey that no one knows;
And for the ear, a sound, a pause, a breath,
    A distant hurried footstep moving fast.   10
The hand has touched the slimy face of death.
    The mind is raking at the ragged past.
... A sound of rifles rattles from the south,
And startled orders move from mouth to mouth.

May 24, 1915

                                                                   1917

The Last to Leave

The guns were silent, and the silent hills
    Had bowed their grasses to a gentle breeze.
I gazed upon the vales and on the rills,
    And whispered, 'What of these?' and 'What of these?'
'These long-forgotten dead with sunken graves,   5
    Some crossless, with unwritten memories;

Their only mourners are the moaning waves;
    Their only minstrels are the singing trees.'
And thus I mused and sorrowed wistfully.
    I watched the place where they had scaled the height,   10
That height whereon they bled so bitterly
    Throughout each day and through each blistered night.
I sat there long, and listened — all things listened too.
    I heard the epics of a thousand trees;
A thousand waves I heard, and then I knew   15
    The waves were very old, the trees were wise:
The dead would be remembered evermore —
    The valiant dead that gazed upon the skies,
And slept in great battalions by the shore.

January, 1916
                                                          1917

House-mates

Because his soup was cold, he needs must sulk
From dusk till dark, and never speak to her;
And all the time she heard his heavy bulk
Blunder about the house, making a stir
In this room and in that. She heard him mutter   5
His foolish breathless noises, snarling and thick.
She knew the very words he first would utter;
He always said them, and they made her sick —
Those awkward efforts at a gracious peace
And kindly patronage of high-forgiving.   10
She knew these quarrelling calms would never cease
As long as she could keep his body living;
And so she lay and felt the hours creep by,
Wondering lazily upon her bed,
How cold the world would be if he should die   15
And leave her weeping for her stupid dead.
                                                          1919

LESBIA HARFORD   *(1891–1927)*

Do you remember still the little song

Do you remember still the little song
I mumbled on the hill at Aura, how
I told you it was made for Katie's sake
When I was fresh from school and loving her
With all the strength of girlhood? And you said   5
You liked my song, although I didn't know
How it began at first and gabbled then

In a half-voice, because I was too shy
To speak aloud, much less to speak them out, —
Words I had joined myself, — in the full voice   10
And with the lilt of proper poetry.
You could have hardly heard me. Here's the girl.
The little girl from school you never knew.
She made this song. Read what you couldn't hear.

     How bright the windows are   15
     Where the dear sun shineth.
     They strive to reflect the sun,
     To be bright like the sun,
     To give heat like the sun.
     My heart too has its chosen one   20
     And so to shine designeth.

The windows on the opposite hill that day
Shone bright at sunset too and made me think
Of the old patter I had half forgot,
Do you remember? I remind you now,   25
Who wandered yesterday for half an hour
Into St. Francis, where I thought of you
And how I would be glad to love you well
If I but knew the way. The rhyme came back
Teasing me till I knew I hated it.   30
I couldn't take that way of loving you.
That was the girl's way. Hear the woman now.
Out of my thinking in the lonely church
And the day's labour in a friendly room
Tumbled a song this morning you will like.   35

     I love my love
     But I could not be
     Good for his sake;
     That frightens me.

     Nor could I do   40
     Such things as I should
     Just for the sake
     Of being good.

     Deeds are too great
     To serve my whim,   45
     Be ways of loving
     Myself or him.

     Whether my deeds
     Are good or ill
     They're done for their own   50
     Not love's sake, still.

I didn't know it till the song was done,
But that's Ramiro in a nutshell, eh?
With his contempt for individual souls
And setting of the deed above the man. 55
Perhaps I like him better than I thought,
Or would like, if he'd give me leave to scorn
Chameleon, adjectival good and ill
And set the deed so far above the man
As to be out of reach of morals too. 60
There you and I join issue once again.

(written October 1912) 1941

I can't feel the sunshine

I can't feel the sunshine
Or see the stars aright
For thinking of her beauty
And her kisses bright.

She would let me kiss her 5
Once and not again.
Deeming soul essential,
Sense doth she disdain.

If I should once kiss her,
I would never rest 10
Till I had lain hour long
Pillowed on her breast.

Lying so, I'd tell her
Many a secret thing
God has whispered to me 15
When my soul took wing.

Would that I were Sappho,
Greece my land, not this!
There the noblest women,
When they loved, would kiss. 20

(written 1915) 1985

Closing Time — Public Library

At ten o'clock its great gong sounds the dread
Prelude to splendour. I push back my chair,
And all the people leave their books. We flock,
Still acquiescent, down the marble stair
Into the dark where we can't read. And thought 5
Swoops down insatiate through the starry air.

(written 1917) 1941

I'm like all lovers, wanting love to be

I'm like all lovers, wanting love to be
A very mighty thing for you and me.

In certain moods your love should be a fire
That burnt your very life up in desire.

The only kind of love, then, to my mind   5
Would make you kiss my shadow on the blind

And walk seven miles each night to see it there,
Myself within serene and unaware.

But you're as bad. You'd have me watch the clock
And count your coming while I mend your sock.   10

You'd have my mind devoted day and night
To you, and care for you and your delight.

Poor fools, who each would have the other give
What spirit must withhold if it would live.

You're not my slave; I wish you not to be,   15
I love yourself and not your love for me,

The self that goes ten thousand miles away
And loses thought of me for many a day.

And you love me for loving much beside,
But now you want a woman for your bride.   20

Oh, make no woman of me, you who can,
Or I will make a husband of a man!

By my unwomanly love that sets you free
Love all myself, but least the woman in me.

                                        (written 1917) 1941

You want a lily

You want a lily
And you plead with me
'Give me my lily back.'

I went to see
A friend last night and on her mantelshelf   5
I saw some lilies,
Image of myself,
And most unlike your dream of purity.   8

They had been small green lilies, never white
For man's delight   10
In their most blissful hours.
But now the flowers
Had shrivelled and instead

Shone spikes of seeds,
Burned spikes of seeds,   15
Burned red
As love and death and fierce futurity.

There's this much of the lily left in me.

(written 1918) 1985

A Prayer to Saint Rosa

When I am so worn out I cannot sleep
And yet I know I have to work next day
Or lose my job, I sometimes have recourse
To one long dead, who listens when I pray.

I ask Saint Rose of Lima for the sleep   5
She went without, three hundred years ago
When, lying on thorns and heaps of broken sherd,
She talked with God and made a heaven so.

Then speedily that most compassionate Saint
Comes with her gift of deep oblivious hours,   10
Treasured for centuries in nocturnal space
And heavy with the scent of Lima's flowers.

(written 1927) 1985

ZORA CROSS   *(1890–1964)*

From Love Sonnets

III

When first I whispered in your wondering ear,
'I worship you,' God smiled through all His skies,
Flinging a starry challenge in surprise,
'Wilt thou have Heaven or him?' . . . 'O, holy Seer,'
I answered, 'give me him.' Then, tier on tier,   5
The cherub-choir that sang above the rise
Of amber air beneath our Father's eyes,
Shouted a song of praise down all the sphere.

For there is neither Death nor Life in love.
And God, whose finger guides eternity,   10
Lights Paradise with parapets of fire
O'er which He leans His vasty form above,
And, looking through His hills on you and me,
Feeds Heaven upon the flame of our desire.

XLIX

In me there is a vast and lonely place
Where none, not even you, have walked in sight.
A wide, still vale of solitude and light,
Where Silence echoes into ebbing space.

And there I creep at times and hide my face,   5
While in myself I fathom wrong and right,
And all the timeless ages of the night
That sacred silence of my soul I pace.

And when from there I come to you, love-swift,
My mouth hot-edged with kisses fresh as wine,   10
Often I find your longings all asleep
And unresponsive from my grasp you drift.
Ah, Love, you, too, seek solitude like mine,
And soul from soul the secret seems to keep.

                                                        1917

Night-Ride

Faster speed we through the bracken,
Catch me closer to your heart!
Clench the reins before they slacken
Lest the frightened filly start!
Oh, the blazing pennons whirling   5
Ruby jewels on the grass
And the burnished blossoms curling
Into phantoms as we pass!

Down the slender tongue of tracking
Let her fly, she cannot trip!   10
Back of us we hear the cracking
Of the scarlet stockman's whip.
He is rounding up his cattle —
Fiery steers and steeds of gold,
Crimson stallions — hear them rattle   15
Through the forest, fold on fold!

He is groaning with his plunder.
Turn her quickly to the creek!
Though his feet be swift as thunder
We shall hear his angry shriek   20
As we gallop, helter-skelter,
Through the cool and plashing tide,
To the land of peace and shelter
On the safe and southern side.

On he follows. Nearer, nearer   25
Ring his brumby's brazen feet.
Clipping-clopping, clearer, clearer —
Death's the fire we must defeat.
Keep your lips on mine, my darling,
Let the flame-flowers lick my hair;   30
Love can brook the angry snarling
Of their passionate despair.

Cross the creek — he cannot follow!
Love will ever conquer all.
Down we canter through the hollow   35
Safe at last from scathe and fall.

    .   .   .   .

Thus I fancied we were speeding
All night long, with Love's control,
From our Passion and its pleading
To the safety of our soul.   40

                          1917

DOROTHEA MACKELLAR   *(1885–1968)*

Heritage

Though on the day your hard blue eyes met mine
I did not know I had a heart to keep,
    All the dead women in my soul
Stirred in their shrouded sleep.

There were strange pulses beating in my throat;   5
I had no thought of love: I was a child:
    But the dead lovers in my soul
Awoke and flushed and smiled;

And it was years before I understood
Why I had been so happy at your side   10
    With the dead women in my soul
Teaching me what to hide.

For it was not the springtime that had come,
Only one strong flower thrusting through the snows,
    But the dead women in my soul   15
Knew all that summer knows.

                          1923

Once When She Thought Aloud

I've had all of the apple, she said,
   Except the core.
All that many a woman desires —
   All and more.
Children, husband, and comfort enough   5
   And a little over.
Hungry Alice and bitter Anne
   Say I'm in clover.

I've had all of the apple, she said.
   — All that's good.   10

Whiles I feel I'd throw it away,
   The wholesome food,
Crisp sweet flesh snowy-cool, and skin
   Painted bright —
To have a man that I couldn't bear   15
   Out of my sight.

                                                              1926

'FURNLEY MAURICE' (FRANK WILMOT)   *(1881–1942)*

Echoes of wheels and singing lashes

Echoes of wheels and singing lashes
   Wake on the morning air;
Out of the kitchen a youngster dashes,
   Giving the ducks a scare.
Three jiffs from house to gully,   5
   And over the bridge to the gate;
And then a panting little boy
   Climbs on the rails to wait.

For there is long-whipped cursing Bill
   With four enormous logs,   10
Behind a team with the white-nosed leader's
   Feet in the sucking bogs.
Oh it was great to see them stuck,
   And grand to see them strain,
Until the magical language of Bill   15
   Had got them out again!

I foxed them to the shoulder turn,
   I saw him work them round,
And die into the secret bush,
   Leaving only sound.   20

And it isn't bullocks I recall,
   Nor waggons my memory sees;
But in the scented bush a track
   Turning among the trees.

Not forests of lean towering gums,   25
   Nor notes of birds and bees,
Do I remember so well as a track
   Turning among the trees.

Oh track where the brown leaves fall
   In dust to our very knees!   30
And it isn't the wattle that I recall,
Nor the sound of the bullocky's singing lash,

When the cloven hoofs in the puddles splash;
But the rumble of an unseen load,
Swallowed along the hidden road   35
   Turning among the trees!

                                        1913

They've builded wooden timber tracks

They've builded wooden timber tracks,
   And a trolly with screaming brakes
Noses into the secret bush,
Into the birdless brooding bush,
   And the tall old gums it takes.   5

And down in the sunny valley,
   The snorting saw screams slow;
Oh bush that nursed my people,
Oh bush that cursed my people,
That flayed and made my people,   10
   I weep to watch you go.

                                        1913

Nursery Rhyme

One year, two year, three year, four,
Comes a khaki gentleman knocking at the door;
Any little boys at home? Send them out to me,
To train them and brain them in battles yet to be.
Five year, six year, seven year, eight,   5
Hurry up, you little chaps, the captain's at the gate.

When a little boy is born, feed him, train him, so;
Put him in a cattle pen and wait for him to grow;
When he's nice and plump and dear, sensible and sweet,
Throw him in the trenches for the grey rats to eat;   10
Toss him in the cannon's mouth, cannons fancy best
Tender little boy flesh, that's easy to digest.

One year, two year, three year, four,
Listen to the generals singing out for more!
Soon he'll be a soldier-boy, won't he be a toff,   15
Pretty little soldier, with his head blown off!

Mother rears her family on two pounds a week,
Teaches them to wash themselves, teaches them to speak,
Rears them with a heart's love, rears them to be men,
Grinds her fingers to the bone — then, what then?   20

One year, two year, three year, four,
Comes a khaki gentleman knocking at the door;
Little boys are wanted now very much indeed,
Hear the bugles blowing when the cannons want a feed!

Fowl-food, horse-food, man-food are dear,   25
Cannon fodder's always cheap, conscript or volunteer.

When the guns grow rarer, and money's in a fix,
Tax the mother's wages down to twenty-nine and six;
Blood cost, money cost, cost of years of stress,
Heart cost, food cost, cost of all the mess.   30
Captains draw their wages with a penny in the slot,
But big bills and little bills, mother pays the lot.

Parents who must rear the boys the cannons love to slay
Also pay for cannons that blow other boys away!
Parsons tell them that their sons have just been blown to bits,   35
Patriotic parents must all laugh like fits!
Raise the boys for honest men, send them out to die,
Where's the coward father who would dare to raise a cry?
Any gentleman's aware folk rear their children for
Blunderers and plunderers to mangle in a war!   40

One year, two year, three year, four,
Comes a khaki gentleman knocking at the door.
Any little boys at home? Send them out for me
To train them and brain them in battles yet to be!
Five year, six year, seven year, eight,   45
Hurry up, you little chaps, the captain cannot wait!

                                                                      1920

HUGH MCCRAE   *(1876–1958)*

The End of Desire

A flooded fold of sarcenet
    Against her slender body sank,
Death-black, and beaded all with jet
    Across the pleasures of her flank.

The incense of a holy bowl   5
    Flowed round her knees till it did seem
That she was standing on the shoal
    Of some forbidden sunlit stream.

A little gong, far through the wall,
    Complained like one, deep sorrowing,   10
And, from the arras, I saw fall
    The woven swallow, fluttering;

While o'er the room there swam the breath
    Of roses on a trellised tree:
Loose ladies in pretended death   15
    Of sweet abandon to the bee.

Flames filled the hollows of my hands:
    Red blood rushed, hammering, round my heart,
Like mighty sleds when anvil bands
    Gape out, and from their holdings start.   20

No peace had I, and knew not where
    To find a solace that would kill
This sin of flesh so hard to bear,
    This sin of soul against the will.

But ever yet mine eyes would seek   25
    That golden woman built for love,
Whose either breast displayed the beak
    Through pouted plumes, of Venus' dove:

Her heavy hair, as smoke blown down
    Athwart the fields of plenteousness;   30
Her folded lips, her placid frown,
    Her insolence of nakedness.

I took her closely, but while yet
    I trembled, vassal to my lust,
Lo! — Nothing but some sarcenet,   35
    Deep-buried in a pile of dust.

                        1928

Gallows Marriage

The king lay a-bed with his queen one night,
And a snow-white dove came on to the sill:
'I am the lass,' said the bird, 'whom your might
Made the poor plaything one day of your will.

'You left me a corse on the road to Dee,   5
Where the poplars grow and the two ways part;
But a lang-syne gift ye bestowed on me —
The little wee knife they found in my heart.'

'Ye lie!' said the king — but the queen turned pale
And her tears fell down like rain from the sky —   10
'May God be my judge if ever this tale
Have aught in it else save the sound of a lie!'

He sprang from his bed to catch at the dove,
When a bow-string sang to the stars without,
And he fell like a knave to mailèd glove,   15
With his eyes fast shut, as the world went out.

But the dove sailed down to her own true lad,
Who stood in the shade of the Southgate Tree:
'Johnnie,' she whimpered, 'my good is your bad;
The gallows will marry you back to me.'   20

                        1928

JOHN SHAW NEILSON   *(1872–1942)*

You, and Yellow Air

I dream of an old kissing-time
  And the flowered follies there;
In the dim place of cherry-trees,
  Of you, and yellow air.

It was an age of babbling,   5
  When the players would play
Mad with the wine and miracles
  Of a charmed holiday.

Bewildered was the warm earth
  With whistling and sighs,   10
And a young foal spoke all his heart
  With diamonds for eyes.

You were of Love's own colour
  In eyes and heart and hair;
In the dim place of cherry-trees   15
  Ridden by yellow air.

It was the time when red lovers
  With the red fevers burn;
A time of bells and silver seeds
  And cherries on the turn.   20

Children looked into tall trees
  And old eyes looked behind;
God in His glad October
  No sullen man could find.

Out of your eyes a magic   25
  Fell lazily as dew,
And every lad with lad's eyes
  Made summer love to you.

It was a reign of roses,
  Of blue flowers for the eye,   30
And the rustling of green girls
  Under a white sky.

I dream of an old kissing-time
  And the flowered follies there,
In the dim place of cherry-trees,   35
  Of you, and yellow air.

(written 1909) 1919

The Hour of the Parting

Shall we assault the pain?
  It is the time to part:
Let us of Love again
  Eat the impatient heart.

There is a gulf behind   5
  Dull voice and fallen lip,
The blue smoke of the mind,
  The grey light on the ship.

Parting is of the cold
  That stills the loving breath,   10
Dimly we taste the old
  The pitiless meal of Death.

(written 1916) 1919

The Orange Tree

The young girl stood beside me. I
  Saw not what her young eyes could see:
— A light, she said, not of the sky
  Lives somewhere in the Orange Tree.

— Is it, I said, of east or west?   5
  The heartbeat of a luminous boy
Who with his faltering flute confessed
  Only the edges of his joy?

Was he, I said, borne to the blue
  In a mad escapade of Spring   10
Ere he could make a fond adieu
  To his love in the blossoming?

— Listen! the young girl said. There calls
  No voice, no music beats on me;
But it is almost sound: it falls   15
  This evening on the Orange Tree.

— Does he, I said, so fear the Spring
  Ere the white sap too far can climb?
See in the full gold evening
  All happenings of the olden time?   20

Is he so goaded by the green?
  Does the compulsion of the dew
Make him unknowable but keen
  Asking with beauty of the blue?

— Listen! the young girl said. For all   25
  Your hapless talk you fail to see
There is a light, a step, a call
  This evening on the Orange Tree.

— Is it, I said, a waste of love
　　Imperishably old in pain,   30
Moving as an affrighted dove
　　Under the sunlight or the rain?

Is it a fluttering heart that gave
　　Too willingly and was reviled?
Is it the stammering at a grave,   35
　　The last word of a little child?

— Silence! the young girl said. Oh, why,
　　Why will you talk to weary me?
Plague me no longer now, for I
　　Am listening like the Orange Tree.   40

　　　　　　　　　　　　　　　　(written 1916–19) 1934

Schoolgirls Hastening

Fear it has faded and the night:
　　The bells all peal the hour of nine:
The schoolgirls hastening through the light
　　Touch the unknowable Divine.

What leavening in my heart would bide!   5
　　Full dreams a thousand deep are there:
All luminants succumb beside
　　The unbound melody of hair.

Joy the long timorous takes the flute:
　　Valiant with colour songs are born: 10
Love the impatient absolute
　　Lives as a Saviour in the morn.

Get thou behind me Shadow-Death!
　　Oh ye Eternities delay!
Morning is with me and the breath   15
　　Of schoolgirls hastening down the way.

　　　　　　　　　　　　　　　　(written 1922) 1934

To the Red Lory

At the full face of the forest lies our little town:
Do thou from thy lookout to heaven, O lory, come down!

Come, charge with thy challenge of colour our thoughts cool and thin;
Descend with the blood of the sunlight — O lory, come in!

The clouds are away, 'tis October, the glees have begun;   5
Thy breast has the valour of music, O passionate one!

The rhythm is thine, the beloved, the unreason of Spring.
How royal thy raiment! No sorrow is under thy wing.

O thou of intrepid apparel, thy song is thy gown;
Translate thy proud speech of the sunlight — O lory, come down! 10

(written 1924) 1947

The Moon Was Seven Days Down

'Peter!' she said, 'the clock has struck
   At one and two and three;
You sleep so sound, and the lonesome hours
   They seem so black to me.
I suffered long, and I suffered sore: 5
   — What else can I think upon?
I fear no evil; but, oh! — the moon!
   She is seven days gone.'

'Peter!' she said, 'the night is long:
   The hours will not go by: 10
The moon is calm; but she meets her death
   Bitter as women die.
I think too much of the flowers. I dreamed
   I walked in a wedding gown,
Or was it a shroud? The moon! the moon! 15
   She is seven days down.'

'Woman!' he said, 'my ears could stand
   Much noise when I was young;
But year by year you have wearied me:
   Can you never stop your tongue? 20
Here am I, with my broken rest,
   To be up at the break of day:
— So much to do; and the sheep not shorn,
   And the lambs not yet away.'

'Peter!' she said, 'your tongue is rude; 25
   You have ever spoken so:
My aches and ills, they trouble you not
   This many a year, I know:
You talk of your lambs and sheep and wool:
   — 'Tis all that you think upon: 30
I fear no evil; but, oh! the moon!
   She is seven days gone.'

'Peter!' she said, 'the children went:
   My children would not stay:
By the hard word and the hard work 35
   You have driven them far away.
I suffered, back in the ten years
   That I never saw a town:
— Oh! the moon is over her full glory!
   She is seven days down!' 40

'Woman!' he said, 'I want my rest.
  Tis the worst time of the year:
The weeds are thick in the top fallow,
  And the hay will soon be here.
A man is a man, and a child a child: 45
  From a daughter or a son
Or a man or woman I want no talk
  For anything I have done.'

'Peter!' she said, ''twas told to me,
  Long back, in a happy year,   50
That I should die in the turning time
  When the wheat was in the ear;
That I should go in a plain coffin
  And lie in a plain gown
When the moon had taken her full glory   55
  And was seven days down.'

Peter, he rose and lit the lamp
  At the first touch of the day:
His mind was full of the top fallow,
  And the ripening of the hay.   60
He said, 'She sleeps,' — but the second look
  He knew how the dead can stare:
And there came a dance of last beauty
  That none of the living share.

How cool and straight and steady he was: 65
  He said, 'She seems so young!
Her face is fine — it was always fine —
  But, oh, by God! her tongue!
She always thought as the children thought:
  Her mind was made for a town.'   70
— And the moon was out in the pale sky:
  She was seven days down.

He sauntered out to the neighbour's place
  As the daylight came in clear:
'The wheat,' he said, 'it is filling well,'   75
  And he stopped at a heavy ear.
He said, 'A good strong plain coffin
  Is the one I am thinking on.'
— And the moon was over his shoulder:
  She was seven days gone.   80

                                      (written 1925) 1927

The Crane Is My Neighbour

The bird is my neighbour, a whimsical fellow and dim;
There is in the lake a nobility falling on him.

The bird is a noble, he turns to the sky for a theme,
And the ripples are thoughts coming out to the edge of a dream.

The bird is both ancient and excellent, sober and wise,   5
But he never could spend all the love that is sent for his eyes.

He bleats no instruction, he is not an arrogant drummer;
His gown is simplicity — blue as the smoke of the summer.

How patient he is as he puts out his wings for the blue!
His eyes are as old as the twilight, and calm as the dew.   10

The bird is my neighbour, he leaves not a claim for a sigh,
He moves as the guest of the sunlight — he roams in the sky.

The bird is a noble, he turns to the sky for a theme,
And the ripples are thoughts coming out to the edge of a dream.

(written 1934) 1938

You Cannot Go Down to the Spring

The song will deceive you, the scent will incite you to sing;
You clutch but you cannot discover: you cannot go down to the Spring.

The day will be painted with summer, the heat and the gold
Will give you no key to the blossom: the music is old.

It is at the edge of a promise, a far-away thing;   5
The green is the nest of all riddles: you cannot go down to the Spring.

The truth is too close to the sorrow; the song you would sing,
It cannot go into the fever: you cannot go down to the Spring.

1947

Say This for Love

Say this for love, when the great summer time
Is gone, and only winter wisdoms blow:
Fiercely he burned, like some imperious rhyme,
Burned, and he burned, but would not let me go.

Say this, his ominous riddlings were so deep   5
I could not see, I knew not where he trod.
He did from out a thousand centuries creep,
As some insurgent enemy of God.

Say this for love: You who did smite to kill,
And you did lie, it was my soul to soil;   10
Dressed as a hatred you did flog me still,
Chained to the last insanities in toil.

Say this for love: For all the ills in him
I give forgiveness for the lies he told;
Say this for love when both the eyes are dim,   15
And darkness leaves you whimpering in the cold.

(written 1941) 1970

MARY E. FULLERTON ('E')   *(1868–1946)*

The Selector's Wife

The quick compunction cannot serve;
She saw the flash
Ere he had bent with busy hand
And drooping lash.

She saw him mark for the first time,
With critic eye,
What five years' heavy toil had done
'Neath roof and sky.

And always now so sensitive
Her poor heart is,
That moment will push in between
His kindest kiss.

The moment when he realised
Her girlhood done
The truth her glass had long revealed
Of beauty gone.

Until some future gracious flash
Shall let each know
That that which drew and holds him yet
Shall never go.

                                        1921

Body

We fend for this poor thing,
Wash, dress, and give it food,
Love it before all men
Through each vicissitude.

Give it whate'er it ask,   5
Shield it from heat and cold,
And croon above its pains
When time has made it old.

It is but house and home
That for no term we rent;   10
We seldom talk with Him —
Its mighty resident.

Body's the easy one,
That lets the mortal be,
As though the pretty shell   15
Were the essential He.

Sometimes in hardihood,
We touch the inner door —

Two entities in one.
Visited and visitor.   20

Oh, Tenant of my flesh,
I knock, and turn, and fly,
Afraid of the appraisement
Within that solemn eye.

1942

Unit

Had Life remained one whole,
Compact of attributes,
Balanced without excess:
Nor men had been, nor brutes.

Had nought been chipped apart,   5
The fragments found no shapes,
Achieved not temperament:
Men had not been, nor apes.

Undo the forms and lines,
And see the units fall   10
With prisoned attributes
Back to the primal All.

Oh, gone the tiger's fire,
The blue snake's poison sting,
Each nevermore himself,   15
But part of everything.

Rob rose of breath and hue.
Diana's limbs unform:
Up, down, and bad and good,
Lapped in a pointless norm.   20

Hope, and desire, and dread,
The mara, and the grapes
Unfeatured, and annulled!

God keep us struggling shapes.

1942

A Man's Sliding Mood

Ardent in love and cold in charity,
Loud in the market, timid in debate:
Scornful of foe unbuckled in the dust,
At whimper of a child compassionate,

A man's a sliding mood from hour to hour,   5
Rage, and a singing forest of bright birds,
Laughter with lovely friends, and loneliness,
Woe with her heavy horn of unspoke words.

What is he then this heir of heart and mind?
Is this the man with his conflicting moods,   10
Or is there in a deeper dwelling place
Some stilly shaping thing that bides and broods?

1946

MARY GILMORE   *(1865–1962)*

Down by the Sea

The sea has soddened the baby clothes,
    The flannel, the shirt, the band;
The rats have bitten the baby face,
    And eaten the baby hand.

.   .   .   .

It lay at my breast and cried all night   5
    As through the day it had done;
I held it tight, and rose with stealth,
    When the day and the night were one.

And on through the city streets I crept
    (But the hand of fear is strong!)   10
And they mocked my steps with echoing,
    They mouthed as I went along!

I passed where mothers like me slept warm,
    And babies like mine were born;
Where it was not a sin to have loved as I,   15
    And motherhood meant not scorn.

And they drove me fast, those leering streets;
    They took up my baby's cry,
They tossed it about, and flung it up,
    Till it seemed to go God-high.   20

But the cry came back to the mother-heart,
    Knowing that it would hear;
I gathered my baby close and close!
    (What was it I seemed to fear ?)

And down by the sea the sun crept up —   25
    Did you hear a baby cry?
I know where one lies beside the quay,
    But I will not tell — not I!

And down by the sea the sun crept up —
    There's a child's cry seems to come   30
From the darkness, there, beyond the wall —
    But I know the dead are dumb !

And down by the sea the sun crept up ...

1910

Eve-Song

I span and Eve span
A thread to bind the heart of man;
But the heart of man was a wandering thing
That came and went with little to bring:
Nothing he minded that we made   5
As here he loitered and there he stayed.

I span and Eve span
A thread to bind the heart of man;
But the more we span the more we found
It wasn't his heart but ours we bound!   10
For children gathered about our knees:
The thread was a chain that stole our ease.
And one of us learned in our children's eyes
That more than man was love and prize.
But deep in the heart of one of us lay   15
A root of loss and hidden dismay.

He said he was strong. He had no strength
But that which comes of breadth and length.
He said he was fond. But his fondness proved
The flame of an hour when he was moved.   20
He said he was true. His truth was but
A door that winds could open and shut.

And yet, and yet, as he came back,
Wandering in from the outward track,
We held our arms, and gave him our breast   25
As a pillowing place for his head to rest.
I span and Eve span,
A thread to bind the heart of man!

                                                          1918

The Hunter of the Black

Softly footed as a myall, silently he walked,
All the methods of his calling learned from men he stalked;
Tall he was, and deeply chested, eagle-eyed and still,
Every muscle in his body subject to his will.

Dark and swarthy was his colour; somewhere Hampshire born;   5
Knew no pity for the hunted, weakness met his scorn;
Asked no friendship, shunned no meetings, took what life might bring;
Came and went among his fellows something like a king;

Paid each debt with strict exactness, what the debt might be;
Called no man employed him master; master's equal, he;   10
Yet there was not one who sought him, none who held his hand;
Never father calling, bid him join the family band.

Tales and tales were told about him, how, from dawn till dark,
Noiselessly he trailed his quarry, never missed a mark,
How the twigs beneath his footstep 'moved but never broke',   15
How the very fires he kindled 'never made a smoke'.

Men would tell with puzzled wonder, marked on voice and brow,
How he'd stand a moment talking, leave, and none knew how;
'He was there!' and then had vanished, going as he came,
Like the passing of a shadow, like a falling flame.   20

Once (I heard it when it happened,) word was sent to him,
Of a lone black on Mimosa — O the hunting grim!
Through three days and nights he tracked him, never asking sleep;
Shot, for him who stole the country, him who killed a sheep.

Tomahawk in belt, as only adults needed shot,   25
No man knew how many notches totalled up his lot;
But old stockmen striking tallies, rough and ready made,
Reckoned on at least a thousand, naming camps decayed.

Time passed on, and years forgotten whitened with the dust;
He whose hands were red with slaughter sat among the just,   30
Kissed the children of his children, honoured in his place,
Turned and laid him down in quiet, asking God his grace.

                                                                1930

The Yarran-tree

The Lady of the Yarran-tree,
    She built herself a house,
And, happy in it, there she lived
    As tidy as a mouse;
She set a stool against the fire,   5
    And hung the broom beside,
And yet, although she sat alone,
    The door was open wide.

And she beside the Yarran-tree
    Was busy as could be;   10
She kept her sheep, she carded wool,
    Her bleach was white to see;
She baked her bread from wheat she grew,
    She tanned the good ox-hide;
And still, for all she sat alone,   15
    Her door was open wide.

The Lady of the Yarran-tree
    Looked out, one night, and saw
The dark hand of a stranger reach
    To lay on her his law;   20

She rose and drew the curtain close,
    Her little lamp to hide —
And yet, for all she was alone,
    The door stood open wide.

I asked her if she didn't know   25
    The fears of woman-kind,
That, though by day they come and go,
    Are still within the mind.
She looked at me and slowly said,
    'Such fears in me abide!'   30
And yet I knew she sat alone,
    The door left open wide.

The Yarran-tree against the spring
    Put on its amber green,
Like golden berries, on each twig,   35
    Its blossoms all were seen;
I saw the stranger watch the tree,
    The woman there inside —
And still, although she sat alone,
    The door was open wide.   40

To her beside the Yarran-tree,
    I said, 'Go buy a ring,
A ring of silver laced with steel,
    From which a shot may sing;
Then, when the stranger hears the song,   45
    As winds shall bear it wide,
It will be safe to sit alone,
    The house-door open wide.'

Then she beside the Yarran-tree,
    She turned and looked at me,   50
She laid the spinning from her hand,
    And spake as still could be;
'Go you,' she said, 'and make the ring,
    And make of it your pride;
That I may safely sit alone,   55
    The door set open wide.'

I took the woman at her word,
    And straitly there I made
A ring of silver laced with steel,
    That sang as trumpets played;   60
I set it down against the step,
    And, though the door is wide,
The Lady of the Yarran-tree
    Dwells ever safe inside.

                  1939

Nationality

I have grown past hate and bitterness,
I see the world as one;
But though I can no longer hate,
My son is still my son.

All men at God's round table sit,   5
And all men must be fed;
But this loaf in my hand,
This loaf is my son's bread.

                                                                    1954

Fourteen Men

Fourteen men,
And each hung down
Straight as a log
From his toes to his crown.

Fourteen men,   5
Chinamen they were,
Hanging on the trees
In their pig-tailed hair.

Honest poor men,
But the diggers said 'Nay!'   10
So they strung them all up
On a fine summer's day.

There they were hanging
As we drove by,
Grown-ups on the front seat,   15
On the back seat I.

That was Lambing Flat,
And still I can see
The straight up and down
Of each on his tree.   20
                                                                    1954

---

17 **Lambing Flat**   on the Burragorang goldfields, near the present town of Young: the site of riots directed against Chinese diggers in 1860–61. Although serious beatings occurred, the suggestion of lynchings has not been verified.

ANONYMOUS

Click Go the Shears

Out on the board the old shearer stands,
Grasping his shears in his long, bony hands,
Fixed is his gaze on a bare-bellied 'Joe',
Glory if he gets her, won't he make the ringer go.

> *Chorus*
> Click go the shears, boys, click, click, click,   5
> Wide is his blow and his hands move quick,
> The ringer looks around and is beaten by a blow,
> And curses the old snagger with the blue-bellied 'Joe.'

In the middle of the floor, in his cane-bottomed chair
Is the boss of the board, with eyes everywhere;   10
Notes well each fleece as it comes to the screen,
Paying strict attention if it's taken off clean.

The colonial experience man, he is there, of course,
With his shiny leggin's, just got off his horse,
Casting round his eye like a real connoisseur,   15
Whistling the old tune, 'I'm the Perfect Lure.'

The tar-boy is there, awaiting in demand,
With his blackened tar-pot and his tarry hand;
Sees one old sheep with a cut upon its back,
Here's what he's waiting for, 'Tar, here, Jack!'   20

Shearing is all over and we've all got our cheques,
Roll up your swag for we're off on the tracks;
The first pub we come to, it's there we'll have a spree,
And everyone that comes along it's 'Come and drink with me!'

Down by the bar the old shearer stands,   25
Grasping his glass in his thin bony hands;
Fixed is his gaze on a green-painted keg,
Glory, he'll get down on it, ere he stirs a peg.

There we leave him standing, shouting for all hands.
Whilst all around him every 'shouter' stands;   30
His eyes are on the cask, which is now lowering fast,
He works hard, he drinks hard, and goes to hell at last!

---

1 board shearing floor
3 Joe ewe
4 ringer fastest shearer
6 blow stroke of the shears
8 snagger rough shearer

JACK MATHIEU   *(1873–1949)*

That Day at Boiling Downs

He was driving Irish tandem, but perhaps I talk at random —
I'd forgotten for a moment you are not all mulga-bred:
What I mean's he had his swag up through his having knocked his nag up;
He had come in off the Cooper — anyhow that's what he said.

And he looked as full of knowledge as a thirty-acre college   5
As he answered to the question — 'How's things look the way you come?'
'Well, they *were* a trifle willing for a bit. There's been some killing;
In fact, I'm the sole survivor of the district ... mine's a rum!'

Then we all got interested in the chap as he divested
Himself of a fat puppy that he carried in his shirt;   10
But he said no more until he had put down his swag and billy,
And had taken off his bluchers just to empty out the dirt.

Bits of cork were tied with laces round his hat in many places,
Out of which he gave the puppy some refreshment, and began —
'Sammy Suds was bound'ry-riding, quite content and law-abiding,   15
Till he bought some reading-matter one day off a hawker man.

'Then he started to go ratty, and began to fancy that he
Was an Injun on the warpath; so he plaited a lassoo,
Shaved and smeared his face with raddle, and knocked up a greenhide saddle,
After creeping on his belly through the grass a mile or two.   20

'Then he decked himself in feathers, and went out and scalped some wethers
Just to give himself a lesson in the sanguinary art;
Sammy then dug up the hatchet, chased a snake but couldn't catch it,
Killed his dog, lassooed a turkey, scalped the cat and made a start.

'And he caused a great sensation when he landed at the station;   25
And the boss said, "Hello! Sammy, what the devil's up with you?"
"I am Slimy Snake the Snorter! wretched pale-face, crave not quarter!"
He replied, and with a shot-gun nearly blew the boss in two.

'Next, the wood-and-water joey fell a victim to his bowie,
And the boss's weeping widow got a gash from ear to ear;   30
And you should have seen his guiver when he scalped the bullock-driver
And made openings for a horse-boy, servant-maid, and overseer.

'Counting jackaroos and niggers, he had put up double figures,
When ensued his awful combat with a party of new-chums,
All agog to do their duty, with no thought of home or beauty —   35
But he rubbed them out as rapid as a school-boy would his sums.

'Out across the silent river, with some duck-shot in his liver,
Went the store-man, and a lassooed lady left in the same boat.
Sam then solved the Chinese question — or at least made a suggestion —
For he dragged one from a barrel by the tail and cut his throat.   40

'But, with thus the job completed, Sammy he got over-heated
And dropped dead of apoplexy — I felt better when he did!
For I'd got an awful singein' while I watched this mulga engine
Doing all that I've related — through a cracked brick oven-lid.

And when now I find men strangled, or I come across the mangled   45
Corpses of a crowd of people or depopulated towns,
Or ev'n a blood-stained river, I can scarce repress a shiver,
For my nerves were much affected that day out on Boiling Downs.'

                                                        (1899) 1927

'RITA SUNYASEE'

Bush Courtin'

When the milkin' music's ended, and the big cans stacked away,
An' the poddies have done drinkin', an' the neddies chew their hay,
Then I eat my snack while dressin', for Dad's always on the growl,
An' the cow-hairs from my love-lock brush, ere to my tryst I prowl.

Through my doss-room windy leavin', for the old man's ears are cocked,   5
I negotiate the pickets as the garden gate is locked;
For I hear the bittern's boomin' from the lily beds afar,
And my heart-strings are a-tingle to old Cupid's sweet guitar.

Jake is waitin' in the timber, where the lace-like shadows fall;
'Tis his signal that is stealin' like the mopoke's croakin' call;   10
Then he clasps me to his shirt-front with a bushman's brawny squeeze,
An' his whiskers sweep my freckles like soft tangles off the trees!

We discuss the price of sorghum; will there be a rise in wheat?
(Just a crumb or two of love-talk, for this fare is awful sweet!)
An' Jake's gettin' in his taters – half a patch a day he digs –   15
While his poddies feed themselves now; an' he's goin' to sell his pigs!

Then we let the world go hang there, as together close we cling
An' swear we'll love each other whate'er prices Fate may bring
(Jake's old trusty dog is watchin' where the shadows dim the track),
An' into Life's old, grey portmanteau a thousand joys we pack.   20

How the saucy moonbeams mock us, an' the grey bats tauntin' fly –
Seems they know that we are wanted, that we're courtin' on the sly;
We'll be married 'after harvest' if the wheat will only rise,
An' Dad will get what he's expectin' – that's a mighty big surprise!

                                                        (1904)

ANONYMOUS

Wallaby Stew

Poor Dad, he got five years or more, as everybody knows,
And now he lives in Maitland gaol, broad arrows on his clothes;
He branded old Brown's cleanskins and he never left a tail
So I'll relate the family's fate since Dad got put in gaol.

Chorus:
So stir the wallaby stew, make soup of the kangaroo tail;   5
I tell you things is pretty tough since Dad got put in gaol.

Our sheep all died a month ago, of footrot and the fluke;
Our cow got shot last Christmas day by my big brother Luke;
Our mother's got a shearer cove forever within hail;
The family will have grown a bit when Dad gets out of gaol.   10

Our Bess got shook upon some bloke, but he's gone, we don't know where;
He used to act about the sheds, but he ain't acted square;
I sold the buggy on my own, and the place is up for sale;
That won't be all that has been junked when Dad comes out of gaol.

They let Dad out before his time to give us a surprise.   15
He came and slowly looked around, then gently blessed our eyes;
He shook hands with the shearer cove, and said that things seemed stale,
And left him here to shepherd us, and battled back into gaol.

ARTHUR H. ADAMS   *(1872–1936)*

The Australian

Once more this Autumn-earth is ripe,
Parturient of another type.

While with the Past old nations merge
His foot is on the Future's verge;

They watch him, as they huddle pent,   5
Striding a spacious continent,

Above the level desert's marge
Looming in his aloofness large.

No flower with fragile sweetness graced —
A lank weed wrestling with the waste.   10

Pallid of face and gaunt of limb,
The sweetness withered out of him.

Sombre, indomitable, wan,
The juices dried, the glad youth gone.

A little weary from his birth; 15
His laugh the spectre of a mirth.

Bitter beneath a bitter sky,
To Nature he has no reply.

Wanton, perhaps, and cruel. Yes,
Is not his sun more merciless? 20

Joy has such niggard dole to give,
He laughs, a child, just glad to live.

So drab and neutral is his day
He gleans a splendour in the grey,

And from his life's monotony 25
He lifts a subtle melody.

When earth so poor a banquet makes
His pleasures at a gulp he takes.

The feast is his to the last crumb;
Drink while he can ... the drought will come. 30

His heart a sudden tropic flower,
He loves and loathes within an hour.

Yet you who by the pools abide,
Judge not the man who swerves aside.

He sees beyond your hazy fears; 35
He roads the desert of the years.

Rearing his cities in the sand,
He builds where even God has banned.

With green a continent he crowns,
And stars a wilderness with towns. 40

His gyves of steel the great plain wears:
With paths the distances he snares.

A child who takes a world for toy.
To build a nation, or destroy.

His childish features frozen stern, 45
A nation's task he has to learn,

From feeble tribes to federate
One splendid peace-encompassed State.

But if there be no goal to reach?
The way lies open, dawns beseech! 50

Enough that he lay down his load
A little further on the road.

So, toward undreamt-of destinies
He slouches down the centuries.

1899

CHRISTOPHER BRENNAN   *(1870–1932)*

From Poems 1913

From *Towards the Source*

Where star-cold and the dread of space
in icy silence bind the main
I feel but vastness on my face,
I sit, a mere incurious brain,

under some outcast satellite,   5
some Thule of the universe,
upon the utter verge of night
frozen by some forgotten curse.

The ways are hidden from mine eyes
that brought me to this ghastly shore: 10
no embers in their depths arise
of suns I may have known of yore.

Somewhere I dream of tremulous flowers
and meadows fervent with appeal
far among fever'd human hours   15
whose pulses here I never feel:

that on my careless name afar
a voice is calling ever again
beneath some other wounded star
removed for ever from my ken: 20

vain fictions! silence fills my ear,
the deep my gaze: I reck of nought,
as I have sat for ages here,
concentred in my brooding thought.

(written 1894) 1897

From *Towards the Source*

The yellow gas is fired from street to street
past rows of heartless homes and hearths unlit,
dead churches, and the unending pavement beat
by crowds — say rather, haggard shades that flit

round nightly haunts of their delusive dream,   5
where'er our paradisal instinct starves: —
till on the utmost post, its sinuous gleam
crawls in the oily water of the wharves;

where Homer's sea loses his keen breath, hemm'd
what place rebellious piles were driven down —   10
the priestlike waters to this task condemn'd
to wash the roots of the inhuman town! —

where fat and strange-eyed fish that never saw
the outer deep, broad halls of sapphire light,
glut in the city's draught each nameless maw: 15
— and there, wide-eyed unto the soulless night,

methinks a drown'd maid's face might fitly show
what we have slain, a life that had been free,
clean, large, nor thus tormented — even so
as are the skies, the salt winds and the sea.   20

Ay, we had saved our days and kept them whole,
to whom no part in our old joy remains,
had felt those bright winds sweeping thro' our soul
and all the keen sea tumbling in our veins,

had thrill'd to harps of sunrise, when the height   25
whitens, and dawn dissolves in virgin tears,
or caught, across the hush'd ambrosial night,
the choral music of the swinging spheres,

or drunk the silence if nought else — But no!
and from each rotting soul distil in dreams   30
a poison, o'er the old earth creeping slow,
that kills the flowers and curdles the live streams,

that taints the fresh breath of re-risen day
and reeks across the pale bewilder'd moon:
— shall we be cleans'd and how? I only pray,   35
red flame or deluge, may that end be soon!

1897

From *The Forest of Night*

Fire in the heavens, and fire along the hills,
and fire made solid in the flinty stone,
thick-massed or scatter'd pebble, fire that fills
the breathless hour that lives in fire alone.

This valley, long ago the patient bed   5
of floods that carv'd its antient amplitude,
in stillness of the Egyptian crypt outspread,
endures to drown in noon-day's tyrant mood.

Behind the veil of burning silence bound,
vast life's innumerous busy littleness   10
is hush'd in vague-conjectured blur of sound
that dulls the brain with slumbrous weight, unless

some dazzling puncture let the stridence throng
in the cicada's torture-point of song.

(1899) 1914

From *The Wanderer*

When window-lamps had dwindled, then I rose
and left the town behind me; and on my way
passing a certain door I stopt, remembering
how once I stood on its threshold, and my life
was offer'd to me, a road how different   5
from that of the years since gone! and I had but
to rejoin an olden path, once dear, since left.
All night I have walk'd and my heart was deep awake,
remembering ways I dream'd and that I chose,
remembering lucidly, and was not sad,   10
being brimm'd with all the liquid and clear dark
of the night that was not stirr'd with any tide;
for leaves were silent and the road gleam'd pale,
following the ridge, and I was alone with night.
But now I am come among the rougher hills   15
and grow aware of the sea that somewhere near
is restless; and the flood of night is thinn'd
and stars are whitening. O, what horrible dawn
will bare me the way and crude lumps of the hills
and the homeless concave of the day, and bare   20
the ever-restless, ever-complaining sea?

                                                            (1902) 1914

From *The Wanderer*

I cry to you as I pass your windows in the dusk;

Ye have built you unmysterious homes and ways in the wood
where of old ye went with sudden eyes to the right and left;
and your going was now made safe and your staying comforted,
for the forest edge itself, holding old savagery   5
in unsearch'd glooms, was your houses' friendly barrier.
And now that the year goes winterward, ye thought to hide
behind your gleaming panes, and where the hearth sings merrily
make cheer with meat and wine, and sleep in the long night,
and the uncared wastes might be a crying unhappiness.   10
But I, who have come from the outer night, I say to you
the winds are up and terribly will they shake the dry wood:
the woods shall awake, hearing them, shall awake to be toss'd and riven,
and make a cry and a parting in your sleep all night
as the wither'd leaves go whirling all night along all ways.   15
And when ye come forth at dawn, uncomforted by sleep,
ye shall stand at amaze, beholding all the ways overhidden
with worthless drift of the dead and all your broken world:
and ye shall not know whence the winds have come, nor shall ye know
whither the yesterdays have fled, or if they were.   20

                                                            (1902) 1914

From *The Wanderer*

The land I came thro' last was dumb with night,
a limbo of defeated glory, a ghost:
for wreck of constellations flicker'd perishing
scarce sustain'd in the mortuary air,
and on the ground and out of livid pools   5
wreck of old swords and crowns glimmer'd at whiles;
I seem'd at home in some old dream of kingship:
now it is clear grey day and the road is plain,
I am the wanderer of many years
who cannot tell if ever he was king   10
or if ever kingdoms were: I know I am
the wanderer of the ways of all the worlds,
to whom the sunshine and the rain are one
and one to stay or hasten, because he knows
no ending of the way, no home, no goal,   15
and phantom night and the grey day alike
withhold the heart where all my dreams and days
might faint in soft fire and delicious death:
and saying this to myself as a simple thing
I feel a peace fall in the heart of the winds   20
and a clear dusk settle, somewhere, far in me.

                                        (1902) 1914

Epilogue

1897

Deep in my hidden country stands a peak,
and none hath known its name
and none, save I, hath even skill to seek:
thence my wild spirit came.

Thither I turn, when the day's garish world   5
too long hath vex'd my sight.
and bare my limbs where the great winds are whirl'd
and life's undreaded might.

For there I know the pools of clearest blue,
glad wells of simple sooth,   10
there, steep'd in strength of glacier springs, renew
the lucid body of youth.

there I alone may know the joy of quest
and keen delight of cold,
or rest, what time the night with naked breast   15
and shaken hair of gold,

folds me so close, that her great breath would seem
to fill the darkling heart
with solemn certainty of ancient dream
or whisperingly to impart   20

aeonian life, larger than seas of light,
more limpid than the dawn:
there, when my foot hath touch'd the topmost height,
the fire from heaven is drawn.

If any murmur that my 'sdainful hand   25
withholds its sacrifice
where ranged unto the Law the peoples stand,
let this blown word suffice:

The gift of self is self's most sacred right:
only where none hath trod,   30
only upon my secret starry height
I abdicate to God.

                                                          1914

Because she would ask me why I loved her

If questioning could make us wise
no eyes would ever gaze in eyes;
if all our tale were told in speech
no mouths would wander each to each.

Were spirits free from mortal mesh   5
and love not bound in hearts of flesh
no aching breasts would yearn to meet
and find their ecstasy complete.

For who is there that lives and knows
the secret powers by which he grows?   10
Were knowledge all, what were our need
to thrill and faint and sweetly bleed?

Then seek not, sweet, the *If* and *Why*
I love you now until I die:
For I must love because I live   15
And life in me is what you give.

                                          (written 1923) 1960

MARIE E. J. PITT   *(1869–1948)*

The Keening

We are the women and children
  Of the men that mined for gold,
Heavy are we with sorrow,
  Heavy as heart can hold;
Galled are we with injustice,   5
  Sick to the soul of loss —
Husbands and sons and brothers
  Slain for the yellow dross!

We are the women and children
    Of the men that died like sheep,   10
'Stoping' the stubborn matrix,
    Piling the mullock heap,
Stifling in torrid 'rises,'
    Stumbling with stupid tread
Along the Vale of the Shadow   15
    To the thud of the stamper-head!

We are the women and children
    Of the miners that delved below —
Main-shaft and winze and crosscut —
    Opening the deadly 'show.'   20
Look at us! Yea, in our faces!
    God! Are ye not ashamed
In the sight of your godless fellows
    Of the men ye have killed and maimed?

They moiled like gnomes in the 'faces,'   25
    They choked in the ''fracteur' fumes,
And your dividends paved the pathways
    That led to their early tombs.
With Death in the sleepless night-shifts
    They diced for the prize ye drew;   30
And the Devil loaded the pieces —
    But the stakes were held by you!

Ye were the lords of Labor;
    They were the slaves of Need.
Homes had they for the keeping,   35
    Children to clothe and feed!
Ye paid them currency wages —
    Shall it stand to your souls for shrift
That ye bought them in open market
    For 'seven-and-six a shift?'   40

Wise in your generation,
    Cunning are ye in your day!
But 'ware of the stealthy vengeance
    That never your wealth shall stay!
They won it — yea, with their life-blood;   45
    Ye laughed at the sacrifice;
But by every drop of your spilling
    We shall hold you to pay the price!

Ye have sown the wind, to your sorrow;
    Ye have sown by the coward's code,   50
Where the glimmering candles gutter,
    And the rock-drill bites on the lode!
Ye have sown to the jangle of stampers,
    To the brawl of the Stock Exchange,

And your children shall reap the whirlwind   55
  On the terms that the gods arrange.

And ye, who counsel the nation,
  Statesmen who rule the State!
Foolish are ye in your weakness,
  Wise are we in our hate!   60
Traitors and false that pander
  To the spillers of human life,
Slaying with swords of silence
  Who dared not slay with the knife!

And ye of the House of Pilate,   65
  Ye who gibber of Christ
At the foot of the golden crosses
  Where the sons of men are triced!
Ye who whimper of patience,
  Who slay with a loose-lipped lie   70
At the word of the fat blasphemers
  Whose poppet-heads mock the sky!

We are the women and children
  Of the men that ye mowed like wheat;
Some of us slave for a pittance —   75
  Some of us walk the street;
Bodies and souls, ye have scourged us;
  Ye have winnowed us flesh from bone:
But, by the God ye have flouted,
  We will come again for our own!   80

                                                           1911

City Hunger

A tent 'neath the gum trees? — O No! No!
Give me the stream of which I am part —
The red stream filling the old world's heart
With life and laughter, with rapture and glow.
Give me the battle the strivers ken   5
With comrades beside and the goal before.
O tears and laughter and strife to the core —
I love you! love you, cities of men!

Fair are the halls where the white stars peer
Through green arched casements from kindly skies!   10
But the cities of men have a thousand eyes
That beacon and beckon the distant near.
With Life on the march and Time on the wing
To a wild world measure, what matter the odds?
Or roses strewn by the hands of the gods?   15
Or hyssop and rue that the seasons bring?

Sing not of far-folden hills agleam,
Of sun-kissed valleys where Strife is not,
The sylvan Nirvanas where ripe to rot
The fruits of Toil and the flowers of Dream.   20
A leaf among leaves I had rather be tossed
With the soul-ships cleaving a treacherous tide
Or freighted for ports of the Barmecide,
Or bound for the deep sea docks o' the lost.

A tent 'neath the gum trees? No! not I!   25
I'll march with the rabble, clean and unclean,
Judas, Barrabas or Nazarene —
And die as I lived when it's time to die.
Till from the banquet that mortals ken
The lights wane low and the guests depart —   30
O tears and laughter and strife to the heart,
I love you! love you, cities of men!

                    1911

R. H. CROLL   *(1869–1947)*

Australia (In Contemporary Literature)

Whalers, damper, swag and nosebag, Johnny-cakes and billy-tea,
Murrumburrah, Meremendicoowoke, Yoularbudgeree,
Cattle-duffers, bold bushrangers, diggers, drovers, bush race-courses,
And on all the other pages horses, horses, horses, horses.

                    (1899)

J. K. MCDOUGALL   *(1867–1957)*

The White Man's Burden

Written 1902

Take up the White Man's burden,
    Lift high the blazing cross;
For Greed must have his guerdon,
    Whoever counts the loss.
Beneath the White Man's banner,   5
    Enlist, ye sons of blood,
Leave cot and peaceful manor
    And march by field and flood.

---

23 Barmecide   name of a rich family of Baghdad who prepared a lavish illusory meal of empty dishes for a pauper, in 'The Barber's Story of his Sixth Brother' from *The Arabian Nights*
The White Man's Burden   title of a poem (1899) on imperial responsibility by Rudyard Kipling

Let War and War's dread rumour
   Bring light and Christian hope   10
To crowds ye deftly humour
   With sword and gallow's rope.
Send forth, with blood anointed,
   The butchers that ye breed,
To push the frauds appointed   15
   To gild the hand of Greed.

Your sires were gods of slaughter;
   Where still their altars are,
On shudd'ring land and water,
   Be yours their bloody star.   20
Turn on the crouching savage
   Your cannon gorged with shot;
Let Might and Murder ravage,
   God sleeps and hears you not.

Spur on the war-horse plunging   25
   Proud crested o'er the slain;
With sword blades, fiercely lunging,
   Wet earth with rose red rain.
Let nations see your sabres
   Turn flashing in the sun,   30
Cut down your Christian neighbours
   High Mammon's will be done!

Ride down the rebel workers,
   Ride down their children, too;
Ye are the tools of shirkers,   35
   Whose red behests ye do.
Ye are the rich men's beagles,
   Kill while your hirers gloat;
Feed ye the wolves and eagles
   On dead men – till they bloat.   40

Ride down — ye have the horses —
   Strike down with lances keen;
Fill up the gaps with corses,
   Between each still machine.
Drive home the mob like cattle,   45
   Take ye the spoilers' pay;
Ride grimly into battle
   And slay, and slay, and slay.

Ye are the White Man's engines;
   Ye fight and force for him;   50
Fill up his cup of vengeance,
   Yea, fill it to the brim.
Paid bullies of the robbers,
   Your murders are not sin;

Kill for the Trusts and Jobbers —   55
   Sock ye the bay'nets in.

Take up the White Man's burden,
   Hired slaves march forth and slay;
The gear of battle gird on,
   Loose Hell and darken day.   60
Thrust brand at breast of brother,
   And hear above the strife
The wail of some White Mother,
   The sob of some White Wife.

Let conquest be your charter   65
   To force the rights of Trade;
(Arise ye rogues who barter,
   And track the conqu'ror's blade.)
Fresh plunder lies before you;
   Law quits the stricken land;   70
A Christian flag waves o'er you
   To back the thieving hand.

Ye are the sordid killers,
   Ye murder for a fee;
Ye prop like rotten pillars   75
   Trade's lust and treachery.
Hog souled and dirty handed
   Ye sell yourselves for gain,
And stand forever branded,
   Red felons after Cain.   80

Ye are the fools and flunkeys;
   Ye die to serve the great —
The rooks and gilded monkeys
   Who eat the fat of State.
Ye fall on alien places;   85
   On foreign wastes ye lie,
Stiff-limbed, with battered faces
   Turned livid to the sky.

The shouts of yobs and wenches —
   Loose cheer and blare of brass   90
Have died beyond the trenches,
   Have passed as echoes pass.
Long lines of helmets gleaming,
   A march in battle played,
Ye see and hear and dreaming   95
   Your lives swoon out in shade.

Fill up your foaming glasses
   With blood instead of wine,
And pledge the robber classes
   And kings as base as swine.   100

Drink to each paid defender,
  While loyal boozers rant;
And veil with flow'rs and splendour,
  The spectre face of Want.

Race ever race is spoiling;   105
  The strong hand triumphs still;
Let Progress cease her toiling,
  Man's mission is to kill.
Shed blood and let it curd on
  The patriot's tear-wet cheek   110
Take up the White Man's burden,
  And rob and wrong the weak.

                                                  (1915) 1922

HENRY LAWSON   *(1867–1922)*

Middleton's Rouseabout

Tall and freckled and sandy,
  Face of a country lout;
This was the picture of Andy,
  Middleton's Rouseabout.

Type of a coming nation,   5
  In the land of cattle and sheep,
Worked on Middleton's station,
  'Pound a week and his keep'.

On Middleton's wide dominions
  Plied the stockwhip and shears;   10
Hadn't any opinions,
  Hadn't any 'idears'.

Swiftly the years went over,
  Liquor and drought prevailed;
Middleton went as a drover   15
  After his station had failed.

Type of a careless nation,
  Men who are soon played out,
Middleton was: — and his station
  Was bought by the Rouseabout.   20

Flourishing beard and sandy,
  Tall and solid and stout:
This is the picture of Andy,
  Middleton's Rouseabout.

Now on his own dominions   25
    Works with his overseers;
Hasn't any opinions,
    Hasn't any idears.

                                 (1890) 1896

Freedom on the Wallaby

Our fathers toiled for bitter bread
    While idlers thrived beside them;
But food to eat and clothes to wear
    Their native land denied them.
They left their native land in spite   5
    Of royalties' regalia,
And so they came, or if they stole
    Were sent out to Australia.

They struggled hard to make a home,
    Hard grubbing 'twas and clearing.   10
They weren't troubled much with toffs
    When they were pioneering;
And now that we have made the land
    A garden full of promise,
Old greed must crook his dirty hand   15
    And come to take it from us.

But Freedom's on the Wallaby,
    She'll knock the tyrants silly,
She's going to light another fire
    And boil another billy.   20
We'll make the tyrants feel the sting
    Of those that they would throttle;
They needn't say the fault is ours
    If blood should stain the wattle.

                                 (1891) 1913

Up the Country

I am back from up the country — very sorry that I went —
Seeking for the Southern poets' land whereon to pitch my tent;
I have lost a lot of idols, which were broken on the track,
Burnt a lot of fancy verses, and I'm glad that I am back.
Further out may be the pleasant scenes of which our poets boast,   5
But I think the country's rather more inviting round the coast.
Anyway, I'll stay at present at a boarding-house in town,
Drinking beer and lemon-squashes, taking baths and cooling down.

'Sunny plains!' Great Scott! — those burning wastes of barren soil and sand
With their everlasting fences stretching out across the land!   10

On the Wallaby   on the wallaby track: tramping the outback to find work

Desolation where the crow is! Desert where the eagle flies,
Paddocks where the luny bullock starts and stares with reddened eyes;
Where, in clouds of dust enveloped, roasted bullock-drivers creep
Slowly past the sun-dried shepherd dragged behind his crawling sheep.
Stunted peak of granite gleaming, glaring like a molten mass   15
Turned from some infernal furnace on a plain devoid of grass.

Miles and miles of thirsty gutters — strings of muddy water-holes
In the place of 'shining rivers' — 'walled by cliffs and forest boles'.
Barren ridges, gullies, ridges! where the everlasting flies —
Fiercer than the plagues of Egypt — swarm about your blighted eyes!   20
Bush! where there is no horizon! where the buried bushman sees
Nothing — Nothing! but the sameness of the ragged, stunted trees!
Lonely hut where drought's eternal — suffocating atmosphere —
Where the God-forgotten hatter dreams of city life and beer.

Treacherous tracks that trap the stranger, endless roads that gleam and glare, 25
Dark and evil-looking gullies, hiding secrets here and there!
Dull dumb flats and stony rises, where the toiling bullocks bake,
And the sinister 'gohanna', and the lizard, and the snake.
Land of day and night — no morning freshness, and no afternoon,
When the great white sun in rising brings the summer heat in June.   30
Dismal country for the exile, when the shades begin to fall
From the sad heart-breaking sunset, to the newchum worst of all.   32

Dreary land in rainy weather, with the endless clouds that drift
O'er the bushman like a blanket that the Lord will never lift —
Dismal land when it is raining — growl of floods, and, O the woosh   35
Of the rain and wind together on the dark bed of the bush —
Ghastly fires in lonely humpies where the granite rocks are piled
In the rain-swept wildernesses that are wildest of the wild.

Land where gaunt and haggard women live alone and work like men,
Till their husbands, gone a-droving, will return to them again: 40
Homes of men! if homes had ever such a God-forgotten place,
Where the wild selector's children fly before a stranger's face.
Home of tragedy applauded by the dingoes' dismal yell,
Heaven of the shanty-keeper — fitting fiend for such a hell —
And the wallaroos and wombats, add, of course, the curlew's call   45
And the lone sundowner tramping ever onward through it all!

I am back from up the country, up the country where I went
Seeking for the Southern poets' land whereon to pitch my tent;
I have shattered many idols out along the dusty track,
Burnt a lot of fancy verses — and I'm glad that I am back.   50
I believe the Southern poets' dream will not be realized
Till the plains are irrigated and the land is humanized.
I intend to stay at present, as I said before, in town
Drinking beer and lemon-squashes, taking baths and cooling down.

                                                    (1892) 1896

The Sliprails and The Spur

The colours of the setting sun
    Withdrew across the Western land —
He raised the sliprails, one by one,
    And shot them home with trembling hand;
Her brown hands clung — her face grew pale —   5
    Ah! quivering chin and eyes that brim! —
One quick, fierce kiss across the rail,
    And, 'Good-bye, Mary!' 'Good-bye, Jim!'

O he rides hard to race the pain
    Who rides from love, who rides from home;   10
But he rides slowly home again,
    Whose heart has learnt to love and roam.

A hand upon the horse's mane,
    And one foot in the stirrup set,
And, stooping back to kiss again,   15
    With 'Good-bye, Mary! don't you fret!
When I come back' — he laughed for her —
    'We do not know how soon 'twill be;
I'll whistle as I round the spur —
    You let the sliprails down for me.'   20

She gasped for sudden loss of hope,
    As, with a backward wave to her,
He cantered down the grassy slope
    And swiftly round the dark'ning spur.
Black-pencilled panels standing high,   25
    And darkness fading into stars,
And blurring fast against the sky,
    A faint white form beside the bars.

And often at the set of sun,
    In winter bleak and summer brown,   30
She'd steal across the little run,
    And shyly let the sliprails down,
And listen there when darkness shut
    The nearer spur in silence deep;
And when they called her from the hut   35
    Steal home and cry herself to sleep.

A great white gate where sliprails were,
    A brick house 'neath the mountain brow,
The 'mad girl' buried by the spur
    So long ago, forgotten now.   40

And he rides hard to dull the pain
    Who rides from one that loves him best;
And he rides slowly back again
    Whose restless heart must rove for rest.

(1899) 1900

To Victor Daley

I thought that silence would be best,
    But I a call have heard,
And, Victor, after all the rest,
    I well might say a word:
The day and work is nearly done,   5
    And ours the victory,
And we are resting, one by one,
    In graveyards by the sea.

You made a jest on that last night,
    I met it with a laugh: 10
You wondered which of us should write
    The other's epitaph.
We filled the glasses to the brim —
    'The land's own wine' you know —
And solemnly we drank to him   15
    Who should be first to go.

No ribald jest; we were but two —
    The royst'ring days were past —
And in our heart of hearts we knew
    That one was going fast.   20
We both knew who should win the race —
    Were rest or fame the prize —
As with a quaint smile on your face
    You looked into my eyes.

But then you talked of other nights,   25
    When, gay from dusk to dawn,
You wasted hours with other lights
    That went where you have gone.
You spoke not of the fair and 'fast',
    But of the pure and true —   30
'Sweet ugly women of the past'
    Who stood so well by you.

You talked about old struggles brave,
    But in a saddened tone —
The swindles editors forgave   35
    For laughter's sake alone.
You talked of humorous distress
    And bailiffs that you knew,
But with a touch of bitterness
    I'd never seen in you.   40

No need for tears or quick-caught breath —
    You sleep not in the sand —
No need for ranting song of death,
    With the death drink in our hand.

No need for vain invective hurled
    At 'cruel destiny';   45
Though you seem dead to all the world
    You are not dead to me.

I see you walk into the room —
    We aye remember how —   50
And, looking back into the gloom,
    You'll smile about it now.
'Twas Victor's entry, solemn style —
    With verse or paragraph:
Though we so often saw your smile   55
    How many heard you laugh?

They dare to write about the man
    That they have never seen:
The blustering false Bohemian
    That you have never been;   60
Some with the false note in their voice
    And with the false tear shed,
Who in their secret heart rejoice
    For one more rival — dead.

They miss the poems, real and true,   65
    Where your heart's blood was shed,
And rave of reckless things that you
    Threw out for bitter bread.
They 'weep' and 'worship' while you 'rest',
    They drivel and they dote —   70
But, Victor, we remember best
    The things we never wrote.

The things that lie between us two,
    The things I'll never tell.
A fool, I stripped my soul, but you —   75
    You wore your mask too well.
(How strangely human all men be,
    Though each one plays a part.)
You only dropped it once for me,
    But then I saw your heart.   80

A souls'-match, such as one might strike
    With or without intent
(How strangely all men are alike —
    With masks so different).
No need to drop the mask again,   85
    On that last night, I know —
It chanced when we were sober men,
    Some seven years ago.

They slander you, fresh in the sand,
    They slander me alive;   90
But, when their foul souls flee the land,
    Our spirits shall arrive.

In slime and envy let them rave,
    And let the worst be said:
'A drunkard at a drunkard's grave,'   95
    'A brilliant drunkard dead.'

Because we would not crawl to them,
    Their hands we would not shake,
Because their greed we would condemn,
    Their bribes we would not take: 100
Because unto the fair and true
    Our hearts and songs we gave —
But I forgot them when I threw
    My white flower on your grave.

So let us turn, and with a smile   105
    Let those poor creatures pass,
While we, the few who wait awhile,
    Drink to an empty glass.
We'll live as in the days gone by,
    To no god shall we bow —   110
Though, Victor, there are times when I
    Feel jealous of you now.

But I'll have done with solemn songs,
    Save for my country's sake;
It is not meet, for all the wrongs,   115
    That any heart should break.
So many need to weep and smile,
    Though all the rest should frown,
That I'd take your burden up awhile
    Where you have laid it down.   120

                                          (1906) 1913

ANONYMOUS

The Bastard from the Bush

As night was falling slowly on city, town and bush,
from a slum in Jones's Alley came the Captain of the Push,
and his whistle, loud and piercing, woke the echoes of the Rocks,
and a dozen ghouls came slouching round the corners of the blocks.

Then the Captain jerked a finger at a stranger by the kerb,   5
whom he qualified politely with an adjective and verb.
Then he made the introduction: 'Here's a covey from the bush;
fuck me blind, he wants to join us, be a member of the Push!'

The Bastard from the Bush   This ballad has survived in several forms through oral transmission and fugitive publication. Its similarity to Henry Lawson's 'The Captain of the Push' (1892) has prompted speculation that he may be the author.

Then the stranger made this answer to the Captain of the Push:
'Why, fuck me dead, I'm Foreskin Fred, the Bastard from the Bush!   10
I've been in every two-up school from Darwin to the Loo;
I've ridden colts and blackgins; what more can a bugger do?'

'Are you game to break a window?' said the Captain of the Push.
'I'd knock a fucking house down!' said the Bastard from the Bush.
'Would you out a man and rob him?' said the Captain of the Push.   15
'I'd knock him down and fuck him!' said the Bastard from the Bush.

'Would you dong a bloody copper if you caught the cunt alone?
Would you stoush a swell or Chinkie, split his garret with a stone?
Would you have a moll to keep you; would you swear off work for good?'
Said the Bastard: 'My colonial silver-mounted oath I would!'   20

'Would you care to have a gasper?' said the Captain of the Push.
'I'll take that bloody packet!' said the Bastard from the Bush.
Then the Pushites all took council, saying, 'Fuck me, but he's game!
Let's make him our star basher; he'll live up to his name.'

So they took him to their hideout, that Bastard from the Bush,   25
and granted him all privileges appertaining to the Push.
But soon they found his little ways were more than they could stand,
and finally their Captain addressed the members of his band:

'Now listen here, you buggers, we've caught a fucking Tartar.
At every kind of bludging, that Bastard is a starter.   30
At poker and at two-up he's shook our fucking rolls;
he swipes our fucking likker and he robs our bloody molls!'

So down in Jones's Alley all the members of the Push
laid a dark and dirty ambush for that Bastard from the Bush.
But against the wall of Riley's pub the Bastard made a stand,   35
a nasty grin upon his dial; a bike-chain in each hand.

They sprang upon him in a bunch, but one by one they fell,
with crack of bone, unearthly groan, and agonising yell,
till the sorely battered Captain, spitting teeth and gouts of blood,
held an ear all torn and bleeding in a hand bedaubed with mud.   40

'You low polluted Bastard!' snarled the Captain of the Push,
'Get back where your sort belongs — that's somewhere in the bush.
And I hope heaps of misfortunes may soon tumble down on you;
may some lousy harlot dose you till your ballocks turn sky-blue!

'May the itching piles torment you; may corns grow on your feet!   45
May crabs as big as spiders attack your balls a treat!
And when you're down and outed, to a hopeless bloody wreck,
may you slip back through your arsehole and break your fucking neck!'

(from 1880s–1914)

BARCROFT BOAKE   *(1866–92)*

Where the Dead Men Lie

Out on the wastes of the Never Never —
   That's where the dead men lie!
There where the heat-waves dance for ever —
   That's where the dead men lie!
That's where the Earth's loved sons are keeping   5
Endless tryst: not the west wind sweeping
Feverish pinions can wake their sleeping —
   Out where the dead men lie!

Where brown Summer and Death have mated —
   That's where the dead men lie!   10
Loving with fiery lust unsated —
   That's where the dead men lie!
Out where the grinning skulls bleach whitely
Under the saltbush sparkling brightly;
Out where the wild dogs chorus nightly —   15
   That's where the dead men lie!

Deep in the yellow, flowing river —
   That's where the dead men lie!
Under the banks where the shadows quiver —
   That's where the dead men lie!   20
Where the platypus twists and doubles,
Leaving a train of tiny bubbles;
Rid at last of their earthly troubles —
   That's where the dead men lie!

East and backward pale faces turning —   25
   That's how the dead men lie!
Gaunt arms stretched with a voiceless yearning —
   That's how the dead men lie!
Oft in the fragrant hush of nooning
Hearing again their mothers' crooning,   30
Wrapt for aye in a dreamful swooning —
   That's how the dead men lie!

Only the hand of Night can free them —
   That's when the dead men fly!
Only the frightened cattle see them —   35
   See the dead men go by!
Cloven hoofs beating out one measure,
Bidding the stockman know no leisure —
That's when the dead men take their pleasure!
   That's when the dead men fly!   40

Ask, too, the never-sleeping drover:
   He sees the dead pass by;

Hearing them call to their friends — the plover,
  Hearing the dead men cry;
Seeing their faces stealing, stealing,   45
Hearing their laughter pealing, pealing,
Watching their grey forms wheeling, wheeling
  Round where the cattle lie!

Strangled by thirst and fierce privation —
  That's how the dead men die!   50
Out on Moneygrub's farthest station —
  That's how the dead men die!
Hardfaced greybeards, youngsters callow;
Some mounds cared for, some left fallow;
Some deep down, yet others shallow;   55
  Some having but the sky.

Moneygrub, as he sips his claret,
  Looks with complacent eye
Down at his watch-chain, eighteen-carat —
  There, in his club, hard by: 60
Recks not that every link is stamped with
Names of the men whose limbs are cramped with
Too long lying in grave mould, camped with
  Death where the dead men lie.

(1891) 1897

A. B. PATERSON ('THE BANJO')   *(1864–1941)*

Clancy of the Overflow

I had written him a letter which I had, for want of better
  Knowledge, sent to where I met him down the Lachlan, years ago,
He was shearing when I knew him, so I sent the letter to him,
  Just 'on spec,' addressed as follows, 'Clancy, of The Overflow.'

And an answer came directed in a writing unexpected,   5
  (And I think the same was written with a thumb-nail dipped in tar)
'Twas his shearing mate who wrote it, and *verbatim* I will quote it:
  'Clancy's gone to Queensland droving, and we don't know where he are.'

.   .   .   .   .

In my wild erratic fancy visions come to me of Clancy
  Gone a-droving 'down the Cooper' where the Western drovers go;   10
As the stock are slowly stringing, Clancy rides behind them singing,
  For the drover's life has pleasures that the towns-folk never know.

And the bush hath friends to meet him, and their kindly voices greet him
  In the murmur of the breezes and the river on its bars,
And he sees the vision splendid of the sunlit plains extended,   15
  And at night the wond'rous glory of the everlasting stars.

.   .   .   .   .

I am sitting in my dingy little office, where a stingy
   Ray of sunlight struggles feebly down between the houses tall,
And the foetid air and gritty of the dusty, dirty city
   Through the open window floating, spreads its foulness over all.   20

And in place of lowing cattle, I can hear the fiendish rattle
   Of the tramways and the 'buses making hurry down the street,
And the language uninviting of the gutter children fighting,
   Comes fitfully and faintly through the ceaseless tramp of feet.

And the hurrying people daunt me, and their pallid faces haunt me   25
   As they shoulder one another in their rush and nervous haste,
With their eager eyes and greedy, and their stunted forms and weedy,
   For townsfolk have no time to grow, they have no time to waste.

And I somehow rather fancy that I'd like to change with Clancy,
   Like to take a turn at droving where the seasons come and go,   30
While he faced the round eternal of the cash-book and the journal —
   But I doubt he'd suit the office, Clancy, of 'The Overflow.'

                                   (1889) 1895

The Man From Snowy River

There was movement at the station, for the word had passed around
That the colt from old Regret had got away,
And had joined the wild bush horses — he was worth a thousand pound,
So all the cracks had gathered to the fray.
All the tried and noted riders from the stations near and far   5
Had mustered at the homestead overnight,
For the bushmen love hard riding where the wild bush horses are,
And the stock-horse snuffs the battle with delight.

There was Harrison, who made his pile when Pardon won the cup,
The old man with his hair as white as snow;   10
But few could ride beside him when his blood was fairly up —
He would go wherever horse and man could go.
And Clancy of the Overflow came down to lend a hand,
No better horseman ever held the reins;
For never horse could throw him while the saddle-girths would stand,   15
He learnt to ride while droving on the plains.

And one was there, a stripling on a small and weedy beast,
He was something like a racehorse undersized,
With a touch of Timor pony — three parts thoroughbred at least —
And such as are by mountain horsemen prized.   20
He was hard and tough and wiry — just the sort that won't say die —
There was courage in his quick impatient tread;
And he bore the badge of gameness in his bright and fiery eye,
And the proud and lofty carriage of his head.

But still so slight and weedy, one would doubt his power to stay,   25
And the old man said, 'That horse will never do
'For a long and tiring gallop — lad, you'd better stop away,
'Those hills are far too rough for such as you.'
So he waited sad and wistful — only Clancy stood his friend —
'I think we ought to let him come,' he said;   30
'I warrant he'll be with us when he's wanted at the end,
'For both his horse and he are mountain bred.'

'He hails from Snowy River, up by Kosciusko's side,
'Where the hills are twice as steep and twice as rough,
'Where a horse's hoofs strike firelight from the flint stones every stride,   35
'The man that hold his own is good enough.
'And the Snowy River riders on the mountains make their home,
'Where the river runs those giant hills between;
'I have seen full many horsemen since I first commenced to roam,
'But nowhere yet such horsemen have I seen.'   40

So he went — they found the horses by the big mimosa clump —
They raced away towards the mountain's brow,
And the old man gave his orders, 'Boys, go at them from the jump,
'No use to try for fancy riding now.
'And, Clancy, you must wheel them, try and wheel them to the right.   45
'Ride boldly, lad, and never fear the spills,
'For never yet was rider that could keep the mob in sight,
'If once they gain the shelter of those hills.'

So Clancy rode to wheel them — he was racing on the wing
Where the best and boldest riders take their place,   50
And he raced his stock-horse past them, and he made the ranges ring
With the stockwhip, as he met them face to face.
Then they halted for a moment, while he swung the dreaded lash,
But they saw their well-loved mountain full in view,
And they charged beneath the stockwhip with a sharp and sudden dash,   55
And off into the mountain scrub they flew.

Then fast the horsemen followed, where the gorges deep and black
Resounded to the thunder of their tread,
And the stockwhips woke the echoes, and they fiercely answered back
From cliffs and crags that beetled overhead.   60
And upward, ever upward, the wild horses held their way,
Where mountain ash and kurrajong grew wide;
And the old man muttered fiercely, 'We may bid the mob good day,
'*No* man can hold them down the other side.'

When they reached the mountain's summit, even Clancy took a pull,   65
It well might make the boldest hold their breath,
The wild hop scrub grew thickly, and the hidden ground was full
Of wombat holes, and any slip was death.

But the man from Snowy River let the pony have his head,
And he swung his stockwhip round and gave a cheer,   70
And he raced him down the mountain like a torrent down its bed,
While the others stood and watched in very fear.

He sent the flint stones flying, but the pony kept his feet,
He cleared the fallen timber in his stride,
And the man from Snowy River never shifted in his seat —   75
It was grand to see that mountain horseman ride.
Through the stringy barks and saplings, on the rough and broken ground,
Down the hillside at a racing pace he went;
And he never drew the bridle till he landed safe and sound,
At the bottom of that terrible descent.   80

He was right among the horses as they climbed the further hill,
And the watchers on the mountain standing mute,
Saw him ply the stockwhip fiercely, he was right among them still,
As he raced across the clearing in pursuit.
Then they lost him for a moment, where two mountain gullies met   85
In the ranges, but a final glimpse reveals
On a dim and distant hillside the wild horses racing yet,
With the man from Snowy River at their heels.

And he ran them single-handed till their sides were white with foam.
He followed like a bloodhound on their track,   90
Till they halted cowed and beaten, then he turned their heads for home,
And alone and unassisted brought them back.
But his hardy mountain pony he could scarcely raise a trot,
He was blood from hip to shoulder from the spur;
But his pluck was still undaunted, and his courage fiery hot,   95
For never yet was mountain horse a cur.

And down by Kosciusko, where the pine-clad ridges raise
Their torn and rugged battlements on high,
Where the air is clear as crystal, and the white stars fairly blaze
At midnight in the cold and frosty sky,   100
And where around the Overflow the reedbeds sweep and sway
To the breezes, and the rolling plains are wide,
The man from Snowy River is a household word to-day,
And the stockmen tell the story of his ride.

                                                                  (1890) 1895

A Bushman's Song

I'm travellin' down the Castlereagh, and I'm a station-hand
I'm handy with the ropin' pole, I'm handy with the brand,
And I can ride a rowdy colt, or swing the axe all day,
But there's no demand for a station-hand along the Castlereagh.

So it's shift, boys, shift, for there isn't the slightest doubt   5
That we've got to make a shift to the stations further out
With the pack-horse runnin' after, for he follows like a dog,
We must strike across the country at the old jig-jog.

This old black horse I'm riding — if you'll notice what's his brand,
He wears the crooked R, you see — none better in the land.   10
He takes a lot of beatin', and the other day we tried,
For a bit of a joke, with a racing bloke, for twenty pounds a side.

It was shift, boys, shift, for there wasn't the slightest doubt,
That I had to make him shift, for the money was nearly out;
But he cantered home a winner, with the other one at the flog —   15
He's a red-hot sort to pick up with his old jig-jog.

I asked a cove for shearin' once along the Marthaguy:
'We shear non-union, here,' says he. 'I call it scab,' says I.
I looked along the shearin' floor before I turned to go —
There were eight or ten dashed Chinamen a-shearin' in a row.   20

It was shift, boys, shift, for there wasn't the slightest doubt
It was time to make a shift with the leprosy about.
So I saddled up my horses, and I whistled to my dog
And I left his scabby station at the old jig-jog.

I went to Illawarra where my brother's got a farm,   25
He has to ask his landlord's leave before he lifts his arm;
The landlord owns the country side — man, woman, dog, and cat,
They haven't the cheek to dare to speak without they touch their hat.

It was shift, boys, shift, for there wasn't the slightest doubt
Their little landlord god and I would soon have fallen out;   30
Was I to touch my hat to him? — was I his bloomin' dog?
So I makes for up the country at the old jig-jog.

But it's time that I was movin', I've a mighty way to go
Till I drink artesian water from a thousand feet below;
Till I meet the overlanders with the cattle comin' down,   35
And I'll work a while till I make a pile, then have a spree in town.

So, it's shift, boys, shift, for there isn't the slightest doubt
We've got to make a shift to the stations further out;
The pack-horse runs behind us, for he follows like dog,
And we cross a lot of country at the old jig-jog.   40

(1892) 1895

The Geebung Polo Club

It was somewhere up the country, in a land of rock and scrub,
That they formed an institution called the Geebung Polo Club.
They were long and wiry natives from the rugged mountain side,
And the horse was never saddled that the Geebungs couldn't ride;
But their style of playing polo was irregular and rash —   5
They had mighty little science, but a mighty lot of dash:
And they played on mountain ponies that were muscular and strong,
Though their coats were quite unpolished, and their manes and tails were long.
And they used to train those ponies wheeling cattle in the scrub:
They were demons, were the members of the Geebung Polo Club.   10

It was somewhere down the country, in a city's smoke and steam,
That a polo club existed, called 'The Cuff and Collar Team.'
As a social institution 'twas a marvellous success,
For the members were distinguished by exclusiveness and dress.
They had natty little ponies that were nice, and smooth, and sleek,   15
For their cultivated owners only rode 'em once a week.
So they started up the country in pursuit of sport and fame,
For they meant to show the Geebungs how they ought to play the game;
And they took their valets with them — just to give their boots a rub
Ere they started operations on the Geebung Polo Club.   20

Now my readers can imagine how the contest ebbed and flowed,
When the Geebung boys got going it was time to clear the road;
And the game was so terrific that ere half the time was gone
A spectator's leg was broken — just from merely looking on.
For they waddied one another till the plain was strewn with dead,   25
While the score was kept so even that they neither got ahead.
And the Cuff and Collar Captain, when he tumbled off to die,
Was the last surviving player — so the game was called a tie.

Then the Captain of the Geebungs raised him slowly from the ground,
Though his wounds were mostly mortal, yet he fiercely gazed around;   30
There was no one to oppose him — all the rest were in a trance,
So he scrambled on his pony for his last expiring chance,
For he meant to make an effort to get victory to his side;
So he struck at goal — and missed it — then he tumbled off and died.

.   .   .   .   .

By the old Campaspe River, where the breezes shake the grass,   35
There's a row of little gravestones that the stockmen never pass,
For they bear a crude inscription saying, 'Stranger, drop a tear,
'For the Cuff and Collar players and the Geebung boys lie here.'
And on misty moonlit evenings, while the dingoes howl around,
You can see their shadows flitting down that phantom polo ground;   40
You can hear the loud collisions as the flying players meet,
And the rattle of the mallets, and the rush of ponies' feet,
Till the terrified spectator rides like blazes to the pub —
He's been haunted by the spectres of the Geebung Polo Club.

                                                                    1895

Waltzing Matilda

(Carrying a Swag)

Oh! there once was a swagman camped in a Billabong,
    Under the shade of a Coolabah tree;
And he sang as he looked at his old billy boiling,
    'Who'll come a-waltzing Matilda with me?'

Waltzing Matilda   The words sung today, which differ slightly from Paterson's poem, are from an
adaptation by Marie Cowan in 1903.

Who'll come a-waltzing Matilda, my darling,   5
   Who'll come a-waltzing Matilda with me?
Waltzing Matilda and leading a water-bag —
   Who'll come a-waltzing Matilda with me?

Down came a jumbuck to drink at the water-hole.
   Up jumped the swagman and grabbed him in glee;   10
And he sang as he stowed him away in his tucker-bag,
   'You'll come a-waltzing Matilda with me!'

Down came the Squatter a-riding his thoroughbred;
   Down came Policemen — one, two, and three.
'Whose is the jumbuck you've got in the tucker-bag?   15
   You'll come a-waltzing Matilda with me.'

But the swagman, he up and he jumped in the water-hole,
   Drowning himself by the Coolabah tree;
And his ghost may be heard as it sings in the Billabong
   'Who'll come a-waltzing Matilda with me?'   20

(written 1895) 1917

W.T. GOODGE *(1862–1909)*

Federation

   Let us sing of Federation
     ('T is the theme of every cult)
   And the joyful expectation
     Of its ultimate result.
   'Twill confirm the jubilation   5
   Of protection's expectation,
   And the quick consolidation
   Of freetrade with every nation;
   And teetotal legislation
   Will achieve its consummation   10
   And increase our concentration
   On the art of bibulation.
   We shall drink to desperation,
   And be quite the soberest nation
   We'll be desperately loyal   15
   Unto everything that's royal,
   And be ultra-democratic
   In a matter most emphatic.
   We'll be prosperous and easeful,
   And pre-eminently peaceful,   20
   And we'll take our proper station
   As a military nation!
   We shall show the throne affection,
   Also sever the connection,

And the bonds will get no fainter   25
And we'll also cut the painter.
We'll proclaim with lute and tabor
The millennium of labour,
And we'll bow before the gammon
Of plutocracy and Mammon.   30
We'll adopt all fads and fictions
And their mass of contradictions
If all hopes are consummated
When Australia's federated;
For the Federation speeches   35
This one solid moral teach us —
That a pile of paradoxes are expected to result!

                                                                1899

Life

Infant; teething,
    Thrush and croup.
Schoolboy; marbles,
    Top and hoop.
Youth; sweet picnics,   5
    Cigarettes,
Cricket, football,
    Sundry bets!

Young man; courtship
    Lovely she!   10
Married; youngsters
    Two or three
Worry, trouble,
    Smile and frown.
'In memoriam   15
    William Brown!'

                                                                1899

VICTOR DALEY   *(1858–1905)*

The Poet Care

Care is a Poet fine:
He works in shade or shine,
And leaves — you know his sign! —
No day without its line.

He writes with iron pen   5
Upon the brows of men;
Faint lines at first, and then
He scores them in again.

His touch at first is light
On Beauty's brow of white;   10
The old churl loves to write
On foreheads broad and bright.

A line for young love crossed,
A line for fair hopes lost
In an untimely frost —   15
A line that means *Thou Wast.*

Then deeper script appears:
The furrows of dim fears,
The traces of old tears,
The tide-marks of the years.   20

To him with sight made strong
By suffering and wrong,
The brows of all the throng
Are eloquent with song.

                                            (1885) 1947

The Woman at the Washtub

The Woman at the Washtub,
  She works till fall of night;
With soap, and suds and soda
  Her hands are wrinkled white.
Her diamonds are the sparkles   5
  The copper-fire supplies;
Her opals are the bubbles
  That from the suds arise.

The Woman at the Washtub
  Has lost the charm of youth;   10
Her hair is rough and homely,
  Her figure is uncouth;
Her temper is like thunder,
  With no one she agrees —
The children of the alley   15
  They cling around her knees.

The Woman at the Washtub,
  She too had her romance;
There was a time when lightly
  Her feet flew in the dance.   20
Her feet were silver swallows,
  Her lips were flowers of fire;
Then she was Bright and Early,
  The Blossom of Desire.

O Woman at the Washtub,   25
    And do you ever dream
Of all your days gone by in
    Your aureole of steam?
From birth till we are dying
    You wash our sordid duds,   30
O Woman of the Washtub!
    O Sister of the Suds!

One night I saw a vision
    That filled my soul with dread,
I saw a Woman washing   35
    The grave-clothes of the dead;
The dead were all the living,
    And dry were lakes and meres,
The Woman at the Washtub
    She washed them with her tears.   40

I saw a line with banners
    Hung forth in proud array —
The banners of all battles
    From Cain to Judgment Day.
And they were stiff with slaughter   45
    And blood, from hem to hem,
And they were red with glory,
    And she was washing them.

'Who comes forth to the Judgment,
    And who will doubt my plan?'   50
'I come forth to the Judgment
    And for the Race of Man.
I rocked him in his cradle,
    I washed him for his tomb,
I claim his soul and body,   55
    And I will share his doom.'

                                                    (1902) 1947

The Dove

Within his office, smiling,
    Sat JOSEPH CHAMBERLAIN,
But all the screws of Birmingham
    Were working in his brain.

The heart within his bosom   5
    Was as a millstone hard;
His eye was cold and cruel,
    His face was frozen lard.

2 **Joseph Chamberlain**   (1836–1914) British politician. He was mayor of Birmingham, and later
Secretary of State for the Colonies (1895–1903), where he was a strong advocate of Empire. His
period in office encompassed the Boer War, 1899–1902.

He had the map of Africa
   Upon his table spread: 10
He took a brush, and with the same
   He painted it blood-red.

He heard no moan of widows,
   But only the hurrah
Of charging lines and squadrons   15
   And 'Rule Britannia.'

A white dove to his window
   With branch of olive sped —
He took a ruler in his hand,
   And struck the white dove dead.   20

(1902) 1947

LOUISA LAWSON   *(1848–1920)*

Buried Love

The sigh of the wind in the soft belahs,
   Is in tune with my thoughts to-night;
That dwell as I stray 'neath the steel bright stars
   On a love that was pure and white.

And I start and thrill as I backward move,   5
   For a face to me close I see;
Oh, surely the pow'r of a deathless love
   Must be bringing you back to me!

For the thrill of that dear old love is sweet,
   And it sinks to my heart's sad core;   10
As fresh as it did ere a soul's defeat
   O'erwhelmed it in days of yore.

You said I was cold when we said 'good-bye,'
   And you thought that your words were true.
I tell you now, with my face to the sky,   15
   That I loved far better than you.

But the love we buried deep out of sight
   On the day that we said 'good-bye,'
Must go back again whence it came, to-night,
   And its ghost in the grave must lie.   20

For the march of time, and the hand of fate,
   And the growth of the great and free,
Have built up a wall and have barred a gate
   Now and ever 'twixt you and me.

For you love to look on the lotus feast,   25
   And drift in a westering way;
But I've set my face to the pregnant east
   Where I watch for a broad new day.

1905

In Memoriam

White and all waxen a fair maiden lay,
White as the snowdrift her beautiful clay.
White raiment clothed her, and over her bier
White lilies faded, sweet emblems they were.
White was her record, and where she is gone   5
White is the stone that her new name is on.

1905

Back Again

Oh, my boy, come in, do.
    You are back at last:
Years since last we saw you —
    How the time has passed!

Have a bath and shave first?   5
    No? A cup of tea?
Think you want a rest worst?
    Dear, oh deary me.

Look, dear, at your boots, too,
    All cut with the rocks;   10
And you haven't, have you,
    Any mended socks?

They are always tearing?
    Threw them all away?
Alberts you are wearing?   15
    Goodness, what are they?

Felt that you were coming,
    So I wrote to Bob;
He says things are humming,
    And you'll get a job.   20

Now, dear, don't come near me,
    You're all over dust;
Can you smoke? Oh, dear me,
    If you really must.

1905

God Give Me Gold

God give me gold that I may test
The blessed sweets of perfect rest,
For I am ill and hotly pressed.
    God give me gold!

In Memoriam   written for the poet's daughter, Annette, who died aged eight months in 1878

God give me gold that I may ease   5
The sorrow that the city sees —
I cannot help the least of these.
    God give me gold!

God give me gold that I may buy
The thing for which my soul doth sigh —   10
For human love, else, Lord, I die.
    God give me gold!

                                                                        1905

MARY HANNAY FOOTT   *(1846–1918)*

Where the Pelican Builds

[The unexplored parts of Australia are sometimes spoken of by the bushmen of Western Queensland as the home of the pelican, a bird whose nesting place, so far as the writer knows is seldom, if ever found.]

The horses were ready, the rails were down,
  But the riders lingered still, –
    One had a parting word to say,
  And one had his pipe to fill.
Then they mounted, one with a granted prayer,   5
  And one with a grief unguessed.
    'We are going' they said, as they rode away –
  'Where the pelican builds her nest!'

They had told us of pastures wide and green,
  To be sought past the sunset's glow;   10
    Of rifts in the ranges by opal lit;
  And gold 'neath the river's flow.
And thirst and hunger were banished words
  When they spoke of that unknown West;
    No drought they dreaded, no flood they feared,   15
  Where the pelican builds her nest!

The creek at the ford was but fetlock deep
  When we watched them crossing there;
    The rains have replenished it thrice since then
  And thrice has the rock lain bare.   20
But the waters of Hope have flowed and fled,
  And never from blue hill's breast
    Come back – by the sun and the sands devoured –
  Where the pelican builds her nest!

                                          (written 1881) 1885

'AUSTRALIE' (EMILY MANNING)   *(1845–1877)*

From the Clyde to Braidwood

A Winter morn. The blue Clyde river winds
'Mid sombre slopes, reflecting in clear depths
The tree-clad banks or grassy meadow flats
Now white with hoary frost, each jewell'd blade
With myriad crystals glistening in the sun.   5

Thus smiles the Vale of Clyde, as through the air
So keen and fresh three travellers upward ride
Toward the Braidwood heights. Quickly they pass
The rustic dwellings on the hamlet's verge,
Winding sometimes beside the glassy depths   10
Of Nelligen Creek, where with the murmuring bass
Of running water sounds the sighing wail
Of dark swamp-oaks, that shiver on each bank;
Then winding through a shady-bower'd lane,
With flickering streaks of sunlight beaming through   15
The feathery leaves and pendant tassels green
Of bright mimosa, whose wee furry balls
Promise to greet with golden glow of joy
The coming spring-tide.

                Now a barren length   20
Of tall straight eucalyptus, till again
A babbling voice is heard, and through green banks
Of emerald fern and mossy boulder rocks,
The Currawong dances o'er a pebbly bed,
In rippling clearness, or with cresting foam   25
Splashes and leaps in snowy cascade steps.
Then every feature changes — up and down,
O'er endless ranges like great waves of earth,
Each weary steed must climb, e'en like a ship
Now rising high upon some billowy ridge   30
But to plunge down to mount once more, again
And still again.

              Naught on the road to see
Save sullen trees, white arm'd, with naked trunks,
And hanging bark, like tatter'd clothes thrown off,   35
An undergrowth of glossy zamia palms
Bearing their winter store of coral fruit,
And here and there some early clematis,
Like starry jasmine, or a purple wreath
Of dark kennedea, blooming e'er their time,   40
As if in pity they would add one joy
Unto the barren landscape.

But at last
A clearer point is reach'd, and all around
The loftier ranges loom in contour blue,   45
With indigo shadows and light veiling mist
Rising from steaming valleys. Straight in front
Towers the Sugarloaf, pyramidal King
Of Braidwood peaks.

    Impossible it seems   50
To scale that nature-rampart, but where man
Would go he must and will; so hewn from out
The mountain's side, in gradual ascent
Of league and half of engineering skill
There winds the Weber pass.   55

    A glorious ride!
Fresher and clearer grows the breezy air,
Lighter and freer beats the quickening pulse
As each fair height is gain'd. Stern, strong, above
Rises the wall of mountain; far beneath,   60
In sheer precipitancy, gullies deep
Gloom in dark shadow, on their shelter'd breast
Cherishing wealth of leafage richly dight
With tropic hues of green.

    No sound is heard   65
Save the deep soughing of the wind amid
The swaying leaves and harp-like stems, so like
A mighty breathing of great mother earth,
That half they seem to see her bosom heave
With each pulsation as she living sleeps.   70
And now and then to cadence of these throbs
There drops the bell-bird's knell, the coach-whip's crack,
The wonga-pigeon's coo, or echoing notes
Of lyre-tail'd pheasants in their own rich tones
Mocking the song of every forest bird.   75

Higher the travellers rise — at every turn
Gaining through avenued vista some new glimpse
Of undulating hills, the Pigeon-house
Standing against the sky like eyrie nest
Of some great dove or eagle. On each side   80
Of rock hewn road, the fern trees cluster green,
Now and then lighted by a silver star
Of white immortelle flower, or overhung
By crimson peals of bright epacris bells.

Another bend, a shelter'd deepening rift,   85
And in the mountain's very heart they plunge—
So dark the shade, the sun is lost to view.
Great silver wattles tremble o'er the path,

Which overlooks a glen one varying mass
Of exquisite foliage, full-green sassafras,   90
The bright-leaf'd myrtle, dark-hued Kurrajong
And lavender, musk-plant, scenting all the air,
Entwined with clematis or bignonia vines,
And raspberry tendrils hung with scarlet fruit.

The riders pause some moments, gazing down,   95
Then upward look. Far as the peeping sky
The dell-like gully yawns into the heights;
A tiny cascade drips o'er mossy rocks,
And through an aisle of over-arching trees,
Whose stems are dight with lichen, creeping vines,   100
A line of sunlight pierces, lighting up
A wealth of fern trees; filling every nook
With glorious circles of voluptuous green,
Such as, unview'd, once clothed the silent earth
Long milliards past in Carboniferous Age.   105

A mighty nature-rockery! Each spot
Of fertile ground is rich with endless joys
Of leaf and fern; now here a velvet moss,
And there a broad asplenium's shining frond
With red-black veinings or a hart's-tongue point,   110
Contrasting with a pale-hued tender brake
Or creeping lion's-foot. See where the hand
Of ruthless man hath cleft the rock, each wound
Is hidden by thick verdure, leaving not
One unclothed spot, save on the yellow road.

Reluctant the travellers leave the luscious shade
To mount once more. But now another joy —
An open view is here! Before them spreads
A waving field of ranges, purple grey,
In haze of distance with black lines of shade   120
Marking the valleys, bounded by a line
Of ocean-blue, o'er whose horizon verge
The morning mist-cloud hangs. The distant bay
Is clear defined. The headland's dark arms stretch
(Each finger-point white-lit with dashing foam)   125
In azure circlet, studded with rugged isles —
A picturesque trio, whose gold rock sides glow
In noonday sunlight, and round which the surf
Gleams like a silvery girdle.

                              The grand Pass   130
Is traversed now, the inland plateau reach'd,
The last sweet glimpse of violet peaks is lost,
An upland rocky stream is pass'd, and naught
But same same gum-trees vex the wearied eye
Till Braidwood plain is reach'd.   135

                                A township like
All others, with its houses, church, and school —
Bare, bald, prosaic — no quaint wild tower,
Nor ancient hall to add poetic touch,
As in the dear old land — no legend old   140
Adds softening beauty to the Buddawong Peak,
Or near-home ranges with too barbarous names.
But everything is cold, new, new, too new
To foster poesy; and famish'd thought
Looks back with longing to the mountain dream.   145

                                                        1877

ADA CAMBRIDGE   *(1844–1926)*

By The Camp Fire

Ah, 'twas but now I saw the sun flush pink on yonder placid tide;
The purple hill-tops, one by one, were strangely lit and glorified;
And yet how sweet the night has grown, with palest starlights dimly sown!

Those mountain ranges, far and near, enclasp me, — sharply pencilled there,
Like blackest sea-waves, — outlined here, like phantoms in the luminous air,   5
Between that cold and quiet sky, and the calm river running by.

The gum-trees whisper overhead, and, delicately dark and fine,
Their lovely shadow-patterns shed across the paths of white moonshine.
The golden wattles glimmer bright, scenting this cool, transparent night.

What spirits wake when earth is still? I hear wild wood-notes softly swell.   10
There's the strange clamour, hoarse and shrill, that drowns the bull-frogs'
         hollow bell;
And there's the plaintive rise and fall of the lone mopoke's cuckoo-call.

And nearer, an opossum flits above the firelight, pauses, peers —
I see a round ball where he sits, with pendant tail and pointed ears;
And two are gruffly snarling now in hollows of yon upper bough.   15

Hark! that's the curlew's thrilling scream. What mountain echoes it has
         stirred!
The sound goes crying down the stream, the wildest bird-note ever heard.
And there's a crane, with legs updrawn, gone sailing out to meet the dawn.

It croaks its farewell, like a crow, beating the air with soft, wide wings.
On the white water down below its vague grey shadow-shape it flings,   20
And, dream-like, passes out of sight, a lonely vision of the night.

Ah me! how weird the undertones that thrill my wakeful fancy through!
The river softly creeps and moans; the wind seems faintly crying too.
Such whisperings seem to come and pass across the orchis-flower'd grass.

The darkness gather'd all around is full of rustlings, strange and low,   25
The dead wood crackles on the ground, and shadowy shapes flit to and fro;

I think they are my own dim dreams, wandering amongst the woods and
    streams.

The tangled trees seem full of eyes, — still eyes that watch me as I sit;
A flame begins to fall and rise, their glances come and go with it.
And on the torn bark, rough and brown, I hear soft scratchings up and
    down.   30

Sometimes I hear a sound of feet, — a slow step through the darkness steals;
And then I think of yours, my sweet, in spirit following at my heels;
For leagues before, around, behind, part me from all my human-kind.

Coo-ey! — the long vibration throbs in countless echoes through the hills.
The lonely forest wakes and sobs, and then no sound the silence fills, —   35
Only the night-frogs' bubbling shriek in every water-hole and creek;

Only a rush of wind in flight, as startled wild-ducks flutter past,
Quivering and twinkling in the light, skimming the shining water fast;
And ripples from a black swan's breast, darting from out its rushy nest.

How is't in England? — Sunday morn, and organ-music, love, with you.   40
That breath of memory, idly born, like a great storm-wind shakes me through.
Ah darling! bend your head and pray, — it cannot touch you far away.

Why do I care? My house of God, beyond all thought, is grand and great!
My prayerful knees, upon the sod, its flowers and grasses consecrate.
And I can see Him in the stars, undimmed by walls and window-bars.   45

Great Nature spreads her wondrous book, and shows me all her pages fair;
To me the language, when I look, seems but a letter here and there —
The very stones beneath me teach a lore beyond my utmost reach.

For all my pain, and toil, and strife, I see so dimly what is true!
O Art! O Science! O great Life! I grasp thee by so faint a clue!   50
No more of ocean tides I dream than minnows in their shallow stream.

Sea without bottom, without shore, where is the plumb to fathom thee?
O mystery! as I learn thee more, the more thy deeps are dark to me!
But who am I, that I should scan the Divine Maker's mighty plan?

And yet, oh yet, if I could hear that organ-music once again,   55
My soul, methinks, would lose its fear; and on this troubled heart and brain
Some light of knowledge would be shed, and some few riddles would be
    read.

                                                  1875

Unstrung

My skies were blue, and my sun was bright,
And, with fingers tender and strong and light,
He woke up the music that slept before —
Echoing, echoing evermore!

By-and-by, my skies grew grey; —   5
No master-touch on the harp-strings lay, —
Dead silence cradled the notes divine:
His soul had wander'd away from mine.

Idly, o'er strange harps swept his hand,
Seeking for music more wild and grand.   10
He wearied at last of his fruitless quest,
And he came again to my harp for rest.

But the dust lay thick on the golden wires,
And they would not thrill to the old desires.
The chords, so broken and jarred with pain,   15
Could never be tender and sweet again.

                                                    1875

Fallen

For want of bread to eat and clothes to wear —
    Because work failed and streets were deep in snow,
    And this meant food and fire — she fell so low,
Sinning for dear life's sake, in sheer despair.
Or, because life was else so bald and bare,   5
    The natural woman in her craved to know
    The warmth of passion — as pale buds to blow
And feel the noonday sun and fertile air.

And who condemns? She who, for vulgar gain
    And in cold blood, and not for love or need,   10
        Has sold her body to more vile disgrace —
        The prosperous matron, with her comely face —
    Wife by the law, but prostitute in deed,
In whose gross wedlock womanhood is slain.

                                                    1887

The Physical Conscience

The moral conscience — court of last appeal —
    Our word of God — our Heaven-sent light and guide —
    From what high aims it lures our steps aside!
To what immoral deeds it sets its seal!
That beacon lamp has lost its sacred fire;   5
    That pilot-guide, compelling wind and wave,
    By slow, blind process, has become the slave
Of all-compelling custom and desire.

Not so the conscience of the body. This,
    Untamed and true, still speaks in voice and face,   10
In cold lips stiffened to the loveless kiss,
    In shamed limbs shrinking from unloved embrace,
In love-born passion, that no laws compel,
Nor gold can purchase, nor ambition sell.

                                                    1887

Influence

As in the mists of embryonic night,
    Out of the deep and dark obscurities
    Of Nature's womb, the little life-germs rise,
Pushing by instinct upward to the light;
As, when the first ray dawns on waking sight,   5
    They leap to liberty, and recognize
    The golden sunshine and the morning skies
Their own inheritance by inborn right; —

So do our brooding thoughts and deep desires
    Grow in our souls, we know not how or why;   10
        Grope for we know not what, all blind and dumb.
So, when the time is ripe, and one aspires
    To free his thought in speech, ours hear the cry,
        And to full birth and instant knowledge come.

                                                    1887

HENRY KENDALL   *(1839–82)*

Rose Lorraine

Sweet water-moons, blown into lights
    Of flying gold on pool and creek,
And many sounds, and many sights,
    Of younger days, are back this week.
I cannot say I sought to face,   5
    Or greatly cared to cross again,
The subtle spirit of the place
    Whose life is mixed with Rose Lorraine.

What though her voice rings clearly through
    A nightly dream I gladly keep,   10
No wish have I to start anew
    Heart-fountains that have ceased to leap.
Here, face to face with different days,
    And later things that plead for love,
It would be worse than wrong to raise   15
    A phantom far too fain to move.

But, Rose Lorraine — ah, Rose Lorraine,
    I'll whisper now where no one hears.
If you should chance to meet again
    The man you kissed in soft dead years,   20
Just say for once 'he suffered much,'
    And add to this 'his fate was worst
Because of me, my voice, my touch,' —
    There is no passion like the first!

If I that breathe your slow sweet name 25
    As one breathes low notes on a flute
Have vext your peace with word of blame,
    The phrase is dead — the lips are mute.
Yet when I turn towards the wall,
    In stormy nights, in times of rain, 30
I often wish you could recall
    Your tender speeches, Rose Lorraine.

Because, you see, I thought them true,
    And did not count you self-deceived,
And gave myself in all to you, 35
    And looked on Love as Life achieved.
Then came the bitter, sudden change,
    The fastened lips, the dumb despair;
The first few weeks were very strange,
    And long, and sad, and hard to bear. 40

No woman lives with power to burst
    My passion's bonds, and set me free;
For Rose is last where Rose was first,
    And only Rose is fair to me.
The faintest memory of her face, 45
    The wilful face that hurt me so,
Is followed by a fiery trace
    That Rose Lorraine must never know.

I keep a faded ribbon string
    You used to wear about your throat; 50
And of this pale, this perished thing,
    I think I know the threads by rote.
God help such love! To touch your hand,
    To loiter where your feet might fall,
You marvellous girl, my soul would stand 55
    The worst of hell — its fires and all!

                  1869

A Death in the Bush

The hut was built of bark and shrunken slabs
That wore the marks of many rains, and showed
Dry flaws, wherein had crept and nestled rot.
Moreover, round the bases of the bark
Were left the tracks of flying forest-fires, 5
As you may see them on the lower bole
Of every elder of the native woods.

For, ere the early settlers came and stocked
These wilds with sheep and kine, the grasses grew
So that they took the passing pilgrim in, 10
And whelmed him, like a running sea, from sight.

And therefore, through the fiercer summer months,
While all the swamps were rotten — while the flats
Were baked and broken; when the clayey rifts
Yawned wide, half-choked with drifted herbage past,   15
Spontaneous flames would burst from thence, and race
Across the prairies all day long.

                              At night
The winds were up, and then with fourfold speed,
A harsh gigantic growth of smoke and fire   20
Would roar along the bottoms, in the wake
Of fainting flocks of parrots, wallaroos,
And 'wildered wild things, scattering right and left,
For safety vague, throughout the general gloom.

Anon, the nearer hill-side growing trees   25
Would take the surges; thus, from bough to bough,
Was borne the flaming terror! Bole and spire,
Rank after rank, now pillared, ringed, and rolled
In blinding blaze, stood out against the dead
Down-smothered dark, for fifty leagues away.   30

For fifty leagues! and when the winds were strong,
For fifty more! But, in the olden time,
These fires were counted as the harbingers
Of life-essential storms; since out of smoke
And heat there came across the midnight ways   35
Abundant comfort, with upgathered clouds,
And runnels babbling of a plenteous fall.

So comes the Southern gale at evenfall
(The swift 'brickfielder' of the local folk)
About the streets of Sydney, when the dust   40
Lies burnt on glaring windows, and the men
Look forth from doors of drouth, and drink the change
With thirsty haste and that most thankful cry
Of, 'here it is — the cool, bright, blessed rain!'

The hut, I say, was built of bark and slabs,   45
And stood, the centre of a clearing, hemmed
By hurdle-yards, and ancients of the blacks:
These moped about their lazy fires, and sang
Wild ditties of the old days, with a sound
Of sorrow, like an everlasting wind,   50
Which mingled with the echoes of the noon,
And moaned amongst the noises of the night.

From thence a cattle-track, with link to link,
Ran off against the fishpools, to the gap,
Which sets you face to face with gleaming miles   55
Of broad Orara, winding in amongst

Black, barren ridges, where the nether spurs
Are fenced about by cotton-scrub, and grass
Blue-bitten with the salt of many droughts.

'Twas here the shepherd housed him every night,   60
And faced the prospect like a patient soul;
Borne up by some vague hope of better days,
And God's fine blessing in his faithful wife;
Until the humour of his malady
Took cunning changes from the good to bad,   65
And laid him lastly on a bed of death.

Two months thereafter, when the summer heat
Had roused the serpent from his rotten lair,
And made a noise of locusts in the boughs,
It came to this, that, as the blood-red sun   70
Of one fierce day of many slanted down
Obliquely past the nether jags of peaks
And gulfs of mist, the tardy night came vexed
By belted clouds, and scuds that wheeled and whirled
To left and right about the brazen clifts   75
Of ridges, rigid with a leaden gloom.

Then took the cattle to the forest camps
With vacant terror, and the hustled sheep
Stood dumb against the hurdles, even like
A fallen patch of shadowed mountain snow;   80
And ever through the curlew's call afar
The storm grew on, while round the stinted slabs
Sharp snaps and hisses came, and went, and came,
The huddled tokens of a mighty blast
Which ran with an exceeding bitter cry   85
Across the tumbled fragments of the hills,
And through the sluices of the gorge and glen.

So, therefore, all about the shepherd's hut
That space was mute, save when the fastened dog,
Without a kennel, caught a passing glimpse   90
Of firelight moving through the lighted chinks;
For then he knew the hints of warmth within,
And stood, and set his great pathetic eyes,
In wind and wet, imploring to be loosed.

Not often now the watcher left the couch   95
Of him she watched; since, in his fitful sleep,
His lips would stir to wayward themes, and close
With bodeful catches. Once she moved away,
Half-deafened by terrific claps, and stooped,
And looked without; to see a pillar dim   100
Of gathered gusts and fiery rain.

Anon,
The sick man woke, and, startled by the noise,
Stared round the room, with dull delirious sight,
At this wild thing and that; for, through his eyes,   105
The place took fearful shapes, and fever showed
Strange crosswise lights about his pillow-head.
He, catching there at some phantasmic help,
Sat upright on the bolster, with a cry
Of, 'Where is Jesus? — it is bitter cold!'   110
And then, because the thundercalls outside
Were mixed for him with slanders of the Past,
He called his weeping wife by name, and said,
'Come closer, darling! we shall speed away
Across the seas, and seek some mountain home,   115
Shut in from liars, and the wicked words
That track us day and night, and night and day.'

So waned the sad refrain. And those poor lips,
Whose latest phrases were for peace, grew mute,
And into everlasting silence passed.   120

As fares a swimmer who hath lost his breath
In 'wildering seas afar from any help —
Who, fronting Death, can never realise
The dreadful Presence, but is prone to clutch
At every weed upon the weltering wave;   125
So fared the watcher, poring o'er the last
Of him she loved, with dazed and stupid stare;
Half conscious of the sudden loss and lack
Of all that bound her life, but yet without
The power to take her mighty sorrow in.   130

Then came a patch or two of starry sky;
And through a reef of cloven thunder-cloud
The soft Moon looked: a patient face beyond
The fierce impatient shadows of the slopes,
And the harsh voices of the broken hills!   135
A patient face, and one which came and wrought
A lovely silence like a silver mist
Across the rainy relics of the storm.

For in the breaks and pauses of her light
The gale died out in gusts; yet, evermore   140
About the roof-tree, on the dripping eaves,
The damp wind loitered; and a fitful drift
Sloped through the silent curtains, and athwart
The dead.

There, when the glare had dropped behind   145
A mighty ridge of gloom, the woman turned
And sat in darkness face to face with God,

And said — 'I know,' she said, 'that Thou art wise;
That when we build and hope, and hope and build,
And see our best things fall, it comes to pass   150
For evermore that we must turn to Thee!
And therefore now, because I cannot find
The faintest token of Divinity
In this my latest sorrow, let Thy light
Inform mine eyes, so I may learn to look   155
On something past the sight which shuts, and blinds,
And seems to drive me wholly, Lord, from Thee.'

Now waned the moon beyond complaining depths;
And, as the dawn looked forth from showery woods
(Whereon had dropt a hint of red and gold),   160
There went about the crooked cavern-eaves
Low flute-like echoes with a noise of wings
And waters flying down far-hidden fells.
Then might be seen the solitary owl,
Perched in the clefts; scared at the coming light,   165
And staring outward (like a sea-shelled thing
Chased to his cover by some bright fierce foe)
As at a monster in the middle waste.

At last the great kingfisher came and called
Across the hollows loud with early whips,   170
And lighted, laughing, on the shepherd's hut,
And roused the widow from a swoon like death.

This day, and after it was noised abroad,
By blacks, and straggling horsemen on the roads,
That he was dead 'who had been sick so long,'   175
There flocked a troop from far-surrounding runs
To see their neighbour and to bury him.
And men who had forgotten how to cry
(Rough flinty fellows of the native bush)
Now learned the bitter way, beholding there   180
The wasted shadow of an iron frame
Brought down so low by years of fearful pain;
And marking, too, the woman's gentle face,
And all the pathos in her moaned reply
Of 'masters, we have lived in better days.'   185

One stooped — a stockman from the nearer hills —
To loose his wallet-strings, from whence he took
A bag of tea, and laid it on her lap;
Then, sobbing, 'God will help you, missus, yet,'
He sought his horse with most bewildered eyes,   190
And, spurring swiftly, galloped down the glen.

Where black Orara nightly chafes his brink,
Midway between lamenting lines of oak

And Warra's gap, the shepherd's grave was built.
And there the wild-dog pauses, in the midst   195
Of moonless watches: howling through the gloom
At hopeless shadows flitting to and fro,
What time the East Wind hums his darkest hymn,
And rains beat heavy on the ruined leaf.

There, while the Autumn in the cedar trees   200
Sat cooped about by cloudy evergreens,
The widow sojourned on the silent road,
And mutely faced the barren mound, and plucked
A straggling shrub from thence, and passed away,
Heart-broken on to Sydney, where she took   205
Her passage, in an English vessel bound
To London, for her home of other years.

At rest! Not near, with Sorrow on his grave,
And roses quickened into beauty — wrapt
In all the pathos of perennial bloom;   210
But far from these, beneath the fretful clay
Of lands within the lone perpetual cry
Of hermit plovers and the night-like oaks,
All moaning for the peace which never comes.

At rest! And she who sits and waits behind   215
Is in the shadows; but her faith is sure,
And *one* fine promise of the coming days
Is breaking, like a blessed morning, far
On hills 'that slope through darkness up to God.'

                                                    (1865) 1869

Prefatory Sonnets

I

I purposed once to take my pen and write
    Not songs like some tormented and awry
    With Passion, but a cunning harmony
Of words and music caught from glen and height,
And lucid colours born of woodland light,   5
    And shining places where the sea-streams lie;
But this was when the heat of youth glowed white,
    And since I've put the faded purpose by.
I have no faultless fruits to offer you
    Who read this book; but certain syllables   10
    Herein are borrowed from unfooted dells,
And secret hollows dear to noontide dew;
And these at least, though far between and few,
    May catch the sense like subtle forest spells.

II

So take these kindly, even though there be   15
 Some notes that unto other lyres belong:
 Stray echoes from the elder sons of Song;
And think how from its neighbouring, native sea
The pensive shell doth borrow melody.
 I would not do the lordly masters wrong,   20
 By filching fair words from the shining throng
Whose music haunts me, as the wind a tree!
 Lo, when a stranger, in soft Syrian glooms
Shot through with sunset, treads the cedar dells,
And hears the breezy ring of elfin bells   25
 Far down by where the white-haired cataract booms,
He, faint with sweetness caught from forest smells,
 Bears thence, unwitting, plunder of perfumes.

               1869

On a Street

I dread that street! its haggard face
 I have not seen for eight long years —
A mother's curse is on the place:
 (There's blood, my reader, in her tears.)
No child of man shall ever track   5
 Through filthy dust the singer's feet;
A fierce old memory drags me back —
 I hate its name — I dread that street.

Upon the lap of green sweet lands,
 Whose months are like your English Mays,   10
I try to hide in Lethe's sands
 The bitter old Bohemian days.
But Sorrow speaks in singing leaf,
 And trouble talketh in the tide;
The skirts of a stupendous grief   15
 Are trailing ever at my side.

I will not say who suffered there:
 'Tis best the name aloof to keep,
Because the world is very fair —
 Its light should sing the dark to sleep.   20
But — let me whisper — in that street
 A woman, faint through want of bread,
Has often pawned the quilt and sheet,
 And wept upon a barren bed.

On a Street Charlotte Kendall wrote in a private note dated 1882: 'The whole of this poem is correct and our own case except with the exception of hunting for chips of wood in the alley. I never did only that my husband begged me not to suppress a single line.'

How gladly would I change my theme,   25
   Or cease the song and steal away
But on the hill, and by the stream
   A ghost is with me night and day!
A dreadful darkness full of wild
   Chaotic visions comes to me: 30
I seem to hear a dying child —
   Its mother's face I seem to see.

Here surely on this bank of bloom
   My verse with shine should overflow;
But ah, it comes — the rented room,   35
   With man and wife who suffered so!
From flower and leaf there is no hint —
   I only see a sharp distress:
A lady in a faded print,
   A careworn writer for the Press.   40

I only hear the brutal curse
   Of landlord clamouring for his pay;
And yonder is the pauper's hearse
   That comes to take a child away.
Apart, and with the half-grey head   45
   Of sudden age, again I see
The father writing by the dead
   To earn the undertaker's fee.

No tear at all is asked for him —
   A drunkard well deserves his life;   50
But voice will quiver — eyes grow dim
   For her, the patient, pure young wife,
The gentle girl of better days,
   As timid as a mountain fawn,
Who used to choose untrodden ways,   55
   And place at night her rags in pawn.

She could not face the lighted square,
   Or show the street her poor thin dress;
In one close chamber, bleak and bare,
   She hid her burden of distress.   60
Her happy schoolmates used to drive
   On gaudy wheels the town about:
The meal that keeps a dog alive
   She often had to go without.

I tell you this is not a tale   65
   Conceived by me, but bitter truth!
Bohemia knows it pinched and pale
   Beside the pyre of burnt-out Youth!
These eyes of mine have often seen
   The sweet girl-wife, in winters rude,   70

Steal out at night through courts unclean,
   To hunt about for chips of wood.

Have I no word at all for him
   Who used down fetid lanes to slink,
And squat in taproom corners grim,   75
   And drown his thoughts in dregs of drink?
This much I'll say, that, when the flame
   Of Reason re-assumed its force,
The hell the Christian fears to name
   Was heaven to his fierce remorse.   80

Just think of him — beneath the ban,
   And steeped in sorrow to the neck!
Without a friend — a feeble man
   In failing health — a human wreck!
With all his sense and scholarship,   85
   How could he face his fading wife?
The devil never lifted whip
   With stings like those that scourged his life!

But He, in whom the dying thief
   Upon the Cross did place his trust,   90
Forgets the sin and feels the grief,
   And lifts the sufferer from the dust.
And now because I have a dream
   The man and woman found the light,
A glory burns upon the stream —   95
   With gold and green the woods are bright.

But — still I hate that haggard street —
   Its filthy courts, its alleys wild!
In dreams of it I always meet
   The phantom of a wailing child.   100
The name of it begets distress —
   Ah, Song, be silent! show no more
The lady in the perished dress —
   The scholar on the taproom floor!

                            (1879) 1886

Orara

The strong sob of the chafing stream,
   That seaward fights its way
Down crags of glitter, dells of gleam,
   Is in the hills today.   4

But, far and faint, a gray-winged form   5
   Hangs where the wild lights wane:
The phantom of a bygone storm —
   A ghost of wind and rain.

The soft white feet of Afternoon
   Are on the shining meads:
The breeze is as a pleasant tune   10
   Amongst the happy reeds.

The fierce, disastrous flying fire,
   That made the great caves ring,
And scarred the slope and broke the spire,   15
   Is a forgotten thing.

The air is full of mellow sounds;
   The wet hill-heads are bright;
And, down the fall of fragrant grounds,
   The deep ways flame with light.   20

A rose-red space of stream I see
   Past banks of tender fern:
A radiant brook, unknown to me
   Beyond its upper turn.

The singing silver life I hear,   25
   Whose home is in the green
Far-folded woods of fountains clear
   Where I have never been.

Ah, brook above the upper bend,
   I often long to stand   30
Where you in soft cool shades descend
   From the untrodden Land!

Ah, folded woods that hide the grace
   Of moss and torrents strong,
I often wish to know the face   35
   Of that which sings your song!

But I may linger, long, and look
   Till night is over all:
My eyes will never see the brook,
   Or sweet strange waterfall!   40

The world is round me with its heat,
   And toil, and cares that tire:
I cannot with my feeble feet
   Climb after my desire.

But, on the lap of lands unseen,   45
   Within a secret zone,
There shine diviner gold and green
   Than man has ever known.

And where the silver waters sing,
   Down hushed and holy dells,   50
The flower of a celestial Spring —
   A tenfold splendour, dwells.

Yea, in my dream of fall and brook
  By far sweet forests furled,
I see that light for which I look   55
  In vain through all the world.

The glory of a larger sky
  On slopes of hills sublime
That speak with God and Morning, high
  Above the ways of Time!   60

Ah! haply, in this sphere of change
  Where shadows spoil the beam
It would not do to climb that range
  And test my radiant Dream.

The slightest glimpse of yonder place,   65
  Untrodden and alone,
Might wholly kill that nameless grace
  The charm of the Unknown.

And therefore, though I look and long,
  Perhaps the lot is bright   70
Which keeps the river of the song
  A beauty out of sight.

                                                                  1880

The Song of Ninian Melville

Sing the song of noisy Ninny — hang the Muses — spit it out!
(Tuneful Nine ye needn't help me — poet knows his way about!)
Sling me here a penny whistle — look alive, and let me slip
Into Ninny like a father — Ninny with the nimble lip.
Mister Melville, straight descendant from Professor Huxley's ape,   5
Started life as mute for daddy — pulling faces, sporting crape;
But, alas, he didn't like it — lots of work and little pay!
Nature whispered, 'you're a windbag — play your cards another way.'

Mister Melville picked the hint up — pitched the coffin 'biz' to pot:
Paid his bills, or didn't pay them — 'doesn't matter now a jot—   10
Twigging how the bread was buttered, he commenced a 'waiting game':
Pulled the strings upon the quiet — no one 'tumbled' to his aim.
Paine, he purchased, Strauss, he borrowed — read a page or two of each:
Posed before his father's porkers — made to them his maiden speech.
Then he spluttered, '*Ninny has it!* Nin will keep himself in clothes, 15
Like that gutter Tully, Bradlaugh, leading noodles by the nose!'

In the fly-blown village pothouse, where a dribbling bag of beer
Passes for a human being, Nin commenced his new career —
Talked about the 'Christian swindle' — cut the Bible into bits —
Shook his fist at Mark and Matthew — give the twelve Apostles fits: 20

Ninian Melville (1843–97) a radical member of parliament in New South Wales 1880–94

Slipped into the priests and parsons — hammered at the British Court —
Boozy boobies were astonished: lubbers of the Lambton sort!
Yards of ear were cocked to listen — yards of mouth began to shout,
'*Here's a cove as is long-headed — Ninny knows his way about!*'

Mister Melville was delighted — game in hand was paying well: 25
Fools and coin don't hang together — Nin became a howling swell!
Took to 'stumping' on the Racecourse — cut the old debating club:
Wouldn't do for mighty Ninny now to mount a local tub!
Thornton's Column was his platform: here our orator began
Hitting at the yellow heathen — cracking up the 'working man' —   30
Spitting out at Immigration: roaring, like a worried bull,
At the lucre made on tallow — at the profit raised on wool!

Said our Ninny to our Ninny, 'I have not the slightest doubt
Soaping down the "'orny-'anded" is the safest "bizness" out!
Little work for spanking wages — this is just the thing they like,   35
So I'll prop the eight hours swindle — be the boss in every strike.
In the end, I'll pull a pot off — what I'm at is bound to take:
Ninny sees a bit before him — Ninny's eyes are wide-awake!
When the boobies make me member, Parkes, of course, will offer tip —
I will take the first fat billet — then my frouzy friends may rip!'   40

So it came to pass that Melville—*Mister* Melville, I should say —
Dodged about with deputations, half a dozen times a day!
Started strikes and bossed the strikers — damned employers, every one,
On the Column — off the Column — in the shanty — in the sun
'Down with masters — up with wages! keep the "pigtail" out of this!'   45
This is what our Ninny shouted — game, you see, of hit or miss!
World, of course, is full of noodles — some who bray at Wallsend sent
Thing we know to be a windbag bouncing into Parliament!

Common story, this of Ninny! many fellows of his breed
Prowl about to bone the guinea, up to dirty tricks indeed!   50
Haven't now the time to tan them; but, by Jove, I'd like to tan
Back of that immense impostor that they call the 'working man'!
Drag upon our just employers — sponger on a worn-out wife —
Boozing in some alley pothouse every evening of his life!
Type he is of Nin's supporters: tot him up and tot him down,   55
He would back old Nick to-morrow for the sake of half a crown!

House with high, august traditions — Chamber where the voice of Lowe,
And the lordly words of Wentworth sounded thirty years ago —
Halls familiar to our fathers, where, in days exalted, rang
All the tones of all the feeling which ennobled Bland and Lang —   60
We in ashes — we in sackcloth, sorrow for the insult cast
By a crowd of bitter boobies on the grandeur of your past!
Take again your penny whistle — boy, it is no good to me:
Last invention is a bladder with the title of M.P.!

                                                                    (1880)

ADAM LINDSAY GORDON   *(1833–70)*

Cui Bono

Oh! wind that whistles o'er thorns and thistles,
  Of this fruitful earth like a goblin elf;
Why should he labour to help his neighbour
  Who feels too reckless to help himself?
The wail of the breeze in the bending trees   5
  Is something between a laugh and a groan;
And the hollow roar of the surf on the shore
  Is a dull, discordant monotone;
I wish I could guess what sense they express,
  There's a meaning, doubtless, in every sound,   10
Yet no one can tell, and it may be as well —
  Whom would it profit? the world goes round!

On this earth so rough, we know quite enough,
  And, I sometimes fancy, a little too much;
The sage may be wiser than clown or than kaiser,   15
  Is he more to be envied for being such?
Neither more nor less, in his idleness,
  The sage is doom'd to vexation sure;
The kaiser may rule, but the slippery stool
  That he calls his throne, is no sinecure;   20
And as for the clown, you may give him a crown,
  Maybe he'll thank you, and maybe not,
And before you can wink, he may spend it in drink —
  To whom does it profit? — We ripe and rot!

Yet under the sun much work is done   25
  By clown and kaiser, by serf and sage;
All sow and some reap, and few gather the heap
  Of the garner'd grain of a by-gone age.
By sea or by soil man is bound to toil,
  And the dreamer, waiting for time and tide,   30
For awhile may shirk his share of the work,
  But he grows with his dream dissatisfied;
He may climb to the edge of the beetling ledge,
  Where the loose crag topples and well-nigh reels
'Neath the lashing gale, but the tonic will fail, —   35
  What does it profit? — Wheels within wheels!

Aye! work we must, or with idlers rust,
  And eat we must our bodies to nurse;
Some folk grow fatter — what does it matter?
  I'm blest if I do — quite the reverse;   40

Cui Bono   Latin: 'to whose profit?'

'Tis a weary round to which we are bound,
  The same thing over and over again;
Much toil and trouble, and a glittering bubble,
  That rises and bursts, is the best we gain;
And we murmur, and yet, 'tis certain we get   45
  What good we deserve — can we hope for more? —
They are roaring, those waves in their echoing caves, —
  To whom do they profit? — Let them roar!

                                                          1867

The Sick Stockrider

Hold hard, Ned! Lift me down once more, and lay me in the shade.
  Old man, you've had your work cut out to guide
Both horses, and to hold me in the saddle when I sway'd
  All through the hot, slow, sleepy, silent ride.
The dawn at 'Moorabinda' was a mist rack dull and dense,   5
  The sunrise was a sullen, sluggish lamp;
I was dozing in the gateway at Arbuthnot's bound'ry fence,
  I was dreaming on the Limestone cattle camp.
We crossed the creek at Carricksford, and sharply through the haze,
  And suddenly the sun shot flaming forth;   10
To southward lay 'Katâwa' with the sandpeaks all ablaze
  And the flush'd fields of Glen Lomond lay to north.
Now westward winds the bridle path that leads to Lindisfarm,
  And yonder looms the double-headed Bluff;
From the far side of the first hill, when the skies are clear and calm,   15
  You can see Sylvester's woolshed fair enough.
Five miles we used to call it from our homestead to the place
  Where the big tree spans the roadway like an arch;
'Twas here we ran the dingo down that gave us such a chase
  Eight years ago — or was it nine? — last March.   20

'Twas merry in the glowing morn, among the gleaming grass
  To wander as we've wander'd many a mile,
And blow the cool tobacco cloud, and watch the white wreaths pass,
  Sitting loosely in the saddle all the while.
'Twas merry 'mid the blackwoods when we spied the station roofs, 25
  To wheel the wild scrub cattle at the yard,
With a running fire of stockwhips and a fiery run of hoofs;
  Oh! the hardest day was never then too hard!

Aye! we had a glorious gallop after 'Starlight' and his gang,
  When they bolted from Sylvester's on the flat;   30
How the sun-dried reed-beds crackled, how the flint-strewn ranges rang
  To the strokes of 'Mountaineer' and 'Acrobat.'
Hard behind them in the timber, harder still across the heath,
  Close beside them through the tea-tree scrub we dash'd;
And the golden-tinted fern leaves, how they rustled underneath!   35
  And the honeysuckle osiers, how they crash'd!

We led the hunt throughout, Ned, on the chestnut and the grey,
    And the troopers were three hundred yards behind,
While we emptied our six-shooters on the bushrangers at bay,
    In the creek with stunted box-tree for a blind!   40

There you grappled with the leader, man to man and horse to horse,
    And you roll'd together when the chestnut rear'd;
He blaz'd away and missed you in that shallow watercourse —
    A narrow shave — his powder singed your beard!

In these hours when life is ebbing, how those days when life was young   45
    Come back to us; how clearly I recall
Even the yarns Jack Hall invented, and the songs Jem Roper sung;
    And where are now Jem Roper and Jack Hall?

Ay! nearly all our comrades of the old colonial school,
    Our ancient boon companions, Ned, are gone;   50
Hard livers for the most part, somewhat reckless as a rule,
    It seems that you and I are left alone.

There was Hughes, who got in trouble through that business with the cards,
    It matters little what became of him;
But a steer ripp'd up MacPherson in the Cooraminta yards,   55
    And Sullivan was drown'd at Sink-or-swim;
And Mostyn — poor Frank Mostyn — died at last a fearful wreck,
    In 'the horrors' at the Upper Wandinong,
And Carisbrooke the rider at the Horsefall broke his neck,
    Faith! the wonder was he saved his neck so long !   60

Ah! those days and nights we squandered at the Logans in the Glen —
    The Logans, man and wife, have long been dead.
Elsie's tallest girl seems taller than your little Elsie then;
    And Ethel is a woman grown and wed.

I've had my share of pastime and I've done my share of toil,   65
    And life is short — the longest life a span;
I care not now to tarry for the corn or for the oil,
    Or for the wine that maketh glad the heart of man.
For good undone and gifts misspent and resolutions vain,
    'Tis somewhat late to trouble. This I know —   70
I should live the same life over, if I had to live again;
    And the chances are I go where most men go

The deep blue skies wax dusky and the tall green trees grow dim,
    The sward beneath me seems to heave and fall;
And sickly, smoky shadows through the sleepy sunlight swim,   75
    And on the very sun's face weave their pall.
Let me slumber in the hollow where the wattle blossoms wave,
    With never stone or rail to fence my bed;
Should the sturdy station children pull the bush flowers on my grave,
    I may chance to hear them romping overhead.   80

                        1870

A Dedication

To The Author of 'Holmby House'

They are ryhmes rudely strung with intent less
        Of sound than of words,
In lands where bright blossoms are scentless,
        And songless bright birds;
Where, with fire and fierce drought on her tresses,   5
Insatiable Summer oppresses
Sere woodlands and sad wildernesses,
        And faint flocks and herds.

Where in dreariest days, when all dews end,
        And all winds are warm,   10
Wild Winter's large floodgates are loosen'd,
        And floods, freed by storm;
From broken-up fountain heads, dash on
Dry deserts with long pent up passion —
Here rhyme was first framed without fashion,   15
        Song shaped without form.

Whence gather'd? — The locust's glad chirrup
        May furnish a stave;
The ring of a rowel and stirrup,
        The wash of a wave.   20
The chaunt of the marsh frog in rushes
That chimes through the pauses and hushes
Of nightfall, the torrent that gushes,
        The tempests that rave.

In the deep'ning of dawn, when it dapples   25
        The dusk of the sky,
With streaks like the redd'ning of apples,
        The ripening of rye.
To eastward, when cluster by cluster,
Dim stars and dull planets, that muster,   30
Wax wan in a world of white lustre
        That spreads far and high.

In the gathering of night gloom o'er head, in
        The still silent change,
All fire-flush'd when forest trees redden   35
        On slopes of the range.
When the gnarl'd knotted trunks Eucalyptian
Seem carved like weird columns Egyptian
With curious device — quaint inscription.
        And hieroglyph strange.   40

Holmby House an adventure novel by the British author G. H. Whyte-Melville, published in 1860

In the Spring, when the wattle gold trembles
        'Twixt shadow and shine,
When each dew-laden air draught resembles
        A long draught of wine;
When the skyline's blue burnish'd resistance   45
Makes deeper the dreamiest distance,
Some song in all hearts hath existence, —
        Such songs have been mine.

They came in all guises, some vivid
        To clasp and to keep;   50
Some sudden and swift as the livid
        Blue thunder-flame's leap.
This swept through the first breath of clover
With memories renew'd to the rover —
That flash'd while the black horse turn'd over   55
        Before the long sleep.

To you (having cunning to colour
        A page with your pen,
That through dull days, and nights even duller,
        Long years ago ten;   60
Fair pictures in fever afforded) —
I send these rude staves, roughly worded
By one in whose brain stands recorded
        As clear now as then.

'The great rush of grey "Northern water,"   65
        The green ridge of bank,
The "sorrel" with curved sweep of quarter
        Curl'd close to clean flank,
The Royalist saddlefast squarely,
And, where the bright uplands stretch fairly,   70
Behind, beyond pistol-shot barely,
        The Roundheaded rank.

'A long launch, with clinging of muscles,
        And clenching of teeth!
The loose doublet ripples and rustles!   75
        The swirl shoots beneath!'
Enough. In return for your garland —
In lieu of the flowers from your far land —
Take wild growth of dreamland or starland,
        Take weeds for your wreath.   80

Yet rhyme had not fail'd me for reason,
        Nor reason for rhyme;
Sweet Song! had I sought you in season,
        And found you in time.
You beckon in your bright beauty yonder,   85
And I, waxing fainter yet fonder,

Now weary too soon when I wander —
              Now fall when I climb.

It matters but little in the long run,
              The weak have some right —   90
Some share in the race that the strong run,
              The fight the strong fight.
If words that are worthless go westward,
Yet the worst word shall be as the best word,
In the day when all riot sweeps restward,   95
              In darkness or light.

                          1870

ANONYMOUS

The Banks of the Condamine

Oh, hark the dogs are barking, love,
I can no longer stay,
The men are all gone mustering
And it is nearly day.
And I must off by the morning light   5
Before the sun doth shine,
To meet the Sydney shearers
On the banks of the Condamine.

Oh Willie, dearest Willie,
I'll go along with you,   10
I'll cut off all my auburn fringe
And be a shearer, too,
I'll cook and count your tally, love,
While ringer-o you shine,
And I'll wash your greasy moleskins   15
On the banks of the Condamine.

Oh, Nancy, dearest Nancy,
With me you cannot go,
The squatters have given orders, love,
No woman should do so;   20
Your delicate constitution
Is not equal unto mine,
To stand the constant tigering
On the banks of the Condamine.

Oh Willie, dearest Willie,   25
Then stay back home with me,
We'll take up a selection
And a farmer's wife I'll be:

---

23 tigering   roughing it

I'll help you husk the corn, love,
And cook your meals so fine   30
You'll forget the ram-stag mutton
On the banks of the Condamine.

Oh, Nancy, dearest Nancy,
Please do not hold me back,
Down there the boys are waiting,   35
And I must be on the track;
So here's a good-bye kiss, love,
Back home here I'll incline
When we've shore the last of the jumbucks
On the banks of the Condamine.   40

(from 1860s)

The Eumerella Shore

There's a happy little valley on the Eumerella shore,
    Where I've lingered many happy hours away,
On my little free selection I have acres by the score,
    Where I unyoke the bullocks from the dray.

    To my bullocks then I say   5
    No matter where you stray,
      You will never be impounded any more;
    For you're running, running, running on the duffer's piece of land,
    Free selected on the Eumerella shore.

When the moon has climbed the mountains and the stars are shining bright,   10
    Then we saddle up our horses and away,
And we yard the squatters' cattle in the darkness of the night,
    And we have the calves all branded by the day.

    Oh, my pretty little calf,
    At the squatter you may laugh.   15
      For he'll never be your owner any more;
    For you're running, running, running on the duffer's piece of land,
    Free selected on the Eumerella shore.

If we find a mob of horses when the paddock rails are down,
    Although before they're never known to stray,   20
Oh, quickly will we drive them to some distant inland town,
    And sell them into slav'ry far away.

Eumerella 'Numerella' in some versions

3 free selection (or simply, 'selection') the low-price allocation, mainly from the late 1850s to the 1870s, of crown land for small farms: a policy opposed by the squatters (line 12), pastoralists with large land-holdings already established. The poem has been read both as a selector's snub to the squatter and as a squatter's satire on the selector.

8 duffer livestock thief

To Jack Robertson we'll say
You've been leading us astray
  And we'll never go a-farming any more;   25
For it's easier duffing cattle on the little piece of land
  Free selected on the Eumerella shore.

(from 1860s)

CHARLES R. THATCHER   *(1831–78)*

Cooking v Digging

John Jenkins was a digger,
  And a married man beside,
And whilst his wife kept house at home,
  The pick and spade he plied;
Sometimes he had a stunning hole,   5
  With an ounce unto the tub,
And frequently he found it hard
  To go and knock out grub.

One day to dinner he came home,
  But the dinner wasn't done,   10
He then abused his patient wife,
  And blew her up like fun:
Says he, it's monstrous, 'pon my word,
  You're lazy, I can see,
I'll do as much work in one day   15
  As you can do in three.

Says she, if you think so, my dear,
  I do not care a fig,
You stay at home and do the work,
  And I'll go out and dig: 20
I'll just use the pick and spade,
  With them I'll be expert,
You throw out the slops, my dear,
  And I'll pitch out the dirt.

You wash up the dishes, whilst   25
  I go and *wash up* too,
Then you'll dress the children, dear
  And dress the dinner too;
Drive the goats away, my love,
  Whilst I *drive* in the claim,   30
Mind you rock the cradle too,
  And I will do the same.

Agreed, says he, it's easier
　　To stay and cook the grub,
Than go to work with pick and spade,　　　　　　　　　35
　　And dirty puddling tub;
So off she went, now mind says she,
　　I shall be home by one,
I'm certain I'll be hungry, so
　　John, have the dinner done.　　　　　　　　　　　40

Now when his wife had gone, poor John
　　Had quite a clouded brow,
He tried to make a pudding, but
　　I'm bless'd if he knew how;
The baby then began to cry,　　　　　　　　　　　45
　　And that made him quite wild,
For with dough up to his elbows
　　He'd to go and nurse the child.

The cat drank all the milk; the child
　　Made litters on the floor;　　　　　　　　　　50
A goat walked off the cabbage,
　　So he had to go for more;
He let the fire go out, alas!
　　And cursed his bitter lot,
'Twas half-past twelve when poor John put　　　　　55
　　The pudding in the pot.

The wife came home at one o'clock,
　　And he was very wroth,
But he went and got the knives and forks,
　　And laid the table cloth;　　　　　　　　　　60
Of course the pudding wasn't done
　　Though he took it up in haste,
But instead of such a nice rich crust,
　　'Twas only sticky paste.

Now naturally he made sure　　　　　　　　　　65
　　·She'd blow him up sky high,
But instead of taking him to task
　　She then began to cry;
Says she, you've spoilt the dinner,
　　But together we'll condole,　　　　　　　　　70
For because I had no miner's right
　　They've been and jumped my hole.

　　　　　　　　　　　　　　　　1859

WILLIAM FORSTER   *(1818–82)*

From The Genius and the Ghost

When in his gay barouche, or tandem neat,
Some fat insolvent whirls adown the street,
Thinking the while, no doubt, what charming sport
He had with Law Commissioner and Court,
And meets some wretch his arts to ruin led,   5
Whom his false schedule robbed of clothes and bread,
Who in his threadbare vesture shrinks, and feels
The sprinkled blessings of his chariot wheels;
When he, rich rogue, whose keen commercial eye
Each passing object glances gaily by,   10
That creeping wretch so pale and so forlorn
Shall dare accost with fashionable scorn,
Or to his victim impudently dole
The base compassion of his knavish soul,
When he shall still be honored and caressed   15
At social boards — a sleek and favoured guest —
When crowds around him bend in servile style,
Awed by his frown and flattered by his smile —
When such the bays that crown a villain's brow,
I ask — Is this your moral city now?   20
At midnight balls, where mirth is faint and hot,
See yonder flushed and fashionable sot;
Behold him, staggering with his weight of wine,
Mid laughing crowds pre-eminently shine.
The devil that obscures his slender sense   25
Inspires a more than usual impudence.
Then see him boldly mix with drunken skill
In the mad polka or the stale quadrille —
See some fair creature's palpitating waist
By his hot arm lasciviously embraced —   30
See the soft cheek of virgin beauty blaze,
With the wild babble of his senseless praise —
See aged dames his battered jokes beguile —
See sober matrons chuckle at his smile —
Hear sons and fathers praise his 'cheerful mood' —   35
'A little swipy,' or 'a little screwed' —
See next at church some slender victim stand,
Whose parents liked the honor of his hand —
See, too, her fond and drooping eyes approve
His worn-out vows of mercenary love —   40
Hear, in his praise, relations loud and warm,
'A little wild, but certain to reform.'
Then turn away where stocks and dungeons bind
The wretched dregs and rabble of mankind —

Where the low sons of vulgar drunkenness   45
Are taught the guilt of unrefined excess,
And dare you still, without a pang of shame,
Your virtue and morality proclaim?

(1847)

CHARLES HARPUR *(1813–68)*

The Beautiful Squatter

Where the wandering Barwin delighteth the eye,
   Befringed with the myal and golden bloom'd gorse,
Oh, a beautiful Squatter came galloping by,
   With a beard on his chin like the tail of his horse;
And his locks trained all round to so equal a pitch,   5
   That his mother herself, it may truly be said,
Had been puzzled in no small degree to find which
   Was the front, or the back, or the sides of his head.

Beside a small fire, 'neath a fair-spreading tree
   (A cedar, I think, but perhaps 'twas a gum,)   10
What vision of love did that squatter now see,
   In the midst of a catch, so to render him dumb?
Why, all on the delicate herbage asquat,
   And smiling to see him so flustered and mute,
'Twas the lovely Miss 'Possum-skin having a chat   15
   With the elegant Lady of Lord Bandicoot.

The squatter dismounted — what else could he do?
   And, meaning her tender affections to win,
'Gan talking of dampers, and blankets quite new,
   With a warmth that soon ruin'd poor Miss 'Possum-skin;   20
And Lord Bandicoot also, whilst dining that day
   On a bak'd kangaroo, of the kind that is red,
At the very third bite to king Dingo did say —
   Oh, how heavy I feel all at once in the head!

But, alas, for the belles of the Barwin! — the youth   25
   Galloped home, to forget all his promises fair;
Whereupon Lady Bandicoot told the whole truth
   To her lord, and Miss 'Possum-skin raved in despair!
And mark the result! Royal Dingo straightway,
   And his warriors, swore to avenge them in arms!   30
And that beautiful squatter, one beautiful day,
   Was waddied to death in the bloom of his charms!

(1845) 1984

Charles Harpur 'A Flight of Wild Ducks', 'The Creek of the Four Graves' and 'A Mid-Summer Noon in the Australian Forest' are given here in substantially revised versions from holographs of the late 1860s

A Flight of Wild Ducks

Far up the River — hark! 'tis the loud shock
Deadened by distance, of some Fowler's gun:
And as into the stillness of the scene
It wastes now with a dull vibratory boom,
Look where, fast widening up at either end   5
Out of the sinuous valley of the waters,
And o'er the intervenient forest, — up
Against the open heaven, a long dark *line*
Comes hitherward stretching — a vast Flight of Ducks!
Following the windings of the vale, and still   10
Enlarging lengthwise, and in places too
Oft breaking into solitary dots,
How swiftly onward comes it — till at length,
The River, reaching through a group of hills,
Off leads it, — out of sight. But not for long: 15
For, wheeling ever with the water's course,
Here into sudden view it comes again
Sweeping and swarming round the nearest point!
And first now, a swift airy rush is heard
Approaching momently; — then all at once   20
There passes a keen-cutting, gusty tumult
Of strenuous pinions, with a streaming mass
Of instantaneous skiey streaks; each streak
Evolving with a lateral flirt, and thence
Entangling as it were, — so rapidly   25
A thousand wings outpointingly dispread
In passing tiers, seem, looked at from beneath,
With rushing intermixtures to involve
Each other as they beat. Thus seen o'erhead
Even while we speak — ere we have spoken, — lo!   30
The living cloud is onward many a rood,
Tracking as 'twere in the smooth stream below
The multifarious shadow of itself.
Far coming — present — and far gone at once!
The senses vainly struggle to retain   35
The impression of an Image (as the same)
So swift and manifold: For now again
A long dark *line* upon the utmost verge
Of the horizon, steeping still, it sinks
At length into the landscape; where yet seen   40
Though dimly, with a wide and scattering sweep
It fetches eastward, and in column so
Dapples along the steep face of the ridge
There banking the turned River. Now it drops
Below the fringing oaks — but to arise   45
Once more, with a quick circling gleam, as touched

By the slant sunshine, and then disappear
As instantaneously, — there settling down
Upon the reedy bosom of the water.

(1845) 1984

The Creek of the Four Graves

Part I

I verse a Settler's tale of olden times —
One told me by our sage friend, Egremont,
Who then went forth, meetly equipt, with four
Of his most trusty and adventurous men
Into the wilderness, — went forth to seek   5
New streams and wider pastures for his fast
Augmenting flocks and herds. On foot were all,
For horses then were beasts of too great price
To be much ventured upon mountain routes,
And over wild wolds clouded up with brush,   10
Or cut with marshes, perilously pathless.

  So went they forth at dawn: and now the sun
That rose behind them as they journeyed out,
Was firing with his nether rim a range
Of unknown mountains that, like rampires, towered   15
Full in their front; and his last glances fell
Into the gloomy forest's eastern glades
In golden masses, transiently, or flashed
Down on the windings of a nameless Creek,
That noiseless ran betwixt the pioneers   20
And those new Apennines; — ran, shaded up
With boughs of the wild willow, hanging mixed
From either bank, or duskily befringed
With upward tapering feathery swamp-oaks —
The sylvan eyelash always of remote   25
Australian waters, whether gleaming still
In lake or pool, or bickering along
Between the marges of some eager stream.

  Before them, thus extended, wilder grew
The scene each moment — and more beautiful!   30
For when the sun was all but sunk below
Those barrier mountains, — in the breeze that o'er
Their rough enormous backs deep fleeced with wood
Came whispering down, the wide upslanting sea
Of fanning leaves in the descending rays   35
Danced interdazzlingly, as if the trees
That bore them, were all thrilling, — tingling all
Even to the roots for very happiness:

---

21 **Apennines**   the mountains that form the backbone of peninsular Italy

So prompted from within, so sentient, seemed
The bright quick motion — wildly beautiful.   40

   But when the sun had wholly disappeared
Behind those mountains — O what words, what hues
Might paint the wild magnificence of view
That opened westward! Out extending, lo,
The heights rose crowding, with their summits all   45
Dissolving, as it seemed, and partly lost
In the exceeding radiancy aloft;
And thus transfigured, for awhile they stood
Like a great company of Archeons, crowned
With burning diadems, and tented o'er   50
With canopies of purple and of gold!

   Here halting wearied, now the sun was set,
Our travellers kindled for their first night's camp
The brisk and crackling fire, which also looked
A wilder creature than 'twas elsewhere wont,   55
Because of the surrounding savageness,
And soon in cannikins the tea was made,
Fragant and strong; long fresh-sliced rashers then
Impaled on whittled skewers, were deftly broiled
On the live embers, and when done, transferred   60
To quadrants from an ample damper cut,
Their only trenchers, — soon to be dispatched
With all the savoury morsels they sustained,
By the keen tooth of healthful appetite.

   And as they supped, birds of new shape and plume,   65
And wild strange voice, nestward repairing by,
Oft took their wonder; or betwixt the gaps
In the ascending forest growths they saw
Perched on the bare abutments of the hills,
Where haply yet some lingering gleam fell through,   70
The wallaroo look forth: till eastward all
The view had wasted into formless gloom,
Night's front; and westward, the high massing woods
Steeped in a swart but mellowed Indian hue —
A deep dusk loveliness, — lay ridged and heaped   75
Only the more distinctly for their shade
Against the twilight heaven — a cloudless depth
Yet luminous from the sunset's fading glow;
And thus awhile, in the lit dusk, they seemed
To hang like mighty pictures of themselves,   80
In the still chambers of some vaster world.

   The silent business of their supper done,
The Echoes of the solitary place,
Came as in sylvan wonder wide about
To hear, and imitate tentatively,   85
Strange voices moulding a strange speech, as then

Within the pleasant purlieus of the fire
Lifted in glee — but to be hushed erelong,
As with the night in kindred darkness came
O'er the adventurers, each and all, some sense —   90
Some vague-felt intimation from without
Of danger, lurking in its forest lairs.

   But nerved by habit, and all settled soon
About the well-built fire, whose nimble tongues
Sent up continually a strenuous roar   95
Of fierce delight, and from their fuming pipes
Full charged and fragrant with the Indian weed,
Drawing rude comfort, — typed without, as 'twere,
By tiny clouds over their several heads
Quietly curling upward; — thus disposed   100
Within the pleasant firelight, grave discourse
Of their peculiar business brought to each
A steadier mood, that reached into the night.

   The simple subject to their minds at length
Fully discussed, their couches they prepared   105
Of rushes, and the long green tresses pulled
Down from the boughs of the wild willows near.
Then four, as pre-arranged, stretched out their limbs
Under the dark arms of the forest trees
That mixed aloft, high in the starry air,   110
In arcs and leafy domes whose crossing curves
And roof-like features, — blurring as they ran
Into some denser intergrowth of sprays, —
Were seen in mass traced out against the clear
Wide gaze of heaven; and trustful of the watch   115
Kept near them by their thoughtful Master, soon
Drowsing away, forgetful of their toil,
And of the perilous vast wilderness
That lay around them like a spectral world,
Slept, breathing deep; — whilst all things there as well   120
Showed slumbrous, — yea, the circling forest trees,
Their foremost boles carved from a crowded mass
Less visible, by the watchfire's bladed gleams,
As quick and spicular, from the broad red ring
Of its more constant light they ran in spurts   125
Far out and under the umbrageous dark;
And even the shaded and enormous mountains,
Their bluff brows glooming through the stirless air,
Looked in their quiet solemnly asleep:
Yea, thence surveyed, the Universe might have seemed   130
Coiled in vast rest, — only that one dim cloud,
Diffused and shapen like a huge spider,
Crept as with scrawling legs along the sky;
And that the stars, in their bright orders, still
Cluster by cluster glowingly revealed   135

As this slow cloud moved on, — high over all, —
Looked wakeful — yea, looked thoughtful in their peace.

Part II

Meanwhile the cloudless eastern heaven had grown
More and more luminous — and now the Moon
Up from behind a giant hill was seen   140
Conglobing, till — a mighty mass — she brought
Her under border level with its cone,
As thereon it were resting: when, behold
A wonder! Instantly that cone's whole bulk,
Erewhile so dark, seemed inwardly a-glow   145
With her instilled irradiance; while the trees
That fringed its outline, their huge statures dwarfed
By distance into brambles, and yet all
Clearly defined against her ample orb, —
Out of its very disc appeared to swell   150
In shadowy relief, as they had been
All sculptured from its substance as she rose.

    Thus o'er that dark height her great orb arose,
Till her full light, in silvery sequence still
Cascading forth from ridgy slope to slope,   155
Like the dropt foldings of a lucent veil,
Chased mass by mass the broken darkness down
Into the dense-brushed valleys, where it crouched,
And shrank, and struggled, like a dragon doubt
Glooming some lonely spirit that doth still   160
Resist the Truth with obstinate shifts and shows,
Though shining out of heaven, and from defect
Winning a triumph that might else not be.

    There standing in his lone watch, Egremont
On all this solemn beauty of the world   165
Looked out, yet wakeful; for sweet thoughts of home
And all the sacred charities it held,
Ingathered to his heart, as by some nice
And subtle interfusion that connects
The loved and cherished (then the most, perhaps,   170
When absent, or when passed, or even when *lost*)
With all serene and beautiful and bright
And lasting things of Nature. So then thought
The musing Egremont: when sudden — hark!
A bough crackt loudly in a neighbouring brake,   175
And drew at once, as with a 'larum, all
His spirits thitherward in wild surmise.

    But summoning caution, and back stepping close
Against the shade-side of a bending gum,
With a strange horror gathering to his heart,   180
As if his blood were charged with insect life

And writhed along in clots, he stilled himself,
Listening long and heedfully, with head
Bent forward sideways, till his held breath grew
A pang, and his ears rang. But Silence there   185
Had recomposed her ruffled wings, and now
Brooded it seemed even stiller than before
Deep nested in the darkness: so that he
Unmasking from the cold shade, grew erelong
More reassured from wishing to be so,   190
And to muse, Memory's suspended mood,
Though with an effort, quietly recurred.

But there again — crack upon crack! And hark!
O Heaven! have Hell's worst fiends burst howling up
Into the death-doom'd world? Or whence, if not   195
From diabolic rage, could surge a yell
So horrible as that which now affrights
The shuddering dark! Beings as fell are near!
Yea, Beings, in their dread inherited hate
And deadly enmity, as vengeful, come   200
In vengeance! For behold, from the long grass
And nearer brakes, a semi-belt of stript
And painted Savages divulge at once
Their bounding forms! — full in the flaring light
Thrown outward by the fire, that roused and lapped   205
The rounding darkness with its ruddy tongues
More fiercely than before, — as though even *it*
Had felt the sudden shock the air received
From those dire cries, so terrible to hear!

A moment in wild agitation seen   210
Thus, as they bounded up, on then they came
Closing, with weapons brandished high, and so
Rushed in upon the sleepers! three of whom
But started, and then weltered prone beneath
The first fell blow dealt down on each by three   215
Of the most stalwart of their pitiless foes!
But One again, and yet again, heaved up —
Up to his knees, under the crushing strokes
Of huge-clubbed nulla-nullas, till his own
Warm blood was blinding him! For he was one   220
Who had with Misery nearly all his days
Lived lonely, and who therefore, in his soul,
Did hunger after hope, and thirst for what
Hope still had promised him, — some taste at least
Of human good however long deferred,   225
And now he could not, even in dying, loose
His hold on life's poor chances of to-morrow —
Could not but so dispute the terrible fact
Of death, even in Death's presence! Strange it is:
Yet oft 'tis seen that Fortune's pampered child   230

Consents to his untimely power with less
Reluctance, less despair, than does the wretch
Who hath been ever blown about the world
The straw-like sport of Fate's most bitter blasts,
Vagrant and tieless; — ever still in him   235
The craving spirit thus grieves to itself:

  'I never yet was happy — never yet
Tasted unmixed enjoyment, and I would
Yet pass on the bright Earth that I have loved
Some season, though most brief, of happiness;   240
So should I walk thenceforward to my grave,
Wherever in her green maternal breast
It might await me, more than now prepared
To house me in its gloom, — resigned at heart,
Subjected to its certainty and soothed   245
Even by the consciousness of having shaped
Some personal good in being; — strong myself,
And strengthening others. But to have lived long years
Of wasted breath, because of woe and want,
And disappointed hope, — and now, at last,   250
To die thus desolate, is horrible!'

  And feeling thus through many foregone moods
Whose lines had in the temper of his soul
All mixed, and formed *one* habit, — that poor man,
Though the black shadows of untimely death,   255
Inevitably, under every stroke,
But thickened more and more, — against them still
Upstruggled, nor would cease: until one last
Tremendous blow, dealt down upon his head,
As if in mercy, gave him to the dust   260
With all his many woes and frustrate hope.

  Struck through with a cold horror, Egremont,
Standing apart, — yea, standing as it were
In marble effigy, saw this, saw all!
And when outthawing from his frozen heart   265
His blood again rushed tingling, — with a leap
Awaking from the ghastly trance which there
Had bound him, as with chill petrific bonds,
He raised from instinct more than conscious thought
His death-charged tube, and at that murderous crew   270
Firing! saw one fall ox-like to the earth; —
Then turned and fled. Fast fled he, but as fast
His deadly foes went thronging on his track!
Fast! for in full pursuit, behind him yelled
Wild men whose wild speech hath no word for *mercy*!   275
And as he fled, the forest beasts as well,
In general terror, through the brakes a-head
Crashed scattering, or with maddening speed athwart

His course came frequent. On — still on he flies —
Flies for dear life! and still behind him hears   280
Nearer and nearer, the so rapid dig
Of many feet, — nearer and nearer still.

Part III

So went the chase! And now what should he do?
Abruptly turning, the wild Creek lay right
Before him! But no time was there for thought: 285
So on he kept, and from a bulging rock
That beaked the bank like a bare promontory,
Plunging right forth and shooting feet-first down,
Sunk to his middle in the flashing stream —
In which the imaged stars seemed all at once   290
To burst like rockets into one wide blaze
Of interwrithing light. Then wading through
The ruffled waters, forth he sprang and seized
A snake-like root that from the opponent bank
Protruded, and round which his earnest fear   295
Did clench his cold hand like a clamp of steel,
A moment, — till as swiftly thence he swung
His dripping form aloft, and up the dark
O'erjutting ledge went clambering in the blind
And breathless haste of one who flies for life: 300
When in its face — O verily our God
Hath those in his peculiar care for whom
The daily prayers of spotless Womanhood
And helpless Infancy, are offered up! —
When in its face a cavity he felt,   305
The upper earth of which in one rude mass
Was held fast bound by the enwoven roots
Of two old trees, — and which, beneath the mould,
Just o'er the clammy vacancy below,
Twisted and lapped like knotted snakes, and made   310
A natural loft-work. Under this he crept,
Just as the dark forms of his hunters thronged
The bulging rock whence he before had plunged.

  Duskily visible, thereon a space
They paused to mark what bent his course might take   315
Over the farther bank, thereby intent
To hold upon the chase, which way soe'er
It might incline, more surely. But no form
Amongst the moveless fringe of fern was seen
To shoot up from its outline, — up and forth   320
Into the moonlight that lay bright beyond,
In torn and shapeless blocks, amid the boles
And mixing shadows of the taller trees,
All standing now in the keen radiance there
So ghostly still, as in a solemn trance.   325

But nothing in the silent prospect stirred —
No fugitive apparition in the view
Rose, as they stared in fierce expectancy:
Wherefore they augured that their prey was yet
Somewhere between, — and the whole group with that   330
Plunged forward, till the fretted current boiled
Amongst their crowding trunks from bank to bank;
And searching thus the stream across, and then
Lengthwise, along the ledges, — combing down
Still, as they went, with dripping fingers, cold   335
And cruel as inquisitive, each clump
Of long-flagged swamp-grass where it flourished high, —
The whole dark line passed slowly, man by man,
Athwart the cavity — so fearfully near,
That as they waded by the Fugitive   340
Felt the strong odor of their wetted skins
Pass with them, trailing as their bodies moved
Stealthily on, — coming with each, and going.

  But their keen search was keen in vain. And now
Those wild men marvelled, — till, in consultation,   345
There grouped in dark knots standing in the stream
That glimmered past them, moaning as it went,
His vanishment, so passing strange it seemed,
They coupled with the mystery of some crude
Old fable of their race; and fear-struck all,   350
And silent, then withdrew. And when the sound
Of their receding steps had from his ear
Died off, as back to the stormed Camp again
They hurried to despoil the yet warm dead,
Our Friend slid forth, and springing up the bank,   355
Renewed his flight, nor rested from it, till
He gained the welcoming shelter of his Home.

  Return we for a moment to the scene
Of recent death. There the late flaring fire
Now smouldered, for its brands were strewn about,   360
And four stark corses, plundered to the skin
And brutally mutilated, seemed to stare
With frozen eyeballs up into the pale
Round visage of the Moon, who, high in heaven,
With all her stars, in golden bevies, gazed   365
As peacefully down as on a bridal there
Of the warm Living — not, alas! on them
Who kept in ghastly silence through the night
Untimely spousals with a desert death.

  O God! and thus this lovely world hath been   370
Accursed for ever by the bloody deeds
Of its prime Creature — Man. Erring or wise,

Savage or civilised, still hath he made
This glorious residence, the Earth, a Hell
Of wrong and robbery and untimely death!   375
Some dread Intelligence opposed to Good
Did, of a surety, over all the earth
Spread out from Eden — or it were not so!
For see the bright beholding Moon, and all
The radiant Host of Heaven, evince no touch   380
Of sympathy with Man's wild violence; —
Only evince in their calm course, their part
In that original unity of Love,
Which, like the soul that dwelleth in a harp
Under God's hand, in the beginning, chimed   385
The sabbath concord of the Universe;
And look on a gay clique of maidens, met
In village tryst, and interwhirling all
In glad Arcadian dances on the green —
Or on a hermit, in his vigils long,   390
Seen kneeling at the doorway of his cell —
Or on a monster battle-field where lie
In sweltering heaps, the dead and dying both,
On the cold gory ground, — as they that night
Looked in bright peace, down on the doomful Wild.   395

   Afterwards there, for many changeful years,
Within a glade that sloped into the bank
Of that wild mountain Creek — midway within,
In partial record of a terrible hour
Of human agony and loss extreme,   400
Four grassy mounds stretched lengthwise side by side,
Startled the wanderer; — four long grassy mounds
Bestrewn with leaves, and withered spraylets, stript
By the loud wintry wingéd gales that roamed
Those solitudes, from the old trees which there   405
Moaned the same leafy dirges that had caught
The heed of dying Ages: these were all;
And thence the place was long by travellers called
The Creek of the Four Graves. Such was the Tale
Egremont told us of the wild old times.   410

                                                        1853

To Myself, June 1855

What's the Crimean War to thee,
   Its craft and folly, blame and blunder?
Its aims are dodges plain to see,
   Its victories shams with all their thunder.

Heed not its proud but passing things,   5
   The royal mischiefs of their day;

But give thou Thought's immortal wings
   To glories of a purer ray:

To Freedom in her future prime,
   To Nature's everlasting lore,   10
To Science from her tower in Time
   Surveying the Eternal's shore.

Be such the subjects of thy thought,
   Not Old World Kings and ruling sets,
And liberties that flounder, caught   15
   Like fish in diplomatic nets.

For these, if pondered, can but hurt
   The straightness of thy moral view,
And foul as with the Old World's dirt
   The virgin nature of the New.   20

                    1984

Modern Poetry

How I hate those modern Poems
   Vaguer, looser than a dream!
Those pointless things that look like proems,
   Only, to some held-back theme!
Wild, unequal, agitated   5
As by steam ill-regulated —
   Balder-dashic steam!
And if (in fine) not super-lyrical,
Then vapid, almost to a miracle.

                    1984

Early and Late Art

When Art is young, it slighteth Nature;
When old, it loves her every feature.

                    1984

A Mid-Summer Noon in the Australian Forest

Not a bird disturbs the air,
There is quiet everywhere;
Over plains and over woods
What a mighty stillness broods.

   Even the grasshoppers keep   5
Where the coolest shadows sleep;
Even the busy ants are found
Resting in their pebbled mound;
Even the locust clingeth now
In silence to the barky bough: 10
And over hills and over plains
Quiet, vast and slumbrous, reigns.

Only there's a drowsy humming
From yon warm lagoon slow coming:
'Tis the dragon-hornet — see!   15
All bedaubed resplendently
With yellow on a tawny ground —
Each rich spot nor square nor round,
But rudely heart-shaped, as it were
The blurred and hasty impress there,   20
Of a vermeil-crusted seal
Dusted o'er with golden meal:
Only there's a droning where
Yon bright beetle gleams the air —
Gleams it in its droning flight   25
With a slanting track of light,
Till rising in the sunshine higher,
Its shards flame out like gems on fire.

   Every other thing is still,
Save the ever wakeful rill,   30
Whose cool murmur only throws
A cooler comfort round Repose;
Or some ripple in the sea
Of leafy boughs, where, lazily,
Tired Summer, in her forest bower   35
Turning with the noontide hour,
Heaves a slumbrous breath, ere she
Once more slumbers peacefully.

   O 'tis easeful here to lie
Hidden from Noon's scorching eye,   40
In this grassy cool recess
Musing thus of Quietness.

                                                    (1858) 1883

LOUISA ANNE MEREDITH   *(1812–95)*

Sun-dew

Jewelled with rubies small and bright,
        Each on a crimson stem
Upheld, to catch the chequer'd light,
The Sun-dew dwells by the river's rim,
        And with silver blossoms there   5
She tempts the dragon-flies, that skim,
        And flash like darts through sultry air
        Into the forest dim,
To fold their wings of bright unrest
        Upon her breast.   10
                                                    1860

Water Beaux

'Hist! grave-eyed frogs!
Demurely squatting upon floating leaves,
And greener than their couches. Their round backs
Of many-shaded chrysoprase, all moist,
Change with each throbbing inner pulse, that waves   5
And varies that rare pattern in gold thread,
Till to our puzzled eyes it seems to fuse
And run in other shapes. Anon, a note,
Deep, full and thrilling, as a harp-string, twanged
I' the bass by a firm finger, rings along,   10
And after a due interval — all's done
With marvellous dignity — another voice,
In bell-like monosyllable, replies;
Then, up and down the brook, the solemn tones,
In quaint, uneven melody, resound;   15
Else, all is still.'

Ah! do you laugh, because I say these frogs
Are Water Beaux? In sooth, I do not know
That mortal exquisite, who pranks himself
In comparable bravery of garb.   20
Broadcloth and velvet are prosaic, dull,
Nowhere in competition! Even those
Supreme high-priests of Nature's mysteries
The scientists, who usually delight
In giving hardest names to fairest things,   25
Calling a butterfly by such a string
Of big, rough, heavy Greek and Latin words
As well might overweight an elephant; —
E'en they, throned high in professorial chairs
Have gracefully unbending, recognised   30
My frog-friend's right to an illustrious name,
And dubbed him Hylas, after the fair youth
Beloved and stol'n by water-nymphs of yore.
Brightly he wears his honours. Not a bird
Floating on radiant pinions to the sun,   35
Nor fish illumining the azure deeps
Of ocean with rich iridescent hues,
Nor tropic fly's superbest pencilled wings
May venture rivalry. I have said it oft,
A 'thrice-told tale' indeed. A tale, told first   40
When Austral climes and forms to me were new,
And life, all throbbing and aglow with youth

1–16 self-quoted from 'A Summer Sketch', published in 1860

And newly wedded love and cloudless hope,
Seemed more of Heaven than earth.
　　　　　　　　　One day I stood　　　　　　　　45
Amidst an arid, grassless plain, beside
The well-nigh dried-up river-pools, and saw —
For the first time — with eager, wondering eyes
The Water Beaux! 'Tis fifty years ago!
Life, then so bright, is wan and weary now;　　　　50
And I — left all alone — grey, feeble, old —
Saddened by sorrow, worn and bent with pain,
Await the nearing end — the sleep below the sod.
Yet — you may deem it childish — so to dream —
'Tis as a written story of the past,　　　　　　55
The chequered — shadowed — but most happy past —
To fancy that I even now look down
Once more, in hushed and cautious silence, where
On the still waters, broad leaves lie afloat
And drooping streamers of fair sweet wild flowers　60
Wave in the sunlit air above the forms
Of these — dear friends for half a century —
My peerless Water Beaux!

　　　　　　　　　　　　　　　　　　　　1891

Incompleteness

Fair were the classic lands, where Song had birth,
　　And chorused plaudits greeted bards sublime,
As crowned with garlands, led in triumph forth,
　　They basked in glory — heroes for all time.

And doubtless well content were they, who wove　　5
　　The fragrant Bay-leaves for the victor's brow,
Unconscious that in any earthly grove
　　Aught fairer, or more fitting, bloomed below.

They wot not of an undiscovered isle,
　　Far — far remote in Austral Orient sea,　　　　10
Where many a river gorge and dim defile
　　Bore worthier guerdon for high minstrelsy.

Had dream or charm revealed to them a sight
　　Of our Tasmanian Laurel's pearly bells,
What urgent prayers had clomb Olympus' height,　　15
　　That God-sent gatherers might invade these dells!

'Tis ever so. In life's unfinished course,
Perfect completeness is a thing unknown:
　　They lacked our Laurel for the Poet's verse,
And we, possessing it, lack Bards to crown!　　　20

　　　　　　　　　　　　　　　　　　　　1891

ROBERT LOWE   *(1811–92)*

From Songs of the Squatters

2

The Commissioner bet me a pony — I won,
So he cut off exactly two thirds of my run,
For he said I was making a fortune too fast;
And profit gained slower, the longer would last.

He remarked as, devouring my mutton, he sat,   5
That I suffered my sheep to grow sadly too fat;
That they wasted waste land, did prerogative brown,
And rebelliously nibbled the droits of the Crown.

That the creek that divided my station in two
Showed that Nature design'd that two fees should be due.   10
Mr Riddell assured me 'twas paid but for show,
But he kept it, and spent it — that's all that I know.

The Commissioner fined me, because I forgot
To return an old ewe that was ill of the rot,
And a poor wry-necked lamb that we kept for a pet,   15
And he said it was treason such things to forget.

The Commissioner pounded my cattle, because
They had mumbled the scrub with their famishing jaws
On the part of the run he had taken away,
And he sold them by auction the costs to defray.   20

The Border Police they were out all the day
To look for some thieves who had ransack'd my dray,
But the thieves they continued in quiet and peace,
For they'd robb'd it themselves had the Border Police.

When the white thieves were gone, next the black thieves appeared,   25
My shepherds they waddied, my cattle they speared;
But for fear of my License I said not a word,
For I knew it was gone if the Government heard.

The Commissioner's bosom with anger was filled
Against me, because my poor shepherd was killed;   30
So he straight took away the last third of my run,
And got it transferred to the name of his son.

The son had from Cambridge been lately expell'd,
And his license for preaching most justly withheld;
But this is no cause, the Commissioner says,   35
Why he should not be fit for my license to graze.

The cattle that had not been sold at the pound
He took with the run, at five shillings all round,

And the sheep the blacks left me, at sixpence a head —
And a very good price, the Commissioner said.   40

The Governor told me I justly was served,
That Commissioners never from duty had swerved;
But that if I'd a fancy for any more land,
For one pound an acre he'd plenty on hand.

I'm not very proud, I can dig in a bog,   45
Feed pigs, or for firewood can split up a log,
Clean shoes, riddle cinders, or help to boil down,
Any thing that you please — but graze lands of the Crown!

3

    The Gum has no shade,
    And the Wattle no fruit;
    The parrot don't warble
    In trolls like the flute;
    The Cockatoo cooeth   5
    Not much like a dove,
    Yet fear not to ride
    To my station, my love.
    Four hundred miles off
    Is the goal of our way,   10
    It is done in a week,
    At but sixty a day.
    The plains are all dusty,
    The creeks are all dried,
    'Tis the fairest of weather   15
    To bring home my bride.
    The blue vault of heaven
    Shall curtain thy form,
    One side of a Gum tree
    The moonbeam *must* warm;   20
    The whizzing Mosquito
    Shall dance o'er thy head,
    And the Guana shall squat
    At the foot of thy bed;
    The brave Laughing Jackass   25
    Shall sing thee to sleep,
    And the Snake o'er thy slumber
    His vigils shall keep!
    Then sleep, lady, sleep,
    Without dreaming of pain,   30
    Till the frost of the morning
    Shall wake thee again.
    Our brave bridal bower
    I built not of stones,
    Though like old Doubting Castle,   35
    'Tis paved with bones:

The bones of the sheep
On whose flesh I have fed,
Where thy thin satin slipper
Unshrinking may tread;   40
For the dogs have all polished
Them clean with their teeth,
And they're better, believe me,
Than what lies beneath.
My door has no hinge,   45
And the window no pane —
They let out the smoke,
But they let in the rain!
The frying pan serves us
For table and dish,   50
And the tin pot of tea stands
Still filled to your wish;
The sugar is brown,
The milk is all done,
But the stick it is stirred with   55
Is better than none.
The stockmen *will* swear,
And the shepherds *won't* sing,
But a dog's a companion
Enough for a king.   60
So fear not, fair Lady,
Your desolate way,
Your clothes will arrive
In three months with my dray.
Then mount, lady, mount, to the wilderness fly —   65
My stores are laid in, and my shearing is nigh;
And our steeds that through Sydney exultingly wheel,
Must graze in a week on the banks of the Peel.

                                              (1845) 1885

'FREDERICK'

North Brisbane Advance!

'Tis not often we hear of a flourishing town
Now-a-days, when the price of the wool has come down,
And the merchants and squatters are low in their pockets,
Like candles burnt down to the grease in their sockets.
But the fact is, North Brisbane keeps going ahead,   5
Though the stores and the streets sometimes seem rather dead:
There's a Judge coming down in his ermine and wig,
To punish all scoundrels who quarrel or prig,
While, to better our souls, and to save us from lurches,
We'll shortly have Methodist chapels and churches.   10

But Government, fearing such diverse religions
Will turn topsy-turvy the souls in these regions, —
And knowing how quickly long-faces fall out,
(Though seldom aware *what* they quarrel about),
Have taken good care, in foreseeing our rackets,   15
And so will send down a small squad of red jackets.

With no less than three lights in Morality's line,
Our lives — and our pockets — to cleanse and refine,
And a town-clock, which looks on the Brisbanites toiling,
Unmov'd, — which never needs setting or oiling;   20
And a Court, where they punish all wicked marauders
And doctors and lawyers to cure all disorders, —
And carriages flying by every fine day, —
It must surely be granted we're making our way;
And as money will quickly increase on our hands,   25
From our prosperous trade, and our flourishing lands,
The Sydney Directors, — whose kindness we thank —
Have promised ere long to establish a Bank;
Where they, — the kind souls — out of pity alone,
Will care for our money as if 'twere their own.   30

      (1848)

'COLONIENSIS'

Melbourne

Melbourne! unclassic, anti-native name!
And yet, as by Magician's spell, upsprung,
Thee have I chosen, subject fit for song.
No antique relics, pyramids sublime
May be thine to boast. But who thy hist'ry   5
Knows? Whether primal city, embattled
Tower, or imperial throne on which have
Sate, of tyrant Czars, a long succession; the
Muse informs me not. No seer am I, nor
Doth my vision scan time past: sufficient   10
'Tis the present to describe. Then aid me
Austral Muse, if such exist.
                 The swarthy
Tribe appeas'd, remov'd; or with force of arms
Into the Interior driven back;   15
(For power, the law of right, too oft o'ercomes)
A savage, to a civil race gives way.
    At first, selected, is large patch of land
Deem'd suitable, and for water standing
Well. A weather-boarded hut is rear'd, or   20

One of turf; shingled, or thatched, not to rain,
Or penetrating wind impervious;
Or against the sweeping storm secure; round
It, the electric fluid, fork'd or sheet
Is seen terrific; while above is heard   25
Of thunder loud, peal after peal: Meantime
The lonely hut shakes at its very base,
If base it may be nam'd. The affrighted
Inmates now, their isolated thoughts, in
Turn, express, and other neighbours wish. They   30
Wish not long. Man must not dwell alone. So
Hut unites to hut, to acre, acre:
A site thus fix'd, a Town is plan'd; the streets
At angles right are then divided off.
And Anglicised, the whole a Stateman's name   35
They give, and call it Melbourne. It's fame now
Sounded far; Emigration's tide rolls in,
And population swells. Lot after lot
Is sold. The lonely weather-boarded hut
Is lost. The turf built house is taken down.   40
Now brick to turf succeeds, and stone to wood
Now spacious stores, and dwellings palace-like
On every hand are seen. Enacted now
Are laws, and Magisterial rod, the
Rights of each, protects. Tis thus men form the   45
Future Empire; the central City build.
    Melbourne! thy rise an Austral Poet sings;
But who thy *fall shall see*, and thus record?
I leave thee now, and distant be the day,
When, 'Here stood Melbourne,' shall the Trav'ler say.   50

                                              (1839)

'FRANK THE POET' (FRANCIS MACNAMARA) *(b ?1811)*

A Convict's Tour to Hell

Nor can the foremost of the sons of men
Escape my ribald and licentious pen.
                              Swift

You prisoners all of New South Wales
Who frequent watchhouses and gaols
A story to you I will tell
'Tis of a Convict's Tour to Hell
Whose valour had for years been tried   5
On the highway before he died.
At length he fell to death a prey
To him it proved an happy day

Downwards he bent his course I'm told
Like one destined for Satan's fold   10
And no refreshment would he take
Till he approached the Stygian lake.
A tent he then began to fix
Contiguous to the River Styx
Thinking that no one could molest him   15
He leaped when Charon thus addressed him
Stranger I say from whence art thou
And thy own name pray tell me now.
Kind sir I came from Sydney gaol
My name I don't mean to conceal   20
And since you seem anxious to know it
On earth I was called Frank the Poet.
Are you that person? Charon cried
I'll carry you to the other side
So Stranger do not troubled be   25
For you shall have a passage free
Five or sixpence I mostly charge
For the like passage in my barge.
Frank seeing no other succour nigh
With the invitation did comply   30
And having a fair wind and tide
They soon arrived at the other side
And leaving Charon at the ferry
Frank went in haste to Purgatory
And rapping loudly at the gate   35
Of Limbo or the Middle State
Pope Pius the 7th soon appeared
With gown beads crucifix and beard
And gazing at the Poet the while
Accosts him in the following style   40
Stranger art thou a friend or foe
Your business here I fain would know.
Quoth the Poet for Heaven I'm not fitted
And here I hope to be admitted.
Pius rejoined vain are your hopes   45
This place was made for Priests and Popes
Tis a world of our own invention
But friend I've not the least intention
To admit such a foolish elf
Who scarce knows how to bless himself.   50
Quoth Frank were you mad or insane
When first you made this world of pain
For I can see nought but brimstone and fire
A share of which I can't desire
Here I see weeping wailing gnashing   55
And torments of the newest fashion

Therefore I call you silly elf
Who made a rod to whip yourself
And may you like all honest neighbours
Enjoy the fruit of all your labours.   60
Frank then bade the Pope farewell
And hurried to that place called Hell
And having found the gloomy gate
Frank rapped aloud to know his fate
He louder knocked and louder still   65
When the Devil came, pray what's your will?
Alas cried the Poet I've come to dwell
With you and share your fate in Hell.
Says Satan such can't be, I'm sure
For I detest and hate the poor   70
And none shall in my kingdom stand
Except the grandees of the land
But Frank I think you're going astray
For convicts never come this way
But soar to Heaven in droves and legions   75
A place so called in the upper regions
So Frank I think with an empty purse
You shall go farther and fare worse.
Well cried the Poet since tis so
One thing of you I'd like to know   80
As I'm at present in no hurry
Have you one here called Captain Murray?
Yes Murray is within this place
Will you said Satan see his face?
May God forbid that I should view him   85
For on board the Phoenix Hulk I knew him.
Who is that Sir in yonder blaze
Who on fire and brimstone seems to graze?
Tis Captain Logan of Moreton Bay
And Williams who was killed the other day   90
He was overseer at Grosse Farm
And done poor prisoners no little harm
Cook who discovered New South Wales
And he that first invented gaols
Are both tied to a fiery stake   95
Which stands in yonder boiling lake.
Hark do you hear this dreadful yelling
It issues from Doctor Wardell's dwelling
And all those fiery seats and chairs
Are fitted up for Dukes and Mayors   100
And nobles of Judicial orders
Barristers Lawyers and Recorders.
Here I beheld legions of traitors
Hangmen Gaolers and Flagellators

Commandants Constables and Spies   105
Informers and Overseers likewise
In flames of brimstone they were toiling
And lakes of sulphur around them boiling
Hell did resound with their fierce yelling
Alas how dismal was their dwelling   110
Then Major Morriset I espied
And Captain Cluney by his side
With a fiery belt they were lashed together
As tight as soles to upper leather
Their situation was most horrid   115
For they were tyrants down at the Norrid
Prostrate I beheld a petitioner
It was the Company's Commissioner.
Satan said he my days are ended
For many years I've superintended   120
The Australian Company's affairs
And I punctually paid all arrears
Sir should you doubt the hopping Colonel
At Carrington you'll find my journal
Legibly penned in black and white   125
To prove that my accounts were right
And since I've done your will on earth
I hope you'll put me in a berth.
Then I saw old Serjeant Flood
In Vulcan's hottest forge he stood   130
He gazed at me his eyes with ire
Appeared like burned coals of fire
In fiery garments he was arrayed
And like an Arabian horse he brayed
He on a bloody cutlass leaned   135
And to a lamp-post he was chained
He loudly called out for assistance
Or begged me to end his existence.
Cheer up said I be not afraid
Remember No. Three Stockade   140
In the course of time you may do well
If you behave yourself in Hell
Your heart on earth was fraught with malice
Which oft drove convicts to the gallows
But you'll now atone for all the blood   145
Of prisoners shed by Serjeant Flood.
Then I beheld that well known Trapman
The Police Runner called Izzy Chapman
Here he was standing on his head
In a river of melted boiling lead.   150
Alas he cried behold me stranger
I've captured many a bold bushranger

And for the same I'm suffering here
But lo, now yonder snakes draw near
On turning round I saw slow worms   155
And snakes of various kinds and forms
All entering at his mouth and nose
To devour his entrails as I suppose.
Then turning round to go away
Bold Lucifer bade me to stay   160
Saving Frank by no means go man
Till you see your old friend Dr Bowman
Yonder he tumbles groans and gnashes
He gave you many a thousand lashes
And for the same he does bewail   165
For Osker with an iron flail
Thrashes him well you may depend
And will till the world comes to an end.
Just as I spoke a coach and four
Came in full post haste to the door   170
And about six feet of mortal sin
Without leave or licence trudged in
At his arrival 3 cheers were given
Which rent I'm sure the highest Heaven
And all the inhabitants of Hell   175
With one consent rang the great bell
Which never was heard to sound or ring
Since Judas sold our Heavenly King
Drums were beating flags were hoisting
There never before was such rejoicing   180
Dancing singing joy or mirth
In Heaven above nor on the earth
Straightway to Lucifer I went
To know what these rejoicings meant.
Of sense cried Lucifer I'm deprived   185
Since Governor Darling has arrived
With fire and brimstone I've ordained him
And Vulcan has already chained him
And I'm going to fix an abode
For Captain Rossi he's on the road   190
Frank don't go till you see the novice
The magistrate from the Police Office.
Oh said the Poet I'm satisfied
To hear that he is to be tied
And burned in this World of Fire   195
I think tis high time to retire
And having travelled many days
O'er fiery hills and boiling seas
At length I found that happy place
Where all the woes of mortals cease   200
And rapping boldly at the wicket
Cried Peter, where's your certificate

Or if you have not one to shew
Pray who in Heaven do you know?
Well I know Brave Donohue   205
Young Troy and Jenkins too
And many others whom floggers mangled
And lastly were by Jack Ketch strangled.
Peter, says Jesus, let Frank in
For he is thoroughly purged from sin   210
And although in convict's habit dress'd
Here he shall be a welcome guest.

    Isiah go with him to Job
    And put on him a scarlet robe
    St Paul go to the flock straightway   215
    And kill the fatted calf today
    And go tell Abraham and Abel
    In haste now to prepare the table
    For we shall have a grand repast
    Since Frank the Poet has come at last   220
    Then came Moses and Elias
    John the Baptist and Mathias
    With many saints from Foreign lands
    And with the Poet they all join hands.

Thro' Heaven's Concave their rejoicings rang   225
And hymns of praise to God they sang
And as they praised his glorious name
I awoke and found twas but a dream.

(written 1839)

For the Company Under Ground

Francis MacNamara of Newcastle to J. Crosdale Esq. greeting

When Christ from Heaven comes down straightway
All his Father's laws to expound
MacNamara shall work that day
For the Company under ground.

When the man in the moon to Moreton Bay   5
Is sent in shackles bound
MacNamara shall work that day
For the Company under ground.

When the Cape of Good Hope to Twofold Bay
Comes for the change of a pound   10
MacNamara shall work that day
For the Company under ground.

J. Crosdale   probably William Croasdill, superintendent of the Australian Agricultural Company's
mines in the Newcastle area in the late 1830s

When cows in lieu of milk yield tea
And all lost treasures are found
MacNamara shall work that day   15
For the Company under ground.

When the Australian Company's heaviest dray
Is drawn 80 miles by a hound
MacNamara shall work that day
For the Company under ground.   20

When a frog a caterpillar and a flea
Shall travel the globe all round
MacNamara shall work that day
For the Company under ground.

When turkey cocks on Jews harps play   25
And mountains dance at the sound
MacNamara shall work that day
For the Company under ground.

When milestones go to church to pray
And whales are put in the Pound   30
MacNamara shall work that day
For the Company under ground.

When Christmas falls on the 1st of May
And O'Connell's King of England crown'd
MacNamara shall work that day   35
For the Company under ground.

When thieves ever robbing on the highway
For their sanctity are renowned
MacNamara shall work that day
For the Company under ground   40

When the quick and dead shall stand in array
Cited at the last trumpet's sound
Even then, damn me if I'd work a day
For the Company under ground

    Nor over ground.   45

(written late 1830s)

'HUGO'

The Gin

'Where spreads the sloping shaded turf
  By Coodge's smooth and sandy bay,
And roars the ever-ceaseless surf,
  I've built my gunya for to-day.

'The gum-tree with its glitt'ring leaves 5
   Is sparkling in the sunny light,
And round my leafy home it weaves
   Its dancing shade with flow'rets bright.

'And beauteous things around are spread;
   The burwan, with its graceful bend 10
And cone of nuts, and o'er my head
   The flowering vines their fragrance lend.

'The grass-tree, too, is waving there,
   The fern-tree sweeping o'er the stream,
The fan-palm, curious as rare, 15
   And warretaws with crimson beam.

'Around them all the glecinæ
   Its dainty tendrils careless winds,
Gemming their green with blossoms gay,
   One common flower each bush-shrub finds. 20

'Fresh water, too, is tumbling o'er
   The shell-strewn rocks into the sea;
'Midst them I seek the hidden store,
   To heap the rich repast for thee.

'But where is Bian? — where is he? — 25
   My husband comes not to my meal:
Why does he not the white man flee,
   Nor let their god his senses steal?

'Lingers he yet in Sydney streets?
   Accursed race! to you we owe, 30
No more the heart contended beats,
   But droops with sickness, pain, and woe.

'Oh! for the days my mother tells,
   Ere yet the white man knew our land;
When silent all our hills and dells, 35
   The game was at the huntsman's hand.

'Then roamed we o'er the sunny hill,
   Or sought the gully's grassy way,
With ease our frugal nets could fill
   From forest, plain, or glen, or bay. 40

'Where sported once the kangaroo,
   Their uncouth cattle tread the soil,
Or corn-crops spring, and quick renew,
   Beneath the foolish white man's toil.

'On sunny spots, by coast and creek, 45
   Near the fresh stream we sat us down;
Now fenced, and shelterless, and bleak,
   They're haunted by the white man's frown.'

She climbed the rock — she gazed afar —
 The sun behind those mountains blue
Had sunk; faint gleamed the Western star,
 And in the East a rainbow hue

Was mingling with the darkling sea;
 When gradual rose the zodiac light,
And over rock, and stream, and tree,
 Spread out its chastened radiance bright.

So calm, so soft, so sweet a ray,
 It lingers on the horizon's shore;
The echo of the brighter day,
 That bless'd the world an hour before.

But sudden fades the beam that shone,
 And lit the earth like fairy spell;
Whilst in the East, the sky's deep tone
 Proclaims the daylight's last farewell.

'Fast comes the night, and Bian yet
 Returns not to his leafy bed;
My hair is with the night-dew wet —
 Sleep comes not to this aching head.

'The screeching cockatoo's at rest;
 From yonder flat the curlew's wail
Comes mournful to this sorrowing breast,
 And keenly blows the Southern gale.

'Avaunt ye from our merry land!
 Ye that so boast our souls to save,
Yet treat us with such niggard hand:
 We have no hope but in the grave.'

Thus sung Toongulla's wretched child,
 As o'er her sleeping babe she hung,
Mourning her doom, to lead a wild
 And cheerless life the rocks among.

Their health destroyed — their sense depraved —
 The game, their food, for ever gone;
Let me invoke religion's aid
 To shield them from this double storm

Of physical and moral ill;
 We owe them all that we possess —
The forest, plain, the glen, the hill,
 Were theirs; — to slight is to oppress.

50

55

60

65

70

75

80

85

(1831)

ANONYMOUS

Australian Courtship

The Currency Lads may fill their glasses,
And drink to the health of the Currency Lasses;
But the lass I adore, the lass for me,
Is a lass in the Female Factory.

O! Molly's her name, and her name is Molly,   5
Although she was tried by the name of Polly;
She was tried and was cast for death at Newry,
But the Judge was bribed and so were the Jury.

She got 'death recorded' in Newry town
For stealing her mistress's watch and gown;   10
Her little boy Paddy can tell you the tale,
His father was turnkey of Newry jail.

The first time I saw this comely lass
Was at Parramatta, going to mass;
Says I, 'I'll marry you now in an hour,'   15
Says she, 'Well, go and fetch Father Power.'

But I *got into trouble* that very same night!
Being drunk in the street I got into a fight;
A constable seized me — I gave him a box —
And was put in the watch-house and then in the stocks.   20

O! It's very unaisy as I remember,
To sit in the stocks in the month of December;
With the north wind so hot, and the hot sun right over,
O! sure, and it's no place at all for a lover!

'It's worse than the tread-mill,' says I, 'Mr Dunn,   25
To sit here all day in the *hate* of the sun!'
'Either that or a dollar,' says he, 'for your folly', —
But if I had a dollar I'd drink it with Molly.

But now I am out again, early and late
I sigh and I cry at the Factory gate.   30
'O! Mrs Reordan, late Mrs Farson,
O! won't you let Molly out very soon?'

---

1 **Currency Lads   Currency Lasses**   Australian-born (in the sense of local currency as opposed to British sterling)

4 **the female factory**   a place where female convicts manufactured cloth. There were several in the Australian colonies in the convict period; the best known was at Parramatta.

7 **Newry**   a town in northern Ireland

'Is it Molly McGuigan?' says she to me,
'Is it not?' says I, for she know'd it was she.
'Is it her you mean that was put in the stocks   35
For beating her mistress, Mrs Cox?'

'O! yes and it is, madam, pray let me in,
I have brought her a half-pint of Cooper's best gin.
She likes it as well as she likes her own mother,
O! now let me in, madam, I am her brother.'   40

So the Currency Lads may fill their glasses,
And drink the health of the Currency Lasses;
But the lass I adore, the lass for me,
Is a lass in the Female Factory.

(1831)

JOHN DUNMORE LANG   *(1799–1878)*

D'Entrecasteaux' Channel, Van Dieman's Land

Now D'Entrecasteaux' Channel opens fair,
    And Tasman's Head lies on your starboard bow;
Huge rocks and stunted trees meet you where e'er
    You look around; 'tis a bold coast enow.
With foul wind and crank ship 'twere hard to wear: 5
    A reef of rocks lies westward long and low.
At ebb tide you may see the Aetæon lie
A sheer hulk o'er the breakers, high and dry.

'Tis a most beauteous Strait. The Great South Sea's
    Proud waves keep holiday along its shore,   10
And as the vessel glides before the breeze,
    Broad bays and isles appear, and steep cliffs hoar
With groves on either hand of ancient trees
    Planted by Nature in the days of yore:
Van Dieman's on the left and Brunè's isle   15
Forming the starboard shore for many a mile.

But all is still as death! Nor voice of man
    Is heard, nor forest warbler's tuneful song.
It seems as if this beauteous world began
    To be but yesterday, and the earth still young   20
And unpossessed. For though the tall black swan
    Sits on her nest and sails stately along,
And the green wild doves their fleet pinions ply,
And the grey eagle tempts the azure sky,

Yet all is still as death! Wild solitude   25
    Reigns undisturbed along that voiceless shore,
And every tree seems standing as it stood
    Six thousand years ago. The loud wave's roar

Were music in these wilds. The wise and good
   That wont of old, as hermits, to adore 30
The God of Nature in the desert drear,
Might sure have found a fit sojourning here.

(written 1823) 1872

From Colonial Nomenclature.

'Twas said of Greece two thousand years ago,
   That every stone i' the land had got a name.
Of New South Wales too, men will soon say so too;
   But every stone there seems to get the same.
'Macquarie' for a name is all *the go:* 5
   The old Scotch Governor was fond of fame,
Macquarie Street, Place, Port, Fort, Town, Lake, River:
   'Lachlan Macquarie, Esquire, Governor,' for ever!

I like the native names, as Parramatta,
   And Illawarra, and Woolloomoolloo; 10
Nandowra, Woogarora, Bulkomatta,
   Tomah, Toongabbie, Mittagong, Meroo;
Buckobble, Cumleroy, and Coolingatta,
   The Warragumby, Bargo, Burradoo;
Cookbundoon, Carrabaiga, Wingecarribbee, 15
   The Wollondilly, Yurumbon, Bungarribbee.

I hate your Goulburn Downs and Goulburn Plains,
   And Goulburn River and the Goulburn Range,
And Mount Goulburn and Goulburn Vale! One's brains
   Are turned with Goulburns! Vile scorbutic mange 20
For immortality! Had I the reins
   Of Government a fortnight, I would change
These Downing Street appellatives, and give
   The country names that should deserve to live.

I'd have Mount Hampden and Mount Marvell, and 25
   Mount Wallace and Mount Bruce at the old Bay.
I'd have them all the highest in the land,
   That men might see them twenty leagues away,
I'd have the Plains of Marathon beyond
   Some mountain pass yclept Thermopylæ, 30
Such are th' immortal names that should be written
   On all thy new discoveries, Great Britain!

---

17 **Goulburn** Henry Goulburn, British Under-Secretary for the Colonies 1812–21

25–30 John Hampden (1594–1643) and the poet Andrew Marvell (1621–78) were on the parliamentary side in the British Civil War. Sir William Wallace (c. 1270–1305) and Robert the Bruce (1274–1329) fought successfully for Scots independence from England. The battles of Thermopylae (490 BC) and Marathon (480 BC) were crucial in thwarting an invasion of Greek city states by Persia.

Yes! let some badge of liberty appear
  On every mountain and on every plain
Where Britain's power is known, or far or near,   35
  That freedom there may have an endless reign!
Then though she die, in some revolving year,
  A race may rise to make her live again!
The future slave may lisp the patriot's name
And his breast kindle with a kindred flame!   40

                          (written 1824) 1872

ELIZA HAMILTON DUNLOP   *(1796–1880)*

The Aboriginal Mother

(from Myall's Creek)

Oh! hush thee — hush my baby,
  I may not tend thee yet.
Our forest-home is distant far,
  And midnight's star is set.
Now, hush thee — or the pale-faced men   5
  Will hear thy piercing wail,
And what would then thy mother's tears
  Or feeble strength avail!

Oh, could'st thy little bosom,
  That mother's torture feel,   10
Or could'st thou know thy father lies
  Struck down by English steel;
Thy tender form would wither,
  Like the *kniven* on the sand,
And the spirit of my perished tribe   15
  Would vanish from our land.

For thy young life, my precious,
  I fly the field of blood,
Else had I, for my chieftain's sake,
  Defied them where they stood;   20
But basely bound my woman arm,
  No weapon might it wield:
I could but cling round him I loved,
  To make my heart a shield.

I saw my firstborn treasure   25
  Lie headless at my feet,
The goro on this hapless breast,
  In his life-stream is wet!

Myall's Creek   a place in the NSW northern tablelands, where 28 Aboriginal people were shot, and
their bodies burned, by a party of twelve white stockmen on 9 June 1838

And thou! I snatch'd thee from their sword,
   It harmless pass'd by thee!   30
But clave the binding cords — and gave,
   Haply, the power to flee.

To flee! my babe — but whither?
   Without my friend — my guide?
The blood that was our strength is shed!   35
   He is not by my side!
Thy sire! oh! never, never
   Shall *Toon Bakra* hear our cry:
My bold and stately mountain-bird!
   I thought not he could die.   40

Now who will teach thee, dearest,
   To poise the shield, and spear,
To wield the *koopin*, or to throw
   The *boommerring*, void of fear;
To breast the river in its might;   45
   The mountain tracks to tread?
The echoes of my homeless heart
   Reply — the dead, the dead!

And ever must their murmur
   Like an ocean torrent flow: 50
The parted voice comes never back,
   To cheer our lonely woe:
Even in the region of our tribe,
   Beside our summer streams,
'Tis but a hollow symphony —   55
   In the shadow-land of dreams.

Oh hush thee, dear — for weary
   And faint I bear thee on —
His name is on thy gentle lips,
   My child, my child, *he's gone!*   60
Gone o'er the golden fields that lie
   Beyond the rolling cloud,
To bring thy people's murder cry
   Before the Christian's God.

Yes! o'er the stars that guide us,   65
   He brings my slaughter'd boy:
To shew their God how treacherously
   The stranger men destroy;
To tell how hands in friendship pledged
   Piled high the fatal pire;   70
To tell — to tell of the gloomy ridge!
   And the *stockmen's human fire.*

                   (1838)

FIDELIA S. T. HILL   *(1790–1854)*

Recollections

Yes, South Australia! three years have elapsed
Of dreary banishment, since I became
In thee a sojourner; nor can I choose
But sometimes think on thee; and tho' thou art
A fertile source of unavailing woe,   5
Thou dost awaken deepest interest still. —
Our voyage past, we anchor'd in that port
Of our New Colony, styled Holdfast Bay.
In part surrounded by the range sublime
Of mountains, with Mount Lofty in their centre: —   10
Beautiful mountains, which at even-tide
I oft have gazed upon with raptur'd sense,
Watching their rose-light hues, as fleeting fast
Like fairy shadows o'er their verdant sides
They mock'd the painter's art, and to pourtray   15
Defied the utmost reach of poet's skill! —
The new year open'd on a novel scene, —
New cares, new expectations, a new land! —
Then toil was cheer'd, and labour render'd light,
Privations welcom'd, every hardship brav'd,   20
In the blest anticipation of reward: —
(Which some indeed deserv'd, but ne'er obtain'd)
Some who unceasingly, had lent their aid,
And time, and information, to promote
The interests of the rising Colony —   25
Still flattering hope on the dark future smil'd,
Gilding each object with fallacious dyes,
And picturing pleasure, that *was not to be!*
They bore me to the future Capitol,
Ere yet 'twas more than desart — a few tents,   30
Scatter'd at intervals, 'mid forest trees,
Marked the abode of men. 'Twas a wide waste,
But beauteous in its wildness. — Park-like scenery
Burst on the astonish'd sight; for it did seem
As tho' the hand of art, had nature aided,   35
Where the broad level walks — and verdant lawns,
And vistas grac'd that splendid wilderness!
'Twas then they hail'd me as the *first* white lady
That ever yet had enter'd Adelaide. —
Can time e'er teach me to forget the sound,   40
Of gratulations that assail'd me then,

1–8 Hill and her husband arrived with the first main party of colonists at Holdfast Bay (now Glenelg)
on 28 December 1836 and moved to the site of Adelaide soon after.

And cheer'd me at the moment, or efface
The welcome bland of the distinguish'd one —
Who fixed the site, and form'd the extensive plan
Of that young City? — He hath passed away   45
To the dark cheerless chambers of the tomb!
But Adelaide if crown'd with fortune, shall
To after age perpetuate his name! —

            .   .   .   .   .

One tent was pitch'd upon the sloping bank
Of the stream Torrens, in whose lucid wave   50
Dipp'd flow'ring shrubs — the sweet mimosa there
Wav'd its rich blossoms to the perfum'd breeze,
High o'er our heads — amid the stately boughs
Of the tall gum tree — birds of brightest hues
Or built their nests, or tun'd 'their wood-notes wild,'   55
Reposing on the rushes, fresh and cool,
Which a lov'd hand had for my comfort strew'd: —
This, this methought shall be my happy home!
Here may I dwell, and by experience prove,
That tents with love, yield more substantial bliss   60
Than Palaces without it, can bestow.

                                                                    1840

ANONYMOUS

The Female Transport

Come all young girls, both far and near, and listen unto me,
While unto you I do unfold what proved my destiny,
My mother died when I was young, it caused me to deplore,
And I did get my way too soon upon my native shore.

Sarah Collins is my name, most dreadful is my fate,   5
My father reared me tenderly, the truth I do relate,
'Till enticed by bad company along with many more,
It led to my discovery upon my native shore.

My trial it approached fast, before the judge I stood,
And when the judge's sentence passed it fairly chill'd my blood,   10
Crying, you must be transported for fourteen years or more,
And go from hence across the seas unto Van Dieman's shore.

It hurt my heart when on a coach I my native town passed by,
To see so many I did know, it made me heave a sigh,
Then to a ship was sent with speed along with many more,   15
Whose aching hearts did grieve to go unto Van Dieman's shore.

43–48 Colonel William Light (1786–1839)

The sea was rough, ran mountains high, with us poor girls 'twas hard,
No one but God to us came nigh, no one did us regard.
At length, alas! we reached the land, it grieved us ten times more,
That wretched place Van Dieman's Land, far from our native shore.   20

They chained us two by two, and whipp'd and lashed along,
They cut off our provisions if we did the least thing wrong,
They march us in the burning sun until our feet are sore,
So hard's our lot now we are got to Van Dieman's shore.

We labour hard from morn to night until our bones do ache,   25
Then every one they must obey, their mouldy beds must make,
We often wish when we lay down we ne'er may rise no more,
To meet our savage governor upon Van Dieman's shore.

Every night when I lay down I wet my straw with tears,
While wind upon that horrid shore did whistle in our ears,   30
Those dreadful beasts upon that land around our cots do roar,
Most dismal is our doom upon Van Dieman's shore.

Come all young men and maidens, do bad company forsake,
If tongue can tell our overthrow it will make your heart to ache;
Young girls I pray be ruled by me, your wicked ways give o'er.   35
For fear like us you spend your days upon Van Dieman's shore.

(from c.1820s)

Van Dieman's Land

Come all you gallant poachers, that ramble void of care
That walk out on moonlight night with your dog, gun and snare,
The lofty hare and pheasants you have at your command,
Not thinking of your last career upon Van Dieman's land.

Poor Tom Brown, from Nottingham, Jack Williams, and poor Joe,   5
We are three daring poachers, the country does well know,
At night we were trepan'd by the keepers hid in sand,
Who for 14 years, transported us unto Van Dieman's land.

The first day that we landed upon that fatal shore,
The planters they came round us full twenty score or more,   10
They rank'd us up like horses, and sold us out of hand
They yok'd us unto ploughs, my boys, to plough Van Dieman's land.

Our cottages that we live in were built of clod and clay,
And rotten straw for bedding, & we dare not say nay,
Our cots were fenc'd with fire, we slumber when we can,   15
To drive away wolves and tigers upon Van Dieman's land.

It's often when I slumber I have a pleasant dream,
With my sweet girl a setting down by a purling stream,
Thro' England I've been roaming with her at command,
Now I awaken broken-hearted on Van Dieman's land.   20

God bless our wives and families likewise that happy shore,
That isle of great contentment which we shall see no more,
As for our wretched females, see them we seldom can,
There's twenty to one woman upon Van Dieman's land.

There was a girl from Birmingham, Susan Summers was her name,   25
For fourteen years transported we all well know the same,
Our planter bought her freedom and married her out of hand,
She gave to us good usage upon Van Dieman's land.

So you gallant poachers give ear unto my song
It is a bit of good advice altho' it is not long.   30
Throw by your dogs & snare for to you I speak plain,
For if you know our hardships you'd never poach again.

(from c.1820s)

BARRON FIELD   *(1786–1846)*

Sonnet

On visiting the spot where Captain Cook and Sir Joseph Banks first landed in Botany Bay

Here fix the tablet. This must be the place
Where our Columbus of the South did land;
He saw the Indian village on that sand,
And on this rock first met the simple race
Of Australasia, who presum'd to face   5
With lance and spear his musquet. Close at hand
Is the clear stream, from which his vent'rous band
Refresh'd their ship; and thence a little space
Lies Sutherland, their shipmate; for the sound
Of Christian burial better did proclaim   10
Possession, than the flag, in England's name.
These were the *commelinæ* Banks first found;
But where's the tree with the ship's wood-carv'd fame?
Fix then th' Ephesian brass. 'Tis classic ground.

1819

---

commelinæ   plural of 'commelina', an order of herbaceous plants, a number of species of which are native to Australia

14 'The Ephesians were the first who erected brazen trophies. The Greeks and Romans preferred wood, as not perpetuating hostility' (author's note).

On Reading the Controversy Between Lord Byron and Mr. Bowles

Anticipation is to a young country what antiquity is to an old.

Whether a ship's poetic? — Bowles would own,
If here he dwelt, where Nature is prosaic,
Unpicturesque, unmusical, and where
Nature-reflecting Art is not yet born; —
A land without antiquities, with one,   5
And only one, poor spot of classic ground,
(That on which Cook first landed) — where, instead
Of heart-communings with ancestral relicks,
Which purge the pride while they exalt the mind,
We've nothing left us but anticipation,   10
Better (I grant) than utter selfishness,
Yet too o'erweening — too American;
Where's no past tense; the ign'rant present's all;
Or only great by the *All hail, hereafter!*
One foot of Future's glass should rest on Past;   15
Where Hist'ry is not, Prophecy is guess —
If here he dwelt, Bowles (I repeat) would own
A ship's the only poetry we see.
For, first, she brings us 'news of human kind,'
Of friends and kindred, whom perchance she held   20
As visitors, that she might be a link,
Connecting the fond fancy of far friendship,
A few short months before, and whom she may
In a few more, perhaps, receive again.
Next is a ship poetic, forasmuch   25
As in this spireless city and prophane,
She is to my home-wand'ring phantasy,
With her tall anch'ring masts, a three-spir'd minster,
Vane-crown'd; her bell our only half-hour chimes.
Lastly, a ship is poetry to me,   30
Since piously I trust, in no long space,
Her wings will bear me from this prose-dull land.

                                                                    1823

Controversy   *Byron's Letter . . . on the Rev. W. L. Bowles's Strictures on the Life and Writings of
Pope* (1821) contested Bowles's view that figures of nature and passion are more 'poetical' than others. Bowles claimed that a ship is not in itself poetical; Byron's reply is that no image is poetical in
itself — poetry is a combination.

BIOGRAPHICAL NOTES

Rebecca Edwards b 1969 Batlow, south-eastern NSW; she grew up in Nambucca Heads, Nauru, Sydney, New Guinea, Katherine and Darwin. She was a student in Brisbane 1990–96 and now lives in Townsville.

Jacinta Le Plastrier b 1965 Melbourne; grew up at Maryknoll, Gippsland, and on a farm near Benalla, central Victoria. She works in Melbourne as a journalist and book editor.

Coral Hull b 1965 Sydney. A poet, an amateur photographer, and an animal rights activist, she lives in Melbourne.

John Kinsella b 1963 Perth. A poet and poetry editor, he is based in Western Australia and travels extensively.

Alison Croggon b 1962 Carltonville, Transvaal, South Africa; moved to England in 1966 and to Australia in 1969 where she grew up near Ballarat. She lives in Melbourne and works as a journalist and as a poet, novelist and librettist.

Emma Lew b 1962 Melbourne, where she lives. She has worked as a proofreader and secretary.

Jordie Albiston b 1961 Melbourne, where she lives. She is a musician and teaches creative writing.

Dipti Saravanamuttu b 1960 Sri Lanka. She has worked in Sydney in journalism, scriptwriting and tertiary teaching, and moved to Melbourne in the mid-1990s.

Lionel G. Fogarty b 1959 Barambah, south-east Queensland, in the Wakka Wakka tribal land. He worked at labouring jobs from the age of 16 and published his first book of poetry at 22. He is based in Brisbane. The themes and language of his poetry are central to his project of speaking for Aboriginal rights and culture.

Philip Hodgins 1959–95 b near Shepparton, northern Victoria, where he grew up on a dairy farm. He worked for ten years in book publishing in Melbourne, then lived near Maryborough, central Victoria, from 1990. From his mid-twenties until his death he was under treatment for leukemia.

Sarah Day b 1958 Lancashire, England; grew up in Hobart. She has worked as a teacher of English, and currently teaches creative writing at the University of Tasmania.

Marcella Polain b 1958 Singapore, of Irish and Armenian parents; arrived in WA in 1960. She has worked as a screen writer and teacher, and lives in Perth.

Anthony Lawrence b 1957 Tamworth, NSW. He has worked as a jackeroo and landscape gardener, and has taught English and creative writing in schools. He has lived for periods in Sydney, Wagga and Carnarvon, and is now based in the Blue Mountains.

Judith Beveridge b 1956 London, moved to Australia 1960 and lives in Sydney. She has worked as a research officer and library assistant, and as a teacher of creative writing in secondary, tertiary and adult education.

Gig Ryan b 1956 Melbourne. She moved to Sydney in 1978, and returned to Melbourne in the early 1990s. She has been an office worker, and also a songwriter and rock musician.

Peter Rose b 1955 Wangaratta, Victoria, where he grew up. He works as a publisher in Melbourne.

Kevin Hart b 1954 London; arrived in Australia aged eleven and grew up in Brisbane. He teaches literature and literary theory at Monash University, Melbourne.

Dorothy Porter b 1954 Sydney. She is a teacher of creative writing and a poet who writes book-length poetic narratives as well as shorter poems. She moved recently from Sydney to Melbourne.

John Foulcher b 1952 Sydney. He is a teacher of English at a secondary school in Canberra.

Myron Lysenko b 1952 Heyfield, Gippsland, Victoria, of Ukrainian parents; moved to Melbourne as a child. He has worked as a labourer, clerk and teacher of creative writing, and is a frequent performer of his work. He lives in Blackwood, central Victoria.

Stephen Edgar b 1951 Sydney. Since 1974 he has lived in Hobart, where he has worked as a librarian, a freelance editor and proofreader.

Peter Boyle b 1951 Melbourne; at the age of twelve he moved to Sydney, where he has worked as a teacher.

Ania Walwicz b 1951 Świdnica Ślaska, Poland; arrived in Australia 1963 and lives in Melbourne. She is a noted performer of her own writing, and is also a visual artist.

Jenny Boult b 1951 England. She arrived in Australia 1966 and has lived in Adelaide since 1977. She has read and taught the writing of poetry to a wide array of community groups.

ΠO b 1951 Katerini, Greece. He arrived in Australia in 1954, and lives in Fitzroy in inner Melbourne. He is active in promoting and performing poetry within a range of local communities and also works as a draughtsperson in the Victorian public service.

Peter Goldsworthy b 1951 Minlaton on the Yorke peninsula, SA. A poet and writer of novels and short fiction, he is also a medical doctor in Adelaide.

Robert Harris 1951–93 b Melbourne. He worked at a variety of jobs, including teaching creative writing, and was active in Christian lay ministry.

Philip Salom b 1950 Perth; grew up on a dairy farm at Brunswick Junction, WA south-west coast. A graduate in agricultural science, he is a teacher of creative writing, based in Perth.

John Forbes 1950–98 Melbourne; educated in New Guinea, Malaya and Sydney. He worked as a literary reviewer and a teacher of creative writing. He moved from Sydney to Melbourne in 1989.

Alan Gould b 1949 London, of a British father and Icelandic mother; arrived in Australia 1966. A poet, novelist and critic, he lives in Canberra.

Jennifer Maiden b 1949, Penrith NSW, where she lives. She is a poet, novelist and teacher of creative writing.

Edith Speers b 1949 Canada; arrived in Australia 1974. A biochemist by training, she lives in southern Tasmania.

Tony Lintermans b 1948 Melbourne, and lives there. He grew up on a farm at Lysterfield, outside Melbourne. A poet and a writer of short fiction, he works also as a scriptwriter.

Alex Skovron b 1948 Katowice, Poland; arrived in Sydney 1958 and moved to Melbourne 1979. He has worked since 1972 as a book editor.

Alan Wearne b 1948 Melbourne, and lives there. A poet and a novelist in both verse and prose, he has worked as an emergency teacher and as a teacher of literature and creative writing in the TAFE system.

John A. Scott b 1948 Sussex, England; arrived in Melbourne 1959, where he worked as a scriptwriter and as a teacher in media studies. He writes fiction and teaches creative writing at the University of Wollongong.

Michael Dransfield 1948–73 b Sydney. He worked briefly in the public service, then led an itinerant life, mainly in NSW. A prolific poet in his early twenties, he died of complications from drug use and a road injury.

Martin Johnston 1947–90 b Sydney. He grew up on the Greek island of Hydra from 1954 and was based in Sydney again from 1964. A poet and the author of one novel, he worked as a journalist and a translator.

Rhyll McMaster b 1947 Brisbane, where she grew up. She has worked as a secretary, a nurse, and as a sheep farmer at Braidwood, south-eastern NSW.

Kris Hemensley b 1946 Isle of Wight, England; arrived in Australia 1966 and lives in Melbourne. He is a poet, dramatist, critic, poetry editor, teacher of poetry, and bookseller.

Diane Fahey b 1945 Melbourne, where she grew up. She has worked as a teacher in secondary and tertiary education. After spending several years based in England and also in Adelaide, she now lives in Melbourne.

Mark O'Connor b 1945 Ararat, western Victoria, and grew up there and in Melbourne. A noted environmentalist who has travelled in and written poetry about many of the regions of Australia, he is based in Canberra.

Robert Gray b 1945 Coffs Harbour, north-coast NSW, where he grew up. He lives in Sydney, where he has worked in advertising and as a bookseller.

Caroline Caddy b 1944; early childhood in USA and Japan. She worked in Road Dental Units throughout WA, and then as a farmer on the state's south coast, where she now lives.

Robert Adamson b 1944 Sydney. A poet, poetry editor and publisher, he lives in the Hawkesbury River district.

John Tranter b 1943 Cooma, south-coast NSW. A poet and literary editor, he has worked in publishing and as a radio producer. He lives in Sydney.

Lee Cataldi b 1942 Sydney. Since 1983 she has worked as a teacher-linguist with the Warlpiri people at Lajamanu School, NT.

Roger McDonald b 1941 Young, NSW. He worked in radio and television in Sydney, and was an influential poetry editor with UQP 1969–76. Already known as a poet, he turned to novel writing from 1976, living from 1979 on a farm at Braidwood, south-eastern NSW. He returned to Sydney in 1992.

Geoffrey Lehmann b 1940 Sydney. He has worked as a solicitor and as a lecturer in law and is now a partner in an accounting firm. He lives in Sydney.

Geoff Page b 1940 Grafton NSW; grew up on a cattle station on the Clarence River. A poet, novelist and literary reviewer he has taught English since 1964 at secondary schools in Canberra.

Jan Owen b 1940 Adelaide, where she lives. She has worked as a librarian, and has held positions as a teacher of creative writing.

Kate Llewellyn b 1940 Tumby Bay on the Eyre Peninsula, SA. She worked in Adelaide as a nurse and as a gallery owner. She writes both poetry and prose, and lives at Leura, in the Blue Mountains, NSW.

Aileen Kelly b 1939 Portsmouth, England, and grew up in Winchester; arrived in Australia 1961 and settled in Melbourne. She works as an adult educator in a number of fields, including poetry and creative writing.

Peter Steele b 1939 Perth. Since 1957 he has been based mainly in Melbourne. A Jesuit priest, he teaches literature at the University of Melbourne.

J. S. Harry b 1939 Adelaide, and educated there. She has lived in Sydney since the late 1960s, where she has worked as a bookseller.

Mudrooroo b 1938 Narrogin, south-west WA; formerly known as Colin Johnson. He moved to Melbourne in the 1950s, and later spent seven years in India, three as a Buddhist monk, returning to Australia in 1975. A poet, novelist and playwright, he has taught Aboriginal culture and literature at several universities.

Les Murray b 1938 Nabiac, north-central coast NSW; grew up on a dairy farm at Bunyah, between Forster and Gloucester. He was based in Sydney from 1957 to 1985, when he returned to Bunyah. A poet, essayist and literary editor, he has been a full-time writer since 1971.

Judith Rodriguez b 1936 Perth; grew up in Brisbane. A poet and literary editor, she has taught at a number of universities, including La Trobe University, Melbourne, 1969–86. She currently teaches professional writing at Deakin University in Melbourne.

Mal Morgan b 1936 London, England; arrived in Australia 1948. He is a pharmacist, and is a long-time promoter of poetry readings in Melbourne.

Thomas Shapcott b 1935 Ipswich, Queensland. He worked there as an accountant, and later, as a literary editor and arts administrator in Sydney and Melbourne. A poet and novelist, he teaches creative writing at the University of Adelaide.

Randolph Stow b 1935 Geraldton, WA. A novelist and poet, he has taught literature at several universities, and since 1966 has lived in England.

David Malouf b 1934 Brisbane, of an English mother and Lebanese father. After living for a decade in Europe, he taught literature at the University of Sydney 1968–77. A novelist, poet and librettist, he resides alternately in Sydney and Tuscany.

Margaret Scott b 1934 Bristol, England; arrived in Australia 1959. She worked as a research assistant in Hobart, and taught literature at the University of Tasmania 1966–89.

Chris Wallace-Crabbe b 1934 Melbourne. A poet and critic, he taught literature and Australian studies at the University of Melbourne 1961–97.

Jennifer Strauss b 1933 Heywood, south-western Victoria. She has taught literature at Monash University, Melbourne, since 1964.

Fay Zwicky b 1933 Melbourne. She was a concert pianist for several years, and subsequently taught literature at the University of WA 1972–87. She lives in Perth.

Kevin Gilbert 1933–93 b Condobolin, central NSW; father Irish, mother part-Aboriginal of the Wiradjuri tribe. He left school early, worked as a labourer and spent time in jail. A poet, playwright and visual artist, he became a leading advocate of Aboriginal rights and culture.

Philip Martin b 1931 Melbourne. He taught literature at Monash University 1964–88, and has also been a writer and presenter of literary programmes on radio. He lives in Sydney.

Evan Jones b 1931 Melbourne. He taught literature at the University of Melbourne 1963–89 and lives in Melbourne.

Bruce Dawe b 1930 Geelong, Victoria. He was in the RAAF 1959–68, and taught from 1972 in Toowoomba at Darling Downs IAE, which became the University of Southern Queensland. As well as poetry he has written short fiction.

Bruce Beaver b 1929 Manly, Sydney, and lives there. He has worked in various manual and clerical jobs, and since the early 1960s has been a freelance journalist.

Peter Porter b 1929 Brisbane. He has lived in London since 1951, at first working in advertising, and then as a freelance writer and reviewer.

Jill Hellyer b 1925 Sydney, where she lives. She was the founding executive secretary of the Australian Society of Authors 1963–71.

Vincent Buckley 1925–89 b Romsey, central Victoria, of Irish lineage. A poet, critic and literary editor, he taught literature at the University of Melbourne.

Francis Webb 1925–73 b Adelaide; grew up in Sydney. He lived in Canada and England in the mid to late 1940s, and again in England 1953–60. Diagnosed as schizophrenic from 1949, he spent much of his subsequent life in psychiatric hospitals.

Dorothy Hewett b 1923 Perth; grew up on a wheat farm at Wickepin, southwest WA. She was a member of the Communist Party 1942–68. A poet and playwright, she lived in Sydney 1949–60, then returned to Perth and taught literature at the University of WA. She has lived in Sydney since 1974.

Nancy Keesing 1923–93 b Sydney. She worked in Sydney as a social worker, then as a literary editor, critic, children's novelist and arts administrator.

Geoffrey Dutton b 1922 Anlaby Station, Kapunda, SA. He taught literature at the University of Adelaide 1955–62, then worked, mostly in Adelaide, as a freelance writer, literary editor, publisher, arts administrator and novelist.

Dimitris Tsaloumas b 1921 island of Leros, Greece; arrived in Australia 1952. He taught in secondary schools in Melbourne, where he lives. He has written poetry in the Greek language, published in Greece; some of this poetry, including 'The Return', printed in the present anthology, was translated by Philip Grundy with the assistance of the author. 'Falcon Drinking' and 'Elegy', the other two poems printed here, are from Tsaloumas's later work written directly in English.

Rosemary Dobson b 1920 Sydney. A poet and art historian, she worked in Sydney in publishing in the 1940s and, after a period in London, has lived in Canberra since 1972.

Gwen Harwood 1920–95 b Brisbane; moved to Hobart 1945, where she lived at Oyster Cove. As well as a poet, she was a musician and a librettist.

Oodgeroo of the tribe Noonuccal 1920–93 b Stradbroke Island, south-east Queensland, where she lived for much of her life; formerly known as Kath Walker. She has been an influential national voice for the Aboriginal people.

Anne Elder 1918–76 b Auckland NZ; arrived in Australia at the age of three. In the early 1940s she was a soloist with the Borovansky Ballet. She lived in Melbourne, and later on a farm near Macedon, central Victoria.

'Ern Malley' '1918–43' b Liverpool, England; arrived in Australia about 1920 and grew up in Sydney, where he worked briefly as a mechanic. From about 1935 he was an insurance salesman in Melbourne. After his death, a collection of his poems submitted by his sister was accepted and published as modernist work in the Autumn 1944 issue of the arts and literary journal *Angry Penguins*. James McAuley and Harold Stewart subsequently identified themselves as the hoax creators of author and work, intended as parody.

Jack Davis b 1917 Perth, of Aboriginal, Sikh and Irish lineage. His many occupations have included stockman, lay preacher and actor. Based in Fremantle, he is a poet and playwright, and a prominent advocate of Aboriginal rights.

James McAuley 1917–76 b Sydney. He worked as a government adviser on New Guinea and Pacific affairs in the 1940s and 50s. He worked as a literary editor, and from 1961 taught literature in Hobart at the University of Tasmania.

Judith Wright b 1915 near Armidale, north-eastern NSW; grew up there on the pastoral property of her family. After some periods working in Sydney and Brisbane, she moved to Mt Tamborine in south-east Queensland, and in the early 1970s to Braidwood, south-eastern NSW. She is a poet, critic, historian, and writer of children's books and adult fiction. She is also a prominent long-time activist in the areas of conservation and Aboriginal rights.

David Campbell 1913–79 b Ellerslie Station near Adelong, south-eastern NSW (now ACT). He farmed in the district after wartime service as a pilot.

Dorothy Auchterlonie 1915–91 b Sunderland, England; arrived in Australia in her teens. A broadcaster and journalist in Sydney during the 1940s, she subsequently taught literature at several universities, latterly in Canberra. She published literary studies under her married name, Green.

John Manifold 1915–85 b Melbourne; grew up on the family pastoral property in Western Victoria. He joined the Communist Party in the 1930s. After war service, he lived in Brisbane and worked as a freelance writer. He was a noted scholar of Australian folk song and ballad, and of early English stage music.

John Blight 1913–95 b Adelaide; grew up in Brisbane. He worked variously as an orchardist, an accountant, and part-owner of timber mills in the coastal areas of south-east Queensland; from 1968 he lived in Brisbane.

Douglas Stewart 1913–85 b Eltham, Taranaki Province, NZ; settled in Australia 1938. A poet and writer of verse plays for radio, he was influential as the literary editor of the *Bulletin* in Sydney 1940–61, and then as poetry editor with the publishers Angus & Robertson 1961–71.

Kenneth Mackenzie 1913–55 b Perth; grew up there and in the country town of Pinjarra. A poet and novelist, working occasionally as a journalist and publisher's reader he lived in Sydney from 1934.

Barbara Giles b 1912 Manchester, England; arrived in Australia 1923. She has worked as a teacher and a literary editor and has written children's fiction. She published the first of several books of poetry in 1978.

Roland Robinson 1912–92 b Co. Clare, Ireland, of English parents; arrived in Australia 1921. He left school early, and seems to have worked in most of the jobs available in country Australia from rouseabout to crocodile catcher. He was also a ballet dancer, and ballet and literary reviewer. Much of his work in poetry and prose reflects a deep familiarity with Aboriginal culture.

William Hart-Smith 1911–90 b Tunbridge Wells, England; went to NZ 1924 and thence to Australia 1936. He lived in NZ after the war, in Sydney from 1962, Perth 1970–78, and then again in NZ. He worked mainly in advertising and in radio.

Elizabeth Riddell b 1910 Napier, NZ; arrived in Australia 1928. She worked as a professional journalist in Australia, USA and Europe, including a period in the 1940s as a war correspondent. She lives in Sydney.

A. D. (Alec Derwent) Hope b 1907 Cooma south-eastern NSW. He taught literature at Sydney Teachers College from 1938, then from 1945 at the University of Melbourne, and from 1951 at Canberra University College, later ANU, in Canberra.

Robert D. FitzGerald 1902–87 b Sydney. A professional surveyor, and a poet and literary reviewer, he lived for most of his life in Sydney.

Kenneth Slessor 1901–71 b Orange, central NSW. From 1920 he worked as a journalist in Sydney, becoming a newspaper and literary editor, and in 1940–44 as an official war correspondent.

Leon Gellert 1892–1977 b Adelaide. He was a schoolteacher in Adelaide before the 1914–18 war. He took part in the landing at Gallipoli, and was wounded and evacuated in July 1915. Moving to Sydney, he worked again as a schoolteacher and later became an arts journalist and literary editor.

Lesbia Harford 1891–27 b Melbourne. She studied at the University of Melbourne 1912–16, graduating in law and philosophy. Poor in health from a heart defect, she worked as a teacher and as an office worker, and for a time in a clothing factory. Her association with radical social groups in Melbourne is reflected in her poetry and one novel — all published well after her death.

Zora Cross 1890–1964 b Brisbane. A poet and novelist, she worked as a freelance journalist in Sydney.

Dorothea Mackellar 1885–1968 b Sydney, where she lived for most of her life. The author of poetry and three novels, she wrote little after the mid-1920s.

'Furnley Maurice' (Frank Wilmot) 1881–1942 b Melbourne. He worked in Melbourne as a bookseller from 1895, and from 1932 as publisher at Melbourne University Press.

Hugh McCrae 1876–1958 b Melbourne, where he grew up. He moved to Sydney in 1904 and worked mainly as a freelance writer.

John Shaw Neilson 1872–1942 b Penola, south-eastern SA; grew up there and at Minimay, western Victoria. He worked as an itinerant agricultural labourer, mainly in western Victoria, until 1928, when in recognition of his literary merit and needs he was given a sinecure with the Country Roads Board in Melbourne. From about 1905 his vision was impaired so that he could only read large print.

Mary E. Fullerton 1868–1946 b Glenmaggie, Gippsland, Victoria. A poet and novelist, and a campaigner on feminist issues, she lived in England from 1922, where her last two books of poetry were published under the pseudonym 'E'.

Mary Gilmore 1865–1962 b Cotta Walla near Goulburn, NSW. She taught in country schools and then in Sydney 1890–95. A socialist, she joined William Lane's utopian 'New Australia' community in Paraguay 1896–1902, then farmed in western Victoria, and finally settled in Sydney 1912. As a journalist, and especially as editor of the Women's Page of the Sydney *Worker* 1908–31, she was a radical social campaigner.

Jack Mathieu 1873–1949 b Goulburn Valley, northern Victoria. A writer of bush ballads and short fiction, he worked as a sailor, shearer, drover and digger. He lived in Brisbane for the latter part of his life.

Arthur H. Adams 1872–1936 b New Zealand; arrived in Australia in his twenties. He worked in Sydney as a journalist and literary editor.

Christopher Brennan 1870–1932 b Sydney. He spent two formative years studying in Berlin 1892–94. He was a cataloguer in the Sydney Public Library from 1895, then taught modern comparative literature at the University of Sydney 1909–25.

Marie E. J. Pitt 1869–1948 b Doherty's Corner, Gippsland, Victoria, and grew up there. She lived in rural Tasmania 1893–1905, and subsequently in Melbourne. She was an office worker and journalist, and active in socialist and feminist causes.

R. H. (Robert Henderson) Croll 1869–1947 b Stawell, western Victoria. He worked as a literary editor and education administrator in Melbourne.

J. K. (John Keith) McDougall 1867–1957 b Learmonth, western Victoria. For much of his life he farmed near Ararat. He wrote poetry and political prose, and was the Labor member for Wannon in the federal parliament 1906–13.

Henry Lawson 1867–1922 b Greenfield goldfield, NSW. The eldest child of Louisa Lawson, he grew up mainly at New Pipeclay (later Eurunderee) near Mudgee, central NSW. A poet and writer of short fiction, he lived principally in Sydney from 1883.

Barcroft Boake 1866–92 b Sydney. He worked as a surveyor's assistant, drover and boundary rider 1886–91. Beset by personal and financial problems, he committed suicide shortly after returning to Sydney. A book of his bush ballads was published in 1897.

A. B. (Andrew Barton) Paterson 1864–1941 b Narambla Station near Orange, central NSW; grew up near Yass. He settled in Sydney and graduated as a lawyer, but worked mainly as a journalist, becoming a newspaper editor and war correspondent. His pseudonym, 'The Banjo', was adopted only in his earliest publications in the *Bulletin*.

W. T. (William Thomas) Goodge 1862–1909 b London, England; arrived in Australia 1882 and worked for twelve years in outback NSW. He then settled in Orange, central NSW, as a journalist and newspaper editor.

Victor Daley 1858–1905 b Co. Meath, Ireland; arrived in Australia 1878 and worked as a journalist in Adelaide, Melbourne and Sydney.

Louisa Lawson 1848–1920 b near Mudgee, central NSW; mother of Henry Lawson. She moved to Sydney in 1883 and became a journalist, campaigning on radical social issues. She founded and edited the feminist journal *The Dawn*, 1888–1905.

Mary Hannay Foott 1846–1918 b Glasgow, Scotland; arrived in Australia 1853. She trained as an artist in Melbourne, and worked as a journalist. From 1877 she farmed in south-east Queensland, then moved to Brisbane, where she founded a private school in 1884, and worked as a journalist for a decade from 1887.

Emily Manning 1845–90 b Sydney. She worked as a journalist in Sydney from the early 1870s. Her poetry and some of her journalism were published under the pseudonym 'Australie'.

Ada Cambridge 1844–1926 b Norfolk, England; arrived in Australia 1870 and lived with her clergyman husband in several Victorian country towns before settling in Melbourne 1893. She was a poet and novelist.

Henry Kendall 1839–82 b near Milton, NSW south coast; grew up in the Clarence River district, northern NSW, and then near Wollongong. He worked on a whaling ship 1855–57, and in the public service in Sydney 1862–69. In Melbourne 1869–70, problems of unemployment and alcoholism led to a five-year rift with wife and family, and treatment in a mental hospital. From 1876, restored to family and health, he settled in Camden Haven, NSW north coast, where he worked for a timber company. Kendall consciously followed Harpur in embracing the vocation of poetry as contributing to the emerging sense of a new nation.

Adam Lindsay Gordon 1833–70 b Azores, of British parents; arrived in Australia in 1853. He worked in South Australia as a mounted policeman, and then as an itinerant horse dealer and steeplechase rider, before settling near Mt Gambier. In 1867–68 he ran a livery stable in Ballarat. He died by suicide.

Charles R. Thatcher 1831–78 b Bristol, England; arrived in Australia 1852, and worked unsuccessfully on the Victorian goldfields. Success came as an entertainer and song-writer. He lived in New Zealand 1861–66, then returned to Victoria and in 1869 to England.

William Forster 1818–82 b Madras, India; arrived in Australia 1829. He was a member of the NSW parliament from 1856, and Premier 1859–60.

Charles Harpur 1813–68 b Windsor, outside Sydney, of emancipist parents; grew up in the Hawkesbury River district. He worked as a clerk in Sydney 1837–39, then moved to the Hunter Valley where he worked at farming and for a time as a schoolteacher. From 1859 to 1866 he was a Gold Commissioner for the Tuross River area, south of Sydney. In about 1863 he settled on a farm at Eurobodalla. He dedicated himself to becoming the first major poet of Australia in terms both of landscape and of emerging nation.

Louisa Anne Meredith 1812–95 b Birmingham, England. Already established as a poet in England, she arrived in Sydney in 1839 and settled in Tasmania from 1840. A botanist and botanic artist, she illustrated several of her own books of poetry and prose.

Robert Lowe 1811–92 b Nottinghamshire, England; arrived in Australia 1842. A barrister and a member of the NSW parliament 1843–50, he initially supported, then from 1847 opposed, the land monopoly of the squatters. He wrote political satires and founded a newspaper, the *Atlas*. Returning to England in 1850, he entered the British parliament and was made Viscount Sherbrooke in 1880.

'Frank the Poet' (Francis MacNamara) b ?1811 Ireland. He was transported to NSW 1832 and spent time at several penal settlements. A recalcitrant prisoner, he was sent to Port Arthur in 1842, finally receiving his freedom in 1849. His life thereafter is unknown, and rumour. He may be the balladeer seen by the writer Marcus Clarke in a doss-house in Melbourne in 1868. The poems printed in this anthology are (except for one line from a transcript) from manuscripts in the poet's hand in the Mitchell Library, Sydney.

John Dunmore Lang 1799–1878 b Greenock, Scotland; arrived in Australia 1823. Based in Sydney, he was a Presbyterian minister and became a member of the NSW parliament. He wrote poetry, and voluminous essays on religion, politics and history. He was a stirrer in the intellectual life of the colony, advocating the abolition of transportation, a system of national education, federation and republicanism.

Eliza Hamilton Dunlop 1796–1880 b Ireland; arrived in Sydney February 1838 and moved to Wollombi in the Hunter Valley in 1839 when her husband was appointed magistrate and protector of Aborigines for the area. She maintained a close interest in Aboriginal people and their culture.

Fidelia S. T. Hill 1790–1854 b Yorkshire, England; arrived in Australia with the first settlers in the Adelaide area in 1836. She moved briefly to Sydney in 1840, then settled in Tasmania from 1841. Her *Poems and Recollections of the Past* (1840) was the first book of poetry by a woman published in Australia.

Barron Field 1786–1846 b England. He spent 1817–24 in Australia as judge of the Supreme Court of NSW, then returned home. His *First Fruits of Australian Poetry* (1819) was the first book of poetry published in Australia.

ACKNOWLEDGMENTS

Robert Adamson: 'Dead Horse Bay', 'The Home, The Spare Room', 'Dreaming Up Mother' from *Selected Poems*, reprinted by permission of Queensland University Press; Jordie Albiston: 'Headcount', 'Letter Home (Margaret Catchpole) from *Botany Bay Document*, reprinted by permission of Black Pepper; Bruce Beaver: From 'Lauds and Plaints', 'Machine' from *New and Selected Poems 1960-1990*, reprinted by permission of Queensland University Press; Judith Beveridge: 'How to Love Bats' from *Accidental Grace*, reprinted by permission of Queensland University Press; John Blight: 'Sea Level' from *A Beachcombers Diary*, reprinted by permission of Mrs B. M. Blight, 'The Oyster-eaters', 'Crab' from *Selected Poems*, reprinted by permission of Queensland University Press; Peter Boyle: 'First Shift', 'Flying by Night' from *The Blue Cloud of Crying*, reprinted by permission of the author and Hale & Iremonger; Vincent Buckley: From 'Stroke', reprinted by permission of the Estate of Vincent Buckley, 'Small Brown Poem for Grania Buckley', 'The Too-Lateness', 'Seeing Romsey' from *Last Poem*, reprinted by permission of Penolope Buckley; Caroline Caddy: 'Finding My Daughter' from *Conquistadors*, reprinted by permission of Penguin Books Australia, 'Solitude' from *Antarctica*, reprinted by permission of Fremantle Arts Centre Press; David Campbell: 'We Took the Storms to Bed', 'Song for the Cattle', 'Among the Farms', 'Mothers and Daughters', 'The Australian Dream', From 'Kur-ring-gai Rock Carvings', 'The Underground', 'Hands', 'Baiame', 'Crab' from *Collected Poems*, reprinted by permission of HarperCollins Publishers Australia; Lee Cataldi: 'if you stay too long in the third world' from *The Women Who Live on the Ground*, reprinted by permission of Penguin Books Australia; Alison Croggon: 'Ode to Walt Whitman', 'The angle of your face', 'Who was going to save you' from *The Blue Gate*, reprinted by permission of Black Pepper; Zora Cross: From 'Love Sonnets III', From 'Love Sonnets XLIX', 'Night Ride' from *The Lilt of Life*, reprinted by permission of HarperCollins Publishers Australia; Jack Davis: 'Camped in the Bush', from *The First Born and Other Poems*, reprinted by permission of the author; Bruce Dawe: 'Drifters', 'The Raped Girl's Father', 'Homecoming', 'Morning Becomes Electric', 'Going', 'Doctor to Patient' from *Sometimes Gladness*, reprinted by permission of Addison Wesley Longman; Sarah Day: 'Chaos' from *A Madder Dance*, reprinted by permission of Penguin Books Australia; Rosemary Dobson: 'In a Café', ' The Bystander', 'The Birth', 'Cock Crow', 'The Rape of Europa', 'The Sailor' from *Collected Poems*, reprinted by permission of HarperCollins Publishers Australia; Michael Dransfield: 'Bum's rush', 'Fix', 'Parnassus mad ward', 'Endsight', 'Flying' from *Collected Poems* edited by Rodney Hall, reprinted by permission of Queensland University Press; Geoffrey Dutton: From 'A Body of Word' from *A Body of Words*, reprinted by permission of the author; Stephen Edgar: 'Destiny' from *Ancient Music*, reprinted by permission of the author, 'Yet' from *Corrupted Treasures*, reprinted by permission of Random House Australia; Rebecca Edwards: 'Moonboat', 'Eating the Experience: A Reminder', 'Draw a Lion', reprinted by permission of the author; Anne Elder: 'At Amalfi', 'The White Spider' from *Crazy Woman and Poems*, reprinted by permission of John Elder; Diane Fahey: 'Dressmaker', 'Sacred Conversations' from

Turning the Hourglass, reprinted by permission of Dangaroo Press; **R.D. FitzGerald:** ' In Personal Vein', *From* 'Eleven Compositions', 'The Wind at Your Door' from *Forty Years Poems*, reprinted by permission of HarperCollins Publishers Australia; **Lionel G. Fogarty:** 'Su and Du', 'Frisky Poem and Risky' from *New and Selected Poems* reprinted by permission of Hyland House; **John Forbes:** 'Drugs', 'Speed, a pastoral', 'Love Poem' from *New and Selected Poems* ,'The best of all possible poems' from *Stalin's Holidays*, reprinted by permission of the author; **Barbara Giles:** 'In the park, looking', 'Stuff' from *The Hag in the Mirror*, Pariah Press, reprinted by permission of the author, 'Moonlighting' from *A Savage Coast*, reprinted by permission of the author and Hale & Iremonger; **Kevin Gilbert:** 'Consultation', 'The Soldier's Reward', 'Jim B' from *The Blackside* reprinted by permission of Hyland House; **Mary Gilmore:** 'Down by the Sea', 'Eve-Song', 'The Hunter of the Black', 'The Yarran-tree', 'Nationality', 'Fourteen Men' from *Selected Poems*, ETT Imprint, Watson Bay 1997, reprinted by permission of ETT Imprint; **Peter Goldsworthy:** 'Alcohol', 'A Statistician to His Love' from *This Goes With That*, reprinted by permission of HarperCollins Publishers Australia; **Alan Gould:** 'That Move from Shelter' from *Mermaid*, reprinted by permission of Random House Australia, 'Tightrope Walker', 'Demolisher' from *Selected Poems*, reprinted by permission of the author; **Robert Gray:** 'Flames and Dangling', 'Wire', 'Reflection', 'Bondi' from *Selected Poems*, reprinted by permission of the author; **Charles Harpur:** 'A Flight of Wild Ducks', 'The Creek of the Four Graves', 'To Myself, June 1855', 'Modern Poetry', 'Early and Late Art', 'A Mid-Summer Noon in the Australian Forest', from Mitchell Library, Sydney; **J.S. Harry:** 'Picking the Nits' from *The Life on Water and the Life Beneath*, reprinted by permission of HarperCollins Publishers Australia, 'Selling Ethiopia', 'Mousepoem' from *J.S. Harry Selected Poems*, reprinted by permission of Penguin Books Australia; **Robert Harris:** *From* 'Seven Songs for Sydney*', 'Cane-Field Sunday 1959' from *Jane: Interlinear and Other Poems*, reprinted by permission of Paper Bark Press; **Kevin Hart:** 'The Black Telephone', 'The Calm', 'The Room', 'Sunlight in a room' from *New and Selected Poems*, reprinted by permission of Golvan Arts Management; **William Hart-Smith:** 'Kellerberrin 6410', 'Relativity', from *Selected Poems 1936-1984* edited by Brian Dibble, reprinted by permission of Brian Dibble; **Gwen Harwood:** 'Home of Mercy', 'In the Park', 'Boundary Conditions', 'An Impromptu for Ann Jennings', 'Barn Owl', 'Oyster Cove', 'The Sharpness of Death', 'The Sea Anemones', 'Religious Instruction', 'A Music Lesson', 'Thoughts before Sunrise', 'Death Has No Features of His Own', 'Return of the Native', 'A Simple Story', 'Mother Who Gave Me Life', 'The Twins' from *Selected Poems*, ETT Imprint, Watsons Bay 1996, reprinted by permission of ETT Imprint; **Jill Hellyer:** 'Living with Aunts', 'Englynion for Two Friends, and another' from *Song of the Humpbacked Whales: Selected Verse*, reprinted by permission of the author; **Kris Hemensley:** *From* 'A Mile from Poetry', reprinted by permission of the author; **Dorothy Hewett:** 'Grave Fairytale', 'I've Made My Bed, I'll Lie On It', *From* 'Alice in Wormland' from *Collected Poems*, reprinted by permission of Fremantle Arts Centre Press; **Philip Hodgins:** 'Ich Bin Allein', 'Trip Cancelled' from *Blood & Bone,* 'After a Dry Stretch' from *Up On All Fours*, reprinted by permission of HarperCollins Publishers Australia; **A.D. Hope:** 'Australia', 'Flower Poem', 'The Gateway', 'Ascent into Hell', 'The Brides', 'Imperial Adam', 'The Return of Persephone', 'Crossing the Frontier', 'Advice to Young Ladies', 'On an Engraving by Casserius', 'Moschus Moschiferus' from *Collected Poems*, 'Inscription for a War' from *Antechinus*, 'Trees', 'The Mayan Books' from *Orpheus*, reprinted by permission of HarperCollins Publishers Australia; **Coral Hull:** 'Liverpool' from *The Wild Life*, reprinted by permission of Penguin Books Australia; **Martin Johnston:** 'The typewriter, considered as a bee-trap', 'Esprit de l'escalier', 'The recidivist' from *The typewriter, considered as a beetrap*, reprinted by permission of Roseanne Bonney; **Evan Jones:** 'Generations', 'Eurydice Remembered', 'Him', reprinted with permission of Australogia; **Nancy Keesing:** 'Old Hardware Store, Melbourne' from *Hails and Farewells and Other Poems*, 'Darlo and the Cross' from *The Woman I Am*, reprinted by permission of Nancy Keesing and Curtis Brown (Aust.); **Aileen Kelly:** 'Substance', 'Looking for Andy', 'Cross Country' from *Coming Up for Light*, Pariah Press, reprinted by permission of the author; **John Kinsella:** 'Heartbreak Drive' from *Lightning Tree*, reprinted by permission of Fremantle Arts Centre Press; **Anthony Lawerence:** 'The Drive', 'Mark and Lars', 'The Capricorn' from *The Darkwood Aquarium*, reprinted by permission of Penguin Books Australia; **Jacinta Le Plastrier:** 'As a child I invented a book', 'Construction Site', reprinted by permission of the author; **Emma Lew:** 'They Flew Me in on the Concorde from Paris', 'Trench Music' from *The Wild Reply*, reprinted by permission of Black Pepper; **Tony Lintermans:** 'A Bone from the Misty Days', 'The Escape from Youth' from *The Shed Manifesto*, Scribe 1989, reprinted by permission of the author; **Kate Llewellyn:** 'Stupid', 'Finished' from *Selected Poems*, reprinted by permission of Hudson Publishing; **Dorothea Mackellar:** 'Heritage', 'Once When She Thought Aloud' reprinted by permission of Curtis Brown (Aust.); **'Frank the Poet' Francis MacNamara:** 'A Convict's Tour to Hell', 'For the Company Under Ground', from Mitchell Library, Sydney; **Jennifer Maiden:** 'Space Invaders' from *Selected Poems* , 'The Winter Baby', 'A Summer Emotion' from *The Winter Baby*, reprinted by permission of the author; **Ern Malley:** 'Culture as Exhibit', 'Petit Testament' from *Angry Penguins*, reprinted by permission of EET Imprint, Watson Bay; **David Malouf:** 'Difficult Letter', 'Early Discoveries' from *Poems*, reprinted by permission of Queensland University Press; **John Manifold:** 'To Lucasta', 'Camouflage', 'Making Contact', 'Incognito' from *Collected Verse*, reprinted by permission of Queensland University Press; **Philip Martin:** 'A Sacred Way', Nursing Home', 'A Certain Love' from *New and Selected Poems*, reprinted by permission of Addison Wesley Longman; **James McAuley:** 'Envoi', 'In the Twentieth Century', 'Because', 'Pietà', 'Childhood Morning — Homebush', 'In Northern Tasmania' from *Collected Poems*, reprinted by permission of HarperCollins Publishers Australia; **Hugh McCrae:** 'The End of Desire' from *The Best Poems of Hugh McCrae*, reprinted by permission of HarperCollins Publishers Australia; **Roger McDonald:** 'Two Summers in Moravia', 'The hollow theasaurus', 'In the event of autumn' from *Airship*, reprinted with permission of Cameron Creswell Agency on behalf of Roger McDonald; **Rhyll McMaster:** 'Case Number 5', 'Company Man' from *Flying the Corp: New and Selected Poems 1972-1994*, reprinted by permission of Random House Australia; **Mal Morgan:** 'Some Dream It', 'Opening Myself' from *Throwaway Moon: New and Selected Poems* reprinted by permission of Hyland House; **Mudrooroo:** 'Lightning Travels', 'Aussie Dreams a Wakey-wake Time 2' from *The Garden of Gethsemane: Poems From the Lost Decade* reprinted by permission of Hyland House; **Les Murray:** 'The Last Hellos' from *Subhuman Redneck Poems*, reprinted by permission of Duffy and Snellgrove, 'Once in a Lifetime Snow', 'The Broad Bean Sermon', 'The Buladelah-Taree Holiday Song Cycle' 'Bent Water in Tasmanian Highlands', 'The Quality of Sprawl', 'The Tin Wash Dish' from *Collected Poems*, reprinted by permission of Random House Australia; **Mark O'Connor:** 'The Beginning', 'Reef', 'The Grasshopper Man', 'Mating Day', 'Stream so quietly, privately', reprinted by permission of Mark O'Connor and Curtis Brown (Aust.); **Oodgeroo of the tribe Noonuccal (formerly known as Kath Walker):** 'We Are Going', 'No More Boomerang', 'Gifts' from *My People 3rd Edition*, 1990, published by Jacaranda Press, reprinted by permission of Jacaranda Press; **Jan Owen:** 'Schoolgirls Rowing' from *Boy with a Telescope*, 'The Kiss', 'Gone' from *Night Rainbows*, reprinted by permission of

410   *Acknowledgments*

the author; **Geoff Page:** 'Kokoda Correction' from *The Great Forgetting: Poems by Geoff Page*, reprinted by permission of Aboriginal Studies Press, 'Inscription at Villers-Bretonneux', 'Clarence Lyric' from *Selected Poems*, reprinted by permission of HarperCollins Publishers Australia; _.o.: 'vol/fol', reprinted by permission of the author; **Dorothy Porter:** 'Bull-leaping', 'Why I Love Your Body', 'The Water' from *Crete* reprinted by permission of Hyland House; **Peter Porter:** 'Print Out: Apocalypse', 'An Exequy', 'Non Piangere, Liù', 'How Important is Sex?' from *Collected Poems*, 'At Schubert's Grave' from *The Chair of Bebel*, reprinted by permission of Oxford University Press; **Elizabeth Riddell:** 'The Soldier in the Park', 'The Letter', 'Occasions of Birds' from *Selected Poems*, reprinted by permission of EET Imprint, Watson Bay; **Roland Robinson:** 'Inscription', 'And the Blacks are Gone', 'The Cradle' from *Selected Poems*, reprinted by permission of HarperCollins Publishers Australia, 'The Two Sisters (related by Manoowa)', 'Mapooram (related by Fred Biggs, Ngeamba tribe)', 'Billy Bamboo (related by Bill Bamboo)', 'Captain Cook (related by Percy Mumbulla)' from *The Nearest the White Man Gets*, reprinted by permission of the author and Hale & Iremonger; **Judith Rodriguez:** 'Towards fog', 'Eskimo occasion', 'The mudcrab-eaters', 'In-flight note' from *New and Selected Poems: The House of Water*, reprinted by permission of Queensland University Press; **Peter Rose:** 'Vantage', 'The Only Farewell', reprinted by permission of the author; **Gig Ryan:** 'Loose Red' from *Manners of an Astronaut* 'Six Goodbyes', 'The Cross/The Bay' from *Excavation*, reprinted by permission of the author; **Philip Salom:** 'Bicentennial — Living Other Lives', 'The Chamber and Chamberlain', reprinted by permission of the author; **Dipti Saravanamuttu:** 'Like Yeast in Bread', 'Poem' from *Language of The Icons*, reprinted by permission of HarperCollins Publishers Australia; **John A. Scott:** 'The Celebration', 'Price of Erin', 'Polka', 'Reverie' from *Selected Poems*, reprinted by permission of Queensland University Press; **Thomas Shapcott:** 'Near the School for Handicapped Children' from *Selected Poems 1956-1988*, reprinted by permission of Queensland University Press, 'Those who have seen visions' from *Welcome!*, reprinted by permission of Cameron Creswell Agency on behalf of Thomas Shapcott; **Alex Skovron:** From 'Infinite City', reprinted by permission of the author; **Kenneth Slessor:** 'Nuremberg', 'The Night-Ride', From 'Five Visons of Captain Cook', 'Country Towns', 'Up in Mabel's Room', 'A bird sang in the jaws of night', 'Out of Time', 'South Country', 'Five Bells', 'Beach Burial' from *Selected Poems*, reprinted by permission of Paul Slessor and the publishers, ETT Imprint; **Edith Speers:** 'Why I Like Men', reprinted by permission of the author; **Peter Steele:** 'April Fool', 'Playwright', 'Brother', reprinted by permission of the author; **Douglas Stewart:** 'Flying Ants', 'The Fungus', 'B Flat' from *Selected Poems*, reprinted by permission of HarperCollins Publishers Australia; **Randolph Stow:** 'Portrait of Luke', 'Ruins of the City of Hay', 'The Utopia of Lord Mayor Howard' from *A Counterfeit Silence: Selected Poems* (c) Randolph Stow 1969, reprinted by permission of Richard Scott Simon Limited; **Jennifer Strauss:** 'Wife to Horatio' from *Labour Ward*, 'Loving Parents' from *Children and Other Strangers*, 'Life 201: Essay After the Seminar' from *Winter Driving*, reprinted by permission of the author; **John Tanter:** From 'The Poem in Love', From 'Crying in Early Infancy' from *Selected Poems*, reprinted by permission of the author and Hale & Iremonger 'Voodoo', 'Debbie & Co' from *Under Berlin: New Poems*, reprinted by permission of the author; **Dimitris Tsaloumas:** 'Falcon Drinking' from *Falcon Drinking*, reprinted by permission of the author, 'The Return' from *The Observatory: Selected Poems* 'Elegy' from *The Barge*, reprinted by permission of Queensland University Press; **Chris Wallace-Crabbe:** 'Losses and Recoveries', 'Genius Loci', 'There' from *Selected Poems*, reprinted by permission of Oxford University Press; **Ania Walwicz:** 'Australia', 'Little Red Riding Hood', 'The Abbatoir', reprinted by permission of the author; **Alan Wearne:** *From* 'The Nightmarkets', 'Roger', reprinted by permission of the author; **Francis Webb:** 'The Gunner', 'Morgan's Country', 'End of the Picnic', 'Five Days Old', 'Bells of St Peter Mancroft', 'The Horses' *From* 'Ward Two' from *Collected Poems*, reprinted by permission of HarperCollins Publishers Australia; **Judith Wright:** 'Camphor Laurel', 'Woman to Man', 'Woman to Child', 'The Cycads', 'Train Journey', 'At Cooloolah', 'Eve to Her Daughters', 'A Document', 'To Another Housewife', 'This Time Alone', 'Lament for Passenger Pigeons', 'Smalltown Dance', 'For a Pastoral Family', 'Summer' from *Selected Poems*, ETT Imprint, Watsons Bay 1996, reprinted by permission of ETT Imprint, 'The Child' from *Collected Poems*, reprinted by permission of HarperCollins Publishers Australia; **Fay Zwicky:** 'Summer Program', 'Tienanmen Square June 4, 1989', 'Letting Go' from *Poems 1970-1992*, reprinted by permission of Queensland University Press.

Details of the acknowledgments are as supplied by the copyright-holders. Every effort has been made to trace the original source of all material contained in this book. Where the attempt has been unsuccessful the editor and publisher would be pleased to hear from the author/publisher concerned, to rectify any omission.

INDEX OF FIRST LINES

INDEX OF TITLES

INDEX OF POETS